ALL-AMERICAN COLLEGES

Project Director

Jeremy Beer

Editor in Chief

John Zmirak

Contributing Editors

Celeste Behe, Charles A. Coulombe, Alexandria Chiasson,
Michael Brendan Dougherty, Alexandra Gilman, Claudia
Henrie, Anne Larson, Kathryn Dillon Luppi, Angel Millar,
Frank Purcell, Jennifer Roche, Cathy Ryan, Laura Vanderkam

Core Curriculum Consultant

Mark C. Henrie

ALL-AMERICAN COLLEGES

Top Schools for Conservatives,

Old-Fashioned Liberals, and

People of Faith

Produced by the Intercollegiate Studies Institute (ISI)
T. Kenneth Cribb Jr., President

All-American Colleges was supported by grants from the William E. Simon Foundation and Mr. Menlo F. Smith. The Intercollegiate Studies Institute gratefully acknowledges their support.

All-American colleges : top schools for conservatives, old-fashioned liberals, and people of faith / produced by the Intercollegiate Studies Institute (ISI). — 1st ed. — Wilmington, DE : ISI Books, 2006.

    p. ; cm.
    (College guide)
    ISBN-13: 978-1-932236-88-0
    ISBN-10: 1-932236-88-0

    1. Universities and colleges—United States—Directories. 2. Education, Humanistic—United States.

LA226 .A45 2006
378.73—dc22   0607

Library of Congress Control Number: 2006929043

Published by: ISI Books
                    Intercollegiate Studies Institute
                    P.O. Box 4431
                    Wilmington, DE 19807-0431

Book design by Sam Torode/Beer Editorial and Design

CONTENTS

How (and Why) to Use This Guide

John Zmirak

IF YOU'VE PICKED UP THIS BOOK from the store shelves that groan with college guides and test-prep manuals the size of telephone books, chances are you're looking for something special. Indeed, our subtitle is a bit of a giveaway; you are holding in your hands a "niche" guide for a self-selected audience. By crafting a book for "conservatives, old-fashioned liberals, and people of faith," we are reaching out to parents and students with distinctive values and educational goals: people who see education as grounded in a particular vision of the person, or a particular notion of what it means to be a "good" and "free" man or woman. The word "liberty" and the term "liberal arts" have more than an etymological relation; the liberal arts are the proper study of someone who hopes to achieve true liberty, which consists in the capacity and inclination to *choose* the good. A liberal arts education must therefore be both formative as well as informative. It builds up one's character as well as one's resumé.

This is something on which all educated Westerners used to agree, regardless of which political party they supported. It was part of the great American consensus, which allowed for civic cooperation across the political spectrum. However, this common understanding of the meaning and purpose of education was largely abandoned in the 1960s and '70s, with the radicalization first of college campuses, then of the faculty, and finally of the classroom. Since then, the very notions of abstract truth, disinterested scholarship, and even pluralism have come under attack by professors in thrall to esoteric ideologies—making reasoned debate difficult, and turning the seminar hall into a political battlefield rather than a place where free minds meet. The task of preserving the fragile ideal of humane education thus has fallen to those intellectual conservatives, religious believers, and honorable "old-fashioned liberals" (in the tradition of John F. Kennedy, Eugene McCarthy, and George McGovern) who esteem the ideals of liberal education—and who share the egalitarian dream of offering such an education not just to an elite, but to the many.

Most of America's founders received—and advocated—just such an education, from Thomas Jefferson to John Marshall to John Adams to Benjamin Franklin. But the American tradition of liberal education predates the founding generation by centuries. Among the first initiatives undertaken by European settlers when they landed on North American shores was to found colleges and universities—the first being the University of Mexico, which dates to 1551. Harvard College, founded in 1636, began as a seminary staffed by broadly learned theologians who had inherited the Renaissance respect for classical education and infused it with a profound spirituality. As European settlers expanded across the continent, schools and colleges served as anchors in the new communities they founded, marking their commitment to building a republic on the shoulders of educated citizens.

The publisher of this book, the Intercollegiate Studies Institute, has worked for more than fifty years with students and scholars to preserve academic freedom and to introduce young people to the classic texts and great ideas that undergird American civilization; this is what ISI has meant by "educating for liberty." As a membership organization, ISI has built up a broad network of students and teachers at hundreds of American universities. It is to these scholars that we turned in preparing this volume. Their insights and advice helped us decide which institutions to include in this select guide to fifty liberal arts colleges and universities, schools that might—in the deepest, most profound sense of the term—be properly called "all-American."

IN DOING COLLEGE RESEARCH, it's easy enough to figure out which schools are the most selective, which have the most superficial prestige, and which the most impressive alumni; these are the kinds of things colleges talk up on their websites, and most guides to higher education use such factors as the primary criteria by which to select (or rank) schools. It's also true that a school which is already famous has a better chance of attracting students with native smarts from elite high schools, not to mention famous professors who will deliver weekly lectures in between researching their own books and jetting off to conferences. This keeps up a school's reputation—regardless, in many cases, of the actual quality of teaching in the classroom. This fact was noticed by author Loren Pope (an old-fashioned liberal whom we admire). In his justly beloved *Colleges That Change Lives,* Pope pointed out how students often benefit from attending less prestigious schools with smaller classes, professors more oriented to teaching than to research, and close-knit communities that encourage serious study over grade-grubbing and careerism.

In this book, we do pay attention to the esteem a college has earned, and its success in training intellectually awakened young men and women for lives of service, science, and creativity. But there is much, much more to this than simply attracting many students with high SAT scores and turning most of them away. Yet that is how a school's "selectivity" is determined by college guides that "rank" schools accordingly. In ISI's other college guide, *Choosing the Right College,* we cover the most selective schools and many more, exploring the quality of the coursework required of every student, the academic freedom found in the classroom, and the opportunities for serious study offered at each. Consulting professors and students at more than 130 schools, we offer in that book an authoritative reference guide to higher education in America—including its highest peaks and deepest valleys.

In this guide, we're doing something a little different. Instead of looking skeptically at the schools that do well in famous rankings—some of which are simply coasting on reputations won long ago—we have taken a fresh look at the field of higher education. In compiling this guide, we largely ignored our competition and the schools they were writing about every year. Instead, we looked first at the curricula offered at hundreds of schools. We checked which courses each school required of every student, regardless of major, to determine that college's philosophy of education.

You can tell what an institution thinks is important by what it makes mandatory. Does a school require that students acquire a broad background in the liberal arts—in European and American history, politics, philosophy, laboratory science, and religion? Or are those core areas of knowledge left up to chance and consumer choice? Have they been replaced by mandated (and typically politicized) courses informed by "race," "class," and "gender"? We tried to identify those schools that were most serious about offering their students a solid grounding in the traditional disciplines, the precise kind of knowledge that universities in the West were founded to transmit. And we came up with the fifty schools profiled here, nearly all of which require their charges to take a reasonable number of foundational classes in these disciplines.

Of course, even if a school does require its students to take a wide array of classes in the traditional disciplines, that doesn't mean those courses are necessarily taught well, or fairly. Our campus contacts report that professors are often reluctant to teach introductory "survey" courses. For faculty, such classes are less entertaining to offer than seminars tracking their latest research. They also require a professor to pitch his or her teaching at nonspecialists—indeed, at students who may resent the fact that the course is required, who start off the semester with a resounding yawn. Not every historian or literary scholar is really equipped to awaken in his reluctant pupils enthusiasm for an alien discipline. Most universities make their tenure decisions based not on a professor's aptitude at transmitting general knowledge to the average student, but rather on the quality (but mostly the quantity) of specialized books and articles he or she produces for a few hundred advanced colleagues in the field. Since schools do not reward the skills of an eloquent generalist, we should not be surprised that this species of teacher is becoming endangered. But we found fifty schools where they still thrive.

In compiling this volume, we asked another question as well: Once a student selects a major, how solid is the course of study required of him to earn a degree? May an undergraduate specialize too soon, focusing narrowly on the things which interested him in high school, to emerge with a sheepskin and a case of tunnel vision? Are there enough serious courses in each discipline for a student to choose among, or have professors filled the course catalog with esoteric, politicized classes? At the schools we recommend, most departments are still serious, with requirements for majors that are intellectually thorough and well-balanced.

You might be surprised to learn that some of the best schools we have found—academically, socially, spiritually—happen to be less well-known to high school guidance counselors than the fifty "top" schools ranked by selectivity. But think of these colleges as if they were fine wines from regions not yet trumpeted by the critics, or as if they were important writers too long overlooked (just as Melville and Hawthorne were once all but forgotten). These schools have mostly stayed true to their founding visions, attracting scholars and students who aren't driven by fashionable trends and academic fads. By flying "under the radar," they have evaded the pressure to conform, retaining their individual characters. Here you will find schools that really are devoted to such glorious particularities as the Great Books, the Bible, Thomist philosophy, Mennonite peacemaking, Southern military traditions, or Quaker theology. But above all, you'll encounter colleges devoted to the vision of formation in the liberal arts outlined by John Henry Newman in his seminal work *The Idea of a University*. As he wrote in that book:

> Every thing has its own perfection, be it higher or lower in the scale of things; and the perfection of one is not the perfection of another. Things animate, inanimate, visible, invisible, all are good in their kind, and have a best of themselves, which is an object of pursuit. Why do you take such pains with your garden or your park? You see to your walks and turf and shrubberies; to your trees and drives; not as if you meant to make an orchard of the one, or corn or pasture land of the other, but because there is a special beauty in all that is goodly in wood, water, plain, and slope, brought all together by art into one shape, and grouped into one whole. Your cities are beautiful, your palaces, your public buildings, your territorial mansions, your churches; and their beauty leads to nothing beyond itself. There is a physical beauty and a moral: there is a beauty of person, there is a beauty of our moral being, which is natural virtue; and in like manner there is a beauty, there is a perfection, of the intellect. . . . The heroes, of whom history tells, Alexander, or Caesar, or Scipio, or Saladin, are the representatives of that magnanimity or self-mastery which is the greatness of human nature. Christianity too has its heroes, and in the supernatural order, and we call them Saints. The artist puts before him beauty of feature and form; the poet, beauty of mind; the preacher, the beauty of grace: then intellect too, I repeat, has its beauty, and it has those who aim at it. To open the mind, to correct it, to refine it, to enable it to know, and to digest, master, rule, and use its knowledge, to give it power over its own faculties, application, flexibility, method, critical exactness, sagacity, resource, address, eloquent expression. . . .

This passage sums up the goals of the great tradition of liberal (i.e., liberating) education in the West, which in one form or another guided the foundation of the first universities in the Middle Ages, the labors of the Renaissance humanists, the research of scientists from Newton to Einstein, and which should continue to govern universities today. We offer for your consideration schools where this spirit still survives.

· · · · ·

NOW, WE ARE NOT so pessimistic as to think that there are only fifty such schools remaining in the entire United States. What we present here is a *selection* of the best schools, as recommended by the students and teachers we work with and trust, and as confirmed by our own research. In whittling down our list, we concentrated on schools with solid core curricula or reasonably narrow distribution requirements. We also covered a few institutions, such as Princeton University and Deep Springs College, whose overall excellence demanded their inclusion—despite the excessive flexibility of their curricula. With mostly top-notch courses on offer, the education offered at Princeton and Deep Springs may be too much left to student choice, but it's not really left to chance.

Many other schools not included here offer excellent programs, programs in which any student would be privileged to take part. At Yale University, for instance, students in the Directed Studies program read the Great Books in small, Socratic seminars and write a paper every week integrating their major themes. Gustavus Adolphus College offers its students the option of an integrated core that covers Western history, art, literature, and politics from a broadly biblical perspective. Marquette College's honors program offers a similar, well-crafted exploration, guided mainly by principles of Catholic philosophy. There are excellent programs of this sort at dozens of schools around the country—if a student is willing to take on the additional challenges they impose. But is such an effort worthwhile?

In her introductory essay, pioneering scholar and educator Dr. Louise Cowan provides a powerful and persuasive rationale for why every student, regardless of major, should be exposed to the great works and ideas of our civilization. For one thing, a democracy can only function if its citizens understand their own traditions and how they have been articulated, understood, changed, modified, and challenged over the centuries. Much more importantly, every human being develops himself by looking to models of greatness and goodness. For many of us, models are close at hand in the form of parents, pastors, and mentors. However, the great complexities of life and the myriad choices offered by a prosperous, postmodern society call out for something more—and present questions that may not be answered by the examples of those good people we encountered in childhood.

We need more—and it is out there, if a teacher will show us where to look for it. In the annals of history, the works of the great authors, the debates of the philosophers, and the lives of the saints we find stories of men and women like ourselves faced with the shock of the new, the temptations urged on us by our fallen nature, the pressures of public opinion, and the puzzling demands of adulthood. By studying the lives and works of those who have gone before us, we form our very selves. As Cowan writes, "To remake oneself in the image of something that calls to greatness demands a heroic tradition displaying heroic models." For the most part, the schools presented here in *All-American Colleges* understand this model of education, and carry it on.

If human models are essential to forming the young person in excellence, so is the discipline and devotion called forth by serious study of the particulars of knowledge in various fields. No one can think responsibly about the ethical and environmental implications of science, for instance, if he has never stood in a laboratory and labored to conduct a valid experiment. The educated adult requires an intimate, hands-on engagement with each of the modes of knowledge that form our civilization and make possible our prosperity and liberty. For this reason, aspiring poets must study chemistry or physics, and future surgeons require courses in philosophy. A university education is meant both to deepen each student's understanding of a specific field and to bridge the chasms that divide the scientist from the historian and the politician from the prelate. For this reason, most colleges until the 1970s required every student to complete what was called a core curriculum—and even today, nearly all impose upon their students a much weaker set of curricular strictures under the rubric of "distribution requirements."

In "A Student's Guide to the Core Curriculum"—a short book, in fact, which ISI Books has published separately, but which is included here as a bonus to the reader—author Mark Henrie explains the rationale for a balanced liberal arts education, describing eight key areas of human inquiry to which every student should be introduced during his or her four years of college. And he explains which courses, available on most every campus, one ought to choose in order to access these intellectual treasures. The ideas presented in Henrie's guide to the core curriculum are what inspired the suggested eight-course core curriculum we offer for every school in this guide. Based on the current course offerings at the school, we suggest one specific class in each of eight critical areas of knowledge:

1. classical literature in translation;
2. introduction to ancient philosophy;
3. the Bible;
4. Christian thought before 1500;
5. modern political theory;
6. Shakespeare;
7. United States history before 1865; and
8. nineteenth-century European intellectual history.

With each profile you will also encounter a list of critical facts about the school under consideration, including the test scores you'll probably need to get in, estimated annual expenses, and the percentage of students who receive need-based aid. In addition, these "vital stats" boxes include information concerning what proportion of courses include fewer than twenty students, what percentage are conducted by graduate teaching assistants rather than professors, the percentage of students who graduate in four and six years, and how many freshmen return for their sophomore years.

In the profiles themselves we offer candid assessments of the strengths and weaknesses of major departments at each school, assessments arrived at through extensive consultation with a network of hundreds of professors and students. You'll learn which departments to seek out and which to skip, and what special programs at each school make for an unforgettable undergraduate experience—whether a semester learning theology through walking tours of Rome, a first-rate honors program, or inner-city internships devoted to putting the Gospel into action. We also explore the pros and cons of dormitory life at each campus, the range of social activities provided (or, in some cases, forbidden) at each school, and the state of religious life at those schools associated with particular faiths.

This point is important. If you're a member of a faith community, chances are you know the four or five most venerable schools sponsored by your denomination—though you may not know how faithful (or faithless) each has proved to the traditions which founded them. Dozens of colleges created by devout religious communities have shed all but the most meaningless traces of their original missions; at such institutions, clergy and creed are only emphasized in fundraising materials sent to alumni—if then. These schools could now best be described as Catholic- or Baptist- or Methodist-*themed* institutions, reminiscent of cheddar-flavored "cheese food." Some are scant steps away from becoming entirely secular, and a few (such as Marist College in New York) have already been defrocked, so to speak. Expect that to happen more often during the next few years, as churches try to retain or regain control over the colleges they founded and funded—and as secular-minded administrators and faculty push back.

It's worth recalling that schools such as Harvard and Yale were founded as Congregationalist seminaries. What happened to them can happen to the college your pastor or parents attended; in fact, it may have happened already. That is why in choosing schools for this guide we looked for those which carry on the creeds of their founders, and thus help students deepen the faith of their mothers and fathers. To achieve that, a school needn't be a seminary, nor need it relentlessly drive home the lessons of faith in subjects where reason rightly prevails. Academic freedom also needs to be honored—in fact, we can think of several religiously affiliated institutions we declined to include in these pages for failing to understand that point sufficiently.

Rather, it means that where these schools do teach theology, they accurately present the broadly accepted tenets of a given faith, presenting dissenting opinions *as* dissent. It also implies that the vision of human dignity enshrined in the religious beliefs treasured by the college's founders guides how the school manages student life. It may mean that certain student organizations are not permitted on campus, that intervisitation between the sexes is restricted, that an honor code governs grading and questions of academic honesty, or even that chapel attendance is mandatory. Various religious traditions will make different demands of a student. We lay out what they are, so that parents and prospective undergrads can choose for themselves. Where religious services offered on campus leave something lacking, or do not accommodate every faith tradition, we suggest local alternatives.

It's an open secret among the largely secular intellectual class that men and women of faith are responsible for many of the achievements that made the West great and good. From the preservation of ancient learning after the fall of Rome to the abolition of slavery and the end of segregation, the power of faith in a life after life has transfigured and ennobled earthly existence. Men and women of faith peopled the first American colonies, fought for the nation's independence—and founded most of the best colleges in the country. *All-American Colleges* includes those schools which best carry on this great tradition.

But this guide also includes many secular institutions that share in the old consensus about the purpose of education and demonstrate it through their solid curricula, devotion to teaching, and commitment to academic freedom. This last point is important to students of a conservative bent, who report to us that they do not feel welcome or free to express their beliefs at a number of this country's elite universities. In the worst cases, they report being publicly rebuked (not simply challenged) by faculty, or else given poor grades as a result of their beliefs—rather than as a consequence of how well or badly they are able to defend them. Speaking one's mind in such circumstances takes great courage and, sometimes, a willingness to accept four years of relative ostracism—which is asking too much of most students. In this book, you'll find fifty schools where free debate prevails, from the most left-leaning campus covered in these pages (probably Whitman College) to the most conservative (perhaps the Citadel). At none of these schools have our contacts reported a suffocating orthodoxy, pressure to conform, or abusive grading. Instead, they are characterized by the presence of lively, free-wheeling, and passionate search for the truth conducted in an atmosphere of mutual respect. And that should make old-fashioned liberals happy, too.

JOHN ZMIRAK *took his bachelor's degree from Yale and a doctorate in English literature from Louisiana State University. He has worked as a journalist for fifteen years, writing for periodicals such as* Investor's Business Daily *and the* American Conservative, *where he is a contributing editor. He is also the author of* Wilhelm Röpke: Swiss Localist, Global Economist *and* The Bad Catholic's Guide to Good Living.

The Necessity of the Classics

Louise Cowan

IN *Kagemusha*, the Japanese film director Akira Kurosawa portrays a beggar called upon to impersonate a powerful warlord. About to be put to death for thievery, this lowly figure is snatched from execution by royal officers who detect in him an uncanny physical resemblance to their chief. They hide him in the palace to understudy the great man and to master the ways of the court. On the death of the warlord, the officers pass this double off as the ruler himself, hoping by this deception to conceal from their enemies their vulnerability. The beggar learns to act the part of a noble and fearless leader and, as he grows in his understanding of his role, acquires its internal as well as external dignity. He successfully continues the impersonation until—after the monarch's death has been discovered and the ruse is no longer useful—he is driven away from the palace, a beggar once more.

But a strange thing has happened: this pretender has developed a genuine sense of responsibility that cannot so lightly be dismissed. The burden of leadership, with its peculiar blend of selflessness and pride, has become his own. Despite his low station, he follows along after the troops in battle and stands at the last defending the banner of his defeated people, exposing himself to the enemy's onslaughts when all others have fallen. The film makes us question: Is this heroic gesture still part of the act? Where does it come from, this apparent greatness of soul that finally requires in a counterfeit role an authentic death? Kurosawa implies that it issues from the depths of human nature itself. But if so, as the film makes clear, it hardly arises naturally. On the contrary, its realization has come about through schooling in a tradition. Such magnanimity, we are shown, requires *mimesis*—imitation. To remake oneself in the image of something that calls to greatness demands a heroic tradition displaying heroic models. *Kagemusha* is, in fact, despite its Japanese subject matter, in the line of the Western and Roman epics, an extension of the Greek heroic code. Like these classics, it uncovers the innate nobility of the soul as a driving force that issues in noble action. *Kagemusha*, a modern classic, speaks to us with a peculiar power in a time when all energies seem to be devoted to self-preservation and to bodily comfort.

THE WORD *CLASSICS*, IF USED WITH strict accuracy, refers to academic studies in Greek and Latin, though it is frequently applied to a list of great books, largely philosophical, that have been assembled for their ability to promote dialectic. Further, *classics* is sometimes employed in reference to a curricular syllabus, under whose auspices works such as *To Kill a Mockingbird* and *Catcher in the Rye* come to assume inordinate importance. These meanings are related of course, and even somewhat overlapping—though they also have clearly different implications. But one use of the word *classic* in our society is often considered to be a kind of idealistic pretentiousness, despite the truth, the reality, that it conveys. I am speaking of the meaning Matthew Arnold ascribed to the term in his effort to identify poetic works of unquestioned quality that deserve a place in what is simply "the class of the best." Despite any appearance to the contrary, these master-pieces, Arnold thought, would never lose "currency."

Some forty years after Arnold, from a position of high modernism, T. S. Eliot further extended the idea of the "best" in literature when he spoke of an identifiable ideal body of texts from Homer to the present, having what he called a "simultaneous existence" and a "simultaneous order," and making up a tradition that can be acquired only through hard labor. Eliot was speaking within and to a world in which, as he well knew, this tradition *had* lost currency. Hence, addressing himself to poets, he reminded them of their need for its retrieval.

What Eliot wrote at that crucial moment we should now be ready to acknowledge as applicable to us all. We have begun to see a world in which the classics have virtually disappeared—though they have been woven so tightly into the patterns of our culture that *meaning*, for us, is hardly separable from them. For a while we may be able to get by on the echoes of their past glory; but when they finally have become perfectly silent, what sort of world shall we inhabit? To lose the classics is to lose a long heritage of wisdom concerning human nature, something not likely to be acquired again. Yet most college curricula now remain sadly untouched by their august presence, or at best make a gesture in their direction with a few samplings for select students. Such neglect is one of the most serious threats our society faces today.

IN SPEAKING OF THE CLASSICS as the primary curricular need in our time, then, I prefer to designate them not as *literature* but as *poetry,* the generic term used by the ancients for mimetic (fictional) writing. Since the advent of Renaissance humanism this kind of writing has been thought of as *belles lettres*, or in English as *literature,* and given until fairly recently a privileged if narrow position—along with proper speech and table manners—in the education of the few. But since the Enlightenment, *literature* has been increasingly marginalized as the "real work" of the university came to be dominated by analysis, measurement, factuality, competition: the sciences.

But when the Greeks spoke of *poetry*, they meant not so much a graceful polish of style, an artful use of language, as an entire cast of mind. *Poiesis* was considered to be a making process governed by *mimesis*, the envisioning, or imagining, of fictional analogies, a kind of *knowing* different from philosophy or history and yet occupying an irreplaceable position in the quest for wisdom. "Poetry is a more philosophical and a higher thing than history," Aristotle tells us in his *Poetics*. "For poetry tends to express the universal, history the particular." Hence, "it is not the function of the poet to relate what has happened, but what ought to happen."

Poetry appeals to the imagination, that faculty of the mind which enables the intellect to know the things of the senses *from the inside*—in other words, to experience by empathy things other than ourselves and to make of that experience a new form. This is the action that Coleridge calls the primary imagination ("the repetition in the finite mind of the infinite I AM"). In contrast, the rational intellect, musing on things from above, sees the structure of a phenomenon with a certain detachment that prevents any knowledge of objects on their own terms. It must abstract from them, reason about them, analyze them in order to reach its conclusions. Only through the agency of the imagination, which begins always with cherishing the things of sense—with finding a fullness of being in such lowly acts as seeing and touching—can the intellect know what John Crowe Ransom has called "the true *dinglichkeit*, the thinginess of things." This active functioning of the imagination is not the act of a child, a kind of make believe; nor is it fantasy; nor is it fancy. It is a mature and vigorous act of the mind and heart, oriented toward reality, expanding the cosmos within which the knowing mind dwells.

Yet this mode of knowledge—poetry ordering the passions so as to make them "philosophical" and hence matters for reflection—is increasingly dismissed in higher education. Consequently, American colleges and universities have ceased performing one of their most important functions: not to be simply a repository of past thought or a sponsor of the new, but to serve as a guide for the otherwise wayward poetic impulse always present in the human community. For if this energy is unchanneled, it tends to flow in one of two directions: toward a dionysiac frenzy or toward the banality of *kitsch*. *Poiesis* is part of the human make-up, ineradicable and yet vulnerable to debasement in the absence of tradition. We rightly sense that this wildly creative faculty, if ungoverned, will end by making golden calves or bronze serpents—or, as in Dostoevsky's *Possessed*, burning down the city.

Thus, if we could imaginably discover the *telos* of liberal education, the underlying purpose for which communities sponsor so impractical and expensive an endeavor as a university, we might find, surprisingly, that it is not so much to further individual success or to produce "new knowledge" or even to preserve the monuments of the past. Rather, it is to give form to this creative impulse in human culture. As we have always secretly suspected, democracy has imposed upon us from the beginning an obligation to provide a liberal education for *every* citizen—a charge that implies not simply literacy but an ability to judge the high from the low, the genuine from the shoddy. We are now failing to perform this task, largely because our schools have discarded the great staple of our education, the poetic mode of thought.

THE TWO FOUNTAINHEADS OF poetic wisdom for the West have been the Greek and Hebrew writings. One speaks of nobility; the other of humility. Both are necessary. And in both it is primarily in poetry that they communicate their hearts and enable us to find our own. The Hebrew heritage looks inward, seeking the hidden God; the Greek heritage looks outward, aspiring to divinity. Greek poetry thus shows forth—in symbol, in *mimesis*, in the *eikon*—what it is that lies behind appearances. I have written at another time [*Intercollegiate Review*, vol. 36, nos. 1–2] of the splendor of our Hebrew legacy and the necessity of including it in today's curriculum. What I want to emphasize now is the importance of the Greek *paideia*, the leading out of the soul and directing it upward.

For it was unmistakably the Greeks who discovered *eros*, desire and aspiration, as the path toward the highest good. It was the Greeks who saw both the poverty and the profundity of the soul, and who proclaimed, as Aeschylus put it, that we must "suffer into wisdom." It was the Greeks who intuited the underlying generic patterns of poetry: who gave us epic, tragedy, and comedy. Homer, in inventing the epic, invented an entire civilization; and Aeschylus, Sophocles, and Euripides produced the most profound tragedies in existence at the moment of that civilization's greatness, just before the decline. It was an encounter with the Greeks (through Rome, and later, Constantinople) that led diverse European peoples to know themselves and that taught the American founders the meaning of the *polis*. It is a return to the Greeks from time to time in history that reanimates those same peoples and allows them to remember who they are.

And the poetic process goes on. The sublime Greek writings have attracted to themselves others from various places and epochs and in response to new additions reveal fresh insights, transforming all sorts of heterogeneous texts into an organic, if polyphonic, whole. Diverse works from various cultures, such as *The Divine Comedy*, *Hamlet*, *Paradise Lost*, *Faust*, *The Scarlet Letter*, *Moby-Dick*, *Madame Bovary*, *The Brothers Karamazov*, *Go Down Moses*, *One Hundred Years of Solitude*, and *Beloved*, among many others, strike sparks from the earlier works, revealing nuances hitherto concealed. Then these later texts themselves, after they have settled into the community of immortals, select their associates and invite them in, continuing to unlock within themselves meanings inaccessible without their fellows. This body of writing, until recently considered the very center of European and American education, has stood guard over the march of Western civilization, preserving its ideals of truth and justice, whatever its lapses may have been. And the later writers included in this remarkable group of texts have continued the unsparing examination of conscience that the Greeks inaugurated three thousand years ago. Hence, the Greeks make up the unmistakable foundation of our body of classics. To be ignorant of Homer, Aeschylus, and Sophocles is to be ignorant of the range and depth of human possibility.

IN *The Oldest Dead White European Males,* Bernard Knox, one of our foremost classical scholars, recounts the story of how the Greek texts survived for the Western world: "When in the third and second centuries B.C. after the great age of Greek literary achievement, the scholars and critics of the Alexandrian library set to work to establish the texts of the classical authors and equip them with commentaries," he writes, "they also established select lists." They did not use the word *canon*, though it is a Greek word, meaning a carpenter's rule; rather, they spoke of the writings they chose as *hoi enkrithentes*, "the admitted," or "the included." Knox goes on to say, "In the final, desperate centuries of classical civilization, the years of civil wars and massive foreign invasions, the vast bulk of ancient Greek literature [vanished], including, to our everlasting loss, most of the work of the nine lyric poets. . . . Only those works transferred to the more durable (and expensive) material of parchment could survive . . . Homer, Hesiod, Herodotus, Thucydides, seven tragedies each for Aeschylus and Sophocles, ten for Euripides, eleven comedies of Aristophanes; . . . all of Plato and much of his successor Aristotle."

It is strange, Knox comments, to find these works today attacked as reactionary and to hear the charge that they dominate the curriculum by "enforced conformity." For as he points out, their role in the history of the West has always been "innovative, sometimes indeed subversive, even revolutionary." Surely this is so. The list of rebels is long: the lonely hero Achilles, challenging the authority of the warlord Agamemnon; the swineherd Eumaeus, whose wisdom and honor the poet respects so greatly as to address him directly in the *Odyssey*; Antigone, defying the tyrant Creon; Dionysus, destroying the narrowminded Pentheus; the Titan Prometheus ignoring the prohibitions of Zeus himself for love of the human race. One thinks, also, of the comic takeover by women in *Lysistrata* when they deny their beds to their husbands and put a stop to war—and of the lonely little old men—the *poneroi*—who are the heroes of Aristophanes' comedies. All of these instances represent something like putting the bottom rail on top, hardly a vindication of some conservative establishment.

This is most plain in comedy. In contrast to only seven plays each from the tragedians, eleven of Aristophanes' comedies survive—all naughty and all subversive (and all much beloved by the early Church Fathers). We sometimes tend to underplay the importance of Aristophanes' remarkable comic genius, primarily, one supposes, because the genre of comedy seems inherently less important and—of course, mistakenly—less serious. It is the distinguishing mark of comedy that, as Aristophanes argued in his choruses, it sifts the truly degrading from the merely shocking and protects the health of the city. Obscene, bawdy, risqué matters have their rightful place in the purifying heart of the comic; pornography dwells only in deadpan seriousness.

The primacy of the Greeks in the Western curriculum, then, as Knox insists, is not a result of any decree by a higher authority; neither Church nor State has imposed them, nor even men of money and power. The Greek texts hardly compose a "master narrative" enforced by conservative tradition. Nor has any ethnic group gained power or prestige from their study. They have had their effect, quite simply, from their intrinsic quality: and it is that quality—to which the classics call us all—that makes them immortal.

· · · · ·

THE LATE PROFESSOR CEDRIC WHITMAN of Harvard maintained that it is from the ancient classics that our culture inherited its idea of the heroic. "The notion of the hero," he writes, is "the center of one of the most powerful clusters of ideas that ancient culture has bequeathed to Western literature and art." We could probably with justice maintain that without poetry, we would have no real notion of the heroic. Admittedly, in America we are heirs to multiple traditions of the hero. Every group of people migrating to this continent brings with it legends and myths of heroes; and these imported stories and ideals have combined with the myths and tales of the native Americans to make up a complex mixture perhaps unique in human culture. But two major strands of heroic ideals composed the founding fathers' heritage when our nation came into being, the Greek and the Roman, and these, along with the biblical view, have shaped the fabric of our society for more than three centuries.

A recent poet, Robert Creeley, in a work entitled "Heroes" replies to the challenge of the Latin poet Virgil across the centuries:

> In all those stories the hero
> is beyond himself into the next
> thing, be it those labors
> of Hercules, or Aeneas going into death.
> I thought the instant of the one humanness
> in Virgil's plan of it
> was that it was of course human enough to die,
> yet to come back, as he said, *hoc opus, hic labor*
> *est* [here the work, here is the labor]
> That was the Cumaean sibyl speaking
> This is Robert Creeley, and Virgil
> is dead now two thousand years, yet Hercules
> and the *Aeneid*, yet all that industrious wisdom
> lives in the way the mountain
> and the desert are waiting
> for the heroes, and death also
> can still propose the old labors.

Creeley is referring to the sixth book of the *Aeneid*, when the sibyl tells Aeneas that to go to the underworld is fairly easy (everyone has to do so eventually), but "to retrace your steps and return to the upper air, this is work, this is labor." And, the poem implies, this is as difficult in the twentieth century as in the first. Yet the *Aeneid* calls us to it; and "the mountain and the desert" are still waiting for the heroic action. All the "industrious wisdom" of the *Aeneid* reminds us that we are destined to something beyond death, harder than death, requiring heroic labor.

We might call this the Roman view of the heroic life, one that had immense influence on the West. The *Aeneid* was for centuries the most popular book in Europe, the book for the formation of Europe during the development of Christian culture. T. S.

Eliot considered it "our classic"; it has been woven into western thought and institutions. The *Aeneid*'s two great features are *pietas* and *fatum*, duty and mission, as we might translate the Latin. No two words could more accurately describe America's deepest sense of what some have pejoratively called "manifest destiny," but which others have believed to be a true mission.

In America, as in Europe, the *Aeneid* has been our dominant classic; until the 1920s it was taught to every schoolboy and schoolgirl. It offers us the image of the person of duty, of *pietas,* who lives not for his own self-fulfillment but for others: for the gods, for the city, for family. Aeneas loses city, wife, father, and the beautiful Queen Dido in his quest to do the will of the gods—to found a new Troy, which will be the great Rome. Virgil does not spare us Dido's suffering; she is a noble queen, with her own city, tricked by the cruel goddess Aphrodite into an infatuation with Aeneas. Yet Aeneas is a man of duty and responsibility who cannot relinquish his god-given task of founding Rome. Part of the poem's power lies in its ability to own up to the dreadful cost of civilization: the damage that has to be done to the family and to women in order to move on to the new: "Such hard work it was to found the Roman city." As his father's shade tells him in the underworld, his is a demanding calling: "Remember, Roman, these will be your arts/ To teach the ways of peace to those you conquer/ to spare defeated peoples, tame the proud."

Hence, as Thomas Greene wrote in *The Descent from Heaven*: "The loss of Virgil to the modern world is an immeasurable cultural tragedy. . . . [F]ar more than Homer, Virgil has been the classic of Western civilization. This has been true partly because he is more fitly a poet of maturity than of youth, because his work continues to educate as the understanding ripens. Fully to know him one must know him long. If he teaches the schoolboy style, to the man he imparts nobility." Western man has found his ideal of the public virtues in "pious Aeneas," the man of destiny chosen for a great task: strong, brave, generous. He is resolute enough to turn his back on personal happiness; he fights skillfully and bravely; he is in fact a great hero. But he is a hero for a cause, for others, having accepted his role in life, his duty. Virgil taught the Western world the civilizing arts and incorporates the softness of our hearts (our Trojan ancestry) into the dynamism of civilization. As T. S. Eliot has reminded us, the prophecy of the *Aeneid* has not failed; we are still in a sense citizens of that city, the eternal Rome. But many current readers cannot accept the poem's ambiguity; perhaps the loss of the ability to bear subtle distinctions stems from the loss of the poem itself in our culture.

BUT THERE IS ANOTHER STRAIN of the heroic that we inherit from antiquity, the one that I quoted Cedric Whitman as commending: the Greek, which, as Whitman writes, gives us that "inviolable lonely singleness, half repellent because of its almost inhuman austerity, but irresistible in its passion and perfected selfhood." Another twentieth-century poet, William Butler Yeats, captures this quality in a poem written about Major Robert Gregory, "The Irish Airman Foresees his Death":

> I know that I shall meet my fate
> Somewhere among the clouds above;
> Those that I fight I do not hate,
> Those that I guard I do not love;
> My country is Kiltartan Cross,
> My countrymen Kiltartan's poor
> No likely end could bring them loss
> Or leave them happier than before
> Nor law or duty bade me fight,
> Nor public men nor cheering crowds,
> A lonely impulse of delight
> Drove to this tumult in the clouds;
> I balanced all, brought all to mind,
> The years to come seemed waste of breath,
> A waste of breath the years behind
> In balance with this life, this death.

This choice of a short life lived in pursuit of heroic achievement is a twentieth-century parallel to the classic decision of Achilles, chief protagonist in Homer's *Iliad*, to enter the Trojan war and risk everything on a short but glorious life. It is this tragic choice that makes his situation so unendurable when, at the beginning of the poem, Agamemnon insults him and engenders the famous "wrath of Achilles" which is the focus of our horrified admiration. Achilles becomes so merciless in his wrath that many readers cannot forgive him; in fact, they find it hard to consider him noble when he puts his own honor above the good of his fellow men. But it is an interior quality above all else that concerns Achilles: that *arete*, excellence of soul, which is the mark of the Greek hero—a heroic achievement sought not for mortals but for the gods. And readers are led into enduring the almost unbearable contradiction in Achilles' choice, the "terrible beauty" of his monstrous wrath.

Despite whatever inordinate deeds the hero commits, the poet knows that true heroism is the most glorious thing that can be passed down in memory through poetry. The novelist Caroline Gordon has commented that the writer has his eyes fixed on the hero, sees him when he is about to take that fatal step—the step that will hurl him into the abyss. For the hero as Homer conceived of him (and then the later Greek dramatists) is too large to be contained by the civic order; he is excessive, must go beyond codes. The other warriors in the *Iliad* fight bravely and nobly, but they do not enter into that realm of heroic paradox that is the true abode of the hero. Nor will they, we feel, enter into *kleos*, heroic memory, the only immortality known to Homer's readers. The basis of the Greek heroic paradox is that human beings must aspire to divinity and yet because of their mortality fail to achieve it. "No Greek ever became a god, and no true Greek ever gave up trying," Professor Whitman observed.

Heroism is one of the fundamental patterns built into all of us, a universal potentiality that must, however, be ignited to be realized. America has been steeped in the classical heroic tradition. But it can easily remain merely latent if each generation simply starts over again without the guidance of the classics. Admiration for the heroic principle will surface from time to time in surprising ways; but without a tradition of reverence it is likely to be deformed and misplaced. A godlike aspiration, a selfless desire for a commitment to a calling, a sense that honor is far more valuable than life—these are aspects of the soul that must be awakened by a vision of the high and the noble.

And herein lies one of the great values of studying the classics: our poetic heritage gives imperishable form to the heroic aspiration. Shakespeare's *Henry V,* Melville's *Moby-Dick,* Conrad's *Lord Jim,* Crane's *The Red Badge of Courage,* Faulkner's *The Unvanquished,* Hemingway's *The Sun Also Rises*—these and other works enter into a dialogue with the Greek and Roman classics to kindle the image of the hero within the individual soul. The heroic thus become not a set of rules but a living ideal, incarnated in the lives of us all.

A RECENT BOOK ENTITLED *Who Killed Homer?* takes up this very topic. Written by two classics professors, Victor Davis Hanson and John Heath, this book gives a clear and unequivocal answer to their question: the professors have killed Homer. Their argument is that the academic world has finally "killed" the body of ancient poetic knowledge that had survived sturdily if somewhat precariously for centuries. By fostering a detached and impersonal scholarship, adopting a methodological sophistication, and marking off the territory as fit solely for specialists, the professors have sought to triumph over the texts they teach and write about, without witnessing to the wisdom and vitality of their contents.

What Hanson and Heath say about the demise of the Greek and Roman writings may be declared as well about all the classics—all those works that have depth, that avoid the simple recitation of what people think they already know, that manifest such difficulty that readers, left to their own devices, avoid them. In this way, all the genuine classics, all poetry, is being "killed." By detaching themselves from the texts and yet mastering their every detail, by avoiding assertions, generalizations, and affirmations, by scorning anyone who dares to speak of one of these works without himself being an expert—and, more recently, by purporting to find in these works exclusions, stereotypes, and subterranean messages of dominance—scholars have turned the classics into philological and semiotic quarry. The classics are thus hunted down by specialists who can kill from a great distance by a single shot—kill, that is, by negating their intrinsic meaning, quibbling about esoteric details, rendering it impossible for anyone but fellow specialists to read the texts in question. These masterpieces are thus off limits for the general reader. And certainly the ordinary college student cannot even obtain the license to hunt.

Our loss of the Greeks and Romans is symptomatic of our loss of the idea of *quality* and of *aspiration,* our loss of the heroic which is known in poetry. Yet we need the classics as never before in our history. For what is happening in our time is the making of a new synthesis, much like that large encompassing pattern of culture constructed in the High Middle Ages or in the period we know as the Renaissance. Ours is a time when the human schema and indeed the total world picture are being redefined. Ours is a "postmodern" age, and we live in a time of "globalization." We are called to respond to our *fatum*: to begin the task of sifting from the poetic traditions of the whole world those works that reflect and extend the meaning of our literary tradition.

This process has gone on at various junctures in civilization: European writings have been added to the Greeks and Romans, as have those representing America. Now that there is indeed one world for us, in which economic, educational, and cultural systems are linked as closely as were the different countries of Europe from the Renaissance onward, we are obligated to include writings from the rest of the world in our curricula and our concern. We need not be afraid that by extending generosity to worthy things outside the Western tradition, we shall be debasing our heritage. As Bernard Knox wrote, nothing short of totalitarianism will admit unworthy things into the canon. Placed beside the works that have long been there, the shallow and merely political pieces will gradually fade away, as did the minor works of the past. But we need an active and lively sense of our own heritage if the widening of the Western heritage to the world is to occur. When our society does indeed become "globalized"—when West and East do stand together as equals in the exchange of ideas as well as goods—we had better be ready by having something left to preserve.

Our need for the classics is intense. Yet any defense of them in our time must come from a sense of their absolute necessity—not from a desire to inculcate "cultural literacy," or to keep alive a pastime for an elite, but to preserve the full range of human sensibility. What is needed is to recapture their spirit of high nobility and magnanimity, of order and excellence, but to recapture that spirit in a framework of democracy engendered by a biblical culture of radical openness. The things worth preserving, the things we ought to be passing down, far transcend any single heritage: they partake of the fundamental structures of being itself. Melville called them the "heartless, joyous, ever-juvenile eternities." And if our children do not encounter these realities in their studies, they are not likely to encounter them at all. As *Kagemusha* makes clear, greatness of soul is an aspect of human being as such, but it is not a quality that comes naturally. It must be taught. The classics have become classics because they elicit greatness of soul. Far from being a particular province of the specialist, they are the essential foundation of our educational process and the impulsion toward that forward movement of the human spirit for which schools exist. In an unpoetic age, we have to learn all over again what and how to teach our own children. We need to re-read the Greeks.

LOUISE COWAN *is former chairman of the English department and dean of the Graduate School at the University of Dallas, and a founding fellow of the Dallas Institute of Humanities and Culture. In 1991 she was awarded the Charles Frankel Prize by the National Endowment for the Humanities (now known as the National Humanities Medal). This essay was first delivered as a talk at a gathering of ISI Weaver Fellows at the Russell Kirk Center for Cultural Renewal in Mecosta, Michigan.*

A Student's Guide to
the Core Curriculum

Mark C. Henrie

Introduction

The American university has for some years been an arena for boisterous disputes about the nature of the academic enterprise and a laboratory of experimentation on a range of fundamental social questions. Some praise innovations in student life as heralding a more just and tolerant multicultural society of tomorrow. Others dismiss these innovations as representing nothing but an intrusive form of political correctness. But however we judge these controversial political matters, we all surely agree that the university is a place for education. Yet here, very often, we face a serious problem. For while the advanced research conducted at U.S. universities is the envy of the world, it is also clear that at most institutions the basic undergraduate curriculum has been neglected and consequently experienced a dissolution.

Once, American universities required all students to take an integrated sequence of courses, a core curriculum, bringing coherence to their basic studies. The core often constituted half or more of the credits required for graduation. Through survey introductions to "the best which has been thought and said," the core sought to provide a comprehensive framework by which students could orient their more specialized studies and within which they could locate themselves.

Today however, the core has vanished or been replaced by vague distribution requirements. Students in effect are left to fend for themselves. Thus, after four years of study, all requirements fulfilled and their degrees in hand, countless students now leave college in a state of bewilderment. They sense that somehow they have been cheated, but to whom can they complain? Laudable reform efforts are sporadically undertaken on various campuses, but it may be decades before these will begin to bear fruit. In the meantime, what is a student to do?

A Student's Guide to the Core Curriculum is offered as one response to the predicament facing today's undergraduates. After a preliminary discussion of the end or *telos* of higher education, this guide directs you to the courses generally still available in university departments that may be taken as *electives* to acquire a genuine body of core knowledge. These courses provide a framework that can help you figure out what is going on in the world. Although the contemporary university has often failed in its responsibilities to its students, a motivated student can nonetheless choose his or her courses well and thus reach the goal of a liberal education.

The Idea of a University

All human action is done for the sake of some end. Why then do we go to college? What is our goal? What are we to *become* when we pursue an education in the liberal arts? We may encounter a variety of answers to this fundamental question, but unfortunately these answers are usually rather bad ones. Some say that college is simply preparation for a career. But no human life is defined completely by paid employment. *Professional man*, therefore, cannot be the true end of a university education. Others champion the sophisticate's proud ability to "see through" conventional views, to critique existing society and cultivate one's individuality in the spirit of John Stuart Mill. But the subversive "why not?" which is central to such an intellectual art, actually stands rather low in the ranks of the intellectual virtues. So dogmatically *critical man* cannot be the goal of liberal education, either. And the partisans of today's multicultural diversity education proffer as their goal the amiable relativist *postmodern man*, freed of hang-ups and "beyond" critical judgment. The postmodern theorist Richard Rorty suggests we must come to understand ourselves as nothing but "clever animals." Yet this hardly seems the end of an authentically *higher* education. We must look elsewhere for an answer to our question.

John Henry Newman (1801–90) is the philosophical soul who reflected most deeply and comprehensively about the meaning of a liberal education. Newman was probably the greatest mind, perhaps even the greatest man, of the nineteenth century; and so, to discover the true *telos* of higher education, Newman's *Idea of a University* is the place to begin.

Like today, Newman had to contend with the popular view that higher education must prove itself by a utilitarian standard, and Newman rejected that servile view. Rather, there is a *human* end, a noninstrumental end, to higher education—an end that is valued for its own sake. For Newman, the goal of a university education is always "enlargement of mind," or "illumination," or "philosophy." With none of these terms is he quite content, however. Rather, he gropes in his text for a term that may be predicated to the mind in the same way in which "health" is predicated to the body. The end of liberal education is the *health of the mind*. We desire health for what a healthy body allows us to accomplish, but also *for its own sake;* and so too with an "enlarged" or "illuminated" mind. And just as with bodies health is achieved through exercising all the parts, so, Newman claims, the health of the intellect is achieved through the broadest education possible. In Newman's historical circumstances, his educational ideal was at least partially realized in the classical curriculum of Oxford University—reading "Greats."

Newman's *Idea* offered a nontraditional defense of nineteenth-century England's traditional form of higher education.

In arguing for the value of broad and liberal learning, Newman, a Catholic priest, was in part rejecting the seminary style of education favored by his bishops. But he was also, and more pointedly, addressing the English proponents of the "scientific" style of higher education then beginning to flourish in the German universities—*Wissenschaft*. This German pedagogic regime, which was widely imitated in America in the first half of the twentieth century, had as its *telos* the production of *scientific men*, specialists in the methods of one discipline of inquiry at the expense of broader humanistic studies. Such men could, through the use of their methods, achieve ever more extensive discoveries of new knowledge, particularly in the natural sciences. Such scientific progress with its technological implications, the utilitarians were quick to note, was also very useful to society at large.

Newman's response to the partisans of specialization and *Wissenschaft* was twofold. First, he observed that while the concentrated intellectual development of the German-style scientists had perhaps a practical advantage, the cost was the narrowing, the diminishment—in fact, the partial mutilation—of the mind of each individual. No more could such specialization be recognized as intellectual health, desirable for its own sake, than could an overdeveloped right arm in an otherwise neglected body be understood as bodily health. Second, Newman insisted that a true understanding of the *whole* could be achieved only through a broad and balanced approach to the whole. The specialist, naturally impressed by the explanatory power that his discipline gives him in one narrow area of inquiry, is apt to overestimate his grasp of other matters: the nuclear scientist or the biochemist presumes to speak on moral and political questions, as if ethics is not itself a serious study with methods very unlike those of the natural sciences. In fact, Newman would argue, there is less justification for crediting the ethical judgment of a scientist who has not received a broadly liberal education—even in such debates as nuclear deterrence or cloning—than there is for crediting the judgment of a liberally educated man wholly lacking in any specialized knowledge of either science or ethics.

Lest there be any confusion, we must emphasize that Newman's arguments for broad studies are radically different from the arguments of those who champion pedagogic diversity today. The *telos* of each program differs, and this has concrete effects on the curriculum. For broad studies are, in Newman, undertaken as part of a disciplined effort to come to a view of the *whole*. Learning proceeds with the assumption that there is a unity to all knowledge, and that there is *truth* out there to be found. The mind is *opened* by the variety of studies so that it will at length *close* upon an ordered view of the *whole* that is as capacious and as rigorous as possible. "That only is true enlargement of mind which is the power of viewing many things at once as one whole," he writes. When this philosophical habit of mind is developed, "it makes every thing in some sort lead to every thing else," for a pattern or an order may thereby be discerned in the *cosmos* and in man's historical experience. Newman has precedent for this view in, for example, Thomas Aquinas, who observed that "to be wise is to establish order."

Newman continues by noting that a sheer variety of subjects of study is a necessary but not a sufficient condition for achieving illumination:

> The enlargement [of mind] consists, not merely in the passive reception into the mind of a number of ideas hitherto unknown to it, but in the mind's energetic and simultaneous action upon and towards and

among those new ideas. . . . It is the action of a formative power . . . it is
a making the objects of our knowledge subjectively our own. . . . We feel
our minds to be growing and expanding then, when we not only learn,
but refer what we learn to what we know already.

If we contrast this vision with that of the multiculturalists, we see that those
who educate for *postmodern man* work to "open minds" without any thought that minds
might possibly close on the truth. The *absence* of truth is the point. Rather than an
ordered whole, postmodern man is pure potential, pure instrumentality—and pure resignation in the face of universal chaos and flux.

For Newman, clearly, human beings can be more than mere clever animals. Indeed, Newman ultimately claims that "[t]o have even a portion of this illuminative
reason and true philosophy is the highest state to which nature can aspire, in the way
of intellect." Concretely, the philosophical habit of mind can be recognized in character traits such as "freedom, equitableness, calmness, moderation, and wisdom." The
name Newman gives to this human achievement, the *telos* toward which liberal education aims, is the *gentleman*.

Books on the Crisis of the University

Allan Bloom's *Closing of the American Mind* did more than anything else to ignite current
concerns about higher education in America. The subtitle of the work is telling: *How
Higher Education Has Failed Democracy and Impoverished the Souls of Today's Students*. Bloom
thought it especially important to use the word "soul" in the title, since that is what
education is ultimately about. Read the first section and see if you recognize yourself.

A political and sociological account of the decline of the university was provided
first by Roger Kimball's *Tenured Radicals,* which argued that countercultural radicals of
the 1960s had now grown up and found their way into tenured positions in the academy; from there they pursued their utopian politics by other means. Martin Anderson's
Impostors in the Temple makes a similar argument.

Now Newman's choice of this term, the *gentleman*, to describe the goal of liberal
learning was expedient in nineteenth-century England, for its attractiveness was then
reinforced by the prejudice of his time which honored a particular socioeconomic class
and its habits; but Newman's intent was precisely to bring his contemporaries to re-
evaluate what it was about a certain class of people that was valuable. Newman's *gentleman*, understood philosophically, is not merely a well-born, well-mannered rich man.
But there *is* a connection between the manners we associate with that class of human
beings and the perfected or healthy mind which a liberal education seeks to cultivate.
For the properly educated man knows both what he knows and what he does not know;
and consequently, he displays habits of consideration, courtesy, and fair-mindedness
which are both moral and intellectual virtues. Moreover, there is a certain pleasing
modesty to the philosophical gentleman. Because he possesses a view of the *whole*, he
does not make the mistake of believing that intellectual virtue is the sole criterion of

human value; the perfection of the intellect leads to the realization that intellection is not the whole of a human life.

Since today we too often associate Newman's term, *the gentleman*, with mere dilettantism, it is probably better to say that the *telos* of a liberal education is the *civilized man*. Ultimately, the reason we go to college is to become *civilized*. Does this goal inform how you are approaching your own years in college?

Western Civ. and the Great Books

In early twentieth-century America, when Newman's classical curriculum of Greek and Latin studies was rejected as no longer practical, certain educational leaders sought to retain the spirit of liberal learning as Newman understood it. Amidst the emergent "majors" and "electives" in the first half of the twentieth century, two models of a core curriculum were attempted. One was the "General Education" survey of Western civilization; the other was the study of the Great Books of the West. Both were noble efforts, but neither was perfect. Each tended toward a characteristic vice.

General Education in "Western Civ." was effectively a required sequence of history courses offering a unified narrative of the West. Such a core curriculum arose in American universities between the two world wars and lasted until the core was rejected in the late 1960s. This method had the advantage of providing an approach to one incarnation of the human whole, Western civilization—its art, literature, philosophy, politics, and religion—understood *as a whole*. The approach also had the advantage of locating the individual in historical time, of taking history seriously.

But the purpose of such an education was all too often self-consciously political rather than philosophical, having much to do with the perception of an ideological threat from outside the West in the form of fascism and then of communism. The universities were in effect brought into the struggle against the ideological foe by teaching students "what we are fighting for." Thus, our culture's historical narrative for the purposes of the old-fashioned "Western Civ." consisted of the story of the advance of freedom and democracy, leading to their apotheosis in contemporary America. This educational project is frequently denounced today as having been nothing but a kind of pseudocritical indoctrination into the unexamined "excellences" of one's own culture, and therefore not truly a liberal education at all. While such criticisms are often overdrawn, it is true that the history proffered in "Western Civ." was frequently too pat. For example, the secular academics who developed "Western Civ." curricula at universities such as Columbia systematically understated the role of Christianity in Western history; and given America's wars with Germany in the first half of the twentieth century, the barbarian Gothic tribes' contribution to the "constitution of liberty" was almost completely ignored. The charge against the educational regime of "Western Civ." was ultimately that it had as its *telos* not the cultivation of the *civilized man* with a view of a genuine whole, but merely the production of the *American citizen*.

The other twentieth-century effort to retain a spirit of liberal learning in the American university was the Great Books curriculum. St. John's College in Annapolis,

Maryland, is the college best known for this kind of program. In such a curriculum, certain works of literature and philosophy are read without the mediation of historical consciousness. Students are told that the first step in grappling fruitfully with such monumental works of the human mind is to attempt to understand the author as the author understood himself: to do this, students must *not* begin from the standpoint of what we know now, judging historical events negatively for their failure to measure up to our modern standards (characteristic of the Left) or else judging such events positively for their contribution to the development of our own current practices and beliefs (characteristic of the Right). Rather, to take such texts as seriously as they deserve to be taken, we must approach them alive to the possibility that what is contained in one or the other of them may be simply *true*, and that what we modern men and women believe may be, quite simply, *false*.

In all of this, the Great Books curriculum is superior to the survey approach of "Western Civ.," for a firsthand approach to "the best which has been thought and said" educes far greater mastery of the arguments that have shaped the world. A Great Books core curriculum is as close as we come today to the education Newman championed. In order to become *civilized men*, we should make every effort to acquire an education of this sort; and insofar as current university practices and regulations frustrate this effort we have the measure of our academic corruption.

However, the Great Books approach is also given to a characteristic vice that must be carefully avoided. In their effort to avoid "indoctrination" and to convince students of the more-than-historical value of a small number of truly great books, anti-historicist defenders of those books sometimes go so far as to assert that the history of the West is not a history of "answers," but a history of *questions*—"permanent questions"— that can never have conclusive answers. Indeed, they sometimes conclude that understanding Western history as a record of such unanswerable questions is the *only* basis for believing in the West's superiority to other civilizations, which achieve their unity, it is said, around one or another set of answers. Reading the Great Books of the West in this way has as its *telos*, it is asserted, the *philosopher*—though here, the philosopher is understood in a tendentious way, owing rather more to existentialism than to older exemplars.

But to hold that all important questions remain permanently open is itself to presume, dogmatically, that history does not matter and thought does not progress. It also curiously fails to do justice to the writers of the Great Books, since these writers were without exception in the business of seeking answers and not merely engaged in thought experiments concerning questions they knew to be irresoluble. Like other practitioners of *Wissenschaft*, exponents of the Great Books too often mistake their particular skill in textual interpretation for the whole of intellectual perfection. If the "Western Civ." survey approach reduced the history of the West to the story of *freedom*, the Great Books understanding of the West as the story of *philosophy* is no less reductive. Grand as both narratives are, neither is the whole story.

What is needed in America today for the cultivation of civilized men and women is a university core curriculum exploring the West—its thought, its history, its characteristic institutions—and this curriculum should proceed largely, though not entirely, through the study of Great Books. Such a curriculum must be followed in the right spirit: not to reinforce unreflective prejudices about the superiority of one's own cultural norms, nor to achieve a spurious philosophy that privileges the activity of penetrating readers of texts. Rather, the history and the texts must be approached as disclosing the pattern of a civilization, the highest of human temporal achievements. The history and the texts must be understood as *aids* pointing beyond themselves to the true object of our interest—the truth of things.

A Core of One's Own

The American poet and memoirist William Alexander Percy wrote of his own college experience that it was designed to "unfit one for everything except the good life." Perhaps now you also want to *fit* yourself for nothing less than the good life which requires coming to know what the good life is, a genuine question. Perhaps you have grown weary with the ideology and pseudosophistication that passes for higher education in so many college classrooms. And perhaps this essay has begun to convince you that there may be some wisdom to learn from, and within, our tradition. You now genuinely *want* to acquire a liberal education and become a *civilized man*. You want to achieve that philosophical habit of mind, the illumination of the reason about which Newman wrote. You want to choose the West as your own inheritance, and through that particular civilization, you want to work toward your own view of the *whole*, which is the precondition for genuine understanding. But you also want to be prepared for the "real world"—since practical concerns are part of every human life, part of the human whole, and cannot be ignored. Given all the requirements and pressures of school, how exactly do you *do* this?

Your university will likely do nothing to help you acquire the rudiments of cultural literacy. For the American academy has with very few exceptions rejected the idea of a coherent, required core curriculum in Western civilization. Harvard University long ago replaced its core curriculum with what William Bennett, the former U.S. secretary of education, has described as a "core lite"—the choice of a random assortment of courses proffering "approaches" to knowledge rather than any particular knowledge itself. The idea seems to be to hone students' minds as *instruments*, with nothing particular in their heads for those instruments to operate on—certainly no wisdom. Whether Harvard recognizes it or not, that august institution is now in the business of producing only (very) clever animals rather than civilized men and women.

But all is not lost. If you really set your mind to it, you can still acquire a genuine liberal education, even at Harvard. For in most American universities, scattered across the various departments, you can find courses that explore the central facets of the Western tradition and do so through an engagement with great texts. The trick is to find them. Your college advisor will not point you in the direction of such courses. The course catalog will not highlight them. But the courses are usually still there, waiting to be discovered. One saving grace of the contemporary university is that you have *electives*. That means you have *choices*. And with such choices comes *responsibility*.

Thus, your years of college can end up being nothing but a jumble of disconnected passing enthusiasms, leaving you in the end only confused and disappointed. Or your college years can be a time of serious intellectual growth—the springboard for genuine understanding of where we have come from and where we are going. Either way, the choice is yours. *You are now responsible for the person you will become.*

But even when you make the choice to treat your education as seriously as it deserves to be treated, how do you know where to begin? That is where this guide comes in. The following chapters are a map to guide you into the *terra incognita*, the "unknown land" that is our own civilization. Through the course of studies outlined below, you will begin to grasp the course of the West, both for good and for ill (and coming to understand what is to be praised and what is to be condemned in our history is not as easy as may first appear). You will discover whence you have come. You will begin to relate the unity and the diversity of knowledge, the one and the many. You will encounter the noble and the base. You may even recognize a wrong turn or two in our history. In choosing to devote yourself to studying the civilization of the West, you will be taking the first step to becoming a civilized man or woman.

Indispensable Aids

Civilization, however, is not a series of entries on a college transcript. The philosophical habit of mind that recognizes connections and glimpses the pattern of the whole is something to be found not in the courses you take, but in *you*. How do you come to possess that habit, that virtue? Two things are nearly indispensable, and if you want to make the most of your college education you must actively seek them out.

• *The Teacher.* Within all traditional cultures, the teacher is highly honored, and the obligations existing between teacher and student are a subject for deep reflection. Confucius taught that the teacher-student relationship is one of the five fundamental human forms. The teacher is understood to have something to give to the student—his wisdom—and the student in turn gives the teacher respect, gratitude, and loyalty. The formalities of such a relationship have been obscured in contemporary society. Not only are Americans less mannerly than the ancient Chinese, but we are also skeptical that anyone might actually *possess* wisdom. We tend to understand teachers more as trainers in methods of inquiry than as bearers of an *ethos*.

Nevertheless, however much this fundamental human experience has been obscured, the basic pattern can still be discerned. Each of us has had a teacher who has held a special place in our hearts, one who has shaped us in a very deep way. Years later we can recognize that we would not be the persons we are were it not for our encounter with these exceptional souls. A common mistake of college students is to believe that such intellectual mentorship ends with high school, that university students should somehow become more independent in their work. This is far from the truth. For everything that really matters in the higher learning, having a teacher remains necessary.

So by all means, seek out the good professors, the ones who care both about their subjects and about their students. And once you've found them, cultivate a relationship with them. Make use of office hours—not in search of a better grade, but to *learn* from someone who has devoted himself to the life of scholarship, someone who really is *wiser* than you, someone who can see further, if only because he is older. If you find a professor who is committed to a traditional exploration of the West and who is willing to spend time both in and outside the classroom with you, take every course you can from this professor. You will be surprised to discover how your thinking develops in response to the attention of a true teacher.

• *Friends.* Friendship is so important that Aristotle devoted two books of his *Nicomachean Ethics* to it—and only one book to justice. One of the highest types of friendship is intellectual friendship. When you go off to college, your parents tell you to choose your friends wisely, but they have in mind keeping you away from trouble. You should choose your friends wisely, not only for the negative reason of avoiding moral hazards, but also for the positive reason that if you can find your way into a group of serious intellectual friends, you will learn immensely more than if you try to "go it alone." Indeed, such friendships will change your life.

Too often in American university life we find a shocking anti-intellectualism, even at the most prestigious schools. The young of every age and time face distractions such as the lure of the opposite sex, but in our time the distractions have grown relentlessly: television, video games, sports, extracurricular activities. Surely we are the most *entertained* people in history. But entertainment is not education. Intellectual friendship is the surest means for connecting pleasure with true education.

Beyond distractions, however, an anti-intellectual attitude to the life of the mind is evident even in some of those who work most diligently at their courses. For Americans have learned a habit of work and leisure that is hostile to the intellectual life. Probably owing to America's Puritan foundations, we tend to understand leisure as the absence of work. The ancients, however, understood work as the absence of leisure. Leisure (*otium*, in Latin) was the substantial thing, and work the negation or absence of that (*negotium*). The ancients understood that human beings were made to *enjoy* their leisure seriously: the serious use of leisure is the cultivation of the mind, which is pleasant and good for its own sake. Americans, however, approach university studies as "work," as *negotium*, from which, once the work is done, they are "freed." Free time, such as time spent with friends, is thus kept clean of any trace of the learning of the classroom. This is no way to learn. It isn't even any real way to enjoy yourself.

In the everyday course of intellectual friendship, friends share with each other their moments of insight, present them to each other for testing. Such moments in turn require us to reconsider not just that discrete matter, but everything else in our view of the whole that touches upon the matter. For example, in a conversation about feminism, someone observes that women in recent decades have been treated with greater justice, but that they are also probably less happy. The mind races at such a striking formulation. Is that true? How can justice and happiness conflict? If they do, which is to be preferred? As Socrates knew twenty-five centuries ago, the normal means for penetrating further and synthesizing our knowledge is *dialogue*. Intellectual friendship consists in a great ocean of dialogue and discussion, and those who have tasted it know it is among the highest human pleasures.

So, seek out as friends people who are in the habit of asking questions, even ridiculous questions, and who are willing in turn to share their moments of insight with you. Then you will use your four years of leisure well; just as a true teacher, a true intellectual friendship will inevitably change your life.

The Curriculum

Finally, there is the very practical matter of which courses to select. Most likely, your university will already require courses in the sciences and a foreign language. This is all for the good. In order for you to understand both the power and the limits of natural science—which is the privileged way of knowing in our time—it is important to experience the working of the sciences at first hand. Moreover, while it is devilishly difficult for Americans to learn foreign languages, the struggle really does pay off, if you keep at it, with genuine enlargement of mind. The common saying is actually true: Some thoughts are best expressed in certain languages rather than others. To acquire a foreign language thus opens up, potentially, an entirely new world to you. So take these requirements seriously.

To assemble the elective core curriculum outlined in this guide, then, the Intercollegiate Studies Institute examined course catalogs of public and private colleges and universities, both large and small, from every region in the country. We also consulted literally dozens of distinguished academics in various disciplines. These professors were asked how they would craft a core curriculum aiming to introduce students to the complexities of the Western tradition and to the spirit of liberal learning. These professors were united in their preference for courses emphasizing primary texts and, conversely, in their recommendation that survey courses should generally be avoided. Direct engagement with great books has all the benefits previously described, while students in a survey course are too easily held hostage to a professor's opinions, because they lack any textual basis for challenging him. That is no small difficulty in today's academy.

The eight courses described here (one course each semester in a four-year college career) are generally available in the departmental offerings of most universities in the United States. In each of the following chapters, you will read about how the course content fits into a sophisticated understanding of the West. You will also be given tips for how to get the most out of the course at your school. And secondary reading is suggested in the event that your professors are offering politicized lectures.

While neither this nor any curriculum is entirely comprehensive, this do-it-yourself core curriculum does allow you to encounter much of the history of the West, and to do so from a variety of perspectives. With this curriculum, taken on your own, you have a real opportunity to leave college after four years not just with a diploma but also with *understanding*.

1. Classical Literature in Translation

The French writer Charles Péguy once observed that "Homer is ever new; nothing is as old as the morning paper." One of the best reasons for studying the works of the oldest of dead white European males is their very novelty. Moreover, in reading the literature of ancient Greece and Rome, you are engaging the same texts that influenced virtually every educated person in our history. So if you want to understand the mind of Descartes or Abraham Lincoln or William Faulkner or even Clint Eastwood—and if you want to understand yourself—you need to understand the classics.

Virtually every university's classics department offers an introductory course of classical literature in translation that will cover both the *Iliad* and the *Odyssey*. There will also be a few tragic plays, often Sophocles' *Antigone* or something from the *Oedipus* cycle, and if you are lucky, a comedy or two, such as Aristophanes' *Lysistrata* or else *The Clouds*. Many universities have separate introductory Greek and Roman literature courses, but most will combine the two by covering at least the great classic of Roman literature: Virgil's *Aeneid*.

THE STORY OF THE WEST begins with a story. The blind bard, Homer (c. 8th century B.C.), recited tales so compelling that they seized the Greek imagination for centuries. Homer's *Iliad* is the story of a fair young warrior, Achilles, who takes the leading role in the defeat of a great and ancient city, Troy. Achilles is one ideal of the Greeks. The Greeks were conscious that theirs was a "youthful" civilization. They knew that they inhabited a world in which there existed more ancient civilizations such as Egypt and Persia, and also a world in which civilizations had risen and fallen, such as that of the Minoans—and that the Greeks were implicated in that fall. In Plato's dialogue *Timaeus*, an Egyptian priest says to the lawgiver of Athens, "O Solon, Solon, you Greeks are always children, and there is no Greek who is an old man. You are all young in your souls, and you have in them no old belief handed down by ancient tradition, nor any knowledge that is hoary with age." The Greek spirit was one of youthfulness; they were parvenus in a world that valued the wisdom of age. Consequently, there is a remarkable freshness to Greek writing, and that is a freshness that continues to define the West.

Moreover, Achilles is *not* the leader of the Greek forces—Agamemnon is—and this is important. Achilles is one of many lesser warlords, though certainly the greatest in skill at arms. That at the origin of Western literature lies the story of an exemplary *individual* who is *not* the paramount ruler sets the West apart from other civilizations whose most ancient and formative literatures are accounts of the exemplary and seemingly effortless acts of emperors or gods.

In the *Iliad*, we also see something else peculiar to Western thought: a sympathetic treatment of the enemy, especially the valiant Trojan Hector, who is perhaps the noblest character in the entire epic. The most touching scenes of domestic happiness are portrayed in the doomed city of Troy; the realization that all this will be put to fire and the sword moves us, as it moved the ancient Greeks, to sorrow for their adversaries.

The *Iliad* is about the *wrath* of Achilles: "Tell, Muse, of the wrath of Achilles" is the epic's first line. This anger, which is the root of the great warrior's courage, and therefore of his heroism, proves to be the hero's undoing. This is man's tragic circumstance: whatever his excellences, man cannot escape the limits of his existence. Indeed, all the heroes of the *Iliad* find themselves trapped by their situation and the roles they are called upon by tradition to play. The *Iliad*, however, culminates in an unusual act of magnanimity on Achilles' part: perhaps there is a way for man to "defeat" fate? The *Iliad* is thus the story of a hero contending against the limits of human nature, at least as he knows that nature reflected through the myths of the Greek world. The poem asks, in effect, What is possible for man? What may he hope for? And can he live with the truth of his state? These are questions that are as important for every one of us today as they were to the Greeks more than twenty-five centuries ago.

The companion epic to the *Iliad* is the *Odyssey*, a more entertaining read and the story of another hero—Odysseus—and his wandering search for *home* after the end of the Trojan War. Viewed together, the Homeric epics are a meditation on the human condition. Is the human condition, the human "homeland," fundamentally that of the *Iliad*? Are we all, effectively, naturally, in a world of strife and war? Are we "made" for war? Or is humanity's true home the world of the hearth, of the domestic life of peace—the goal of Odysseus in the *Odyssey*? Or are we natural wanderers, wayfarers? And what is *best* in life—the glory of military victory, or the quiet happiness of family life, or something else? The question of the best life is a very Greek one, which might lead us to ask why it is a question we hardly ever ask today.

The *Iliad* ends tragically while the *Odyssey* ends comically. These may be the two limiting extremes of human experience, and therefore of poetic invention—or perhaps not. In either event, Greek drama soon afterward developed both genres. Tragedy came first, and comedy followed; and that sequence is significant. For the tragic sensibility depends on man's intuition of his own greatness in collision with human limitation, particularly the limit of fate. But Greek comedy emerged with a sudden doubt about the greatness of man. Perhaps man is really a ridiculous creature? If so, it is best not to probe too deeply into his condition. The comic playwright penning his most scatological scenes is in reality issuing a cautionary warning.

Ultimately, attending carefully to the Greeks should lead us to understand both our similarities with *and* our differences from the oldest dead white European males. A great mistake of cultivated minds throughout our history has been to overemphasize continuity. Nineteenth-century Englishmen read their Greeks and found in Athens a culture of proper gentlemen. A well-raised Englishman, it was contended, could have walked into Periclean Athens and felt deeply at home. Germans of the same period read their Greeks and found the romantic souls of German *Volk*. Today, some find the Greeks to be the fathers of a bourgeois liberalism not unlike modern America. There is an element of truth in each of these characterizations, but none is true simply.

• • • • •

EVER SINCE THE RENAISSANCE, a bias against the Romans has prevailed among the learned. The Romans' legal, political, military, architectural, and engineering accomplishments are admittedly great, but what of their philosophy and their art? Derivative of the Greeks, it is said. Yet Virgil's epic, the *Aeneid*, is both an imitation of Homer and also something quite new. We see this in the very first line of the poem. In Homer's epics, the *Muse* sings out. But Virgil's *Aeneid* begins with the line, "I sing of arms and a man...." *I* sing. That is new. And for Virgil, the *destiny* of pious Aeneas is not quite the *fate* of the Homeric heroes. A close comparison of the *Aeneid* with the *Iliad* shows how Virgil (70-19 B.C.) grapples with the Homeric tradition so as to surpass it, and it is this engagement with tradition that led T. S. Eliot to name the *Aeneid* "the classic of all Europe."

One of the best reasons to read the *Aeneid* is that it will disabuse you of a silly notion you may have picked up in high school English classes. Namely, the opinion that what literature is fundamentally about is the struggle of the individual with society. A bright student is apt to get this impression in large part because the works commonly found in high school curricula are designed to connect with young people who are coming to understand and define their individuality. But much great art has nothing to do with this theme. And there is probably no better example than the *Aeneid*, an epic that was actually commissioned by the Emperor Augustus as political propaganda, and in which the hero is individuated by his *service* to society. In the *Aeneid*, we might even say that we find represented that classical ideal against which all the rebellious American high school literature is aimed.

WHAT CAN YOU EXPECT from your professor in the typical introductory classics course? The older generation of classics professors are among the finest members of the academy. The rigor of their language studies and the quality of the texts they have pored over for years have made them perhaps curmudgeonly, but also deeply humane. Not infrequently, however, the younger generation of classicists have learned all the worst habits of postmodern literary critics. You should become suspicious when a professor begins to use code words and catch phrases such as the "social construction of homosexuality" or "retrieving women's experience." Since any great work of literature contains an entire *world*, it is a gross reduction to view that world through the narrowing lens of sex or gender.

The principal error that beginners in the study of literature encounter is that their professors' interpretations of the text, so powerfully presented in expert lectures, overwhelm students so that they can then not really see other possibilities for interpreting and understanding. Despite themselves, students then parrot the professor's line. A good way to combat this natural tendency is to consult several editions or translations of the text and *read the introductions*. Very frequently these introductions are written by some of the finest literary minds—and if they have any biases, the best way to observe them is to read other introductions.

The literature on classical literature is vast, and your library is filled with marvelous introductions to the ancient writers. Cedric Whitman was the author of some of the best works on classical themes in the tradition of the New Criticism, the critical tradition that examines poems as integral pieces of art. Whitman's *Homer and the Heroic Tradition* is an excellent introduction to the *Iliad* and the *Odyssey*, and his *Aristophanes and the Comic Hero* discusses the major themes and plays of that poet. *The Heroic Temper: Studies in Sophoclean Tragedy,* by Bernard Knox, provides a powerful reading of tragedy similar to that of Whitman. For other views, Jasper Griffin's *Homer on Life and Death* is an example of the best of traditional scholarship developed in a life of teaching undergraduates. Louise Cowan's *Terrain of Comedy* includes a wise interpretation of Aristophanes.

T. S. Eliot's essay "Vergil and the Christian World," in his book *On Poetry and Poets*, contains the thoughts of the greatest English-language poet of the twentieth century on the classic of Roman civilization. C. S. Lewis's *Preface to Paradise Lost* contains an excellent chapter on the *Aeneid* as well. For more extended treatment, Brooks Otis's *Virgil: A Study in Civilized Poetry* is a penetrating study of the *Aeneid* and other works.

If you want to understand the social institutions of the Homeric age, M. I. Finley's *World of Odysseus* attempts to uncover the historical facts of life of an age so different from our own. *The Oxford History of the Classical World*, edited by John Boardman, Jasper Griffin, and Oswyn Murray, is likewise a reliable source of such information. For a philosophical view of the meaning of classical civilization in general, Eric Voegelin's *World of the Polis*, while difficult, is illuminating.

2. Introduction to Ancient Philosophy

Having tasted the wisdom of the classical poets, you'll discover something unsettling quite soon in a course on ancient philosophy: virtually every Greek play and countless lines of Homer would have been censored, banished from the ideal political community described in Plato's great work of political philosophy, the *Republic*. Plato's teacher, Socrates (c. 469–99 B.C.), the famous gadfly of Athens condemned to drink poisonous hemlock for corrupting the young men of his city, appears in the *Republic* spiritedly arguing against the poetry of the Greeks, for he believes that such poetry is *corrupting*. Very early in the Western tradition, we already see powerful arguments against the "traditional" curriculum. Such a tradition of examining tradition is one of the signal achievements of the West.

That most ironical philosopher, Socrates, is the one who "brought philosophy down from the heavens and into the city," according to Cicero. Before Socrates, philosophers sought to understand the workings of *nature* (*physis* in Greek)—biology, physics, the motions of the heavens. Socrates, by contrast, turned his attention to man and the meaning of his existence; he sought to uncover the unchanging *nature* of man. In his philosophizing, Socrates opposed a group known as Sophists, who focused their intellectual energies not on the heavens or on man but on lawyerly expertise in rhetoric so as to control the political assemblies of the Greek cities. In effect, the Sophists seem to have held the opinion that there are no universal truths to be found in human af-fairs, all is relative, and so the only thing worth knowing about human affairs is how to manipulate them: the point of learning, for the Sophists, was not wisdom but power. Socrates was the great critic of the Sophists, a *philosopher* or *lover of wisdom* (rather than of power).

Philosophy is sometimes called "Socratism"—Nietzsche called it that—so crucial was Socrates to our understanding of what philosophy is. And it is recorded that Socrates believed that philosophy is something that cannot be written down. Philosophy for Socrates was not some set of asserted doctrines but rather a *way of life*, a life of constant questioning in the quest to determine that which *is*. Conversation is thus the central philosophical activity. This is why Plato (427–347 B.C.), who did write down a philoso-phy, did so in the form of dialogues, which are rather like small dramas or plays.

But whereas poets such as Homer or Sophocles seek to *represent* the human con-dition, to *display* it in all its concrete variety, philosophers are driven by the thought that what we "see," what we *think* we "know" about the world around us, is in some way a mask or an illusion. Philosophers seek to penetrate behind appearances to grasp what is "really real" both in nature and in human nature. For instance, faced with the many differing customs of men in different cities, Socrates did not conclude, as the Sophists did, that all is relative in human affairs. Rather, he redoubled his efforts to discover the unchanging human *nature* behind or within such customs.

At the heart of Plato's *Republic*, Socrates recounts the famous analogy of the cave. In this tale, a group of men have been chained down since birth and forced to watch puppet-shadows playing on their cave wall. These chained men are like us, Socrates says, but we know that this is true only when we are freed and dragged out of the cave, where we can see the truth of things by the light of the sun. Another fundamental contention of all ancient philosophy is, then, that philosophy is the road to liberation, for only by philosophy can we discover *what is*—including the life that is best by nature. In this course, you just might experience that Socratic liberation for yourself.

IN YOUR READINGS YOU WILL first encounter Plato's meditation on the trial of Socrates, the *Apology*, which most directly discusses the philosophical way of life. What does it mean to be a philosopher? Why is the philosopher necessarily a *problem* for the political community? And is the philosopher's life really the best life? The *Crito* and the *Phaedo* then recount the last days of Socrates after his trial and before his execution. These dialogues examine Socrates' political obligation and his thoughts about the soul and the afterlife: philosophy, it seems, is really about learning to *die*.

Plato's other dialogues each address a particular fundamental question. In the *Meno*, we see what the Platonic Socrates understands as knowledge. True knowledge is like a geometrical proof: once it is known, we can't imagine not having known it all along. It is as if we "remembered" this knowledge, though we had never learned it. To know the properties of an isosceles triangle is truer knowledge than to know who won the Battle of Waterloo, for the properties of an isosceles triangle cannot but be. The philosopher wants all his knowledge to be as demonstrable as that, which is why the gate of Plato's Academy bore an inscription warning away anyone ignorant of geometry.

Another characteristically Platonic observation about the philosophical life is the important role of love or desiring—of *eros*. In the *Phaedrus*, the Platonic Socrates describes the erotic element of the philosophical quest in the most powerful way, while the *Symposium* recounts a drinking party with a long and sometimes ribald conversation about love. What is love *for*? Is love good for us? Should we seek to minimize our loves so as to achieve autonomy? These are questions that young men and women naturally wonder about today; they are questions that all human beings must ask, and that all human beings answer in the way they live their lives. Perhaps you will find wisdom in Plato's answers.

The *Republic*, Plato's greatest work, is too complex to describe briefly, but you must keep in mind while reading it that the "politics" of the *Republic* is recounted only in answer to a question about where virtue might reside in the human soul. The *Republic* is a book about the soul. There is actually more attention given to politics as such in the *Gorgias*, which contains the strongest Platonic arguments against the Sophists. Not the least interesting aspect of the *Gorgias* is Plato's depiction of the Sophist Callicles, who is nothing less (or more) than a Nietzschean more than twenty centuries before the fact.

It is almost impossible not to be swept up in the philosophical enthusiasm of Plato. His dialogues are a *joy* to read. Unfortunately, it is more difficult for many students to sustain that interest with Plato's greatest student, Aristotle (384–322 B.C.). Aristotle's works are not dialogues but treatises (perhaps even the notes of his lecture courses) that aim to be complete accounts of every possible subject of inquiry. His goal is apparent when we list his titles: *Politics, Rhetoric, Poetics, Physics, On the Generation of Animals, On the Heavens*, etc. Moreover, whereas Plato is suspicious of appearances and seeks to reach knowledge as certain as a geometric proof, Aristotle is more empirically minded. He too wants to discover *what is*, but he begins his scientific and philosophical inquiries with *observation*. If geometry is the paradigmatic science for Plato, biology seems to be the paradigmatic science for Aristotle. In other words, what is most striking about the *cosmos* to Aristotle is that it contains biological entities, including man.

Most students will profit most immediately from the *Nicomachean Ethics*. Here, Aristotle asks, what is the virtue (*arête*, which means, literally, *excellence*) of a human being? If an excellent knife is one that cuts well, what is an excellent man? Aristotle tries to answer that question completely, describing in the process both moral and intellectual virtues and discussing the importance of friendship for a good human life. What will be most striking for many students is Aristotle's insistence that the moral life aims at *eudaemonia*, the complete happiness of the person. The reason to act morally, the reason to develop virtuous habits, the reason to cultivate the soul is to be *happy*.

Plato's *Republic* is a book about the soul, but Aristotle presents his views on this subject directly, in the work *De Anima (On the Soul)*. For Aristotle, plants, animals, and human beings all have souls, but ascending up from plants to humans, the soul at each stage acquires something not available to the lower form. The human soul is one of the strangest things in the cosmos, and Aristotle finds himself ultimately unable to give a coherent account of it. His perplexity in *De Anima* will be resolved in different ways by later Christian theologians and by Jewish and Islamic philosophers.

You will likely also be required to grapple with at least parts of the *Categories*, the *Physics*, and the *Metaphysics*, which are all difficult works, requiring the guidance of a skilled professor. But do not think for a minute that even the most abstruse points of Aristotelian metaphysics are not relevant! On the contrary, how we imagine the basic structure of reality decisively informs how we may understand God, the self, and human ethics, among other rather relevant concerns. Moreover, Aristotle's account of the basic structure of reality may be *true*. If so, we'll all have to reassess something we've been taught to view as simple fact: atomism.

As early as elementary school, we learn of modern science's heroic quest for the "fundamental building blocks" of matter—the atoms. We soon learn that atoms are composed of even smaller particles: protons, neutrons, and electrons. And if we read popular scientific literature or take physics courses in college, we discover that protons and neutrons are themselves composed of smaller particles, quarks. But here we begin to learn that these tiniest particles are extremely strange; indeed, they hardly exist at all, which is odd indeed for a "fundamental building block." What we do not learn in all this is that the quest for the smallest bits of matter represents a prior commitment by modern science to one of the metaphysical views of ancient philosophy: atomism. From before the time of Socrates, atomism was a good contender for a "Theory of Everything." Atomism, however, was explicitly rejected by Aristotle in favor of his account of substances composed of form and matter. Today's speculative physics has turned up results that raise questions about the adequacy of any kind of atomism, results that seem rather more consistent with Aristotle. Even metaphysics can be very interesting indeed!

POLITICAL CORRECTNESS MAY CREEP into discussions of the *political* philosophy of Plato and Aristotle. Plato is an explicit "elitist" of the first order, and Aristotle gives an account of "natural slaves." Aristotle's discussion of women may raise eyebrows as well. The fact that our intuitions about human equality differ so markedly from those of Plato and Aristotle is significant, and we should certainly consider how and why these differences exist. But we should take care to examine the ancient arguments first and not simply dismiss them out of hand.

But the more pressing problem in ancient philosophy courses is a tendency for some professors to apply modern analytic techniques to the ancient texts, and thus to find them logically wanting—nothing but "brilliant errors." What is compelling and true in the vision of the ancients does not concern these professors. When a course in ancient philosophy is approached merely for historical interest, it can easily become rather boring, and rightly so. What is always important in any philosophical study is to remain open to the possibility of discovering truth, and nothing can dim this prospect more than a professor who himself finds unconvincing the philosophy he is teaching.

If you find your philosophy professor uninspiring, therefore, you might want to talk to a classics professor or to a professor of political science who teaches ancient political theory. Either might provide the inspiration that the philosophy department might lack. (However, the texts you read in the philosophy department's standard introductory course provide the most representative sampling of ancient philosophy.)

As for supplemental reading, it is no exaggeration to say that Plato is the best introduction to Plato. Try first to read him without the mediation of secondary literature. Still, Mary Nichols's *Socrates and the Political Community* is engagingly written and will entice you into genuinely philosophical reading. F. M. Cornford's *Before and After Socrates* is always in print and provides good background on Greek philosophy in general. *The Republic: The Odyssey of Philosophy*, by Jacob Howland, is a brief reading of Plato's great dialogue in relation to the broader Greek literary tradition. Robert E. Cushman's *Therapeia: Plato's Conception of Philosophy* is a thorough treatment of Plato's central teaching: that the practice of the philosophic life entails a radical reorientation—indeed a conversion—of the person toward the Good. In addition, *The Sophists*, by W. K. C. Guthrie, presents those pre-Socratics in the most dispassionate light.

Mortimer Adler was an enthusiastic popularizer of Aristotle's thought, and his *Aristotle for Everybody: Difficult Thought Made Easy* is extremely accessible, so it is a good place to begin. Jonathan Lear's *Aristotle: The Desire to Understand* is an advanced overview of Aristotle's complete works, while Terence Irwin's *Aristotle's First Principles* is a discrete work of philosophy treating Aristotle's first principles first. *The Cambridge Companion to Aristotle*, Jonathan Barnes, ed., contains a variety of solid contemporary essays.

The articles on "Plato" and "Aristotle" in *History of Political Philosophy*, Leo Strauss and Joseph Cropsey, eds., are very sophisticated introductions to the political dimension of these thinkers, but tend to slight their broader philosophical contributions. Eric Voegelin's *Plato and Aristotle* is a monumental introduction to both great minds with particular attention paid to the religious dimension of their thought. Finally, Giovanni Reale's *History of Ancient Philosophy*, translated by John Catan, has a volume devoted to Plato and Aristotle.

3. The Bible

The *nature* or *physis* that is the subject of inquiry for the classical philosophers is by definition that which cannot but be. If something cannot but be, it must always have existed, since nothing can come from nothing. Consequently, in the vision of classical philosophy, the cosmos is "pre-eternal." The cosmos cannot have had a beginning, nor can it have an end. Insofar as there was any Greek philosophy of history, therefore, it necessarily considered history in terms of cycles. Just as nature has cycles, the seasons, so have the affairs of men. In principle, there can be nothing genuinely *new* under the sun. The ancient philosophers were therefore wholly unprepared for the advent of *revealed religion*, and in particular for the incarnation of the Son of God, the Christian revelation. The Gospel, the "good news," is, precisely, *new*.

Christianity changed the world more profoundly than anything ever had or has, and nothing so defines Western thought and practice as the legacy of Christianity. For the believer, Christ's life, death, and resurrection open up nothing less than the only way to salvation, which is eternal life with God. But even without the eyes of faith, the litany of developments generally understood as peculiar to the Christian world is striking: the rise of companionate marriage and the equality of the sexes, the abolition of slavery, an emphasis on the individual and his rights, the separation of church and state, hospitals, universities, and the list goes on. Even modern science can be seen as requiring a Christian intellectual background, for modern science is closely tied to a technological desire to intervene in the natural world, and a belief in the possibility of technological progress is itself only possible if time is understood as *linear* rather than *cyclical*, a thought that is introduced by the revealed religions.

But perhaps it is in everyday personal judgments that the West's Christian heritage is most striking, yet least remarked upon. Consider, for example, the highest moral virtue according to Aristotle: *megalopsychia* or magnanimity—"greatsouledness." This is the virtue of one who takes for himself the honor due him. In other words, something like justified pride is the highest moral virtue for Aristotle. How different this is from Christ's teaching in the Beatitudes—that those who are poor in spirit are blessed, and that the meek shall inherit the earth. How different this is from the Christian humility that acknowledges that any excellence we might possess is a gift from God. How different, in other words, is Aristotle's moral view from ours, even when we aren't believers.

The Muslims refer to Muslims, Christians, and Jews as "People of the Book." All three faiths are unlike Eastern religions in that they are constituted by a revelation of the will of a transcendent God in historical time. But Christianity is also unique, for unlike Moses or Muhammad, Jesus Christ did not come in order to write down a new law. While Jews and Muslims revere their scriptures as the Word of God delivered by patriarchs and prophets, for Christians, Christ was himself "the Word [of God] made flesh." Christ does not *write*; he *is* and he *acts*. Still, for nearly twenty centuries the men and women of the West have found the meaning of their collective and personal existence revealed in the text of the Christian Bible, and no liberal education is complete without an encounter with that Word.

SOME RELIGION DEPARTMENTS offer a combined introductory course on the Old and New Testaments called "The Bible." Others offer only two separate courses—one on "The Hebrew Bible" (the Old Testament), the other on "The Christian Scriptures" (the

New Testament). A course on the whole Bible is preferable, but if you must choose between the Old and New Testaments, opt for the New. For the Christian revelation recorded in the New Testament has served decisively as the lens through which the West has understood the whole Word of God, including that Word recorded in the Old Testament. Besides, if Christ is he who the Christians claim he is, then he is not simply a new kind of hero, greater than either Achilles or Socrates; he is the central axis of all history. Any encounter with this remarkable person must begin, of course, with the New Testament.

Perhaps the saddest fact about the modern (secular) American university is that the standard course offered on the Bible is among the most corrupt and corrupting in the curriculum. Countless college students have lost their faith by studying the Bible in college. The reason for this is the virtually universal acceptance by academic biblical scholars in the modern university of the "historical-critical method," an approach to Scripture study that may be traced to German liberal Protestantism in the nineteenth century.

Essentially, the practitioners of this method of biblical interpretation assert that the biblical text is only "explained" when one has explained the historical situation in which the text was written and to which the text apparently responds. Whereas in Christian tradition the Scriptures were understood to have several layers of meaning—a nuanced approach—for the historical critics, the "real" meaning of the text is to be found only in historical context—which is known definitively, of course, only by the historical critics themselves. Needless to say, theirs is not a subtle approach to the Bible.

Armed with their method, academic biblical critics like to pronounce upon the "misinterpretations" of the Christian churches through the centuries. Eventually they come to such absurdities as the so-called Jesus Seminar, whose members regularly vote on which sayings of Jesus recorded in the Gospels are authentic and which were, well, *made up* by the Gospel writers. The historical critics are perhaps the first deconstructionists, rejecting the *authority* of the biblical text and understanding it instead as the outcome of contending forms of political *power*. But in giving their highly speculative (and often simply fanciful) accounts of how the biblical text came to be, these critics have nothing really useful to say about the reception and interpretation of the canonized text in the centuries-long tradition of believers.

The good news in biblical studies today is that devastating objections have been raised against the historical-critical method. The skepticism that the historical critics wielded so vigorously against traditional faith has now been directed against the tradition of historical criticism itself. The project of historical criticism can now be seen as a pristine example of the Enlightenment effort to displace what it understood to be unreflective "tradition" with an absolute "science" arrived at by open-minded, autonomous, or neutral inquiry. As with so many of the Enlightenment's projects, historical critics' own prior ideological commitments and generally intolerant closed-mindedness are now increasingly clear. Faced with such new post-Enlightenment perspectives, the historical critics must now admit that their submerged intellectual premises frequently have made their interpretative arguments perfectly circular: their secularizing conclusions were implicit in their secular assumptions, which are in no sense either "autonomous" or "neutral." With the emergence of a younger generation of biblical scholars who have absorbed these critiques, the Jesus Seminar, the apogee of the historical critical enterprise, now seems an embarrassment to the historical critics themselves.

IN SECULAR AMERICAN UNIVERSITIES, the history of biblical studies we have described above means that you are more likely to find a genuinely open-minded view of traditional biblical interpretations among the *younger* faculty. That said, however, for believers, it is still best to take a course on the Bible only after they have situated themselves on campus religiously: that is, made contact with an ecclesial community, whether a church or a para-church group, and come to know a clergyman who may be consulted when difficulties or doubts arise. In the end, for the Bible to be read and understood as Sacred Scripture, it must be read with the mind of the community of faith. A local church group or clergyman will also be familiar with the quality of the course offered in your university's religion department. In large cities, they may also know of better Bible courses offered in nearby seminaries which are *not* dominated by the historical-critical method. Such courses may often be taken for easily transferable credit. Sometimes there is also a professor in a university's faculty who would be willing to supervise an independent study of the Bible. This is another way to investigate this indispensable book without the glib reductionism of the historical critics.

There are numerous books you can consult that will help you judge the persuasiveness of the arguments of the historical critics. Mark Powell's *Jesus as a Figure in History* is a textbook offering balanced critiques of the major historical-critical schools from a mildly evangelical Protestant perspective. More polemical is Luke Timothy Johnson's *Real Jesus*. The book's subtitle, "The Misguided Quest for the Historical Jesus and the Truth of the Traditional Gospels," sums up its message. I. H. Marshall's *New Testament Interpretation: Essays on Principles and Methods* is a very sound exploration of the topic from an evangelical viewpoint. William R. Farmer and Denis Farkasfalvy provide an excellent and accessible discussion of redaction questions in *The Formation of the New Testament Canon: An Ecumenical Approach*.

For questions about authorship of the books of the Old Testament, see Umberto Cassuto, *The Documentary Hypothesis and the Composition of the Pentateuch: Eight Lectures* translated by Israel Abrahams, which is an elegant response to liberal and secularizing scholarship.

To get a sense for the many-faceted ways in which Christians in the first centuries understood the biblical message, you may want to consult the series, *Ancient Christian Commentary on Scripture*. These volumes collect statements by the Fathers of the Church on particular passages in the biblical books. Frequently, the statements are taken from sermons, and so there is an immediacy and practicality evident that you may find refreshing yet perhaps strangely familiar. *A Commentary on the Gospels* by Ronald Knox,

ALL-AMERICAN COLLEGES

who is famous for his translation of the Bible, is also an elegant, sophisticated explication of the New Testament from the Catholic perspective.

If you are not a believer, and you find discussions of redaction and hypothetical source documents baffling, try N. T. Wright's *The Challenge of Jesus: Rediscovering Who Jesus Was & Is*. You might even try C. S. Lewis's famous work *Mere Christianity* to see what all the fuss is about.

4. *Christian Thought before 1500*

Believing students perturbed by the contentions of the historical critics of the Bible would be heartened to read the *Contra Celsum* of Origen of Alexandria (A.D. 185–254). Numerous passages in this early work of Christian apologetics demonstrate that the most fashionable objections to biblical faith today are not the advanced achievement of a new and critical scientific age; contemporary criticisms of Christianity are not unprecedented and unanswerable. Rather, many of the most skeptical interpretations and arguments have already been advanced against Christian belief by such pagan philosophers in antiquity as Celsus and answered with elegant dispatch—in Celsus's case by Origen, a philosophical convert to Christianity.

But hardly anyone in America, even with an advanced academic degree, is aware that a man named Origen of Alexandria ever lived. Without any doubt, the most glaring intellectual deficiency of American higher education is an almost total neglect of the discipline of theology—and, with that, of the Age of Faith. To neglect theology is to neglect a study that absorbed the best minds of the West for more than a thousand years. Nothing else about the American university so distorts a student's understanding of the course of Western civilization. Nothing else so hinders a true appreciation of some of the greatest minds in our history. Nothing else so limits our grasp of the intellectual universe that is the object of liberal education. And nothing else so powerfully enforces the glib temporal parochialism that is the besetting vice of America's proudly cosmopolitan intellectual elite. It is impossible to do justice to our history without an acquaintance with theology, and it is impossible to understand the true limits and possibilities of human understanding.

Theology, the study of "the God of the philosophers" and of the God revealed in Scripture, is no idle exercise, nor is it a pursuit that ended with the Enlightenment. Christian theology is still studied with the utmost seriousness *today,* and not only in specialized denominational seminaries or distant monasteries, but also at Oxford and Cambridge and Tübingen and other first-class universities throughout the West. Some of the greatest minds of the twentieth century were Christian theologians, from Karl Barth to Hans Urs von Balthasar, and Americans are frankly unique among Westerners in their ignorance of this fact. As we saw, John Henry Newman's *Idea of a University* was written to demonstrate that a university in which theology is not studied does not merit the title of "university." If you mean to acquire a genuine liberal education, you must find a way to overcome all the obstacles that the American university will put in your way. You must learn at least something of the science of theology.

· · · · ·

IN THE ABSENCE OF A DEPARTMENT of theology in your university, you must turn, however awkwardly, to the religion department. The academic discipline studied in such a department, however, is *not* theology. Rather, it is a variety of comparative social science that focuses on the practices of human communities deemed "religious." We saw in the previous course on the Bible that the presuppositions of the historical-critical method are such as to yield necessarily secular conclusions. The same is true for the academic study of religion more generally. Religion is here understood to be a universal human phenomenon, a set of practices differing from place to place but always serving some social function. That one religion might be true and all others false is unthinkable for the professors in the typical religion department. But the very heart of theology is the attempt to do justice to the *truth* about the God who has been revealed in the Old and New Testaments of the Bible and in the faith and practice of the churches. Theology is, in Saint Anselm's formulation, "faith seeking understanding." To start from disbelief rather than faith is no way to begin theology. But it is the best we can do in most American universities.

In almost all religion departments a course entitled something like "The Christian Tradition" can be found. Such courses can be of some value to those who have had little or no exposure to Christian practice; such courses examine the customs and beliefs of Christians as one would those of Stone Age tribes along the Amazon. To interpret Christian rituals in this anthropological way is a species of social history rather than intellectual history, and it falls far short of theology. There are, however, in many religion departments, courses with names like "Christian Thought before 1500," and these will come closer to a general introduction to theology than any other course in the curriculum. Take this course to gain at least a glancing acquaintance with theology.

THE FIRST CHRISTIAN CENTURIES, called the Patristic Age, witnessed the intellectual explication of Christian orthodoxy by the Fathers of the Church, the bishops-theologians revered as saints who answered heresy with their decisive arguments. The work of the Fathers is distilled for us in the Nicene Creed, which is still recited by many Christian communities during Sunday liturgy. The first Christian creed was simply "Jesus Christ is Lord." But what could that mean? What did it mean to say that Jesus of Nazareth was the Son of God, the Christ? A Christological controversy was one of the major disputed questions of those first centuries. The other main area of theological dispute involved the Trinity: Christians are monotheists who worship a God who is Father, Son, and Holy Ghost. How were Christians to understand this paradox?

In both cases, the challenge faced by the Fathers was twofold. On the one hand, they had to respond to the reductionist solutions of heretics. For example, some contended that Jesus of Nazareth was not really a man, only a spirit pretending to be a man. Others held that only God the Father is truly God, while the Son and Holy Spirit are his creatures. Such formulations ultimately fail to capture the radical claim of the Christian revelation. On the other hand, the Fathers had to avoid falling into logical contradiction that would invalidate the faith.

By the fifth century, with a series of brilliant dialectical developments by such theological giants as Athanasius, Cyril of Alexandria, Basil, Gregory of Nyssa, and Gregory of Nazianzus, the Christian Church defined its central "mysteries"— the rudiments of the faith that could not have been known by unassisted human reason but that can be shown by theology to be free of internal contradiction.

Now, the *supernatural* Christian assertions about God and the redeeming work of Jesus Christ have implications about the *nature* of man and the cosmos. True, philosophy is always the "handmaid of theology." But truer still, theology serves philosophy by enabling philosophy to reach its true end. In the first Christian centuries, the greatest theologian was also the greatest philosopher: Augustine (354–430), a bishop in Roman North Africa and author of literally hundreds of seminal works, the foremost being his *Confessions* and the *City of God*. It is often said that all of Western philosophy consists of footnotes to Plato. This is true in one sense, but it is actually more accurate to say that Western philosophy for the last fifteen hundred years has consisted of footnotes to Saint Augustine. For many of the most important questions in philosophy for more than fifteen centuries could not even have been formulated before the Christian revelation and before Augustine's grappling with the meaning of that revelation. Questions about freedom and the will and their relationship to personal identity, for example, are effectively unthinkable before Augustine; and philosophers from Descartes to Kant may best be understood as "Augustinians." The range of Augustine's interests was stupendous. Who could grapple with them all in college? But not to have read his *Confessions* is to miss perhaps the single greatest book in Western history: so singular a work is the *Confessions* that it seems nobody attempted such an autobiography of his inner life for more than a thousand years thereafter. Yet how difficult it is to find *any* course in an American university that will introduce you to this great Western mind.

THE FALL OF THE WESTERN Roman Empire to invading barbarian tribes brought about the so-called Dark Ages, with classical learning kept barely alive in far-flung monasteries. The Dark Ages were neither so ignorant nor so lengthy as commonly believed, however. Boethius, executed by the Ostrogoth King Theodoric in A.D. 524, was perhaps the last representative of the uninterrupted classical Christian tradition of learning in the West. By the time of Anselm of Canterbury (1033–1109), the great flowering of the "medieval synthesis" was already at hand. Yet even in the dark depths of the ninth century, the writings of John Scotus Eriugena (810–c. 877), a monk from Ireland, demonstrate that philosophical and theological erudition and originality of the highest level were possible in the monastic schools.

Still, the second great moment for theology after the Patristic Age is the period of

scholasticism in the High Middle Ages. With the Christian faith well defined and ad-
hered to throughout Europe, Christian monks and friars in the new universities of
Paris, Oxford, and elsewhere now faced a challenge from Aristotle, whose works were
being translated from Arabic into Latin and thus becoming available to the Western
mind for the first time in centuries. Aristotle's logical treatises, translated into Latin by
Boethius, had been in constant use throughout the Dark Ages, but the newly translated works threw into doubt several of Christianity's (and of theism's) core beliefs,
from the createdness of the world to the life of the soul after death.

This challenge was met most decisively in the *Summa Theologiae*, a summary of
theology, by Saint Thomas Aquinas (c. 1225-1274). This huge undertaking explicates
the Christian faith in the philosophical language of Aristotle and shows that nothing
that reason knows as true must necessarily render Christian faith irrational. As Aquinas
frequently puts it, grace (the supernatural) *perfects* nature; it does not destroy it. The
Summa is justly famous for its style of presentation as well as for its content. By pro-
ceeding through a series of propositions, while noting objections and answering those
objections in detail, Aquinas was able to display the dialectical spirit of scholastic
thought. Aquinas's *Summa* thus belies the common view of the medieval mind as dogmatic or narrow. Far from it. The possibility of alternate universes, whether monogamy
or polygamy is natural for man, and how it is that human beings can know anything at
all are just a few of the surprising topics addressed in the *Summa*. The very first question of the *Summa* asks whether theology is necessary. The answer is yes, of course, but
the objections to which Aquinas must respond are genuine ones.

Because medieval thought and theology are so little studied in American universities, few students are familiar with medieval theologians other than Aquinas. However, the essential continuity of the medieval scholastic enterprise with the theology of
the Patristic Age can best be seen in the writings of Anselm of Canterbury in the century before Aquinas. Moreover, while the *Summa Theologiae* is the most systematic work
of its kind, on several key matters—particularly the nature of the will, both in man and
in God—the theologians of Aquinas's Dominican Order were locked in unresolved dispute with the theologians of the Franciscan Order. Yet both the Dominican and
Franciscan schools of theology are considered orthodox, both authentic ways by which
faith can seek understanding. The first great Franciscan theologian was Saint
Bonaventure (c. 1217-1274), a contemporary of Aquinas. And in the two generations
after Aquinas, the Franciscans Duns Scotus (c. 1266-1308) and William of Ockham (c.
1285-1349) raised what might be called Augustinian objections against Aquinas's
Aristotelianism.

The views of Scotus and Ockham, in turn, are generally understood to have prepared the way for the Protestant Reformation of the sixteenth century. Martin Luther
(1483-1546) was a great Ockhamite Augustinian, and John Calvin (1509-1564) is probably best understood as a brilliant late medieval scholastic theologian attempting to read
Augustine anew. One result of the Reformation theology was that the traditional Christian marriage of theology and philosophy was annulled. In the churches of the Reformation, theology thereafter proceeds almost exclusively by way of scriptural commentary.

• • • • •

PERHAPS THE MOST PERNICIOUS development in the teaching of this material in recent years is the tendency of professors to champion the views of heretics against the orthodox theologians. Certain professors have "rediscovered" the Gnostic gospels and the writings of Arius, Pelagius, and Nestorius and have found these teachings more congenial to the modern mind. They like to suggest that what is considered orthodox Christianity is purely the result of arbitrary exercises of power by the hierarchical and patriarchal Church. In taking this deconstructive view, they profoundly skew a true understanding of the theology of the first centuries. For in fact, on several occasions the orthodox position was a distinctly minority view that won the assent of the faithful primarily by the force of greater logical coherence. To study the controversy between the heretics and the champions of orthodoxy can be useful, however, for in this way you can more readily see how dogmatic theology proceeds "negatively."

There are numerous secondary works that will help you to understand the orthodox theological tradition in a way that does not succumb to trite deconstruction. G. L. Prestige's *God in Patristic Thought* is an exhaustive study, though sometimes quite technical. J. N. D. Kelly's *Early Christian Doctrines* is a balanced and readable account of a range of disputed Patristic questions. Leo Donald Davis, S.J., *The First Seven Ecumenical Councils (325–787): Their History and Theology* is also valuable. Jaroslav Pelikan's monumental *The Christian Tradition: A History of the Development of Doctrine* is an encyclopedic source of information about the formal teaching of the Church. It is particularly good in its account of individual thinkers.

John Henry Newman's *Essay on the Development of Christian Doctrine* is one of the greatest theological treatments of the idea of theological tradition written in any language. It is as much a primary work in the thought of the nineteenth century as it is a work to aid understanding of historical developments. Newman's earlier work, *The Arians of the Fourth Century* is a still-useful model of Patristic scholarship that opens up the heart of the disputed question of those early days.

Vernon Bourke's *Augustine's Love of Wisdom* is an excellent philosophical biography, while Peter Brown's *Augustine of Hippo* represents the findings of the latest scholarship.

It is more difficult to find satisfactory secondary works on medieval theology; the philosophy of that age has been more studied. Josef Pieper's *Scholasticism: Personalities and Problems of Medieval Philosophy*, translated by Richard and Clara Winston, is the place to begin, and Frederick Copleston's *A History of Medieval Philosophy* is a standard reference. Etienne Gilson treats medieval theology and philosophy with the highest seriousness in *The Spirit of Mediaeval Philosophy* translated by A. H. C. Downes, *The Christian Philosophy of St. Thomas Aquinas* translated by G. A. Elrington, and *The Philosophy of St. Bonaventure* translated by Illtyd Trethowan. Gilson in turn recommended to students G. K. Chesterton's biography *Saint Thomas Aquinas*, saying that it captured the spirit of Aquinas's project better than any other book available.

In addition, Aidan Nichols, *The Shape of Catholic Theology*, offers a view of the contemporary course of the discipline of theology.

5. Modern Political Theory

Half a century ago, the political writings of Luther and Calvin would have been prominent on the syllabus of any American college course in modern political thought. Today, that course begins with Machiavelli (1469–1527) and excludes any consideration of the Reformers—or, indeed, of such Catholic thinkers of the sixteenth century as Thomas More (1478–1535) or Robert Bellarmine (1542–1621). In so presenting the history of political philosophy, the contemporary course indicates that its primary concern will be the problem of *modernity*—*die Neuzeit* or "new time," as it is called in German—which is, among other things, an age characterized by a growing secularism. One of the advantages of the current order of presentation is that it enables us to see more clearly how *being modern* might constitute a problem. One of the disadvantages of excluding Christian political theologies is that the dialectical dependence of modernity on Christianity is thereby obscured.

At the beginning of his longest work, the *Discourses on the First Ten Books of Livy*, Machiavelli implicitly compares himself with that icon of the new man, Christopher Columbus. Machiavelli writes that he has set out to discover new continents in the moral and political world: this, in a book that is, on the surface, a commentary on an ancient Roman work of history. In addition, Machiavelli wrote *The Prince*, a handbook for ruthless statecraft in the turbulent world of Renaissance Italy. To be sure, the Renaissance was a rebirth of classical (pre-Christian) learning, but it was also something *new*. Machiavelli's "new modes and orders" were to be instituted *against* Christianity in a way that pagan philosophy and practice never had been. Consequently, to investigate the course of modern political theory is to approach a question of the first importance that nevertheless seldom is considered: What is *modern man?*

ARISTOTLE HELD THAT POLITICAL SCIENCE (or political philosophy) was the architectonic inquiry. Since it is the business of statecraft to oversee all human initiatives and to assign each person to his place, it is therefore the business of political philosophy, after examining all human interests in due order, to provide the overarching pattern into which those activities will be fitted. For Aristotle, the *polis* (the "city") comes into being because of human necessity, but its aim is the good life. According to Greek political philosophy, then, life in the *polis* is the natural *end* for man. But Christianity introduced an unprecedented political and philosophical problem, for Jesus had said, "My Kingdom is not of this world." Life in the city is *not* man's ultimate goal: salvation is, and salvation is personal. Christianity thereby "loosened" the ties that bound men together in their particular political orders.

But unlike either Judaism or Islam, Christianity did not present itself as a divine rule that superintends all the details of life. Had this been the case, political life as the Greeks understood it would simply have been reconstituted at the level of the believing community. In both Judaism and Islam, the political and religious spheres coincide exactly and do so on religion's terms. But for Christianity the secular realm is, in principle, free to organize itself independently. Jesus had also said, "Render unto Caesar the things that are Caesar's," thus bestowing a certain autonomy on secular affairs. Still, the Church's divine mission is to lead all men to salvation. Having renounced secular governance, the Church must nonetheless claim the right to regulate anything that might put salvation in peril. In the Christian dispensation, the secular realm is never, finally, free. An irresolvable conflict between *sacerdotium* and *imperium*, between pope and emperor, seems essential to Christianity. Some twentieth-century commentators, such as Christopher Dawson, have seen this very tension as the driving force of true progress in the West. But the modern political philosophers did not see it this way. Instead, it is just this conflict that they set out to resolve decisively. In the process, modern political philosophy brought into being *modern man*.

Thus, we may speak of a "modern project." For the modern political philosophers did not merely seek to capture the truth about man's place in the cosmos and in society; they also set out to transform the human world. In doing so, modern political philosophy diverges systematically from both ancient and medieval thought. In reaction to both Christian and classical political thought, the moderns begin by "lowering the sights" of political communities. Modern thinkers in various ways insist that the end for man in politics is not the good life but mere life, comfortable security. This end in turn is accomplished, perhaps paradoxically, by the liberation of human passions. Whereas all ancient and medieval political philosophy sought to temper human passions through an education into virtue, understood as a kind of voluntary self-constraint, modern political philosophy seeks to understand and foster *freedom*.

HUMAN FREEDOM IS OF COURSE nothing new. But pursuing freedom as an end, and not merely for the few but for all men equally—that is a radical novelty. For Plato and Aristotle both, freedom was thought neither to be the natural state of man nor to be an unqualified good. After all, it seems obvious that most men, when left free, will seek to satisfy their vulgar desires rather than pursue any higher and specifically human ends. Freedom can only be good for you if you can use your freedom well. Thus, for the ancients *virtue*, not freedom, is the proper pursuit of political men. Any purported natural "right" to liberty would depend upon virtue. Virtue comes *first* in ancient political thought, and it is a public rather than a private concern.

But for the moderns, freedom comes first. And this contention precipitates a "transvaluation of values" beyond the realm of politics. The most obvious example of this concerns the relative valuing of political life and family life. The ancients associated politics with the good life or human flourishing. Political participation was thought intrinsically valuable, an end in itself. In contrast, the family or household (the *oikos*, in Greek) was understood as the realm of slavish "economics," where the mere necessities of life were secured. For modern men, however, something of the reverse is true. We tend to consider politics to be a matter of technical economic division and boundary-setting. Political life is nothing very exalted, more a distraction from "what really matters." Conversely, we hold family life to be the privileged sphere of human fulfillment. Only a modern man would say that the end of all human striving is to be happy at home. Such is the power of political philosophy.

After Machiavelli, the modern pursuit of freedom proceeds by proposing a rival to the biblical Eden—the "state of nature"—from which men emerge not by divine expulsion but by choice, by agreement, by *contract*. In the accounts of Hobbes (1588-1679), Locke (1632-1704), and Rousseau (1712-1778)—each quite distinct in his theorizing—the justice that men construct for themselves is based not on conformity with nature but on reason's cunning overcoming of nature's inconvenience. Talk of the "state of nature" with its "natural rights" secured in civil society by a "social contract" strikes us as a moderate commonplace, but these are frankly revolutionary concepts. David Hume (1711-1776) was the political philosopher in our tradition who called attention to the extremism in these views—*our* views. In the subsequent thought of German philosophers—from Kant (1724-1804) through Hegel (1770-1831) and Marx (1818-1883) to Nietzsche (1844-1900)—the philosophical burden of human freedom grew acute. For human freedom to be truly free, it must be utterly free of the restrictions of nature and tradition. For men to be truly free, these Germans say, each in his own way, men must be, or become, *gods*.

PRACTICALLY SPEAKING, YOU MUST make sure the course you take is in *modern* political theory and not *contemporary* political theory. The modern period begins in the sixteenth century, and some would say that modernity has already come to an end, having been succeeded by a postmodern age. Whatever the case, the work of such contemporary academic political thinkers as John Rawls or Richard Rorty or Jürgen Habermas is of only narrow interest. None is a central figure in the Western tradition.

Frequently the course in modern political theory is well taught, but two pedagogic approaches can misdirect your attention away from the really important questions you must grapple with. On the one hand, there are professors who will so focus their reading of the philosophical texts on the "contexts" of their times that there will be nothing we could possibly learn from them about how to order our life together today. In this case, modern political theory becomes merely a matter of antiquarian interest. On the other hand, there are professors who will spend much of their classroom time judging these great thinkers for their failure to live up to *our* standards of justice and right, particularly their bad record with regard to women and minorities. In this case, modern political theory becomes an exercise in flattering the prejudices of the present age.

The study of political philosophy is most valuable when you make use of the thought of the various philosophers to challenge your own unexamined opinions. Rather than recoiling at Machiavelli's amorality or Hobbes's totalitarianism or Kant's absolutism, ask yourself how these philosophers would react to *your* opinions. Would they find them wanting? Ask yourself what it is about the human world and the nature of man that these thinkers *see* and that you do not see as clearly, or at all. And because our American prejudices reflect the thought of John Locke and John Stuart Mill (1806-1873), you must make an extra effort to be critical when examining those two thinkers.

The readings in this course are difficult and lengthy. Indeed, students often find this course the hardest of the eight courses in this core curriculum. Fortunately, sound secondary literature in political philosophy is widely available. For a straightforward account of what each of the thinkers is actually saying (not always apparent on a first reading), try Dante Germino's *Machiavelli to Marx*. Pierre Manent's *Intellectual History of Liberalism*, translated by Rebecca Balinski, is especially telling concerning the anti-Christian orientation of modern political theory. Charles N. R. McCoy's *The Structure of Political Thought* is the effort of a Thomist to understand the meaning of modernity in light of the permanent structure of human nature. Eric Voegelin's *From Enlightenment to Revolution* examines several less prominent political theorists to illuminate the trajectory of modernity.

For particular modern political thinkers, the essays in Strauss & Cropsey's *History of Political Philosophy* are usually excellent.

6. Shakespeare

In Shakespeare's *Henry VI: Part III*, the magnificently wicked Duke of Gloucester (later Richard III) compares his villainy to the precepts of "the murderous Machiavel"—that is, to Machiavelli, the philosopher we found at the dawn of the modern age. *Julius Caesar* is one of a number of Shakespeare's plays set in antiquity, and the bard populates *A Midsummer Night's Dream* with minor pagan deities. *The Merchant of Venice* is Shakespeare's meditation on the relationship between the revealed Law of the Old Testament and the Law of Grace instituted by the New Covenant in Christ. Shakespeare (1564-1616), in short, is the poet who stands uniquely at the intersection of modern man, ancient man, and Christian man. He also notoriously engages in anachronism, refers to such impossible locales as the "shores of Bohemia," and often indiscriminately mixes pagan and Christian references in the same play. But far from constituting the forgivable "mistakes" of a precritical and uneducated mind, Shakespeare in this way signals his theme: the representation of human nature as such, in all its diversity and its unity.

It is a commonplace to say that Shakespeare's position for us in the English-speaking world is like that of Homer for the Greeks, Virgil for the Romans, Dante for the Italians, or Cervantes for the Spaniards. But this may actually understate Shakespeare's genius; he may simply be more universal even than those who are ranked among his peers. Shakespeare holds the poetic mirror of his imagination up to all of nature and to all of history. He invites us to delight and marvel at what he discovers. And we do. One excellent reason for taking a course on the plays of Shakespeare is the sheer *joy* of it.

We saw that in Plato's *Republic*, Socrates argues for the absolute superiority of philosophy to poetry. He even speaks of an "old quarrel" between the two, noting that since the poets sometimes portray the prospering of the wicked and the misfortunes of the just, the poets are a threat to virtue. Shifting his ground from morals to aesthetics,

Socrates adduces as key evidence for philosophy's superiority the fact that there is no poet among the Greeks who can write both tragedy and comedy well. What the poets relate is striking but one-sided and therefore distorted. Life is *both* tragic and comic, and yet perhaps neither ultimately tragic nor comic. Philosophers, on the contrary, transcend poetic partiality to approach the *whole*. This Socratic observation about poetic limitation proved true for centuries. But among Shakespeare's plays may be counted some of the most profound tragedies and most delightful comedies in all literature. If any poet can challenge Plato's claim about philosophy's supremacy, it is Shakespeare. His vision extends to the whole of man's wide world, while capturing the innermost workings of the human heart.

BY CONVENTION WE DIVIDE Shakespeare's plays into three kinds: tragedies, comedies, and histories. Among the histories, however, there are tragic endings (general woe and death for Richard II), and there are comic endings (Henry V's wooing of the French princess following victory at Agincourt). In Shakespeare, life and art thus mingle. He in effect reveals that the stories of "real life," the life of each historical human being, can hold as much meaning as the most powerful mythic tale. Each human life holds a fascination beyond any archetype. Shakespeare marvels lovingly at humanity, and we in turn share in that wonder.

Here among the striking facts of Shakespeare's work is that he did not invent his plots. Rather, he took well-known historical episodes or popular tales lying ready to hand and retold what was familiar to his audiences. Where, then, is Shakespeare's creativity—if, indeed, creativity is the measure by which to judge a poet? In his incomparable language of course. But beyond that, Shakespeare's genius is expressed primarily in his characterizations. Our deepest interest is drawn by Shakespeare's characters—about 900 of them throughout the plays, and yet each an irreducible individual, each with a life of his own. Falstaff alone is a miracle.

A comparison of MacBeth and Richard III illustrates Shakespeare's unmatched ability to portray the details of our humanity. Both MacBeth and Richard III are soldiers, both usurpers who obtain the throne through treason, both driven by ambition. In both cases, their futures are foretold by supernatural signs and they both lose their thrones in battle with the legitimate heir. Yet where MacBeth is "too full of the milk of human kindness," Richard III is remorselessly evil. MacBeth's ambition is a matter of vanity, revolving around honor; whereas Richard's ambition is oriented to power and driven by pride. MacBeth is soft where Richard is strong. On the surface, their stories are the same, but how different are these two men—or rather, these two fictions who seem so alive in Shakespeare's verse. As Shakespeare's wisest reader, Samuel Johnson, aptly commented, "[H]e that has read Shakespeare with attention will perhaps find little new in the crowded world."

• • • • •

SOME STUDENTS OBJECT TO STUDYING Shakespeare in college because he is so familiar to them from high school. They therefore associate him with a discarded intellectual naiveté, judging themselves "beyond" the bard. Of course this is not true, for Shakespeare is always ahead of us. Harold Bloom goes so far (too far) as to suggest that Shakespeare has "invented" us, for much of what we recognize in human nature has been observed *for* us by Shakespeare. So well has he represented nature that now we may well judge nature by *his* artistic standards. Now that we have begun to grasp the sweep of the Western tradition, however, other questions can also emerge for us. For example, we must now inevitably ask, How do Shakespeare's tragedies compare to those of the Greeks? How do his comedies compare? What can the differences and similarities tell us about the human condition?

Hegel observed that in ancient tragedy, conflict erupts *between* antagonists, such as Creon and Antigone, each representing a principle of action. In the prototypical modern tragedy, *Hamlet*, however, conflict rages *within* the protagonist. There is greater depth to the human soul in Shakespeare's tragedies, and Hegel believed this to be a legacy of Christianity. It is certainly the case that Shakespeare's tragedies appear more horrifying to us than the works of Sophocles. What accounts for this effect? And what does this effect mean for Shakespeare's vision of the world? Is the greater *depth* of Shakespearean tragedy brought about because of the greater *heights* opened up for the human soul by Christian hope?

For often very bad reasons, we tend to consider tragedy a more profound, a more important genre than comedy. This may be one reason we tend to underestimate the mind of the Middle Ages. For medieval men did not write tragedies. When Chaucer attempted one, he set it in the ancient world and used the story to illustrate the difference Christian grace makes. The world is tragic without grace, but since grace has come, it is tragic no longer. The greatest achievement of the medieval mind could only have been a divine *comedy* (Dante). Tragedy returns to the world with the Renaissance, and Shakespeare is a great tragic writer. But Shakespeare is also a writer of *profound* comedies. His comedies, however, are utterly unlike those of the ancients. For in Shakespeare, human love is not simply ridiculous. While love perhaps begins as something low, and while it may lead us astray, it also may be made sublime. His comedies always end with marriage, the hallowed fulfillment of human love. Shakespeare can teach us how to love.

IF THE POET WERE TO RESPOND to the philosopher's claimed supremacy, he would note that human nature is such that poetic representation can stir the moral imagination beyond the deepest philosophy. We may learn in Aristotle's *Ethics* about the virtue of courage, and Aristotle may even convince us—intellectually—that we must become virtuous. But Henry V's Saint Crispin's Day speech *moves* us. We then *know* courage better. We may anatomize human loves with impressive philosophical skill, but everyone knows that love can only be understood from the inside. In our concreteness, somehow artistic representation provides an icon of actual experience, always the best of teachers. And in the end, Shakespeare knows quite well what he thinks about the limitations of the philosophers. In *The Tempest*, he presents for our consideration the philosopher Prospero, whose philosophical island idyll is seen as ultimately irresponsible. Does Plato really comprehend the poet better than Shakespeare comprehends the philosopher?

SHAKESPEARE HAS LARGELY RETAINED his privileged place in the curricula of many university English departments. However, precisely because Shakespeare is the very epitome of a classic or a canonical figure, he seems always the favorite target of the latest vogue in critical theory. Thus, you must beware the theoretical lens through which Shakespeare may be taught to you.

Today, deconstruction has become passé, but it has often merely metamorphosed into a critical school known as "new historicism" or "cultural materialism." For critics of this persuasion, inheritors of Karl Marx, literary texts are cultural artifacts reflecting the power structure of their authors' societies. Like any other author, Shakespeare's works are interrogated to "show" how the bard is merely mouthing the ideology of his day. Shakespeare is an early modern bourgeois. The objections to such an approach are legion, the foremost being that in trapping the poet in his context, there is nothing one could possibly learn from him. There is thus little point in reading him. And of course, if all writers are merely reflections of power relations, isn't that also true of these contemporary academic writers of criticism? Why read them?

Shakespeare's plays have also proven fertile ground recently for the ruminations of feminists and theorists of sex and gender. Some feminists denounce him as a patriarch, but more recently there is an enthusiasm for Shakespeare's alleged ambiguity about sex and gender: so often comic plot developments involve cross-dressing, and of course, in Shakespeare's time, all the women's roles would have been played by boys. But while some of these critics are very intelligent, they push their arguments to farcical extremes. Perhaps the best response to those who claim to discover themes of "sex and gender" in Shakespeare is to respond that he is much more clearly a poet concerned with "love and marriage."

To learn more about Shakespeare and his times, you may consult Andrew Gurr's *William Shakespeare: The Extraordinary Life of the Most Successful Writer of All Time*. Eric Sams' *The Real Shakespeare: Retrieving the Early Years, 1564–1594* sheds new light on the bard's formative influences.

C. S. Lewis's *Discarded Image* is a brilliant and brilliantly crafted account of the late medieval and early modern worldview that formed the background understanding of Shakespeare's audience.

C. L. Barber's *Shakespeare's Festive Comedy* is a classic work exploring the Christian elements of the bard's comedies. R. Chris Hassel's *Faith and Folly in Shakespeare's Romantic Comedies* is a more contemporary work in the same spirit.

A. C. Bradley's *Shakespearean Tragedy* studies the heroes of the tragedies, appreciating their depth and differentiating their plights from the crises found in ancient tragedy. Roy Battenhouse's *Shakespearean Tragedy: Its Art and Christian Premises* argues that the peculiarities of Shakespearean tragedy are a result of the explicitly Christian dimension of Shakespeare's mind.

Robert Ornstein, *A Kingdom for a Stage: The Achievement of Shakespeare's History Plays* is the best general introduction to the history plays, arguing that they contain a political teaching.

For an accessible response to contemporary schools of criticism, see Brian Vickers's *Returning to Shakespeare*. A more sophisticated defense of traditional interpretations of Shakespeare may be found in Anthony David Nuttall, *A New Mimesis: Shakespeare and the Representation of Reality*. The first third of Nuttall's volume constitutes a sophisticated expression of the old argument that art is valuable in its representative function. The remainder of the book is a delightful contemporary reading of Shakespeare freed from the shackles of ideology.

For another perspective, G. Wilson Knight's *Wheel of Fire* is a stunning example of the critical insights that can be gained when attention is paid to the imagery embedded in Shakespeare's poetic language.

7. United States History before 1865

Machiavelli's aim was to institute "new modes and orders" in the moral world, and Shakespeare set his play *The Tempest* on Caliban's mysterious island home across the sea. In both cases these men were reflecting on an historical fact that looms enormous in the history of the West: the discovery of the New World. While ideas certainly have consequences, the facts of historical experience shape no less profoundly the human imagination, and so with the experience of the Discovery.

Columbus had set sail to find a trade route to China, an advanced civilization whose political upheavals had already affected the economy of the Roman Empire in the days of the Caesars. But Columbus encountered something more remarkable than Cathay—an entire continent seemingly in a state of nature and thus, to the European mind, the property of no one. Never before had Western men experienced anything remotely like this. Perhaps no one in history had. The *idea* of America seized the European mind and remains part of all Americans' identity. That idea is of an unconquered but conquerable wilderness where one may escape and start anew in freedom and independence. Peasants leaving the land for the medieval towns had experienced a kind of liberation, but the New World promised something more startling, an opportunity to reform the human situation for all, to overcome at last the weight of the past in the name of freedom and nature.

However much philosophers and humanists had speculated about utopia in previous centuries, utopia had always been "nowhere," situated in the shadowy mental realm of myth or fantasy. Now, a seemingly utopian territory had been discovered that was incontestably *real*. Time and again America has been the home of utopian projects, from the Puritans' Godly Experiment, to Oneida in upstate New York, to David Koresh's apocalyptic commune in Waco. But above these smaller experiments, many of them motivated by religious enthusiasm, there is the overarching political project of the United States itself, the American Experiment of an Empire of Liberty fulfilling its Manifest Destiny as "the last best hope of men on earth." Surely there are utopian (and messianic) elements evident even in our Constitutional prudence. And this peculiarity—extremism embedded in our moderation—is what you will explore in a course on the first "half" of American history.

THE UNITED STATES IS A NATION with a known origin, a *founding*. Our history as a people does not in the first instance run off into an immemorial past, nor do our political practices descend to us from before the dawn of recorded history. America's political forms are the result of a choice. Moreover, that choice was not arbitrary but was guided by principles believed to reflect the moral realities of human life. Whether these principles arose from reason or experience remains a disputed question.

The two questions that naturally face Americans when considering our history are these: (1) Are America's founding principles sound or unsound? and (2) Has America "turned out" as the founders intended (i.e., have America's political principles worked)?

These questions assume that we already know what America's founding principles are; as we shall see, however, such a belief is not really warranted.

These questions have been answered quite differently at different points in our history. Charles Beard, writing in the 1930s in the midst of capitalism's apparent collapse, discerned at work in the U. S. Constitution the unjust self-interest of an early class of powerful possessive individualists. For Beard, America was ill founded, but America had indeed turned out as intended, only to face the "inherent contradictions" of capitalism in the Great Depression.

Today, however, the typical answer to these questions is that America's founding principles were sound but were originally incompletely applied (the equal rights of slaves and women were not secured by the original Constitution). This incompletion may be attributed to the founders' inability to see beyond their historical context, or to a conscious and malign intent on the founders' part, or to their conscious calculation and hope of setting in motion a process leading to "liberty and justice for all." Whatever the case, insofar as America has turned out "badly," it is said to be because of those incomplete applications of the founding principles. In this account of our history, America's core principle is a commitment to equal freedom. The expansion of "rights" is thus America's most important story. Such, for example, is the implication of Eric Foner's widely assigned but dubious book, *Reconstruction: America's Unfinished Revolution*. Such is the promise said to be held by "our living Constitution." Such also, in a slightly different register, is the view of a prominent group of contemporary neoconservative political thinkers.

The narrative of expanding liberty is indeed majestic, and there is much truth to it. But it also neglects much in America's history and therefore obscures full understanding. Above all, this interpretation of America requires us to believe that nothing has been lost in the unfolding of American history except injustice, to lose which, of course, is no loss at all. But in fact, genuine human goods have sometimes waned as our rights and freedoms have waxed. America's progress has a *tragic* dimension as well.

To interpret American history through the lens of a rights-based individualism is to say that America is the historical actualization of the liberal tradition in political theory, a tradition most closely associated with Locke. Louis Hartz's famous book *The Liberal Tradition in America* argued for a Lockean consensus in American history. Because America was a nation "born equal," Hartz claimed that Americans were exclusively devoted to one form or another of bourgeois liberalism; both radical socialism and European-style conservatism were instinctively believed to be un-American. Again, there is some truth in this, but one immediate problem for Hartz's thesis was that he had to write the South and the Civil War *out* of American history.

Two further responses to the liberal thesis have emerged in recent years. One group of scholars argues that early America's authentic political tradition is really civic republicanism, a term that designates strong democracy and political participation of the sort that characterized the ancient Greek *polis*. Samuel Adams spoke of his desire to see America as a "Christian Sparta." For the civic republican interpreters, America's founding aspiration was not the "right to be left alone," but rather the right to participate in decisions affecting the individual and the community. Rights are then a *secondary* concern to democracy.

But Adams spoke of a *Christian* Sparta. The other major interpretive school of recent years has explored the decisive role played by Christianity throughout American history. Both liberalism and civic republicanism have a secular orientation, but many of their themes have correlates in American Christianity's faith and practice. Liberalism speaks of individual freedom, and Christian conversion promises a truth that will set men free. Civic republicanism speaks of self-governing communities, and Congregationalist Christianity is concretely organized in just such a fashion. The religious beliefs of such early national figures as Madison, Jefferson, and Adams are a matter of dispute. But the religious enthusiasm of the ratifying publics of the original states is not, and this fact must be remembered when we seek to discover the original understanding of the American Constitution.

TODAY, AMERICAN HISTORY IS AMONG the most politicized of the disciplines. Fashionable historians vacillate between, on the one hand, denouncing America for its exclusion or marginalization of women, minorities, and the poor from the promise of American life, and, on the other, championing the unsung (and sometimes simply mythical) contributions made by women, minorities, and the poor to the development of American life. But all historians seem united in holding America to be an "exceptional" country, the embodiment of an *idea*. The challenge for an American hoping to develop a genuine historical imagination is to see America as a *not* wholly exceptional country—to note, for example, that the unstable countries of Latin America for the most part adopted variants of the American Constitution, while stable Canada was founded in explicit repudiation of American principles. Such recognitions are where *thought* begins.

The most powerful sustained argument for the classical republican thesis concerning the American founding is Bernard Bailyn's *Ideological Origins of the American Revolution*. Barry Shain's *Myth of American Individualism* in turn provides the evidence and assesses the theoretical importance of exclusivist Reformed Protestant communalism.

Harry Jaffa's *Crisis of the House Divided* is a philosophical reading of the Lincoln-Douglas debates that interprets American experience through the lens of classical natural right. Jaffa sees Lincoln as "completing" the founding. For a powerful rejoinder to Jaffa that champions a strongly states'-rights understanding of America's original compact, see M. E. Bradford, *Original Intentions: On the Making and Ratification of the United States Constitution*.

Willmoore Kendall and George Carey's *Basic Symbols of the American Political Tradition* examines a series of American founding documents of the late eighteenth century in the light of previous American founding moments. Kendall and Carey discern an American tradition of a self-governing "virtuous people."

Herbert Storing's *What the Anti-Federalists Were For* is a brilliant recovery of the views of America's early losing side. A commonplace observation among political theorists is that America now possesses Federalist institutions operating in an anti-Federalist fashion.

The great Southern alternative understanding of the America experiment requires careful study if we are to avoid shallow ideological interpretations of our history. Eugene Genovese's *Roll, Jordan, Roll* is the best book on slavery in America; and his book *The Slaveholders' Dilemma* is a sympathetic account of the way in which the ruling classes in the antebellum South viewed their world. Two books that present Southern views in a striking fashion and that serve to balance the likes of Eric Foner are E. Merton Coulter's *The South during Reconstruction, 1865–1877* and Ludwell Johnson's *Division and Reunion: America 1848–1877*.

For a work arguing for continuity between America and the European past, see Russell Kirk's *Roots of American Order*. Gary L. Gregg's *Vital Remnants: America's Founding and the Western Tradition* collects several notable essays exploring the same theme.

8. Nineteenth-Century European Intellectual History

By about the end of their second year in college, American students have acquired an assortment of concepts and ideas by which they are able to interpret their world, and they are impressed with themselves because of the intellectual *power* such mediating schema, provide. They may be familiar with the Hawthorne Experiment and understand the Oedipal Complex. They may say knowing things about *gemeinschaft* and *gesellschaft* and about alienation. They may analyze their friends' behaviors as the manifestation of sublimated desires. They may speak with assurance about the social construction of reality, and object to a friend's generalization as relying on evidence which is only "anecdotal."

That an individual's thinking proceeds by means of mediating concepts—mental "lenses," if you will—is no surprise. Such mediating concepts may be found in many forms: in scriptural exemplars or in historical knowledge or in literary precedent, for example. What *is* striking about the (very) American minds of American undergraduates is that their common stock of mediating concepts is drawn *overwhelmingly* from the social sciences, which the Europeans call more aptly the "sciences of man" or the "human sciences," those academic disciplines born in the nineteenth century. The American mind of today has thus in large part been constituted by European ideas of very recent and very particular provenance. To study the intellectual history of the nineteenth century provides you with the chance to polish your conceptual lenses for even deeper insight, and also to discover, perhaps, that what you took to be a powerfully useful lens is in fact a *blinder*.

THE GREAT SYNTHETIC MIND WHO stands at the dawn of the nineteenth century is the German philosopher G. W. F. Hegel (1770–1831). Into him flow both the rationalism of the Enlightenment and the insights of the Romantic reaction to the excesses of Enlightenment. For the next century, much Western thought might be understood as a prolonged response to Hegel, and that response is disproportionately undertaken in the German language. In many ways, the nineteenth century was the German century. Even America came under Germany's cultural sway as the institutional Germanization of the American university in the first quarter of the twentieth century led to the Germanization of the American mind.

Hegel is the great nineteenth-century thinker, and therefore the prototypically *modern* thinker, for at least three reasons.

First, Hegel's philosophical system is not just a series of discrete ideas but the elaboration of one Big Idea. The coming to self-consciousness of *Geist* or Spirit in history is the grandest of grand narratives; Hegel's system endeavors to be a Theory of Everything, from the meaning of music to religion to culture to economics. And the modern Western mind has been strongly attracted to such ingenious comprehensive theories resting on the most parsimonious of foundations. We find such theories *impressive*. We accord *respect* to a thinker who can concoct one, but the grounds for our doing so is by no means clear. The idea of the grand narrative is also the point on which turns the contemporary postmodern assault on modern thought. For the postmoderns, grand narrative is now passé. Or is it truer to say that the super-session of all grand narratives *is* the postmodern grand narrative?

Second, Hegel's attempt to understand history philosophically is an example of the secularization of the Western mind. In old-fashioned accounts of nineteenth-century intellectual history, historians would speak of the "coming of age" of modern man, the mind's final liberation from clerical supervision and medieval superstition. The story of the nineteenth century is of course more complex than that. In fact, Christianity was terribly weak throughout the eighteenth century and experienced a robust popular, doctrinal, and institutional revival in the nineteenth century. At the same time, however, it is true that during the nineteenth century the human sciences co-opted Christian categories and concepts. Purporting to uncover the rational truths behind Christian "myths," the practitioners of the human sciences emptied Christian ideas of their content and kept the shells. Hegel's particular appropriation was the doctrine of Providence, and his innovation would have lasting impact on Western thought.

The Renaissance understood itself as a rebirth of classical culture—that is to say, a turning back to the past rather than something new. However, the discoveries of that age soon precipitated the Battle of the Books, a debate about the relative importance of the revived ancient and new modern learning. Nineteenth century men had no such debate. They simply *knew* that modern times were better. They knew this because thinkers like Hegel had devised arguments for the *necessity* of historical progress. In understanding the philosophical or scientific "laws" of history in the manner of Hegel or his successors, one could claim to understand the mind of God better than any priest or bishop.

Third, Hegel's claimed insight into the structure of history meant that he was relieved (as were his epigones, such as Marx and many of us today) of the obligation to argue for the justice or goodness of his preferred social arrangements. Whether we liked it or not, Hegel said, history was heading in a certain direction, and nothing could stop it, much less reverse it. In a time of disputed values, such an argument was an apparent trump. Hegel purported to demonstrate something *objective*, a fact, rather than to argue pointlessly over something *subjective*, values. This dubious intellectual shorthand—claiming to be on the side of the "inevitable" future—remains deeply engrained in us today. But Hegel's understanding of history is also paradigmatic of the modern sciences of man in another way: in its virtual elimination of human agency. Men are no longer understood as free and responsible *causes;* rather, they are understood as *effects* of forces beyond their control. Humanity's coming of age seems to entail for the modern mind a considerable deflation of humanity.

By consensus, the other major figures of modern, or nineteenth-century, intellectual history are Charles Darwin (1809–82), Karl Marx (1818–83), Friedrich Nietzsche (1844–1900), and Sigmund Freud (1856–1939). These four are the paradigmatic figures of their age and ours. Like Hegel, they are intellectual system builders, founders of entirely new academic disciplines, human sciences based on a single insight. All of these thinkers are secularizers. They find they can no longer believe in the biblical religion. Yet try as some may, they cannot simply return to a pre-Christian understanding of nature. And so their naturalism is peculiarly post-Christian. And their humanism has in each case a peculiarly inhuman quality, for in each case man is reduced to an epiphenomenon of other influences, and largely materialist influences at that. Can such as these truly represent the "highest" intellectual achievements of the Western tradition? Or are we not driven, rather, to reconsider precisely that view of historical progress which is so striking a legacy of modern times?

• • • • •

IN HISTORY DEPARTMENTS, the course covering the key thinkers mentioned above might be called something like "Makers of the Modern Mind" or "Western Mind in Crisis." Or you may be able to find only a course in, for example, "European Intellectual History after 1815," which will combine the nineteenth and twentieth centuries. But the twentieth century is less significant intellectually. Beyond some genuine advances in the natural sciences, very few of the currents of twentieth-century thought are original. Communism, nationalism, social democracy, Christian democracy, Darwinism, feminism, neo-paganism, racism, behaviorism, and utilitarianism are just a few twentieth-century movements with roots in the nineteenth century. Focus your attention there.

You may encounter two distinct teaching problems in a modern intellectual history course. First, your professor may provide an excessively narrow interpretation of the modern world, a "big theory" which is inevitably distorting. Perhaps the modern age is thought to be the age of progress, and so progressive texts will be supplied, with each successive radicalization following as if of necessity from the previous. Or perhaps the modern mind is thought to represent the fulfillment of the Enlightenment project, in which case secularism is stressed. Keep in mind that to characterize an age in such a sweeping way is to follow in the footsteps of Hegel. Try to be more critical, while also acknowledging the partial truth in virtually every Big Idea.

Second, the discipline of intellectual history has begun a slow death in American history departments, being displaced by "cultural history." Cultural history is driven by the fashionable theories of Foucault (1926–84) and Derrida (b. 1930) concerning "knowledge/power," the post-Marxian notion that all thinking is a function of the power relations in a society. The cultural historians' project is not to discover what is good and true, or false and pernicious, in a given thinker's work; nor is it to assess how that thinker's work influences later developments of thought. Rather this project seeks to reveal the origin of a thinker's ideas in economic and other power relations. In this way a thinker's views are said to be "explained," rather in the manner of the historical critics of the Bible. But do we ever think of ourselves in this way? Does the cultural historian think of himself in this way? If he does not, and we do not, why ever would we think such a procedure would yield true understanding of the past?

Students also frequently encounter what we might term a "learning problem" in this course. Faced with great minds who appear to see through dearly held views such as those proposed by traditional religion, a student may feel the need to summon all his intellectual resources to refute these "masters of suspicion" in the most direct fashion, to smite them hip and thigh. Yet the same student may secretly fear that the "jig is up" on traditional faiths. For it is quite unlikely that even the brightest of students will be able to achieve anything approaching a demonstrative refutation of some of the world's greatest minds. Undergraduates should therefore focus their attention first on *understanding*—critically, of course. The best defense against unsettling texts is always to *read more*, and to read critically.

Moreover, if a core curriculum pursued in the spirit of Newman has taught a student anything, it should be that temporal parochialism is to be avoided; the most recent thinking is not necessarily the best. A clever and spare theory is also not the same thing as wisdom. And while each of the great nineteenth-century thinkers boasts of removing veils, dispelling illusions, revealing the unvarnished truth about the human condition, one may legitimately wonder whether these thinkers have broken through to new vision or merely propounded new myths. Intellectual equipoise is one of the great fruits of the liberally educated mind.

Karl Lowith's *From Hegel to Nietzsche* is an elegantly written book describing the course of philosophy in the nineteenth century. Robert Nisbet's *Sociological Tradition* and Raymond Aron's *Main Currents in Sociological Thought* both serve as valuable introductions to the sciences of man. Jacques Barzun's *Darwin, Marx, Wagner: Critique of a Heritage* offers judicious assessments. A sweeping religious perspective on such thinkers as Comte and Feuerbach is added by Henri de Lubac's *Drama of Atheist Humanism*. In a more academic idiom, you may find useful James Turner's *Without God, Without Creed: The Origins of Unbelief in America*.

Concerning individual thinkers, Gertrude Himmelfarb's *Darwin and the Darwinian Revolution* places the father of scientific evolution carefully in the context of his time. Adrian Desmond and James Moore's *Darwin: The Life of a Tormented Evolutionist* likewise contextualizes and demythologizes Darwin. Neither book is any sort of handbook refuting evolution, but both can contribute to your understanding of the topic.

Thomas Sowell's *Marxism: Philosophy and Economics* is an accessible introduction to the father of communist doctrine. Leszek Kolakowski's *Main Currents of Marxism* is the definitive work by an ex-Marxist theoretician. The writings of Alexander Solzhenitsyn are also valuable here. That recent years have seen an explosion of work on Nietzsche is a bad sign, given the current politicization of the academy. Two recent thought-provoking exceptions are Fredrick Appel's *Nietzsche contra Democracy* and Peter Berkowitz's *Nietzsche: The Ethics of an Immoralist*, though the latter may paint Nietzsche in colors too attractive.

Two good books on Freud are Frank Sulloway's *Freud: Biologist of the Mind* and Frederick Crews's remarkable collection, *Unauthorized Freud: Doubters Confront a Legend*. Both are critical in the highest sense. Students should actively avoid the frequently assigned Peter Gay, *Freud: A Life for Our Time*, which is uncritical hagiography.

Ten Courses More

The core curriculum is the heart of the matter of undergraduate education. Indeed, as we saw with John Henry Newman, the nonelective, wide-ranging classical Western studies of nineteenth-century Oxford were once thought to be appropriately the whole of the college curriculum. Even as late as the 1950s, a student's core requirements frequently constituted more than half of his college coursework.

Today that is not the case, and you will eventually find yourself navigating through the many requirements of a "major" or "concentration." While presumably you choose your major based on personal interest and motivation, there are still common pitfalls to avoid. And quite often the right word of advice at the right time can prove to be the key that unlocks for you the inner logic of your studies. For expert guidance through your major, similar to that offered here for the core curriculum, the Intercollegiate Studies Institute is publishing a complete series of "Guides to the Major Disciplines." These monographs contain the personal reflections and advice of some of the country's most distinguished scholars. They distill insights gained in decades of award-winning teaching. These guides show you the way to get the most from your major.

Still, having completed the eight courses that here constitute a core of your own, you may find yourself with some remaining electives and a desire to explore the Western tradition further and for its own sake. If so, here are some suggestions for additional courses that can help complete your view of the Western *whole:*

RELIGION: *The Old Testament.* If your college offerings have constrained you to take a course on the New Testament rather than a course on the Bible as a whole, you really must proceed to the Old Testament. (Not to do so is to succumb to one of the oldest Christian heresies: Marcionism.) In the Hebrew scriptures, a fundamental Western paradox is first played out: the tension between the universalism implicit in Abraham's world-shaking discovery of the One God—monotheism—and the particularism of God's special covenant with and gift of the Law to his chosen people, Israel.

HISTORY: *Roman History.* The American founders looked to Greek history primarily for *cautionary* tales—examples of what can go wrong with republics. But in the Roman experience they found virtues and institutions that worked. It is no accident that so many of the early American pamphleteers took Roman names for their pseudonyms, the foremost being Publius, the collective pseudonym of the authors of *The Federalist* (Hamilton, Madison, and Jay).

COMPARATIVE LITERATURE: *The "Divine Comedy."* This great epic has been called the *Summa Theologiae* set to poetry. The cosmic dimension of the Christian faith is made powerfully clear as Dante plumbs the depths of hell and then approaches "the love that moves the sun and the other stars."

PHILOSOPHY: *Introduction to Modern Philosophy.* For an alternative understanding of the nature of modernity, one that focuses on problems of knowledge and the metaphysical legacy of Christianity, you need to encounter such thinkers as Rene Descartes (1596-1650) and David Hume (1711-76) and Immanuel Kant (1724-1804), and here is where you will meet those minds at their best.

POLITICAL SCIENCE: *Constitutional Interpretation.* While America's founders set out to establish *novus ordo saeclorum*, a new order for the ages, they nonetheless took pride in upholding the continuity in America of the main body of English common law, a set of practices and judgments inherited from time immemorial. Regarding the most important things, wisdom is found not only in the minds of singular philosophical geniuses, but sometimes—perhaps more frequently—in the voice of tradition, "the democracy of the dead."

ECONOMICS: *History of Economic Thought.* Those drawn to the life of the mind often view business and economic production with lofty disdain. But since human beings are *embodied* spirits, "getting and spending" is no small matter. Economic policies can mean the difference between wealth and poverty for whole societies. And as the twentieth-century showdown between the followers of Adam Smith (1723-90) and Karl Marx showed, economic systems can also mean the difference between liberty and tyranny.

HISTORY OF SCIENCE: *Introduction to the History of Science*. The prestige of science in the modern world has come at the expense of philosophy and theology. Science was thought capable of an absolute knowledge unavailable to other forms of inquiry. To discover that science can have a *history* is to put science in a more humble but still important place. Scientists already know this. This course lets nonscientists in on that secret.

ENGLISH LITERATURE: *The English Novel*. The novel, the introspective prose epic of everyday life and ordinary people, is the dominant literary form of the modern world. Long after you have completed your last college course, you will continue to read novels for pleasure. Here can be found authors you will want to return to for the rest of your life. And to appreciate the work of the incomparable Jane Austen (1775-1817) is perhaps the surest sign of a civilized soul.

ART HISTORY: *Renaissance Art History*. Exposure to the paintings and sculptures of the most fertile period of artistic production in Western history will give you deeper insight into the classical and Christian themes that are the subjects of these works— and transform your experience of art museums for the rest of your life.

MUSIC: *Music Appreciation*. This is the classic "gut" course, a favorite of seniors looking for light work. But this frequently well-taught course offers so much more. After experiencing the unparalleled achievements of Western classical music, you may be startled to discover that you can no longer listen to your stereo with the inattentive pleasure you could before. You will in any event be able to recognize precisely what it is you like or dislike about certain music. And you may recall—either with alarm or with satisfaction—that according to Plato, a proper musical education is the first step on the path to the health of the soul.

EVEN IF YOU HAVE STOPPED with our eight core courses and gone no further, you still have run the race, fought the good fight, and followed closely the course and contours of the West. You have struggled with some of the best which has been thought and said. You have been introduced to many alternative approaches to knowledge. You have seen questions raised that you did not know could be questions, and you have seen the dramatic differences various answers can make. You have seen that "what everybody knows" isn't always true. As you cross the finish line of the core curriculum, you perhaps will find yourself like Socrates, who could account himself wise only in that he was aware of his ignorance.

Perhaps. But if you have followed Newman's advice, thinking hard how to connect in your own mind all the disparate perspectives and fragments of knowledge you were acquiring through these courses, in wonder you may begin to realize that you do understand something about what is going on in the world. You will have acquired a philosophical habit of mind, and that is a human good that no one can take away.

The good news is that you now know something, not least, about yourself.

The even better news is that you will be able to learn more and more by assimilating new knowledge within an understanding of the Western *whole* which is now your permanent possession.

There is no bad news.

MARK C. HENRIE *is Director of Academic Affairs at the Intercollegiate Studies Institute. He is editor of the* Intercollegiate Review, *senior editor of* Modern Age, *and executive editor of the* Political Science Reviewer. *The editor also of* Doomed Bourgeois in Love: Essays on the Films of Whit Stillman, *he holds degrees from Dartmouth College, the University of Cambridge, and Harvard University.*

ASBURY COLLEGE

WILMORE, KENTUCKY • WWW.ASBURY.EDU

Asbury College proclaims in its bulletin that "every college student should have a well-balanced general education. This prepares a person for living, regardless of vocation or professional interests." Unlike other colleges that wax eloquent about the importance of a liberal education without actually providing one, Asbury takes its idea of balance seriously. By requiring students to spend half of their academic credits studying the liberal arts and the other half meeting requirements for one of a variety of majors, Asbury College helps students prepare not only for careers, but also for lives enriched by a liberal arts education—and by the spirituality of the Methodist Holiness tradition. Christened Kentucky Holiness College at its founding in 1890, the school was later renamed Asbury College to honor Bishop Francis Asbury, the founder of American Methodism. Today, the college would be a strong choice for any student in the region who shares its evangelical Christian faith, and particularly for one who aspires to teach at the secondary-school level.

Academic Life: Setting Standards in Kentucky

Asbury College, unlike many of the Methodist colleges named for John Wesley, remains dedicated to its Wesleyan-Arminian origins, and its student body has traditionally been drawn from the Methodist-Holiness churches and the Salvation Army. This last connection is especially strong; the school notes with pride that "[more] members of the Salvation Army in the USA have attended Asbury College than any other college or university in the country . . . [including] a large number of high-ranking Salvation Army Officers." In fact, the current president of Asbury, alumnus Dr. Paul A. Rader, formerly served as general of the Salvation Army, the highest office in the worldwide organization. Dr. Rader has recently announced his decision to retire, but he has pledged to continue his involvement with the school to ensure a smooth transition to the leadership of successor William Crothers.

Asbury College offers nearly fifty majors, from art to youth ministry, and additional minors. Education and ministry are emphasized, but a number of science and humanities majors are also included. Regardless of major,

1

each student is required to complete the core curriculum of forty-eight to sixty credit hours. This core curriculum includes

- twelve credit hours in English;
- twelve in a foreign language (or demonstrated proficiency to the end of the second year);
- twelve in theology and philosophy;
- three in physical education;
- nine in Western tradition;
- six in science;
- three in mathematics; and
- six in the social sciences.

The required classes include surveys of the Old and New Testaments, research and communication classes, a biology and a physical science class, a music and art appreciation class, and a psychology, sociology, or anthropology class.

The most substantial foundation in the liberal arts, however, comes from two yearlong courses in English and history. The two-semester sophomore sequence in English, "Masterworks: Western Classics" I and II, covers Western literature from the ancients to the present, while the two-semester freshman sequence in history, "Western Civilization" I and II, is a "survey of western social, intellectual, aesthetic, religious, and institutional development from antiquity . . . to the present." While some students regard these requirements as hoops through which to jump, others appreciate the value of comprehensive liberal learning. Some faculty (according to a student, "especially philosophy and history professors") are eloquent advocates for the importance of such an education.

Not surprisingly for a school that emphasizes the liberal arts, many of Asbury's strongest majors are in the humanities. According to both faculty and students, particularly strong departments include communications, education, history, psychology, English, and Bible/theology. Education traditionally has been the most popular major at Asbury, which offers bachelor of arts, bachelor of sciences, and master of arts degrees in the subject. The education department, according to a professor, is "long established as a high-quality small-college program, a standard-setter in Kentucky, with a national reputation." While the education major remains a strong choice for students, the communications department is now the largest at the school, and the media communications major is also popular. Students in the communications department enjoy the opportunity to break real news, including the chance to assist James Owens, the director of the media communications program, in covering the Olympics every four years.

The English program at Asbury is also highly recommended by faculty and students. As one professor in the department notes, "our requirements include a mostly traditional curriculum for our students, a fact which leads to our majors' very high scores on national tests. In the area of electives, we have a good number of nontraditional classes on subjects such as detective fiction, J. R. R. Tolkien, and so on." Students warmly commend a number of teachers in this department, particularly Dan Strait,

Marcia Hurlow, and Devin Brown, a leading C. S. Lewis scholar.

Another strong humanities department at Asbury is history, which offers a wide range of electives in addition to the "Western Civilization" courses. Burnam Reynolds and Edward McKinley are recommended as scholars and teachers. The history department has a reputation for sound academics and is popular with students planning to go on to law or graduate school.

As at many other small liberal arts colleges, Asbury professors focus on teaching, taking on as many as four classes each semester. Despite this heavy course load, the faculty strive to remain active in academic research and publishing. As one professor explains, "teaching is paramount at our college, and in the past it has been the exclusive emphasis. In recent years there has been an emphasis on professional standing, with some increase in resources. . . . Our faculty have done a very good job at professionally competitive academic production over the past twenty years. Even so, the main responsibility for the faculty is to teach small undergraduate classes, and this remains the largest part of the work for almost all of us." Another professor adds, "Teaching is highly valued at Asbury College. Scholarship is, too. And the goal is that these activities should be directly related: that teaching should lead to scholarship and that research should then contribute to teaching."

For the most part, students praise their teachers as dedicated and helpful. As one recent graduate reports, "The professors *want* to be here; since we are a small college, the pay is not great, so professors who stay here do it because they care about the students and the college itself. They are accessible and helpful. Many provide extra study sessions outside of class time. I have been to many professors' homes. I have never had a hard time getting in touch with professors, and they have always been gracious about phone calls received at home. They really are superb." A current student notes that he finds his teachers approachable even about nonacademic concerns: "I would go to one of my professors if I had a problem before I would go to Student Services," he says.

Off campus, Asbury offers students the opportunity to participate in several special academic programs. In the American Studies Program, junior and senior students may earn credit through internships in Washington, D.C. The Oxford Honors Program allows students to experience tutorial study in a variety of fields while attending Oxford University for a semester. Students may also spend a semester abroad in Egypt, China, Russia, or Latin America.

VITAL STATISTICS
Religious affiliation: Wesleyan/evangelical
Total enrollment: 1,278
Total undergraduates: 1,218
SAT/ACT medians: SAT V: 593, M: 560; ACT: 24
Applicants: 1,014
Applicants accepted: 73%
Accepted applicants who enrolled: 71%
Tuition: $17,808
Room and board: $4,498
Freshman retention rate: 80%
Graduation rate: 54% (4 yrs.), 70% (6 yrs.)
Average class size: 18
Student-faculty ratio: 11:1
Courses taught by graduate students: none
Most popular majors: communications, education, ministry
Students living on campus: 85%
Guaranteed housing for four years? yes
Students in fraternities or sororities: none

The college's religious commitment has no negative ramifications for academic freedom. One professor reports that "faculty members are committed to a nondoctrinaire approach to teaching. They do make a concerted effort to integrate faith and learning, but in ways that stimulate rather than stifle inquiry." Another faculty member adds, "There is a kind of orthodoxy, but it is neither pervasive nor oppressive, and is not imposed." Students feel free to ask questions and present various perspectives; one student remarks, "if somebody has an opinion, the professors respect it; if they disagree, they will explain why, but they still respect it." A former student explains: "Campus politics intrude into the classroom at times, but it depends on the professor and whether the class asks questions. Many professors open up time at the beginning of class for students to ask questions about anything, [and] the *Collegian*, the school newspaper, often presents dissenting views as well."

As one professor explains, "Teaching is paramount at our college. . . . The main responsibility for the faculty is to teach small undergraduate classes, and this remains the largest part of the work for almost all of us."

Thus, without curbing academic inquiry or imposing a uniform religiosity, Asbury remains a place where traditional, religious, and conservative students can have their intellects challenged without having their values assaulted. "There are no departments in which conservative young people will feel uncomfortable," a professor says. "Some of our faculty and students are less conservative than others on this or that point, or in general, but even those who are liberal by Asbury standards would seem no more than slightly right of the middle anywhere else—and the very large majority of faculty and students are conservative by every standard except taste in music and casual dress."

Student Life: No Dancing Here

Located in scenic Wilmore, Kentucky (population circa 5,000), Asbury College offers students a small-town setting, one situated some two hours from larger cities such as Lexington and Cincinnati. The school's twenty buildings range from the historic Hager Administration Building, which dates from 1910, to the new Dennis F. and Elsie B. Kinlaw Library, which opened in 2001 and includes a computer lab and a media center.

Because the school is relatively small, with an undergraduate enrollment of 1,218, the sense of community is strong. There is a good deal of class spirit at Asbury. As one graduate explains: "Each incoming class is given a name, class colors, class hymn, etc. These create a huge sense of identification with the others in your class. I have never seen anything like it at any other school; in the fall semester of your freshman year, the class votes on their class hymn. For the rest of their time at Asbury, whenever that hymn is sung in chapel, the class gets to stand and sing by themselves for the first verse. . . . There are also competitions between classes [and] . . . class prayers once a month, class cabinets, and class retreats."

Asbury College takes as its motto the phrase *Eruditio et Religio* (Learning and Religion). While the school is dedicated to providing a high-quality education, it remains concerned with the spiritual as well as the academic development of its students. To this end, the college sets forth a number of "lifestyle standards" for the community that address the topics of Morality, Honor (including rules about church and chapel attendance, and bans on alcohol, drugs, pornography, tobacco, and, yes, dancing), Propriety (including a dress code), and Civics (including regulations regarding college property, registration of vehicles, and the like). In short, Asbury's not a big party school.

Because Asbury College holds "the firm belief that significant learning occurs outside of the classroom," it requires single students to reside on campus in order to foster "an integration of faith, learning and living." A curfew is enforced at the campus residences—eleven o'clock on weeknights and later on weekends. The men may visit the lounges in the women's dorms at regularly scheduled hours; lounges in the men's dorms are open to women only on special occasions. Open houses scheduled throughout the year give men and women the chance to admire the posters in each others' dorm rooms.

SUGGESTED CORE
1. English 210: Masterworks: Western Civilization I
2. Philosophy 211: Ancient and Medieval Philosophy
3. Bible and Theology Old Testament 100 / New Testament 100: Understanding the Old Testament / Understanding the New Testament
4. Theology 310: History of the Early Church
5. Philosophy 343: Political and Social Philosophy (*closest match*)
6. English 332: Shakespeare
7. History 301: History of the United States to 1876
8. No suitable course.

Although Asbury College sees its Methodist-Holiness heritage as essential to its mission "to equip men and women, through a commitment to academic excellence and spiritual vitality, for a lifetime of learning, leadership, and service to the professions, society, the family and the church," the school welcomes students from outside the Wesleyan-Arminian religious tradition, provided they are willing to live within community guidelines and respect the school's unique mission and history. This means joining the believers in chapel at least three times a week. The college mandates attendance at chapel for three fifty-minute services, held on Mondays, Wednesdays, and Fridays. Seats are assigned and attendance is taken. In addition, the Handbook for Community Life states that "members of the community are expected to attend Sunday worship services and encouraged to attend class and campus prayer meetings on Wednesday evenings."

One former student says, "Since Asbury is a conservative school, I don't believe that [traditionally-minded] students would feel uncomfortable or unwelcome here. There are community standards at Asbury which may make some people feel stifled, but it doesn't have to do with political correctness; it has more to do with living a life according to Christian principles."

The rules and regulations of the college certainly do not stifle the social lives or extracurricular activities of the students. Asbury offers a variety of athletic opportunities, both intercollegiate and intramural, and has dedicated 118 acres of campus land to a large equestrian center. The college offers many opportunities for involvement in musical ensembles, both instrumental and choral, as well as special-interest clubs and academic societies, the college newspaper and yearbook, a pro-life group, political clubs, drama groups, and societies focused on particular majors such as history and business. Students may also become involved in a variety of service clubs and mission trips.

Although there will always be students not drawn by the moral and academic standards of a place like Asbury, the fact that the school attracts students who do seek such standards is key to its success. Indeed, Asbury appears to be taking its moral and academic heritage even more seriously than it did in the past. One student, comparing the present state of the college to what he observed when his older siblings were attending, states, "I'm very positive about the future. I think Asbury will continue to refine its focus. The leadership at the college is really working in the direction of standing up for what we believe."

Both the campus and the town offer a safe environment in which students may pursue their studies and social interests. Statistics reveal that Asbury enjoys a very low crime rate. The most common reported crime is burglary, of which there were five cases reported in 2004, the most recent year for which statistics are available. One motor vehicle theft was also reported that year. Otherwise, there is no record of other criminal offenses, nor have there been any reports of hate crimes or arrests on campus. The surrounding community of Wilmore is also reported to be a safe place.

The basic price tag of one year at Asbury is less than $23,000 (room, board, and tuition). The school offers a variety of financial aid programs, including honors scholarships, state and federal grants, loans, and work-study opportunities. In awarding aid, the school takes the need of the student into consideration. More than 90 percent of Asbury students receive some type of financial aid.

AUSTIN COLLEGE

SHERMAN, TEXAS • WWW.AUSTINCOLLEGE.EDU

Churches in the Calvinist tradition have always shown a great respect for learning—perhaps because John Calvin was a Renaissance humanist. That element of the Calvinist legacy remains alive and well at Austin College, which has maintained its affiliation with the Presbyterian Church (USA). In many ways, Austin is a traditional liberal arts school. Located in rural Sherman, Texas, in the extreme north of the Dallas/Fort Worth metroplex, Austin prides itself on both its relative isolation and on the many cultural opportunities provided by its big-city neighbors. Founded in 1849, the college was the first in Texas to award an academic degree, and it continues to operate under its original, Princeton-based charter.

The administration is clear about its mission: "Through liberal arts and sciences coursework, Austin College students learn to question, to think critically, and to arrive at their own informed conclusions." But neither its Christian roots nor its academic aspirations mean that Austin is necessarily a conservative school. The 2004 commencement speaker was Mary Robinson, the feminist former president of Ireland, and a fair percentage of students and teachers seem to equate liberal arts with liberalism. If you're seeking a cozy, conservative Texas environment, look elsewhere (Texas A&M, for instance). That said, Austin has many opportunities to offer students seeking a serious humanistic education.

Academic Life: An Intimate Affair

Austin's curriculum, while not quite a traditional core, does impose serious restrictions on what courses students may take. Students must complete
- one Communication/Inquiry course, such as "The Most Extreme Places in Our Solar System," "Censorship and Expression in American Culture," and "Of Libraries and Labyrinths: Jorge Luis Borges and Other Peculiar Writers and Readers (including you)";
- three Heritage of Western Culture courses: "The Early Western World," "Integrated Science," and "Individual and Society in the Modern World";
- three humanities courses in three different disciplines;

ALL-AMERICAN COLLEGES

- one natural science course;
- two social science courses in two different disciplines;
- a minor or second major;
- three January-term courses, or one for each fall term in residence;
- one course in Lifetime Sports;
- three semesters of a classical language, or a modern language other than their own (students may test out); and
- an approved course that "provides instruction in quantitative techniques" (students may test out).

The three-course, interdisciplinary Heritage of Western Culture program is quite popular; one student describes it as "what makes this school worthwhile." The freshman class, "The Early Western World," is billed as a "study of selected aspects of early Western culture (antiquity to the Enlightenment) with particular attention to critical issues in the study of cultural heritage before the modern era and the legacy of the early West." Depending upon who teaches it, it "may include attention to non-Western culture." Sophomores take "Integrated Science," a "study of notable scientific achievements [undertaken] to develop an understanding of the nature of science, the structure of scientific thought, and the influence of some of the achievements of science on Western ideas from the seventeenth through the twenty-first centuries." Juniors take "The Individual and Society in the Modern World," a "study of the evolution of major facets of Western culture and civilization from the Enlightenment until the present."

According to one participant, these classes "are our largest. . . . In fact, one of the classes has an unheard-of one hundred students. However, their reading list is great and the three professors that split up the course are supposedly great. I would say some are definitely critically respectful of the Western tradition, while others are uncritically respectful. All the professors here strongly encourage the study of Western heritage; there really aren't any who say anything anti-Western. . . . The whole philosophy of the Austin College education is definitely pro-Western." This alone sets Austin apart from most liberal arts colleges, especially those left-leaning ones whose teaching of the Western intellectual tradition is biased towards a grievance-based multiculturalism.

Students seem grateful for the school's integrated approach to learning: "I would say one of the most amazing things [I've received from] Austin College is the ability to draw connections between disciplines," one says. "Because all the classes are small and approached from a liberal arts perspective, there is an overlap between them," showing the relevance of the curriculum in an interdisciplinary manner. "For example," this student continues, "in American history we discussed the Victorian era and Thorstein Veblen's work, *The Theory of the Leisure Class*. In my freshman seminar on consumerism with Dan Nuckols we discussed and read the same book. In that same class (freshman seminar) we read *Buddenbrooks* by Thomas Mann and discussed the style and themes of Thomas Mann's books, which were also read in Heritage of Western Culture, English, and German lit classes." This interdisciplinary reinforcement of the curriculum is widely appreciated among students.

The eighty-three full-time faculty members at Austin are generally popular with their students, who describe them as "accessible" and "challenging mentors" who "have a passion for helping their students succeed." This is made possible by a healthy student-faculty ratio of 12 to 1. Students characterize the school itself as being "big enough to have facilities that larger schools have but small enough that you can really get to know the faculty and other students." The student body has the reputation of being highly focused on academics; 40 percent of students go on to graduate school. The most popular majors are biology, psychology, and business administration, with students also speaking highly of the premed program and the economics department. One economics major say that he "can attest to the excellence of the professors in [my] department, who do not solely focus on research and publishing, but also on teaching and interacting with students. . . . I run into my econ professors daily and always stop for a conversation. They are enthusiastic and very knowledgeable in their fields. Their passion for economics is obvious and their devotion to the subject is inspiring to see."

Highly recommended professors and mentors include Hunt Tooley of the history faculty (lauded by one student as "proficient and concerned, with a keen sense of humor"), Dan Nuckols in economics, Jack Mealy in mathematics, Jackie Moore in history, Truett Cates in German, and Frank Rohmer in political science.

Some 70 percent of students take courses abroad through one of Austin's programs, which send undergraduates to different colleges and cities in Argentina, Australia, Austria, Belgium, Chile, China, Costa Rica, France, Germany, Greece, Ireland, Israel, Italy, Japan, Mexico, New Zealand, Spain, and the United Kingdom.

In a refreshing change from many other schools, all classes at Austin are taught by professors; because the college offers no graduate programs, there are no TAs leading seminars. Furthermore, all faculty keep office hours, which, one student reports, "is a great time to catch them and talk about anything with them, whether it be class-related or not."

There are, however, some weak departments at the school, most notably the media and art deparments. "Neither one of those programs has many professors, nor sufficient equipment for students to do much with," reports one student. Nor is Austin immune to some of the newer and flakier academic disciplines; an interdepartmental gender studies program, offered as a minor, boasts some twenty professors. One English professor teaching in the program explains: "My interests in gender studies in-

VITAL STATISTICS
Religious affiliation: Presbyterian Church in the USA
Total enrollment: 1,370
Total undergraduates: 1,288
SAT midrange: 1100–1290
Applicants: 1,475
Applicants accepted: 69%
Accepted applicants who enrolled: 36%
Tuition: $20,310
Room and board: $7,376
Freshman retention rate: 85%
Graduation rate: 68% (4 yrs.), 75% (6 yrs.)
Courses with fewer than 20 students: 60%
Student-faculty ratio: 12:1
Courses taught by graduate students: none
Most popular majors: biology, psychology, business administration
Students living on campus: 71%
Guaranteed housing for four years? yes
Students in fraternities: 30% sororities: 31%

clude research on feminist activism (conservative, moderate, and radical ones), reverse discrimination against men, women of color, lesbians and gay men, and the literary representations of sexual politics (mostly) in eighteenth-, nineteenth-, and twentieth-century writings/political movements. . . . I also expect to teach Jan-term classes on lesbian and gay literature and on AIDS and literature." In addition to these more exotic interests, this professor teaches a course in the history of Western civilization.

Whether or not the gender studies minor metastasizes into a major, at the moment "Austin College is a fairly balanced school and at times apolitical," according to a libertarian student. "Politics intrude into the classroom every so often, but mostly because a student says something, not a professor. I have never taken a class where I [was] afraid to voice a conservative or religious opinion. There are no doubt some very liberal, left-wing teachers who might shy away from a conservative opinion but they wouldn't make a student feel uncomfortable. The school is very good about respecting religious views of students. The campus is definitely not stultified by political correctness, and political debate is a common theme on campus."

> *"My faculty mentor has really helped shape my personality and my mind, teaching me how to think for myself and form my own opinions. . . . He has really taught me a lot about how to be a critical thinker, how to ask questions, and how to analyze."*

Upon arrival, each student is assigned a faculty mentor who serves as his advisor and teaches him as a freshman in the Communication/Inquiry course. The mentor system is quite popular among students. One tells us that his mentor "has really helped shape my personality and my mind, teaching me how to think for myself and form my own opinions. Because of [him], I have been engaged in an intellectual and fulfilling life since I started at AC." Not surprisingly, the student has chatted with his mentor "about economics, research, books, college life, and many other things. In fact I have gone out to lunch with him and other mentees as well as attending a Christmas party at his house for his mentees. He has really taught me a lot about how to be a critical thinker, how to ask questions, and how to analyze."

Student Life: No More Mayonnaise

Sherman, Texas, is not exactly a vibrant metropolis; one student calls it "pretty much a hell-hole." However, the recent closure of the local mayonnaise factory—whose frequent, if not exactly fragrant, emissions were the butt of many jokes—has left the town in a much better odor. Sherman is an outpost of the Bible Belt, whose blue laws and relative remoteness leave few outlets for those seeking either high culture or low dives.

Although the student body has been characterized as "predominantly white, Texan, and conservative," this description may not jibe completely with media-driven expectations of how white Texan conservatives think and behave. In 2004, for instance, Austin's student assembly passed a resolution opposing the Iraq War. Three years ago, a gay-rights group called PRIDE (People Reaffirming Identity Differences and Educating) was organized; the group arranges for gay movie nights and trips to the Dallas "Pride Parade." Although the current chairman of the county libertarian organization is an Austin College student, the only officially registered political clubs (apart from PRIDE) are the Young Democrats and W.I.S.E. (Women's Issues, Support, and Education).

Politics and cultural issues aside, one of the dominant notes in Austin life is housing. The administration specifically considers dorm life to be part of the overall Austin education: "As anyone will tell you, some of the most important lessons you'll ever learn take place in the residence halls." Among these are "sharing space and ideas, making and enforcing rules, taking care of yourself and others—all with a fully trained residential life staff to back you up."

This arrangement is not optional for the first three years. According to the school catalog, "All full-time, unmarried freshman, sophomore, and junior students under the age of 21 must live in College housing." Exceptions are made for those whose families live nearby. Not surprisingly, 71 percent of students live on campus.

So what is this like? Says one student, "Dorm life is dorm life. Sometimes it's cramped and dirty and irritating, but most of the time it's fun and lively. The school administers the Myers-Briggs Personality Test upon enrollment at AC and so they do a pretty good job of matching students together. The main dorm halls are constructed in a way that each floor has two wings and a T-section. The wings are all freshman and known as the 'clusters.' Each cluster has about nine rooms with two freshmen in each and one RA room, where your RA lives. That cluster shares one bathroom. Most clusters get together and spend time hanging out and a lot of clusters end up being very close." In all-female dorms, male visitation hours run from 10 a.m. to 1 a.m. Sunday through Thursday, and from 10 a.m. to 3 a.m. on weekends. All bathrooms are single-sex. The single coed dorm is segregated by floor. There is also the Jordan Family Language House, in which forty-eight selected German, Spanish, French, or Japanese language students are invited to live in an intense language immersion learning/residence experience. Each language's area is staffed by four native-speaker RAs.

Smoking is forbidden in all buildings, although there are designated smoking areas outside. Students twenty-one and older are permitted to drink alcohol in their

SUGGESTED CORE
1. Classics 110: Greek Literature in Translation. *See also* Heritage of Western Culture 101: The Early Western World.
2. Philosophy 220: History of Philosophy: Ancient/Medieval
3. Religious Studies 135: The Biblical Heritage
4. Religious Studies 250: Topics in Religious Studies: Christian Thought (*closest match*)
5. Political Science 20: Political Theory (*closest match*)
6. English 332: Shakespeare and His Contemporaries
7. History 162: History of the United States to 1876
8. Heritage of Western Culture 301: Individual and Society in the Modern World

rooms if the door is closed. In fact, though Sherman is a dry town, drinking is highly popular on Austin's campus, and Greek life is pretty much the center of the Austin social whirl. All seven of the college's Greek organizations are local—unique to Austin College with no national affiliations, and approximately a third of students belong to a fraternity or sorority. The courtship scene is said to be fairly bleak; one student moaned, "You have to wait four years for a date." But this may be changing, given that fully 28 percent of female students are opting to live in the coed dorm.

Student groups include academic clubs (art, biology, chemistry, prelaw, premed, physics); ethnic, environmental, religious, athletic, cultural, and international relations organizations; *Chromascope*, the Austin College yearbook; the *Observer*, the biweekly student newspaper; Amnesty International, Kiwanis, and Rotary. Moreover, "the Austin College Service Station coordinates community service activities ranging from Habitat for Humanity and the Alternative Spring Break program to the Saturday Morning Program, which pairs Austin College students with low-income children from the Sherman community for tutoring," according to the catalog.

The school's mascot is the Kangaroo. Austin's teams compete at the NCAA Division III level in men's baseball, basketball, football, golf, soccer, swimming and diving, and tennis; and in women's basketball, soccer, swimming and diving, tennis, and volleyball. Austin College also fields a men's lacrosse team (as a club sport), and hosts both cheerleading and spirit squads.

There is quite an active religious life at the college, not restricted to the Presbyterian faith. Among other groups are the Alpha Gamma Omega, the Baptist Student Union, the Catholic Student Organization, the Canterbury Society, the Muslim Students Association, and the Wesley Fellowship. The college chaplain, John Williams, leads a weekly Bible study and presides over a nondenominational Christian communion service planned and led by Austin College students. This is usually followed by dinner at his home or the home of a faculty member. For Catholics, St. Mary's Catholic Church in Sherman is a beautiful Gothic style church with many devotions and an active parish life. Traditionally minded Episcopalians may well find themselves at home at St. Stephen's Episcopal Church, a historic nineteenth-century building with an all-male clergy and a classical (1928 Prayer Book) liturgy.

With regard to crime, small-town Sherman is very quiet, and so too is the college. The biggest single threat to personal safety appears to be liquor law violations in residence rooms, forty-one of which occurred in 2004. In the same year, there was one drug-related offense, three reported cases of burglary, and no rapes or robberies (although one of each was reported the previous year). "The city of Sherman is very safe," says a student, "especially in terms of violent crime. I can easily walk around campus and the surrounding area without feeling unsafe. The biggest problem in the surrounding city is methamphetamine, nothing violent."

As today's private college costs go, Austin is pretty reasonable. The tuition price tag is just over $20,000. On-campus residence, including twenty meals, costs an additional $7,300. Ninety percent of students receive some form of financial assistance.

BELMONT ABBEY COLLEGE

BELMONT, NORTH CAROLINA • WWW.BELMONTABBEYCOLLEGE.EDU

In 1876 the Order of St. Benedict established a monastery and school in Belmont on land donated by missionary priest Father Jeremiah O'Connell. The school was renamed Belmont Abbey College in 1913. Early in the college's history the monks next door ran a dairy farm, the proceeds of which helped fund the school. "For years, the endowment of the college was the monks," Abbot Placid Solari, chancellor of the college, told the *Gaston Gazette* in 2002.

Today the Belmont Abbey monastic community continues to serve as the bulwark of the college. The Benedictines sponsor the school, serve on its board of trustees, and do much of the teaching. The mission of the Abbey is to educate "in the liberal arts tradition as guided by the Catholic intellectual heritage and inspired by the 1,500-year-old Benedictine monastic tradition. This heritage is sustained through fidelity to the Christian message as it comes to us through the Church," says the college catalog. In conformity with Pope John Paul II's 1990 decree *Ex Corde Ecclesiae*, President William Thierfelder has made a public profession of faith and taken an oath of fidelity to the church's magisterium. Every professor of theology has a *mandatum* from the local bishop—official church recognition that they intend to teach in communion with the church. This obedience to a Vatican decree, flouted by most so-called Catholic colleges, sets Belmont Abbey College apart. So does the excellence and seriousness of its core curriculum. Rooted in philosophy, theology, and the classical liberal arts, it encourages the sort of academic well-roundedness that lies at the heart of every good liberal education.

Academic Life: The Rule of Benedict

The Abbey catalog states that, "the skills, knowledge, and values we seek to instill through the core [curriculum] are a tangible manifestation of the spirit of the Benedictine founders of the College, whose basilica, monastery, and original school buildings give architectural shape to their singleness of purpose." The school's core is designed to familiarize students with the history, philosophy, and fundamental texts of Western civilization—all of which the Benedictine order helped save during the Dark Ages—as well as with the life and Rule of St. Benedict. Students must take nineteen core classes, or narrowly targeted electives, and fulfill several other requirements:

- "First-Year Symposium," an "introduction to the values, traditions, and academic culture characteristic of a Catholic, Benedictine liberal arts education";
- "Writing on Contemporary Issues" and "Argumentative Prose";
- one course in mathematics;
- two courses in science;
- a two-semester sequence on Christian thought;
- "Logic";
- an "Introduction to Philosophy" course (students choose either ancient and medieval philosophy or modern and contemporary);
- "Ethics";
- a two-semester sequence on either world civilization or American history;
- "American Government" and another social science course;
- one class in English literature and a course in world or American literature;
- a fine arts course;
- a Global Perspectives requirement, which can be fulfilled by taking an intermediate-level modern language, completing one of several humanities core electives such as "World Literature," "Introduction to Art in Western Civilization," or "World Civilization," or by significant academic experience abroad;
- a computer competency course, exam, or a "technology-intensive" course; and
- a Great Books capstone course, taught in small groups, which focuses on the history of ideas in Western culture with selected readings from ancient, medieval, and modern writers.

"To be liberally educated means not only recognizing the inherent value of these great texts, but also becoming aware of their place in the larger dialectical history. The best way to learn this history is to read and study some of the great books of the Western intellectual tradition. Education in this tradition is ultimately moral in that it examines various teachings regarding the purpose of human life," asserts the college website. Can somebody say "Amen?"

Trendy classes do not get in the way of serious study at the Abbey. "Novelty is not big on this campus," says a professor. "There are no feminist, ethnic, or gay and lesbian studies here."

The honors program at the Abbey allows students to work with professors on independent-study projects and to engage in cultural activities outside the classroom. Honors students are also offered a set of more advanced courses, such as "World Civilization" and "American Polity," which fulfill many of the core curriculum requirements. A student must maintain a minimum GPA of 3.0 in order to remain in the program.

Students highly recommend the teaching in the English department, where requirements for majors are solid, including: "Literature of the English Renaissance," "Restoration and Eighteenth-Century British Literature," "Shakespeare," and "Literary Criticism." The senior faculty members of the English department are known for their strong commitment to teaching.

Another department noted for its attention to teaching is biology, whose faculty "groom their students for medical school and follow their careers," says one professor.

The philosophy department stresses breadth of knowledge and depth of analysis. Students study the systematic disciplines of logic, ethics, metaphysics, and epistemology. With few philosophy majors, advanced courses are taught on a cyclical basis—so you might have to wait a few semesters to fulfill a requirement or to take a desired elective. Theology majors supplement their theology courses with courses in philosophy. After becoming well-acquainted with the Catholic tradition of theological reflection, they write a senior thesis directed by one of the department faculty.

The history department requires students majoring in history to take two survey courses in world civilization and United States history. A comprehensive exam for history majors is taken upon completion of coursework.

The education department has suffered recently from a loss of faculty and is in the process of hiring a new department chair. While the language studies program is not large enough to offer majors, introductory and intermediate courses are taught in Spanish, French, Italian, and Latin. Serious modern-language students can avail themselves of the school's study-abroad program. It offers language, business, history, and science programs in a number of locations, including Germany, India, Europe, Guatemala, and Peru. Students must first qualify academically (a minimum cumulative GPA of 2.5 is required) and have junior status before they can enroll in the program.

Noteworthy faculty members at the Abbey include Elizabeth Baker, Sheila Reilly, and Robert Tompkins in biology; Russell Fowler, Martin Harris, Michael Hood, and Mary Ellen Weir in English; Chris Kirchgessner, O.S.B., Jane Russell, O.S.F., and David Williams in theology; Stephen Brosnan in mathematics and physics; James Giermanski and David Neipert in international business; and Angela Blackwood and Lynne Shoaf in accounting.

First-Year Symposium instructors serve as primary academic advisors for students during their first year. Each student must choose a major field of study by the second

VITAL STATISTICS

Religious affiliation:
  Roman Catholic
Total enrollment: 887
Total undergraduates: 871
SAT/ACT medians:
  SAT V: 500, M: 500;
  ACT: 19
Applicants: 1,016
Applicants accepted: 74%
*Accepted applicants who
  enrolled*: 22%
Tuition: $16,870
Room and board: $8,588
Freshman retention rate: 56%
Graduation rate: 44% (4 yrs.),
  47% (6 yrs.)
*Courses with fewer than 20
  students*: 87%
Student-faculty ratio: 14:1
*Courses taught by graduate
  students*: none
Most popular majors:
  business, education,
  biology
Students living on campus:
  56%
*Guaranteed housing for four
  years?* yes
Students in fraternities: 20%
  sororities: 20%

semester of the sophomore year. After a student declares an academic major, a professor from within the department that supports the major will become his advisor. Students must meet each semester with their advisors to discuss their choices of coursework for the next term. Students find the Academic Resource Center very useful. The center offers tutoring by faculty in core subjects such as math, biology, and English composition.

With a student-faculty ratio of 14 to 1 and an average class size of seventeen, student-faculty relationships are strong at the Abbey. A professor says that John Henry Newman's motto, "heart speaks to heart," could describe faculty-student relationships at the Abbey. "Most of the faculty agree that our students are best served by teachers who want to teach. Our loads are too heavy to engage in research," says the same professor. The faculty report that their level of collegiality is high, that their peers are "really competent and experienced," and that they "live and die by teaching."

"To be liberally educated means not only recognizing the inherent value of these great texts, but also becoming aware of their place in the larger dialectical history. . . . Education in this tradition is ultimately moral in that it examines various teachings regarding the purpose of human life," asserts the college.

The Bradley Institute for the Study of Christian Culture supports the mission of the college by "fostering an understanding of the Catholic intellectual heritage and by advancing the truths of Christian thought and an appreciation of their unique impact upon the development of Western culture," says the institute's website. The institute's symposium topics range from business, legal, and medical ethics to history and philosophy. Recent titles included "The Role of Government in the Moral Development of Citizens," "Faith and Politics Today," and "The New Constitution of Iraq."

Students who receive financial assistance such as grants and scholarships (which includes some 90 percent of students), must attend five cultural events each semester to fulfill a "cultural events requirement." In addition, they must complete ten hours of community service each semester. Attendance at a Bradley Institute lecture will fulfill one cultural requirement. Other events that fulfill this requirement include plays, poetry readings, and musical presentations. Students serve at homeless shelters, schools, domestic violence centers, animal shelters, crisis pregnancy programs, and other nonprofits to fulfill community service obligations. According to the school, the purpose of this requirement is to "encourage students to step beyond their own boundaries and step into the community"

The Charlotte Area Educational Consortium allows Abbey students to take classes at, and faculty to share library resources with, twenty colleges and universities in the greater Charlotte area.

Student Life: Gothic Revival

Charlotte, the largest city in the Carolinas, has become the melting pot of the South. Across the Catawba River, ten miles west of Charlotte, the town of Belmont offers a quaint setting in a small community of 15,000. The town's streets are lined with gracious mansions surrounded by lilac, magnolia, and dogwood trees. Stowe Park in the downtown area is the site of special events like concerts and movies. Belmont is located two hours from the Great Smokey Mountains and four hours from the North Carolina coast.

The Abbey's 650-acre wooded campus is home to the Belmont Abbey Monastery and the Abbey Basilica. Most of the Gothic Revival buildings were designed and built by the monks themselves in the nineteenth century. Priest-architect Michael McInerny, O.S.B., was the monastery's resident builder. Among his most notable contributions is St. Leo Hall, built in 1906. It provides the backdrop for visitors as they get their first glimpse of campus. Today the building houses faculty offices, the college's bookstores, career services, and Grace Auditorium. The college itself and Abbey Basilica are listed on the National Register of Historic Places. The monks host thousands of visitors each year who come for tours and retreats.

For many of the students, the twenty or so monks on campus are confessors, counselors, mentors, and friends who make the college a "real home away from home," as a student reports. (This is fitting, since the family is the model of Benedictine life.) A senior wrote in the *Crusader* student newspaper, "I love the fact that we get to learn from, take classes with, go on retreats with, eat with, watch basketball games with, laugh at, get into snowball fights with, cheer for, and mourn the monks."

The school's plans for the future include several building projects, new majors and minors, sports teams, scholarships, and possibly a masters program, as well as increasing enrollment. While most people on campus applaud the initiatives, there are some who bemoan so many changes. One professor wrote in the *Crusader* that some people feel that "the speeding train is perhaps morphing into a 'product line' that isn't Abbey College at all."

Across the Catawba River from the school, the U.S. National Whitewater Center and Olympic training center is scheduled to open in the spring of 2006. This will be a public park offering the facilities and amenities of an outdoor recreational center with a custom-made whitewater river.

Almost 90 percent of freshmen—but less than half the upperclassmen—live on campus. Housing includes three residence halls and a four-building apartment complex where men and women live on separate floors. Overnight guests in student housing can only stay with students of the same sex. Some students choose to live in close proximity to other students in "households," faith-sharing groups in the residence halls

SUGGESTED CORE
Taking the college's honors program curriculum may cover the contents of courses 1, 2, 5, and 8. See also Theology 103/104: Introduction to Scripture, Old Testament / New Testament; Theology 101: Christian Thought I; English 410: Shakespeare; and History 309: U.S. History, 1492–1877.

ALL-AMERICAN COLLEGES

or apartment buildings. Members of the four households—Faithful Daughter, Brothers in Christ–Sons of Mary, Our Lady of Good Counsel, and One Body in Christ—are committed to living their faith in their daily lives on campus. In addition to the households, 20 percent of students belong to one of the three sororities or three fraternities.

In keeping with the Abbey's Catholic and Benedictine traditions, students are expected to follow school guidelines on conduct between men and women and to wear appropriate attire. "Sexual activity outside of marriage is contrary to the Law of God and the teachings of the Catholic Church, and therefore, not condoned by the College. Promiscuous behavior, depending on the facts and circumstances of each case, may result in disciplinary action including possible dismissal from the College," says the student handbook. Neatness, cleanliness, and good taste are the guiding norms for dress on campus. "Attire that is disrespectful of the College's mission and heritage is not permitted (for example, t-shirts with disrespectful slogans)."

At Belmont Abbey, alcohol is not permitted in public areas of residence halls; however, twenty-one-year-old students are free to imbibe in their rooms. Kegs, bars, drinking games, and punch containing alcohol are prohibited on campus. Events serving alcohol with more than fifteen guests require at least one officer, arranged through campus police, to be on-site and are limited to four hours in duration.

Students describe the student body at Belmont Abbey College as "friendly" and "like a big family." Students know the names of the cafeteria staff, the janitors, and the postal clerk on campus. It is not the kind of place where students fall through the cracks. "The student body at the Abbey has been over the years mostly Protestant rather than Catholic. That is changing now as more Catholics move into this area, but I think that this history has affected the campus culture in a positive way, i.e., towards openness," says a professor. Many Abbey students are originally from the Carolinas, New Jersey, Georgia, New York, or Florida. Home-educated students feel comfortable on campus. President Thierfelder and his wife are themselves parents of nine homeschooled children.

The College Union Board is a student group that sponsors social weekends, dances, comedians, musical performers, coffeehouse performances, lectures, and other special events. Additional groups include the Student Government Association, Senior Class Counsel, Peace and Justice Committee, International Club, the *Agora* (a literary magazine), chess club, Democratic and Republican clubs, BAC Dance Team, Abbey Cheerleaders, and the Commuter Council.

Established in 1883, the Abbey theater is one of the oldest continuously operating theaters in the Southeast. The Abbey Players and Belmont Community Theatre present six productions a year, including dramas, stylish comedies, major musicals, and a Shakespearean production. Recent productions have included the musical *Into the Woods*, the comedy *The Boys Next Door*, *A Man for All Seasons*, and *Macbeth*. The Abbey Chorus, Belmont Abbey Quintet, and Carolina Pro Musica (an instrumental group that plays pre-1800 music on historic instruments) are also active on campus.

The monks gather in the Abbey Basilica to pray or celebrate Mass four times a day, and the Abbey community is welcome to join them for all of these services. The students are under the spiritual care of the monks, one of whom serves as the chaplain for Campus Ministry. Campus Ministry offers an "Alternative Spring Break" program that allows students to travel to the Caribbean or Central America for charitable and pastoral work. Crusaders for Life is the college's pro-life group. Each year a group of faculty, staff, monks, and students attend the March for Life in Washington. The Hintemeyer Program for Catholic Leadership provides full scholarships for freshman and transfer students who demonstrate active Catholic leadership.

The Belmont Abbey College Crusaders participate in athletics at the NCAA Division II level. Abbey Athletics has recently grown from twelve varsity teams to sixteen varsity and two junior varsity teams, and from 160 athletes to 260. This growth has made the college one of the top schools in the Carolina Virginia Athletic Conference. New teams include men's and women's lacrosse, women's golf, men's wrestling, JV baseball, and JV basketball. The other twelve sports offered are men's and women's soccer, basketball, cross-country, and tennis; men's baseball and golf; and women's volleyball and softball. Intramural sports programs at the school include "extreme dodge ball," indoor volleyball, bowling leagues, flag football, aerobics classes, martial arts, softball, table tennis, ultimate frisbee, golf, chess, tennis, and a jogging club. The renovated Wheeler Athletic Center has a new fitness center, an athletic training facility, and auxiliary gyms.

Students can call Campus Police for escorts twenty-four hours a day year round. In 2004, the school reported six burglaries, one aggravated assault, and one sex offense.

Tuition at Belmont Abbey College in 2005–6 was $16,870; room and board averaged $8,588. Eighty percent of students at the college receive need-based financial aid. The average student loan debt of recent graduates is $17,125.

ALL-AMERICAN COLLEGES

Biola University

LA MIRADA, CALIFORNIA • WWW.BIOLA.EDU

Biola University has serious ambitions for a school that got its name from an acronym. Founded in 1908 as the Bible Institute of Los Angeles by oil magnate Lyman Stewart, who served as its first president, Biola describes itself as a Global Center for Christian Thought and Spiritual Renewal. In 1913, the cornerstone was laid for the institute's long-time home in downtown Los Angeles. This was the historic "Church of the Open Door" building, which longtime area residents still recall as the home of an enormous neon sign that flashed "Jesus Saves." (This sign was later acquired by and now adorns the temple of the late and notorious Dr. Gene Scott). Though the school outgrew its Los Angeles location and moved some twenty miles to La Mirada, that neon sign evokes its mission—to train its graduates in theology and the liberal arts in a modern Christian context. A recent alumnus, Scott Derrickson, cowrote and directed the theologically sophisticated 2005 smash hit *The Exorcism of Emily Rose.*

Biola's six schools (Talbot School of Theology, Rosemead School of Psychology, School of Arts and Sciences, School of Intercultural Studies, Crowell School of Business, and School of Professional Studies) offer 145 academic programs for both undergraduate and graduate students. As its catalogue proudly says, "Biola is recognized as a National University (ranked by *U.S. News & World Report*)—one of 229 out of the 3,300 institutions of higher learning in the United States that are called the 'major leagues' of higher education." It is the only member of the Council for Christian Colleges and Universities to attain such a rank. Through its serious curriculum, dedicated faculty, and talented student body, Biola has earned it.

Academic Life: It Works by Faith Alone

In keeping with its theological framework, Biola requires biblical studies of all graduates. As a school with a definite commitment to its own view of Western civilization, Biola also insists that all students in all six schools receive a firm grounding in the liberal arts. The school's idiosyncratic but worthy core curriculum is as follows:

- "First-Year Seminar," designed to help new students begin (or choose) their majors. Students who already have (perhaps prematurely) chosen a major enter appropriate sections;
- ten courses of biblical and theological studies, seven of which are specified: "The Bible and Spiritual Formation," "Foundations of Christian Thought," "Old Testament History and Literature," "New Testament History and Literature," "Christian Thought" I and II, and "Early Christian History—Acts";
- one rhetoric course, such as "Small Group Communication" or "Introduction to Argumentation and Debate";
- four foreign language courses. Spanish and French are the only foreign languages regularly offered, although occasionally Chinese, Japanese, Russian and Korean are taught;
- two courses in English composition;
- one course in literature. Students may choose from "Film and Literature," "Literature in Context," or "American Literature";
- one Fine Arts course, such as "Art Appreciation," "Introduction to Music," or "Introduction to Drama";
- two history courses: "United States History" or "Political Survey of American Government," then either "World Civilizations I" or "World Civilizations II";
- one philosophy course out of seven introductory classes offered: "Introduction to Logic"; "Ancient Philosophy"; "Medieval Philosophy"; "Modern Philosophy"; "Philosophy"; "Ethics"; or "Philosophy and Aesthetics";
- four physical education "skills," such as volleyball and softball (adult students are exempt);
- one behavioral science course, chosen from introductions to anthropology, sociology or psychology; and
- one course each in math and science.

Biola declares that "our general education courses seek to educate students as human beings rather than as prospective members of particular professions. This 'whole person' approach to education is designed to help prepare our students to succeed in their roles in the family, the church, and the larger society of our culturally diverse world. It pays particular attention to the spiritual formation and character development of students by faculty members who are open and honest about their own need for growth." Unfortunately, one student reports that "some of the general education classes we have to take are really, really easy, and you don't feel challenged at all." Here, perhaps, Biola's reach exceeds its grasp.

The university is serious about integrating its view of Christianity into the curriculum: "Our idea of Bible integration is not simply a prayer before class begins, but it is a worldview that impacts the way we see and think about each discipline. In business,

VITAL STATISTICS

Religious affiliation:
evangelical Protestant

Total enrollment: 5,662

Total undergraduates: 3,246

ACT midrange: 24–29

Applicants: 2,057

Applicants accepted: 78%

*Accepted applicants who
enrolled:* 28%

Tuition: $22,602

Room and board: $7,100

Freshman retention rate: 84%

Graduation rate: 51% (4 yrs.),
68% (6 yrs.)

Average class size: 23

Student-faculty ratio: 17:1

*Courses taught by graduate
students:* not provided

Most popular majors: theology, nursing, business

Students living on campus:
71%

*Guaranteed housing for four
years?* no

*Students in fraternities or
sororities:* none

students learn that the business world is a mission field and [they learn] how to minister to co-workers through their service to the company. Students also learn about starting businesses as ministries in third world countries," the school reports.

Classes at Biola run from intimate to largish—thanks to a student-faculty ratio of 17 to 1. Some 68 percent of faculty members have their doctorates. Among the more notable members of that faculty are William Lane Craig and J. P. Moreland in philosophy, Todd Pickett in English, Paul Buchanan in creative writing, and John Mark Reynolds, director of the Torrey Honors Institute.

Academic majors in the liberal arts at Biola include anthropology, art, biblical studies, Christian education, communication studies, education/liberal studies, English, history, humanities, intercultural studies, philosophy, psychology, sociology, and Spanish. As one student says, "There are some really great opportunities to have hands-on experience in your major, and many internships as well."

In the liberal arts, one Biola program stands out: the Torrey Honors Institute, which combines a Great Books approach with Biola's biblical and classical Protestant focus. As the prospectus says, "the inclusion of first-rate Christian thinkers in the Protestant tradition, along with extensive study of the Bible, makes Torrey unique in the area of classical education. Writers such as Calvin, Luther, and Wesley are rarely studied in most 'Great Books' programs." You'll study them here—along with such high-church Anglicans as C. S. Lewis and Dorothy Sayers. Torrey's goal is to teach the student "to love beauty, as well as ideas; doing as well as thinking. Torrey students engage with the worlds of art, commerce, and government. Our goal is to produce citizens for the City of God."

The small classes here are taught by faculty tutors and contribute to the major essay each student must write every semester, synthesizing his knowledge from various fields. The classes offered by Torrey substitute for most of Biola's general education and biblical studies requirements, but supplement (rather than replace) an ordinary major. The program offers its own extracurricular activities, such as discussions with Torrey faculty and students on BUBBS ("Biola University Bulletin Board Service"), outside lectures and retreats, and group outings. The program sponsored a three-day convention for Christian bloggers in 2005 and plans to repeat it. Engagement with modern culture and technology is part of Torrey's stated goal: "to send into contemporary society persons of . . . dedication and courage." On a more old-fashioned note, the program also offers a semester abroad at Oxford University.

Torrey is certainly the spearhead of an institution that has a definite vision. For those who share that vision, it would be hard to imagine a better place. Biola students tend to be highly motivated achievers who see their studies mot merely as preparation for employment, but as a calling. It is not surprising that most graduates rave about the place—though the editors were mildly disturbed at the fact that nearly every current student contacted refused to speak about the school without the explicit approval of Biola's public relations office (which we declined to request).

Student Life: Biblical Instruction

La Mirada, California, is a suburb of Los Angeles. Biola University is made up of modern institutional buildings, but the surrounding campus has been called "park-like," and in southern California natural beauty (and the beach) is never far away. Since even freshmen are allowed to own cars, students can venture out from the Biola bubble to sample what Los Angeles has to offer—in all its tainted glory. But they won't find such decadence on campus, which is regulated by a strict code of Christian ethics, spelled out at great length in a detailed student handbook.

The rules governing behavior are considered to be tools for teaching the student "to exercise individual discernment as demonstrated in thoughts, actions, and lifestyle." The school places heavy emphasis on personal conduct, adopting "Love your neighbor as yourself" as "the foundation stone of community." Biola students are asked to "live with integrity, practice confession and forgiveness, attempt to live in reconciled relationships, accept responsibility for their actions and words, and submit to biblical instruction."

"Our idea of Bible integration is not simply a prayer before class begins, but a worldview that impacts the way we see and think about each discipline. In business, students learn that the business world is a mission field and [they learn] how to minister to co-workers through their service to the company," says the school.

Concretely, this means an environment that will be a "stifling straitjacket to some, and a warm family to others," one student says. "The school can feel pretty claustrophobic sometimes, because everyone knows everyone else's business, and it's hard to get any alone time." Another student counters that "everyone here is really encouraging and supportive; you never feel left in the lurch by anyone.

Biola presents obedience to its standards of behavior as a kind of religious duty. "We at Biola recognize that Scripture condemns sins of the heart, such as covetousness, selfishness, ambition, envy, greed, lust and pride. By their very nature, these sins are more difficult to discern, but because they lie at the heart of relationships, they are of central concern to the Biola community. We confess and repent of these sins as we become aware of them. We also do not condone practices that Scripture forbids, such as occult practices, sexual relations outside of marriage, homosexual behavior, drunkenness, theft and dishonesty. Members of the Biola Community have committed to abstain from these practices. We at Biola recognize that the abuse of tobacco products and alcoholic beverages presents a danger to personal and communal health. Biola students have committed not to use or possess these products while enrolled at our institution." Social dancing is also forbidden.

These standards also apply at home and on vacation: "The University reserves the right to take disciplinary action in response to behavior off campus that violates University standards and policies or adversely affects the University community and/or the pursuit of its objectives." Skateboards and rollerblades may not be used or owned on campus, although burning candles and incense may be done with "special permission from the Office of Campus Safety or [a] member of the Residence Life staff." The student handbook devotes many pages to discipline and its enforcement.

Modesty is of great concern to the administration, since "Biola University seeks to maintain a vital Christian community and witness through its appearance, in particular our standards of dress. . . . As representatives of this community even while outside the Biola campus, we have the desire to present a holistic witness that includes modesty." As a result, short shorts, halter tops, short or tight dresses and skirts, tight, strapless, backless, or low-cut shirts, and visible undergarments are all forbidden. Shirts must be worn at all times, save for the specially designated pool areas.

But all is not rules and regulations at Biola. The university rightly says that it "offers a wealth of opportunities for learning, growing, ministering, and playing that go well beyond the classroom." A number of traditional events enliven the Biola year. Among these are the parents' opening day luncheon, the art department's gallery openings on the first Tuesday of each month, the Parent/Family Weekend in October; the Christmas Tree Lighting during Advent, the Conservatory of Music's Christmas concerts, and the Spring Banquet. This event "is a formal banquet held at a nice location off campus during the spring of every year." Biola students are encouraged to "express their faith through work in off-campus Christian service." Each year students and faculty involve themselves in "nearly 200,000 hours of community service," the school reports. Although Biolans believe in salvation by "faith alone" (that's part of the college's formal creed), they don't neglect good works.

Biola students may be devout, but they are far from humorless. Zany events regularly enliven the campus, such as "Get Your Roommate a Date (GYRAD)," in which each dormitory floor "plans an original group activity for every resident on the hall and the date that his or her roommate sets up to participate in as a group." Other light-hearted festivities punctuate the calendar, such as "Blue Christmas" "Bursting the Bubble," "Freshman Fiesta," "Sophomore Mugging," "Harvest Fest,' "Junior Petition Pizza Party," "Midnight Madness," and "Mock Rock," to name a few.

None of these detract from Biola's serious purpose, which is reinforced by mandatory attendance at chapel, a core element of a Biola education. Typical chapel events— which take place every Monday, Wednesday, and Friday— feature a talented "worship band" that "leads praise," and "acclaimed speakers communicat[ing] God's word in a relevant way." Full-time students must attend a minimum of thirty chapels each semester, and must prove it by swiping their ID cars through bar code readers. Students are also encouraged to belong to off-campus congregations. The Student Ministries Department maintains a southern California church directory (www.biola.edu/admin/stumin/Churches), which includes no Episcopal, Orthodox, or Catholic congregations.

> **SUGGESTED CORE**
>
> The Great Books curriculum in the Torrey Honors Institute suffices.

All unmarried full-time enrolled freshmen and sophomores (under twenty-one years of age) not living with their parents or a legal guardian must live on campus. Unfortunately, there is not space for all upperclassmen to live there, so those who want a dorm room have had to compete in a lottery. (No, this does *not* count as gambling.) In fall 2006, a new residence hall opened that should relieve the housing shortage. Dorms are single-sex either by building or by wing, and limited intervisitation of rooms is permitted. "In the residence halls, there's always some kind of activity going on, from pizza parties to movie nights, late night fast food runs to barbeques on the lawn," the school reports. "Our professional Residence Life staff works with students to organize Bible studies, provide peer counseling, offer training in interpersonal relationships and leadership, and generate lots of good, clean fun."

While there are a number of clubs on campus, no political associations, nor Greek fraternities and sororities, are allowed. The groups that thrive at Biola are those which contribute to the college's mission. Alpha Gamma Theta is a woman's academic group; the Biola Korean Student Association seeks to integrate its members more fully into the life of the school, while keeping their traditions alive in an evangelical Christian context; the local branch of the California Nursing Students Association helps students prepare for a career. There are, of course, a number of spiritual and Bible study groups.

Social centers on campus include the coffee shop, Common Grounds, and a "charming little grill" called the Eagle's Nest. A new state-of-the-art gym, the Biola Fitness Center, has recently opened. Intramural sports are also important to the life of the school. Offerings include flag football, basketball, volleyball, and softball. There is also a lively theater scene at the university.

By and large, given the size of the campus and the student body, the administration's attempts to establish a safe environment have been successful. Although there were twenty burglaries in 2002, eighteen of these were committed by one individual who was later apprehended. Obviously, Biola benefits from the twenty-four-hour campus patrol conducted by trained security personnel.

ALL-AMERICAN COLLEGES

In 2005–6, tuition was $22,602, with room and board another $7,100. Sixty-eight percent of students receive assistance from the school. Some 59 percent of aid comes in scholarship grants, while the rest comes through campus jobs.

BROOKLYN COLLEGE

BROOKLYN, NEW YORK • WWW.BROOKLYN.CUNY.EDU

Brooklyn College got its start in 1926, when, to meet the growing demand for afford-able education for the best and brightest of New York's immigrant children, the city's board of higher education opened branches of Hunter College (then a women's college) and the College of the City of New York (then for men) in Brooklyn. With the merger of the two in 1930, the first public coeducational liberal arts college in New York City was born. Brooklyn College is one of the eleven senior colleges of the City University of New York (CUNY), a state-funded institution and the nation's leading public urban univer-sity with 200,000 students. Located in the borough of Brooklyn, once a major city in its own right, the college's setting puts a student within a subway ride of unparalleled cul-tural opportunities in Manhattan. But Brooklyn also boasts its own first-class orches-tras and museums and a magnificent public library and park, as well as bohemian arts enclaves and enough ethnic restaurants to challenge the most jaded palate. The college itself offers one of the best liberal arts educations available at any public institution in the country.

Academic Life: Loyal to the Core

Brooklyn College may be marked with big govern-ment's footprint—Franklin Roosevelt himself laid the cornerstone of its current campus—but at the time of its founding, civic-minded liberals were using tax dollars for such causes as preserving humanistic higher education in the Western tradition. While the school's curriculum is broader than it used to be and its student body is a cosmopolitan gumbo, Brooklyn College is still one of the more academically tradi-tional—and top-ranked—public academies.

This can be seen in Brooklyn's Core Studies pro-gram, a set of fourteen interrelated courses plus a for-eign language requirement. Distinctive among most universities today, the college's core curriculum is re-quired of all candidates for a baccalaureate degree and has been a national model for general education pro-grams and for faculty and curriculum development.

In 1981, bucking the trend toward cut-and-paste education, the college instituted this foundation program for all undergraduates in order to foster a common base of knowledge in the liberal arts and sciences. The National Endowment for the Humanities praised the college's core in a 1989 report as having "[led] to the revitalization of Brooklyn College and drawn much public attention and praise." One senior academic thinks of the core as "reflecting a sense of our traditional strengths and values. . . . It is intellectually rigorous, sharply focused, and at the forefront of higher education."

While it makes rigorous demands of them—sometimes taking up the better part of their first two years—students seem to appreciate the core program. One undergraduate praises it for "expos[ing] students to the great ideas of the West," and for presenting the Western tradition in a manner he calls "critically respectful."

The required courses are:
- "The Classical Origins of Western Culture";
- "Introduction to Art";
- "Introduction to Music";
- "People, Power, and Politics," which seeks "insight into American society in broad terms, as well as in terms of such specific issues as social class, race, gender, community, equality, and opportunity";
- "The Shaping of the Modern World," which covers "European and American civilization since 1700 in its global context";
- "Introduction to Computer Science";
- "Thinking Mathematically";
- "Landmarks of Literature," which emphasizes "English and American literature" and includes "works of European and non-Western cultures";
- "Science in Modern Life: Chemistry";
- "Science in Modern Life: Physics";
- "Science in Modern Life: Biology";
- "Science in Modern Life: Geology";
- "Philosophy: Knowledge, Existence, and Values"; and
- "Comparative Studies in African, Asian, Middle Eastern, and Latin American Culture."

This last course, known on campus as the Core 9 requirement, concentrates on non-Western regions—which in theory makes perfect sense, given the extent of globalization and America's interactions with every corner of the world. But while at many schools such classes are the locus of an anti-Western multiculturalist ideology, this worldview does not seem to predominate at Brooklyn College, where one student says, "I am glad to report that most of the [sections of the global culture course] are taught by professors from traditional departments—history, anthropology, English—and not from the politically radical 'ethnic studies.' Unfortunately, those few sections that are taught by professors from Latin American studies, black studies and similar disciplines do indeed contain a fairly large amount of anti-Western and anti-American propaganda. If there is one core class that has a very large proportion of radicals, it is the political science section ('People, Power, and Politics')."

According to one student, the tiny anthropology department deserves special note since "the professors are not only non-radicals, but a number of them are openly anti-Marxist." One student claims that his strongest classes have been in "the classics and English departments. The Brooklyn College classics department is very small, but the professors are dedicated, and professors, not graduate students, teach most of the classes. In my experience, all have been very accessible and helpful. The same goes for the English department. Most of its offerings are on the great texts of Western civilization, and there are relatively few courses that are designed for 'multiculturalist' indoctrination. This also applies very much to the history department."

One student says there is not a single department "where religious students would feel unwelcome"—with the possible exception of "certain 'ethnic studies' departments and a tiny women's studies program." Another student notes, "I have never had an experience at BC where campus politics intruded into the classroom. In cases where the professor's views were typically leftist, mostly in sociology and some other social science departments, the professor did not try to stifle debate or ridicule or penalize students with conservative leanings. However, the political science department may be one where a conservative or religious student would feel uncomfortable. The same goes for sociology, though there are certain exceptions."

Throughout its history, Brooklyn College has attracted outstanding professors, earning the college its nickname of "the poor man's Harvard." Some prominent faculty members include Pulitzer prize–winning historian Edwin Burrows, MacArthur Foundation fellow and painter Elizabeth Murray, Pulitzer Prize–winning novelist Michael Cunningham, and nuclear physicist Carl Shakin. Brooklyn College professors do more than just teach. They are known for their availability as mentors, advisors, and even career counselors.

Brooklyn College had an openly conservative leadership for almost thirty years in the person of President Harry Gideonse, who in 1938 ousted left-wing faculty whom he suspected of involvement in the Communist Party. In the 1950s, Gideonse tried again to police faculty politics, in part because professors with Marxist connections were being summoned to Washington, D.C., to appear before the House Un-American Activities Committee. Gideonse also shut down the student newspaper, the *Vanguard*, when its editors refused to publish articles reflecting the school's official anticommunist stance.

VITAL STATISTICS

Religious affiliation: none
Total enrollment: 15,385
Total undergraduates: 11,172
SAT midranges: V: 450–570, M: 490–600
Applicants: 7,083
Applicants accepted: 33%
Accepted applicants who enrolled: 51%
Tuition: $4,000 (in state), $8,640 (out of state)
Room and board: n/a
Freshman retention rate: 79%
Graduation rate: 37% (6 yrs.)
Courses with fewer than 20 students: not provided
Student-faculty ratio: 15:1
Courses taught by graduate students: 2%
Most popular majors: business/management, education, psychology
Students living on campus: none
Guaranteed housing for four years? no
Students in fraternities or sororities: 5%

Things changed quickly and radically at Brooklyn College during the Vietnam War era, when weekly protests disrupted academic life. The faculty here as elsewhere lurched to the left, and New York City politicians began meddling with Brooklyn College and the other CUNY schools. The most destructive change pressed upon the school was the egalitarian "Open Admissions" policy, which allowed any graduate of a New York City public high school admission to a CUNY college, regardless of academic ability. In just a few years enrollment at Brooklyn swelled to more than 30,000 students—and faculty began to complain that quantity was really a poor substitute for quality. Happily, the policy was reversed in 1976, and the CUNY system began a long, steady climb back to its historic standard of excellence.

The college motto, *Nil Sine Magno Labore* (Nothing without Great Effort), reflects the growing number of academically excellent students at Brooklyn College. The freshman class admitted in 2004 had the highest aggregate SAT scores in Brooklyn College history, with an average combined score of 1102.

Besides an excellent core curriculum, Brooklyn College offers fairness in the seminar room. One student notes, "I am happy to report that I have never had an experience at BC where campus politics intruded into the classroom."

The school is advancing on several fronts. In just three years since the launch of a fundraising campaign, Brooklyn College has received awards totaling $9.8 million to support research, training, program development, and institutional improvement. In 1992, the school was one of six, and the only public college, with student winners of both Marshall and Rhodes scholarships. The school's reputation has continued to improve since then. The Princeton Review's 2003 edition of *The Best 345 Colleges* ranked Brooklyn College first for the most beautiful campus in the United States, fifth for best academic value and for the friendly interaction of its diverse student body, and ninth for being situated in "a great college town."

The school has three academic divisions: the College of Liberal Arts and Sciences, the School of General Studies, and the Division of Graduate Studies. Brooklyn College offers more than seventy undergraduate and more than sixty graduate majors, advanced certificates, and programs in the humanities, sciences, performing arts, social sciences, education, and preprofessional and professional studies. Doctoral-level courses are available through the City University of New York Graduate Center in midtown Manhattan, with a number of doctoral courses offered on the Brooklyn College campus.

The college boasts prominent alumni in every field. A 2001 survey by Standard & Poor's ranked Brooklyn College second among the CUNY colleges in the number of graduates who hold major leadership positions in large corporations. The college is able to boast that more than 300 alumni are presidents, vice presidents, or chairmen of the boards of major corporations. Each year the college's graduates receive more than

350 acceptances to law schools and medical schools, including such institutions as Harvard, Yale, Stanford, and the University of Pennsylvania. Its famous graduates include actor Jimmy Smits, painters Mark Rothko, Burgoyne Diller, and Philip Pearlstein, sculptor Lee Bontecou, Congresswoman Shirley Chisholm, Senator Barbara Boxer, Adobe Systems CEO Bruce Chizen, and artful defense attorney Alan Dershowitz.

Student Life: Crossing Brooklyn Bridge

As the college describes its neighborhood, "the Brooklyn College campus merges the surrounding areas of Victorian Flatbush, Hasidic Midwood, and West Indian Flatbush." In spite of this utterly urban setting, the school is often praised for its beauty. Made up of thirteen buildings on a twenty-six-acre tree-lined campus—it was built on the site of a former golf course and circus grounds—Brooklyn College has no dormitories. In fact, a fairly large portion of its students are working adults. One student says, "This very fact means that the student life here is not as intimate an experience as in a typical college where students live on campus." On the positive side, campus politics and social pressures play a much smaller role in the typical student's time here; the same student adds with approval: "There is far less opportunity for the radical left to intimidate."

Brooklyn College's total student population comprises some 15,385 undergraduate and graduate students. Its ethnic, religious, and racial composition reflects New York City's diversity, with students from more than one hundred nations. The college's student body breaks down roughly as 47 percent white, 31 percent black, 11 percent Hispanic, and 11 percent Asian. Says one student, "A very large proportion of the BC student body is Orthodox Jewish, and also a very large portion of the faculty. Many students also come from ethnic Catholic backgrounds. This, I think, goes a long way in explaining why the lunatic left is not as active on the BC campus as it is on many others."

New buildings are going up around the campus as you read this, since Brooklyn College has embarked on a major capital improvement program. In 2003, it completed an extensive renovation and expansion of the Brooklyn College Library, which now boasts the most technologically advanced computer networking system in the City University of New York system. The West Quad Project, begun in 2003 and due for completion in 2007, will provide a second large green space on the quadrangle, as well as a new building for student services and a sports complex, all under one roof.

Many significant cultural events take place at the Brooklyn Center for the Performing Arts, bringing in large audiences from Manhattan. Since 1992, Brooklyn Col-

SUGGESTED CORE
1.–2. Core Studies I: The Classical Origins of Western Culture
3. English 31.2: The Bible as Literature
4. Philosophy 11.2: Medieval Philosophy (*closest match*)
5. Political Science 52: Modern Political Thought
6. English 30.5/30.6: Shakespeare I/II
7. History 13: America to 1877
8. Philosophy 12.2: Nineteenth-Century Philosophy (*closest match*)

lege has secured more than $275 million for capital improvements, including $54.4 million in 1996 for revitalization and expansion. Planning has begun for a new center for the performing arts, which will serve the Conservatory of Music, the Department of Theater, and the school's dance degree program.

Campus crime has been on a steady decline over the past five years. In 2004, the last year for which statistics are available, the school reported only one robbery and one burglary, an impressively low number for any college, let alone an urban one. The college is sufficiently policed and well maintained. One student reports, "Crime on campus is not a big issue, nor is it a huge concern outside of it. After a string of incidents a few years ago, the school implemented a very strict security system, and it is virtually impossible to enter the campus without proper ID. Security is everywhere."

Brooklyn College is a genuine bargain, particularly for New York residents, with in-state tuition only $4,000 per year; out-of-staters pay just $8,640—less than for many high schools. Room and board are not offered by the college, but apartments are plentiful in the diverse and cosmopolitan neighborhoods surrounding the school. Fifty percent of students receive need-based financial aid, and the average student loan debt of a graduate is around $14,000.

CALVIN COLLEGE

GRAND RAPIDS, MICHIGAN • WWW.CALVIN.EDU

Calvin College was founded as a seminary for the Christian Reformed Church in 1876. Strongly influenced by the Reformed tradition, which posits "a world made good by God, distorted by sin, redeemed in Christ, and awaiting the fullness of God's reign," Calvin educates its students in the hope that they might "recapture society, culture, and all creation for Jesus Christ." The college is committed both to academic excellence and to offering a liberal education thoroughly steeped in Christian "faith, thought, and practice."

Calvin maintains a rare unity of thought and mission through its stringent faculty requirements. Faculty are expected to adhere to the college's standards and expression of the Reformed faith. They must be members in good standing of a Christian Reformed church or another denomination in "ecclesiastical fellowship" with it and sign a "synodically approved Form of Subscription" pledging their fidelity to the three principle documents of the Reformed faith: the Heidelberg Confession, the Belgian Confession of 1561, and the Canons of Dordt. They must also send their children to Christian Reformed schools (or receive special permission from the college provost to send them elsewhere). These explicit requirements have helped insulate Calvin from many of the relativist and deconstructionist fads that have swept through other church-related institutions, rendering them religious in name only. The school also offers the opportunity for an outstanding liberal arts education to students who seek it out (for instance, by taking the courses in our suggested core).

Academic Life: Reformed Humanism

In 2001, Calvin adopted a new core curriculum that, according to the catalog, is designed to "equip students with the knowledge and skills required for an informed and effective life of Christian service in contemporary society." In addition to teaching knowledge and skills, the core aspires to "cultivate such dispositions as patience, diligence, honesty, charity, and hope that make for a life well-lived— of benefit to others and pleasing to God." All students must satisfy these requirements:

ALL-AMERICAN COLLEGES

- two "gateway and prelude" orientation classes during the first year: "Developing a Christian Mind" and "First-Year Prelude," which "introduce students to Calvin College as a Christian community of inquiry";
- two courses in biblical or theological foundations, such as "Biblical Literature "or "Theology and Interpreting the Bible";
- "History of the West and the World" I or II;
- "Fundamental Questions in Philosophy";
- one literature course, such as "Survey of British Literature" or "Literature and Women";
- "Written Rhetoric";
- one class in information technology, such as "Introduction to Engineering Design" or "Foundations of Information Technology";
- one health and fitness class, such as "Jogging" or "In-Line Skating";
- courses or tests to show an intermediate competency in a foreign language (Chinese, Dutch, French, German, Greek, Latin, Japanese, or Spanish);
- one course in mathematics, such as "Introduction to Probability and Statistics" or "Differential and Integral Calculus";
- one class in the arts, such as "Introduction to Art History" or "Understanding and Enjoying Music";
- one social science course, such as "Principles of Economics" or "Diversity and Inequality in the United States";
- one course focusing on "societal structures in North America," such as "Sociological Principles and Perspectives" or "American Public Policy";
- one class in global and historical studies, such as"Religion and Politics in Comparative Perspective" or "Ancient Near East";
- one course in the physical world, such as "Oceanography" or "Stars, Galaxies, and the Universe";
- one class in the living world, such as "Human Biology" or "Cell Biology and Genetics";
- one course in the area of "cross-cultural engagement." The guidelines state that these courses teach students to "distinguish between enduring principles of human morality . . . [and] to witness other cultural embodiments of faith." Many students fulfill this requirement through off-campus volunteer programs; and
- a "core capstone" course during the final year. This is typically a small seminar with a major research project undertaken in the student's major field of study; its purpose is to integrate rigorous scholarship and a Christian worldview.

With their many options, navigating among these complex requirements can be tricky. In fact, each year in October the school suspends classes for two "advising days." Nevertheless, the college is serious about its commitment to the liberal arts and to a curriculum that seeks to integrate different disciplines. One professor says, "Will all students get a comprehensive experience in Western history, literature, philosophy, theological and political theory? Probably not, but they will get a serious engagement with such subjects." "Our core requirements are decent, and make for a real, shared educational experience—a platform that can then be assumed in later courses and research," says another professor. "[T]here is a strong sense of shared mission that students encounter across all courses." More than any other factor, it is this clear sense of mission that brings unity to the curriculum and a framework for inquiry.

Calvin's intellectual atmosphere is bracing. Students and faculty agree that there is a lively exchange of ideas on campus. "We reject the anti-intellectualism and defensiveness which characterizes too much of the evangelical community," one professor wishes to make clear. Despite Calvin's 98 percent acceptance rate, professors indicate that most students are earnest about academics and those students who want to be challenged will find ample opportunities. A professor says, "Because the college has such a generous admission policy (as a matter of justice), one finds quite a range of students. At the top are some cream-of-the-crop students who would excel anywhere, are passionate about learning, and who are a delight to teach. These students tend to find one another in the Honors Program and/or through some of the stronger majors on campus (philosophy, English, history, biology), creating a core community of students dedicated to learning. These students also find many faculty receptive to drawing alongside of them and really mentoring them beyond the classroom."

For the most part, Calvin is relatively free of the political extremes that afflict many other campuses. Calvin is shaped more by its shared belief and Christian commitments than by the latest educational innovations or ideological silliness. One professor remarks, "Despite having one of the most stringent sets of faculty requirements of any religious college in the country, Calvin also has the most academic freedom I have ever experienced. I have taught at two other, larger Catholic universities and found them much more dominated by reigning ideologies and political correctness. In fact, I think it is precisely the rigorous confessional requirements for faculty (based on historic creeds) that actually opens the space for quite rigorous, open debate amongst faculty." A retired professor concurs: "Calvin is much more serious about and unified around the idea of serving the Kingdom of God as this is understood in the Reformed theological tradition, through teaching and scholarship and the building of a Christian community of hearts and minds, than it is in advancing the agenda of either conservatives or liberals as those groups are defined in today's political debates."

VITAL STATISTICS

Religious affiliation: Christian Reformed Church

Total enrollment: 4,177

Total undergraduates: 4,125

SAT/ACT midranges: SAT V: 540–663, M: 550–670; ACT: 23–28

Applicants: 2,156

Applicants accepted: 98%

Accepted applicants who enrolled: 48%

Tuition: $20,470

Room and board: $7,040

Freshman retention rate: 88%

Graduation rate: 54% (4 yrs.), 71% (6 yrs.)

Courses with fewer than 20 students: 39%

Student-faculty ratio: 12:1

Courses taught by graduate students: none

Most popular majors: business/marketing, education, health professions

Students living on campus: 58%

Guaranteed housing for four years? yes

Students in fraternities or sororities: none

Students report that, with a few exceptions, professors do not use their classrooms as forums for advancing their personal agendas, and that conservative students are not marginalized. A professor says, "In my experience, there's room for open and honest debate." Students report, however, that liberal groups are generally the most outspoken on campus. Indeed, the Calvin community isn't as politically predictable as one might think, given the school's theological conservatism. When President Bush spoke at the 2005 commencement, nearly a third of the faculty and about one hundred students issued protests about the Iraq war—which they considered unjust by Christian standards. The administration recognized their right to do so and according to one professor there were no lasting repercussions for either side.

Calvin professors are deeply committed to both excellence in teaching and in scholarship. A professor says, "Calvin is one of only a handful of schools that really tries to have it both ways. On the one hand, the expectations for original research are very high; on the other hand, the college continues to think of itself as first and foremost an undergraduate teaching institution." The quality of a professor's teaching weighs heavily in the college's decision to grant tenure and most faculty work to maintain close relationships with students. A professor says, "My experience in tenure decisions has been that a professor's responsibilities to students (in the classroom, through advising, and in mentoring) are very important for tenure decisions. It is much more likely, for tenure and reappointment decisions, that great teaching might compensate for a modest scholarly record than vice versa."

> *"Calvin is much more serious about and unified around the idea of serving the Kingdom of God as this is understood in the Reformed theological tradition . . . than it is in advancing the agenda of either conservatives or liberals as those groups are defined in today's political debates."*

"The college boasts a number of strong departments, with excellent records of sending students on to top graduate programs and into careers in policy, nonprofit agencies, and political life," reports a professor. Calvin's philosophy department, described by one faculty member as the college's "flagship department," has produced four presidents of the American Philosophical Association [and] two Gifford lecturers (Alvin Plantinga and Nicholas Wolterstorff). Faculty from the department have gone on to endowed chairs at Yale, Notre Dame, and elsewhere. Other recommended professors in the department include Kevin Corcoran, Rebecca DeYoung, Lee Hardy, Del Ratzsch, and James K. A. Smith.

The political science department houses the Paul Henry Institute for the Study of Christianity and Politics, which one professor refers to as a major center of intellectual life on campus. The institute is directed by Corwin Smidt, a national expert on religion and politics and an eminent figure at the school. One professor says, "Our departmental teaching evaluations are among the highest in the college. We have an outstanding record of scholarship and actively involve students in our research." The department offers off-campus programs in New York and Washington, D.C., as well as state and local internships. Other recommended professors here include James Penning and Bill Stevenson.

The history department "takes seriously the history of Western thought and early American history without the kind of ideologies that reign at research universities," claims a professor. Notable faculty include Jim Bratt, Bert DeVries, and William VanVugt. The English department is also strong, although, reports a faculty member, the younger professors tend to be more enamored of contemporary academic ideologies than senior faculty, who are generally more rigorous and critical. Students recommend Dale Brown, Susan Felch, Karen Saupe, and James VandenBosch.

The classics department and its professors attract some of Calvin's best students, many of whom double major in classics and either philosophy or religion. Professor Ken Bratt received Calvin's 2006 Presidential Award for Exemplary Teaching. Bratt also directs Calvin's honors program.

According to one professor, the business department "tends to attract our least reflective students, who treat their time here only in terms of professional preparation, with little respect for liberal arts formation." He says that this attitude also infuses some of the business faculty, who tend to a kind of "industry pragmatism." However, the economics department, which is housed with the business department, is reportedly one of Calvin's most demanding. Most of the economics faculty are "deeply respectful of the principles of the classically liberal tradition," says a professor. Recommendations include George Monsma, Kurt Schaefer, and John Tiemstra.

Other strong departments at Calvin include biology, chemistry, and engineering. Students recommend Curt Blankespoor and Stephen Matheson in biology and Ronald Blankespoor in chemistry. According to the college website, engineering majors routinely demonstrate excellence on national and state exams, far exceeding national pass rates.

Students interested in pursuing academic excellence should consider Calvin's honors program. Honors courses are offered in most departments, providing students with the opportunity to undertake research with faculty mentors. A professor says, "The honors program at Calvin is home-base to our best and brightest from across the disciplines. The McGregor Fellows program selects twelve to fifteen of the college's best juniors (and sometimes sophomores) to work with professors for the duration of the summer, doing intensive research aimed toward publication and providing excellent training for graduate school."

Calvin offers extensive study-abroad options, ranking fourth in the nation among baccalaureate institutions for the number of students studying abroad. Nearly 60 percent of the class of 2005 spent time off campus during their tenure at Calvin, either during "January term" or for semester-long stays in England, France, Hungary, China, Honduras, Ghana, and Washington, D.C.

Student Life: Geneva on the Grand

Grand Rapids, with a metro population of 650,000, is located in central Michigan. The city boasts historic neighborhoods, trendy shopping, a downtown riverwalk, four professional sports teams, salmon fishing in the Grand River—and, for those who dare to take a walk on the wild side, the Gerald R. Ford Presidential Library and Museum.

In the summer of 2006, the college celebrated fifty years on its Knollcrest campus, which it purchased from millionaire businessman J. C. Miller. The college has more than doubled the original 166-acre purchase, including the addition of an eighty-acre Ecosystem Preserve. The new Bunker Interpretive Center and extensive trail system draw nearly 5,000 visitors a year to the preserve. The thirty-six-acre Gainey Athletic Facility includes a cross-country course, softball, soccer, and baseball fields, and tennis courts. The H. Henry Meeter Center for Calvin Studies, located in the Hekman Library, contains one of the world's largest collections of works by and about Calvin and other Protestant reformers. Recent campus additions include a 55,000-square-foot DeVos Communication Center, "Calvin's Crossing" (a 400-foot-long skywalk), and the Prince Conference Center.

The Student Life Division at Calvin offers, in its own words, "a wide array of programs and services that are consistent with, and complement, the educational opportunities that abound at Calvin." Musically minded students can join one of five choral ensembles, the orchestra, or a contemporary Christian ensemble. Calvin participates in NCAA Division III athletics and also offers numerous intramural sports. Arts organizations include the Calvin Writers Guild and a theater group. There are a number of campus publications, including a student newspaper, *Chimes*, and a literary journal, *Dialogue*. Students participate in several political groups, such as the College Republicans, College Democrats, and even the fun-loving Calvin Students for Christian Feminism. Wacky annual events include Chaos Day, the Mud Bowl, Airband, the Cold Knight plunge, Siblings Weekend, and a cardboard canoe contest sponsored by the engineering department. The college celebrates Calvin's birthday each year with cake, ice cream, and a two-minute speech by a faculty impersonator of the dour theologian.

Calvin offers a variety of special programs. The award-winning January Series consists of fifteen days of lectures featuring "the world's greatest authorities in their respective fields." It is offered free of charge to students and the community. The college also hosts a biennial conference, the Festival of Faith and Writing, which explores Christianity and the arts. The Student Activities Office sponsors more than fifty performing artists each year.

Unlike the professors, students are not required to sign any pledge regarding belief or behavior; however, the student conduct code is some twenty-seven pages long. The code is based on the idea of "building community" and states that "Calvin seeks to weld its participants together around the beliefs that all are made in God's image and that members of Christ's church need one another." "Responsible freedom" has its limits at Calvin, as demonstrated by a recent controversy on campus regarding student use of online profiles posted in forums such as Facebook or MySpace. Recently, ten

Calvin students were called into a Student Life office and questioned about the content of their profiles in Facebook, creating a campus debate about student privacy. The administration holds that by signing the code, students can be held responsible for any incriminating information posted about them on the web. Vice President of Student Life Shirley Hoogstra said, "There is initially no searching of student [w]eb life unless an incident is reported. Reporters could be RAs or RDs. Student Life will respond to any and all reports of this type."

The religious identity of the student body is overwhelmingly Christian, but is no longer predominantly Reformed; only about half of the student body is affiliated with a Reformed denomination. Students of non-Reformed backgrounds are made to feel welcome, but the Reformed faith is so integrated into the curriculum that it is hard not to be influenced by it. "We are almost all agreed on the central beliefs of the Christian faith," says one such student, "so we get along pretty well." A professor says, "While the vast majority of Calvin students come from conservative, evangelical backgrounds, they also come from a large number of religious denominations and geographic locations (including over forty countries). This makes for an interesting mix and lively debate." The college offers numerous opportunities for worship, including daily chapel services, the student-led LOFT (Living Our Faith Together), foreign language chapels, dorm Bible studies, and a new "Faith" website. "Campus worship is an important part of the life of the college and in fact another aspect of the college that ties it to tradition and history," says a professor. "Chapel attendance is not at all required, but it is an important source of reflection and formation on the campus," he adds.

Calvin students are housed in one of seven resident halls or in the Knollcrest apartments for juniors and seniors. Freshmen and sophomores (except those who are twenty-one or older) are required to live on campus or at home with their parents. Calvin's residence hall policy prohibits, among other things, alcohol, noise (outside of the hours of 4:30–6 p.m.), offensive language or posters, pornography, and premarital sex. In addition, Calvin students are expected to observe Sunday "by keeping the spirit and purpose of the day." Visitation hours are limited and students are not allowed to have members of the opposite sex in their rooms unless the door is open.

The area of Grand Rapids surrounding the Calvin campus is safe. However, one of the popular off-campus neighborhoods for upperclassmen, East Town, has recently experienced some robberies and assaults. The college reported in 2004 a single sexual assault, one burglary, and six stolen cars.

SUGGESTED CORE

1. Classics 211: Classical Literature
2. Philosophy 251: History of Western Philosophy I
3. Religion 121/221: Biblical Foundations I (Biblical Literature and Theology) / Biblical Foundations II (Synoptic Gospels and Acts)
4. Religion 243: History of Christian Theology I
5. Political Science 306: History of Modern Political Thought
6. English 346: Shakespeare
7. History 251/252: Colonial America (1500–1763) / The American Republic (1763–1877)
8. Philosophy 252: History of Western Philosophy II *or* History 266: Nineteenth-Century Europe *(closest matches)*

Calvin was designated in the *Fiske Guide to Colleges* as one of "America's best value colleges." Costs are below the national average for other four-year private colleges, with tuition at $20,470, and room and board just over $7,000. Calvin offers both need-based and merit-based aid to the tune of $43 million each year. There are fifty pages of academic scholarships listed in the college catalog, some of which are open to all students, some restricted to students in certain disciplines. In general, numerous means of support are available at Calvin for diligent students. The average financial aid package is $13,200; 90 percent of students receive some aid; 61 percent receive academic scholarships.

CENTRE COLLEGE

Founded in 1819, Centre College is best known for being a good, solid, Presbyterian school in the center of Kentucky. In recent years Centre has fought to transcend this limited reputation to become better known as a worthy liberal arts college that serves not just local Kentucky Calvinists, but any student eager for an authentic liberal education. Centre has done this, thankfully, not by embracing the postmodern lunacy that permeates elite northeastern schools, but by holding to its own standard of excellence. Here, students are exposed to the best ideas of the Western tradition and important existential issues of faith and doubt in required courses on the humanities and the "fundamental questions." Like it or not, they know their professors and their professors know them. They do have the chance to leave Danville for a semester to study in Europe on one of many Centre-sponsored programs. But by the close of their senior year most come to agree that Centre put them on track for a lifetime of learning and achievement.

Academic Life: Asking Life's Fundamental Questions

Although there is not a fully formed traditional core curriculum, Centre students face a rather structured set of general education requirements. This set of requirements provides for a much broader liberal arts education than they would receive at most schools—including other liberal arts colleges. To fulfill these requirements, students must take:

- a Freshman Studies seminar designed to introduce them to college-level work, with choices ranging from "Stem Cells, Cloning, and You" to "Women and Spirituality" and "An American Obsession: The Lawn";
- two humanities courses, selected from a choice of four courses that study the literature, philosophy, and arts of different eras of Western history;
- two courses in social sciences, including a basic history course, such as "Development of the Modern World," and one social studies course in cultural or physical anthropology, economics, politics, or sociology;

- two courses in Fundamental Questions, either "Biblical History and Ideas" or "History of Christian Thought," along with another course from the philosophy or religion departments such as "Philosophy of Art," "Ancient Philosophy," "Seventeenth- and Eighteenth-Century Philosophy," or "Happiness and Justice: An Introduction to Ethical Thinking";
- two science courses, chosen from the biology, chemistry, physics, and natural sciences departments; and
- two pragmatic but worthy courses: "Personal Safety," designed to prepare students for emergency situations, and "Wellness: A Way of Life," a basic health and fitness class.

Centre students must also demonstrate competency in:

- math, by having an acceptable score on the SAT or ACT or a passing grade in a basic math course;
- a foreign language, by passing an exam or an intermediate language course; and
- expository writing, by taking a writing course in the freshman year, and if necessary, another writing-intensive general education course.

The strongest part of these requirements is the humanities. According to the catalog, Humanities 110 is a "study of literature, philosophy, and the fine arts in classical Greek and Roman civilization with special attention given to ethical and aesthetic values." One professor says that the course gives a "critical overview of classical Greek and Roman civilization." Humanities 120 examines the same topics from the medieval period onwards. An admirable requirement at Centre (one conspicuously absent from most other college curricula) mandates two courses in Fundamental Questions, which exposes students to topics in philosophy and religion, mostly from the Western tradition. The catalog explains, "Becoming educated should include a mature understanding of values and beliefs which have shaped us and our culture, and it should also involve both a heightened awareness of our own values and a critical appraisal of them."

Requirements for the majors, especially in the humanities, are solid. Students majoring in English must be exposed to literature from various centuries. They take two British literature courses, an American literature course, a course in Shakespeare, and upper-level courses in medieval and Renaissance literature, eighteenth- and nineteenth-century works, and twentieth-century writing. There are choices within each section, but whatever they choose students graduate with a broad knowledge of their field. History majors also must take courses concentrating on different eras; the required courses seem particularly strong. Courses such as "Indian Magic" are kept to a minimum and are offered as electives. The religion department requires that majors take "Biblical History and Ideas" and "History of Christian Thought" among other courses. Students can choose important courses like "Biblical Hebrew" and the like, but there are several course choices focused more on social outreach than on theology or religion, such as "Poverty and Homelessness" (which explores "theological and philosophical approaches to economic justice") and "World Hunger and the Environment." In the humanities department, all choices are solid, and several are downright exciting. Talented singers who pass an audition can take Music and Art in the Great Italian Cities, which culminates in "an eleven-day choral performance tour to Italy." Another course sounds like a highly educational junket: "Elsaß, Alsace or Elsass: Forming a Modern Alsatian Identity," in which "[s]tudents spend three weeks exploring and studying Alsatian culture: its history, art and architecture, language, cuisine, geography, demographics, and politics. Conducted in Strasbourg." Where do we sign up?

Centre is, of course, a small school, so most of the academic departments are of modest scale. The philosophy department includes just four faculty members, the history department eight, and the psychology department six. By design, Centre's approach to education is interdisciplinary, and many classes are crosslisted with those in other departments. One student notes, "It really lets you find how inter-related learning truly is."

One sophomore student says that faculty members teaching general education courses do have some degree of flexibility—not every section of Humanities 110 reads the same works—but there is still an overall awareness of "common knowledge" among students on campus. The general education requirements, she says, encourage discussion outside of class, and she and her friends often discuss class topics even when the professor isn't listening, although, she admits, "I'm not sure if I'm normal." Perhaps she isn't. One faculty member complains that there isn't enough intellectual curiosity at Centre—among students *or* faculty. An emphasis on teaching has come at the expense of research. Instructors, who teach on average six courses a year, have little time left for pursuing their own publishing aims. Of course, from a student's perspective this is probably a good thing. The student-faculty ratio is an appealing 11 to 1, and more than half of all classes have fewer than twenty students.

The personal attention students receive from their instructors sets Centre apart from its big-name neighbors. Students are assigned faculty advisors, based on their academic interests, at the start of their freshman year; once a student has declared a major, he is assigned a faculty advisor within that discipline. One student gives an example of the sheer dedication one of her professors displayed when she was struggling with her coursework the day before an exam. "My professor gave up everything that day and sat there patiently with me for two and a half hours, helping me understand everything. You're never 'on your own' here." Teaching, one professor says, is the central focus at Centre and a primary factor in tenure decisions. "A good set of student course evaluations counts about the same as a publication in a peer-reviewed journal," he says.

VITAL STATISTICS
Religious affiliation: Presbyterian
Total enrollment: 1,130
Total undergraduates: 1,130
SAT/ACT midranges: SAT V: 580–678, M: 600–670; ACT: 25–29
Applicants: 1,989
Applicants accepted: 63%
Accepted applicants who enrolled: 25%
Tuition: $23,110
Room and board: $7,700
Freshman retention rate: 92%
Graduation rate: 77% (4 yrs.), 79% (6 yrs.)
Courses with fewer than 20 students: 54%
Student-faculty ratio: 11:1
Courses taught by graduate students: none
Most popular majors: social sciences, history, biology
Students living on campus: 92%
Guaranteed housing for four years? yes
Students in fraternities: 37% sororities: 38%

An advantage of Centre's small academic departments is the close interaction that students experience. One recent alumnus, a graduate student in chemistry, says his department "felt like a family." Taking many classes with the same professor encouraged camaraderie between students and faculty, as did the frequent Frisbee and croquet games they played against the math department. The college's strong focus on teaching yields obvious results among students. One student says that it's the faculty's devotion to their students that makes Centre a "very transformative experience in so many ways." She explains that the school guides students to find their academic interests and to use them wisely. "Before coming to Centre, I had no idea what any of my intellectual passions were. It was not until I had the opportunity to study abroad in London for three months that I realized my passion was rooted in international studies, learning about the world, and in particular advocating human rights and humanitarianism around the world. Now I know the direction of my life will never be the same." The chemistry student mentioned above says that although he entered Centre knowing he wanted to be a chemist, one of his favorite professors, José Workman, showed him that organic chemistry is "more than just memorizing reactions and mechanisms."

One student who was struggling with her coursework reports, "My professor . . . sat there patiently with me for two and a half hours, helping me understand everything. You're never 'on your own' here."

The best departments, according to our sources, are computer science (with a demanding but dedicated faculty) biology, economics (where teachers use research in their courses to energize their classes), and education (whose graduates are very successful as teachers and administrators). Faculty in the religion department are noted for being particularly balanced in presenting their personal views. Professors singled out for praise include Christine A. Shannon in computer science, Preston Miles in chemistry, Jane W. Joyce in classical studies, Robert E. Martin in economics, Ken C. Keffer in French, Donna M. Plummer in education, Stephen E. Asmus in biology, Mark T. Lucas in English, Richard D. Axtell in religion, Stephen R. Powell in art, Lori Hartmann-Mahmoud and Nayef H. Samhat in government, and Michael Hamm and Clarence Wyatt in history.

One important element of a Centre education is the CentreTerm, a three-week spread in January that allows students the flexibility to study particular academic areas in great depth. As sophomores and upperclassmen, many students choose to cooperate closely with professors in independent study or laboratory work, to participate in an internship (one student went to Chicago to work at the stock exchange), or to go overseas on Centre-run study trips. One student heading to Vietnam for CentreTerm planned to do an independent study with her professor to study the Vietnamese health care system. Study-abroad programs in general are popular at Centre, in part due to the school's relatively remote location. Some 70 percent of Centre students study abroad at some point during their college years, most through Centre-run programs. One Centre alumnus reports that his winters abroad allowed him to study the art, music, and architecture of Europe. But as a senior, he says, he also learned the benefits of *true* cultural diversity when he learned how to interact with natives in Samoa while studying the economics of tourism in the South Pacific. This has proved to be a necessary skill in his present job.

Classroom politics, students say, are generally kept to a minimum, though most faculty are more liberal than students. There are no women's or multicultural studies departments: worthwhile courses in these areas are spread throughout the disciplines, not secluded in identity-politics enclaves. One student says the campus has a fairly free exchange of ideas and remembers a few instances when the school itself encouraged political debate. Centre recently sponsored a viewing of Michael Moore's *Fahrenheit 9/11*, but then also presented opposing views. However, a faculty member says it is rare that political ideas are actually exchanged. "Part of that is an inherently southern civility," he says, "and part of it is a student body that is generally rather conservative."

SUGGESTED CORE
1. Classics 321-329: Topics in Classical Literature in Translation
2. Philosophy. 210: Ancient Philosophy
3. Religion 314, 315: Literature of the Hebrew Bible and New Testament Literature
4. Religion 120: History of Christian Thought
5. Government 301: Western Political Theory I
6. English 301, 302: Shakespeare I and II
7. History 230: Development of the United States I
8. History 308: Nineteenth-Century Europe (*closest match*)

Student Life: Walking the Talk

Each fall, the first college event for Centre's new crop of freshmen occurs on the Sunday evening before classes start. "The Walk" is a procession past Olin Hall, the library, and Sutcliffe Hall to Newlin Hall, where the newbies attend the opening convocation. When they become graduating seniors, Centre students march along the same path on their way to the commencement ceremony.

Between these two rituals, Centre students enjoy a fairly traditional and wholesome college experience. Danville has a charming Main Street with plenty of shops and restaurants. The college has a strong relationship with the town, with students often volunteering for community projects and many residents working at Centre. In the surrounding horse country, students can explore the many hiking and equestrian trails and other outdoor activities. Even on campus Centre makes a great effort to keep students occupied and entertained. The impressive Norton Performing Arts Center, renovated ten years ago, recently featured entertainers Dolly Parton and Ben Folds, dancer Mikhail Baryshnikov, the Boston Pops, and musicals *Fiddler on the Roof* and *My Fair Lady*. In 2000, it hosted the vice-presidential debate between Dick Cheney and Joe Lieberman. Students receive free tickets to many performances. Lexington, about half an hour away, offers the attractions of a small city and better shopping than Danville. Louisville is about an hour's drive.

ALL-AMERICAN COLLEGES

To foster community—and perhaps to boost the level of intellectual engagement—the school requires students to attend at least twelve of the thirty or so convocations held each year; recently these have ranged from a discussion on world hunger, to a seminar on how to dress for interviews, to an informational lecture on NASA.

Centre College has a very active religious life, mostly in the Centre Christian Fellowship, with many students participating in group Bible studies and outreach events. Centre has Presbyterian roots, but the college student body has a strong Catholic presence, according to one student—although the Catholic student organization is not as active as other ministries.

Almost 40 percent of Centre students belong to a fraternity or sorority. At larger schools that might suggest a high degree of cliquishness. But at Centre, as one student says, groups can't be too exclusive; with only around 1,130 students, there just aren't enough people to exclude. Fraternity and sorority parties are open to all. College officials exercise some control over alcohol at parties, since all official parties must first be registered with the school.

Although two-thirds of the student body hail from Kentucky, most students tend to stay on campus on the weekends instead of heading home to mom, dad, and their high school buddies. That's one indicator of the campus's healthy social life. More than 90 percent of Centre students live on campus, where they have several options for living arrangements, including traditional dormitories, suite-style residences, and apartments. The most coveted spots are those located on the main quad, but the campus is small enough that everything is within easy walking distance. Some students also live in the fraternity and sorority houses in Greek Park, but space there is limited: the houses are primarily used for social events. One student stresses that students genuinely *want* to be on campus, and it's not just for the sake of convenience that so many of her classmates are also her neighbors. RAs are paid only a minimal stipend, yet competition for these positions is fierce. "Nobody's in it for the money," one RA says. "We genuinely want to help each other out."

The average student-athlete will find plenty of opportunities to compete at Centre. The athletic center is open to all, and sporting events, particularly football, are usually well attended—even by the students of yesteryear. About forty years ago, some members of Phi Delta Theta fraternity decided that the late Fred Vinson, a Centre alumnus and Phi Delt brother who was Chief Justice of the Supreme Court from 1946 to 1953, would still like to attend games, so fraternity members started bringing his portrait to athletic and other campus events. This "Dead Fred" tradition is a favorite at Centre.

Built almost entirely in red brick, the Centre campus's oldest building is Old Centre, a large and majestic building with Greek columns and portico. It once housed the students' sleeping, studying, eating, and recreation quarters, and today is listed in the National Register of Historic Places, along with thirteen other Centre College buildings. Except for one or two buildings dating from the 1960s, the campus is generally pleasant and quaint, and renovations of old buildings and construction of new ones have conformed well to the overall style of the campus. On-campus crime is minimal.

Except for a couple dozen burglaries in 2004 (which was abnormally high), no other crimes are listed in the most recent statistics.

A year at Centre runs around $23,000 for tuition, and another $7,700 for room and board. Forty-three percent of students receive need-based financial aid. Most recently, the school reported that it had met 88 percent of its students' demonstrated financial need.

UNIVERSITY OF CHICAGO

CHICAGO, ILLINOIS • WWW.UCHICAGO.EDU

Of all the colleges profiled in this book, this one is perhaps the toughest and most impressive. While not a member of the Ivy League (originally a football conference, the Ivy League is limited to schools in the northeast), the University of Chicago is every bit the equal of member schools, and in fact exceeds most of them in intellectual rigor and seriousness. Chicago has boasted seventy-seven Nobel Laureates among its faculty, six of whom are still on campus. In the last six years, eight Chicago students have been named Rhodes scholars and five have been named Marshall scholars. A student entering the university as a proud valedictorian will have to get used to the fact that he no longer stands out; some 75 percent of entering first-year students graduated from high school in the top 10 percent of their classes. If you're looking for a community of devoutly intellectual aspiring scholars, there is no better place to begin than here in the Windy City. At the very least, you will no longer be the lone oddball who would rather stay at home finishing a philosophy book than go to the Friday night football game.

On paper, Chicago's academic achievements may be equaled by certain other elite schools, but the university has a different approach to education than most, one guided by a still-vital core curriculum that allows each student to acquire a holistic base of knowledge and understanding in a variety of fields. Future lawyers will emerge with a comfortable knowledge of literature and science; biologists will leave Chicago with a feel for the great traditions in art and music. Chicago's motto is *Crescat scientia; vita excolatur* (Let knowledge grow from more to more; and so let human life be enriched). This university stands apart from other top-notch schools because of its broader, truer picture of what learning really is, and its mission to impart that standard of learning to all who enroll. As one student explains, "I have a strong foundation upon which I can build—I can study any subject potentially, mostly because I have been taught how to *talk* about ideas." Mission accomplished.

Academic Life: Drilling through the Core

The University of Chicago is so well known as an intellectual powerhouse that its method of educating young men and women once set the standard for other liberal arts colleges. (In succeeding decades, of course, many schools followed the example of Harvard in dismantling their core curricula.) The university's Common Core has been around since 1931, and although Chicago acknowledges that it has since undergone several revisions, the university catalog makes clear that the school's objective is "not to transfer information, but to raise fundamental questions and to encourage those habits of mind and those critical, analytical, and writing skills that are most urgent to a well-informed member of civil society." Even after recent changes to the core, the university is still able to offer that kind of broad, comprehensive education—not one measured easily by Scantron results, but rather by individual contributions to engaging and answering the larger questions of society.

The Common Core is a set of general education requirements that every undergraduate must take in order to graduate. The academic requirements are divided into three main areas, and within each area students are granted only a small degree of flexibility. Where there is a choice of courses for a particular requirement, students can select from ten or so available options. Students must complete the following:

- six quarters of Humanities, Civilization Studies, and the Arts, including at least one course in each of the following three areas:

  A. Interpretation of Historical, Literary, and Philosophical Texts, offering sequences such as "Philosophical Perspectives on the Humanities" and "Greek Thought and Literature";

  B. Musical, Visual, and Dramatic Arts, including everything from the basic "Introduction to Art" to "Drama: Embodiment and Transformation" and "Introduction to World Music"; and

  C. Civilization Studies, with such courses as "Introduction to Islamic Civilization," "History of European Civilization," "Science, Culture, and Society in Western Civilization," and "Judaic Civilization";

- six quarters of natural and mathematical sciences, including at least two in the physical sciences, two in the biological sciences, and at least one in the mathematical sciences;

- three quarters in the social sciences, taken as a sequence, with choices such as "Democracy and Social Science," "Classics of Social and Political Thought," and "Self, Culture, and Society," among others;

- coursework or tests demonstrating competency in a foreign language at the intermediate level; and

- three quarters of physical education.

VITAL STATISTICS

Religious affiliation: none

Total enrollment: 14,150

Total undergraduates: 4,671

SAT/ACT midranges: SAT V: 680–770, M: 670–760; ACT: 29–30

Applicants: 9,011

Applicants accepted: 40%

Accepted applicants who enrolled: 33%

Tuition: $33,336

Room and board: $10,608

Freshman retention rate: 96%

Graduation rate: 82% (4 yrs.), 89% (6 yrs.)

Courses with fewer than 20 students: 57%

Student-faculty ratio: 4:1

Courses taught by graduate students: none

Most popular majors: social sciences, biology, foreign languages and literature

Students living on campus: 56%

Guaranteed housing for four years? yes

Students in fraternities: 12% sororities: 5%

Some courses are certainly more stimulating than others. The best way to satisfy one of the Humanities, Civilization Studies, and the Arts requirements is by taking the three-course "History of Western Civilization" sequence, which, says one student, "is famous for a reason—it was one of the best courses I've taken here and provides a comprehensive approach to the intellectual historical tradition of the West." (But take it while you can—once lecturer Katy Weintraub stops teaching, it may be the end of the course at the university.) The humanities sequence "Human Being and Citizen," taught by Herman Sinaiko, a popular professor, is also quite good.

While some students resent the strictness of the core, many others attend Chicago because of it. Regardless of their expectations when they enter the school, and in spite of the fact that the curriculum has been dumbed down somewhat in recent years, the core remains a transformative academic experience. One student testifies, "The core has been crucial to my own intellectual awakening. I spent time at Oxford later on, and found myself to be so much better prepared than my peers, both British and American. I attribute this to the Common Core and Fundamentals." Fundamentals is an optional interdisciplinary concentration in which, according to the school, "students focus on certain fundamental questions of human existence and certain fundamental books."

> *The core curriculum remains a transformative academic experience for students: "The core has been crucial to my own intellectual awakening. I spent time at Oxford later on, and found myself to be so much better prepared than my peers. . . . I attribute this to the Common Core. . . ."*

Majors (or "concentrations," as they are known at Chicago) are wide and varied here. The choices range from the most common, like history and economics, to the more obscure, like Early Christian Literature or Cinema and Media Studies. The New Collegiate Division offers Law, Letters, and Society, and Fundamentals: Issues and Texts, cross-disciplinary majors that allow students to take a wide variety of courses in the law school and other graduate colleges. The curricula in both of these areas are more self-directed, so students have more flexibility in creating their majors. If a student can't find a major that suits him, the university, through the New Collegiate Division, allows him to create his own major in tutorial studies. With the guidance of a faculty tutor, the student proposes a set of courses that contribute to a nontraditional major or one that is not offered at the university, like education or American studies.

Well-known departments like economics are very strong, and have been for years. One student advises incoming students not to graduate without having taken a course in the department—best would be the sequence in micro and macroeconomics taught by Allen Sanderson, who, according to another student, "teaches the basic principles of economics with irreverent wit and a trove of real-world examples. Many a bleeding heart has entered his classroom, been horrified at what he has to say (about the minimum wage, just for starters), but absolutely unable to argue against him."

The many great professors of the philosophy department seem to suffer their students reluctantly, being distracted by the drive to research and publish. This comes at the expense of their teaching and out-of-class time with students. The philosophy department offers different paths for different students: the intensive track is much more structured and comprehensive in its requirements, and students in this program may take courses that are available only to students in the same track.

Students interested in foreign policy will find many worthy courses and professors in Chicago's famous political science department—although, according to one undergrad, many of the upper-level political science courses are full of graduate students who "tend to dominate discussions and are pretty insufferable."

Highly recommended professors include Leon Kass, who teaches in the Fundamentals: Issues and Texts program; Jonathan Lear and Nathan Tarcov in Fundamentals and Social Thought; and José Quintans, who is head of the biological sciences division and "made fulfilling the core biology requirement *fun*," recalls one student. Other excellent faculty include John Mearsheimer in political science; Ralph Lerner, Mark Lilla, and Mark Strand of the Committee on Social Thought; Amy Kass and Jonathan Smith of the humanities division; Peter Vandervoort in astronomy and astrophysics; Paul J. Sally Jr. in mathematics; Gary S. Becker (a Nobel winner) and James Heckman in economics; Michael Fishbane in Jewish studies; Isaac D. Abella in physics; Robert Pippin in philosophy; Jean Bethke Elshtain, Jean-Luc Marion, and David Tracy in religion; David Bevington in comparative literature; and Lawrence McEnerney of the Little Red Schoolhouse writing program.

Because of its obsession with intellectual rigor, Chicago tends to be more traditional than many other elite schools. Even so, students looking for an education and not ideological harangues might want to steer clear of some anthropology and most gender studies courses. One student says, "There are courses and departments that might have red flags, but avoiding them isn't difficult." The English department has become increasingly more politicized in recent years. Although the English major does not require such courses, electives have crept into the catalog like "Problems in the Study of Gender," "Problems in the Study of Sexuality," and "Introduction to Theories of Sex and Gender: Ideology, Culture, and Sexuality"—courses that belong, if anywhere, in the sociology department. Something similar has happened in the history department, which allows students to concentrate in History of Gender and Sexuality by taking six courses related to the theme. Overall, however, the history department remains solid, offering many important, traditional courses in the field.

The school assigns each incoming student a professional advisor, and each student is required to meet with his advisor during his first year at Chicago. Once a student has declared a major, the department assigns a faculty advisor to guide the student in what courses to take and in other issues of academic life. Many departments require their students to write a B.A. essay, due in the final quarter of a student's university

ALL-AMERICAN COLLEGES

SUGGESTED CORE

1. and 2. Humanities 12000, 12100, 12200: Greek Thought and Literature
3. Religious Studies 12000: Introduction to Biblical Studies
4. Theology 604 30100: History of Christian Thought I *and* Theology 604 30300: History of Christian Thought III
5. Social Sciences 15100, 15200, 15300: Classics of Social and Political Thought
6. English 16500, 16600: Shakespeare I and II
7. History 18700: Early America to 1865
8. History 13001, 13002: History of European Civilization

career, and the faculty advisor helps in this project as well. It's much easier to avoid one's everyday professors. However, as one recent graduate counsels, "You can get really close to professors as long as you take a bit of initiative. *Go to office hours!*" Getting to know professors is easier here than at other large schools because there are so many of them; the student-faculty ratio is an intimate 4 to 1.

Chicago offers a number of study-abroad programs—twenty-seven through the university and nine others through the Associated Colleges of the Midwest, mostly quarter-length trips, but also a few full-year programs in Berlin, Bologna, Kyoto, Paris, Seville, and various places in the United Kingdom. Chicago shines in foreign language study in general, offering courses and exams in fifty-two tongues, including some taught at few other American institutions—such as Akkadian, Hittite, and Old Church Slavonic.

The university selected a new president, Robert Zimmer, in spring 2006. Most recently a mathematics professor at Brown, Zimmer had previously taught at the University of Chicago for twenty-five years, and is said to be deeply imbued with its traditions and ethos.

Student Life: Nerds Gone Wild

Students choose the University of Chicago—and Chicago chooses them—because of the school's high standards and reputation for academic rigor. Nobody goes to Chicago for sports or for wild parties. Instead, professors in the humanities offer public lectures, and students actually attend out of sheer interest, not for the sake of apple-polishing. Intellectual discussions do not stop at the classroom door; for many students such talks make up the core of social life at Chicago. Students expecting much more than that may be sadly disappointed. Some students complain of their peers' lack of social skills. One student gripes, "U of C unfortunately attracts a high concentration of those students so convinced of their own brilliance that they never shut up." But engaging in debate and discussion is part of being a Chicago student. Political debate is "free and rigorous," says a student. Organized political clubs include the Anti-Sweatshop Coalition, the Campaign to End the Death Penalty, Chicago Friends of Israel, the Federalist Society, the College Republicans, the College Democrats, and the especially excellent, philosophically oriented debate club, the Edmund Burke Society. Campus opinion mostly skews to the left, but conservative students here are not afraid to let their voices be heard.

For all that, there is some semblance of a social life outside the libraries. It is the University of *Chicago* after all, and the museums (particularly the Art Institute and the nearby Museum of Science and Industry), the cultural attractions, the restaurants, and the architectural and natural beauty of the city are certainly enough to keep students occupied and away from campus obligations. On campus, student organizations like the *Chicago Maroon* newspaper, political organizations, and academic societies are especially popular. Indeed, with 433 organizations—and counting—listed, it shouldn't be too hard for students who wish to get involved in something besides coursework to find a congenial group. Many religions are represented on campus, including Buddhist, Muslim, Jewish, Episcopalian, Roman Catholic, and Protestant groups. The Orthodox Christian Fellowship holds meetings and services on campus once a week, and students with a fondness for Gregorian chant can take in a sung Latin Mass each Sunday at the local parish of St. John Cantius.

First-year students (as they are called at Chicago) live on campus in college houses. After the first year, students have a choice whether or not to live on campus, but close to two-thirds of the student body live in university housing. Dorm life varies greatly, depending both on the student's place in the housing lottery and on his own housing selection. The ten residence halls at Chicago are divided into thirty-seven houses intended to promote community life beyond the larger, less manageable dorms. While some buildings are traditional hall-style, others have suites, and some suites have coed bathrooms. "Do your research," says one student, in order to avoid such surprises. The university tries to promote community life in another way by requiring students to eat together in one of three dining commons.

Although there are no athletic scholarships offered to student athletes at Chicago, the school does compete in eight women's and nine men's intercollegiate teams. The women's soccer team has been strong in recent years, and in 2005 placed third in the country in NCAA Division III competition.

Crime on campus and in the surrounding Hyde Park–Kenwood area has long been a concern. Some shrug it off as the inevitable drawback of attending an urban university, and while there's some truth to that proposition, the area has been particularly dangerous in the last two decades. The most recent on-campus crime statistics (2004) include two arsons, one aggravated assault, two robberies, and thirty-nine burglaries. During that time, however, the only crime in the residence halls was a lone burglary. The campus is clearly not as threatening as the blocks surrounding it, where there were reported seventy-three motor vehicle thefts in 2004 alone. The school does what it can to protect its students. An extensive evening bus system is available from 6 p.m. to 1 a.m. on weekdays and longer on the weekends. Students staying up later than that can call for the late-night van service, or in an emergency they can call for "Umbrella Coverage," meaning a police car will escort the student to wherever he needs to go. The police department notes that 135 white emergency phones dot the campus; when activated, a police car will arrive at the student's location in less than four minutes.

Chicago isn't cheap, with tuition at around $33,000, and room and board almost $11,000. But the school, like most of its rivals in the Ivy League, is generous with aid. Admission is "need-blind," and the school meets the demonstrated financial need of admitted students. That makes it an excellent choice for high-achieving children of working-class families.

CHRISTENDOM COLLEGE

FRONT ROYAL, VIRGINIA • WWW.CHRISTENDOM.EDU

A visitor to Christendom senses an enthusiasm that transcends time and season, grounded in the quest for truth and animated by faith. The cultural revolution of the late 1960s all but eradicated this feeling in most Catholic academies, at the same time triggering a rejection of the liberal arts tradition to which they had been devoted. The sudden, shocking collapse of Catholic higher education prompted groups of Catholic laymen and women around the country to found colleges that would integrate religious orthodoxy and classical education—and one of the first such schools was Christendom College. The driving force behind its founding was Dr. Warren H. Carroll, a historian and convert to Catholicism who envisioned a curriculum "centered on faith and reason, on the truths of Divine Revelation as taught by the Roman Catholic Church and the truths of natural reason as derived from natural law and human experience," a curriculum that would "integrate harmoniously the knowledge acquired from these sources." In 1977, with the opening of Christendom College, this vision came to fruition.

Academic Life: Swimming the Tiber

The vision of a revitalized Christian society kindled by a committed lay apostolate gave this college its name. "Christendom" (the old term for what we now call "the West") means a Christianized social order. In the classic liberal arts tradition, the mission of Christendom College is to "form the whole person for a life spent in the pursuit of truth and wisdom." Steve Snyder, vice president for academic affairs, says that a Christendom education gives "the solid moral principles, core knowledge and skills, and intellectual flexibility suited to a liberally educated person in a rapidly changing and often confused modern world." While the effective (if unstated) aim of most colleges today is to provide vocational and professional training, Christendom's goal is to lead its students to "the discovery and appropriation of the True, the Good, and the Beautiful for their own sakes" and to help them live "as faithful, informed, and articulate members of Christ's Church and society," dedicated "to the task of transforming the social order in Christ." A tall order for a small school.

As one can see, this is not a college for occasional churchgoers or uncommitted seekers who simply want a solid liberal arts education (though they'll find that here). Such students would be better off at, for example, Deep Springs or St. John's College.

Christendom's core curriculum totals eighty-four credit hours and takes up two-thirds of a student's coursework—one of the highest percentages of any school in the country. But it's a balanced and well-thought-out program, constituted from seven areas of discipline. The courses required are:

- "Literature of Western Civilization" I, II, III, and IV, where students are immersed in classic works from the ancient Greek playwrights through modern novelists;
- elementary and intermediate French, Greek, Latin, or Spanish;
- "The Ancient and Biblical World," "The Formation of Christendom," "The Division of Christendom," and "Church and World in the Modern Age";
- "Principles of Political Theory" and "Social Teachings of the Church";
- "Euclidean Geometry," "Logic," or other college-level mathematics, and "Introduction to Scientific Thought" or other college-level science;
- "Introduction to Philosophy," "Philosophy of Human Nature," "Metaphysics," "History of Medieval Philosophy," and "History of Modern Philosophy"; and
- "Fundamentals of Catholic Doctrine" I and II, "Introduction to the Old Testament," "Introduction to the New Testament," "Moral Theology," and "Catholic Apologetics."

Except by special permission, all Christendom students are expected to take these classes in a set sequence.

As one can see, theology and philosophy courses dominate the curriculum. During the thirty-six semester hours required in these disciplines, students explore the writings of such thinkers as St. Augustine, John Henry Newman, and G. K. Chesterton. They are steeped even more deeply in the works of St. Thomas Aquinas, whose categories of learning shape the curriculum itself. Students thus exposed to traditional Catholic philosophy and theology and guided by able faculty are expected to learn to "use reason to understand the nature of reality and to illumine further the truths of revelation."

VITAL STATISTICS

Religious affiliation:
  Roman Catholic
Total enrollment: 435
Total undergraduates: 379
SAT/ACT midranges: SAT V:
  600–720, M: 530–630;
  ACT: 23–29
Applicants: 309
Applicants accepted: 73%
*Accepted applicants who
  enrolled:* 57%
Tuition: $15,368
Room and board: $5,776
Freshman retention rate: 88%
Graduation rate: 69% (4 yrs.),
  70% (6 yrs.)
*Courses with fewer than 20
  students:* 59%
Student-faculty ratio: 12:1
*Courses taught by graduate
  students:* none
Most popular majors:
  history, philosophy,
  political science
Students living on campus:
  95%
*Guaranteed housing for four
  years?* yes
*Students in fraternities or
  sororities:* none

ALL-AMERICAN COLLEGES

55

Christendom's history curriculum reflects a reverence for the traditions of Christian Europe that is rare, to say the least, on today's college campuses. "Christendom is very respectful of the Western heritage," notes one student, adding that, after all, the Western tradition is the cradle of the Catholic faith. Christendom's "philosophy of history" requires the study of Hebrew, Greek, and Roman history as preludes to the history of the church and of the West.

In literature courses, students read complete works rather than selections. The freshman at Christendom acquires writing and critical reading skills through the study of classics such as the *Iliad*, Aristotle's *Poetics*, and selected plays of Shakespeare. Works by Chaucer, Milton, and Cicero round out the literature core and support the program's goal of fostering an appreciation and understanding of the "rich patrimony of Western culture."

Outside of the core curriculum, students may choose from courses in Italian, German, and Hebrew. Christendom maintains an excellent classical and early Christian studies department, which, according to one student, "has recently been highlighted by several students receiving scholarships and stipends for graduate work."

By the time a student reaches the end of his sophomore year, he is ready to declare a major. Christendom students may major in theology, philosophy, history, or English literature, classical and early Christian studies, or political science—this last with either a politics or an economics subspecialty. One program of note for seniors is Politics Practica, which includes lectures and workshops given by nationally recognized authorities and offers students internship opportunities in their chosen fields.

Students in their junior year have the opportunity to spend a semester in Rome. In addition to their philosophy and theology core classes, students take courses in art, architecture, and the Italian language. "It was one of the main highlights of my career at Christendom," says one student, whose semester in Rome coincided with the funeral of Pope John Paul II and the election of Benedict XVI.

Since its 1997 merger with the Notre Dame Institute, Christendom has also been able to offer master's-level programs in theological and catechetical studies at its Notre Dame Graduate School, some seventy-five miles north in Alexandria, Virginia.

Faculty members are always available to help students meet the rigorous demands of the curriculum. Says one student, "The teachers are very approachable." All classes at Christendom are taught by professors rather than graduate students. Despite the dedication of teachers to their students, however, this practice can be burdensome to faculty whose departments are already short-staffed. "Our theology, political science, and classics departments are in need of more professors," says one senior. (Recent hires may resolve this problem, one teacher reports.) This places more work on the current professors," but "does not diminish the value of each major." One history major feels that, although the quality of teaching is not affected, "the demand of the core curriculum has limited the number of upper division courses" offered by his department. Christendom students name several favorites among the faculty. In theology, Eric Jenislawski is a "down to earth" and "fun" teacher, while Raymund O'Herron is said to be "challenging" and a "good motivator." Students also laud John Cuddeback, J. Michael

Brown, and Anthony Andres in philosophy, William Fahey in classical and early Christian studies, and Rafael Madan in political science.

The most qualified faculty members also engage in cross-disciplinary teaching. There is a "synergy" among departments, reports one professor, which allows strengths in one field to be shared with departments in closely related fields. A few outstanding courses that embrace several disciplines are "Latin Readings in Saint Thomas," "Byzantine History," and "Roman Perspectives." The interrelatedness of the core curriculum discourages the overspecialization common at other colleges.

Also absent is the pressure on faculty members to publish their research. "All Christendom professors engage in ongoing research to enhance the content of their classes," says one professor. "It is that kind of research upon which retention and promotion decisions are made." Nevertheless, nearly all the members of Christendom's faculty have published at one time or another. Many remain active and respected scholars, and quite a few are in demand as speakers. The college's most widely published professors include Tony Andres and John Cuddeback in philosophy, Christopher Blum, Adam Schwartz, and Christopher Shannon in history, and Christendom president Timothy O'Donnell. Besides the aforementioned faculty, students should seek out courses with these teachers. Christendom requires all professors to affirm their loyalty to the teachings of the church by making both a profession of faith and an oath of fidelity at the beginning of every academic year.

Christendom's history curriculum reflects a reverence for the traditions of Christian Europe that is rare on college campuses. Christendom's "philosophy of history" requires the study of Hebrew, Greek, and Roman history as preludes to the history of the church and of the West.

Graduates of the college have become successful leaders in fields as varied as education, nutrition, law, computer technology and film production—while others have pursued graduate studies at Catholic University, Notre Dame, St. Louis University, and the University of Virginia School of Law. Still others have entered the religious life; a full 15 percent of alumni serve as priests and religious in dioceses and orders around the world.

Christendom is not all things to all men. It is emphatically *not* a vocational school. "A student who has a functional career goal will find that he must build on his Christendom education after graduation by taking the technical courses of his chosen profession," says one professor. However, "Christendom graduates find that they are better prepared as learners and as Catholic citizens" because of their liberal arts background.

Student Life: Meticulous Dress Code

Christendom is located in Front Royal, Virginia, a once-pastoral town that has been relentlessly overdeveloped in recent years, with woods and ponds giving way to strip malls, shopping centers, and chain stores. Except for the chapel, the campus itself is unexceptional (all the buildings are less than thirty years old). But it does overlook the legendary Shenandoah Valley, and it boasts nearly seventy acres of woodland laced with walking, hiking, and jogging trails. One is never far away from a vista of breathtaking natural beauty.

The education shared by all its students, and the devotion of its faculty, contribute to the "extended family" feel of the Christendom community. With an enrollment limit of 450 set at its founding, the college is clearly committed to maintaining an institution "in which every faculty member and student may be known personally to one another." Professors and students take their meals together in the common dining room, and teachers often open their homes for class parties and other socials.

Despite the apparent uniformity of religious belief in the Christendom community, many issues are open to debate. "Christendom faculty and students share a common love of learning and of the church," says one professor, but the college provides an "environment of critical enquiry" where "discussion and debate, and the disagreements that are part of the human condition, are encouraged." A popular forum for debate is the *Rambler*, a student-run newspaper that addresses contemporary issues. Formal debates are held on campus several times per year, and impromptu symposia, whether in dorms, dining halls, or classrooms, spring up like mushrooms after a rainstorm. With debate, as with all intellectual ventures at the college, the goal is the discovery of truth. Christendom College, says one professor, is "a truly academic community" set apart from its peers by its "freedom and civility."

Although it is Thomas Aquinas's light that guides Christendom's academics, it is Hilaire Belloc's insight that inspires its social life. "Wherever a Catholic sun doth shine," wrote Belloc, "there's always laughter and good red wine. At least I have always found it so. *Benedicamus Domino*." Church feast days are campus-wide holidays at Christendom. Most social events, such as the St. Joseph–San Francesco Italian Feast, the St. Patrick's Day Celebration, and the St. Cecilia's Night Talent Show, are tied to the liturgical life of the church. Christendom's "zeal for Catholic culture" is apparent in its annual MedievalFest and Oktoberfest celebrations. The 2005 MedievalFest brought out the entire student body, attracted droves of visitors, and featured jugglers, morality plays, folktales, and a pig roast. Professor Sharon Hickson recited an "Ode to the Pig" prior to the roast, in which two "heretic" pigs named "Madonna" and "Britney" were "burned at the stake." Hey, it's all in good fun. And to be fair, the burning was preceded by the recitation of a moving prayer for the heretics' conversion. The Oktoberfest festivities customarily include German foods, a keg race, lively polkas, and mugs of foaming (root) beer.

Students who would prefer beer of a different variety, however, will be disappointed by Christendom's unconventional idea of "partying." Real beer, along with Belloc's "good red wine," are rarely tasted on campus. Alcoholic beverages are forbidden, except for those served at school-sanctioned events to students who have reached legal drinking age. Students found with alcohol, or who return intoxicated from an off-campus spree, are instantly suspended. "Because Christendom's 'no-alcohol' policy is so strict, it's hard to enforce," says one student. "For the administration to suspend a student for a single infraction is pretty severe. On the other hand, relaxing the rules isn't a good idea, either. So a lot of the time, the administration just turns a blind eye." One chronic problem has been seniors buying alcohol for freshmen. "Last year's graduating class was especially troublesome," he continued. "They had problems with their own drinking, as well as giving alcohol to younger students." Any incidents involving illegal drugs, either on or off campus, result in immediate expulsion.

High standards of decorum, civility, and modesty are expected of students. According to the college handbook, Christendom students "practice all virtues and enjoy all things in moderation." When attending class or campus events, students adhere to a meticulous dress code that, says one professor, reflects "the seriousness of the education they are pursuing." "It is interesting for a professor to watch the evolution of freshman tugging at their ties and sneaking out their shirt tails into young adults who are proud to project an adult appearance." The dress code for women is quite rigorous, with a detailed "modesty dress code" that must be followed at all times, including bans on miniskirts, jeans, and tank tops.

"Romantic displays of affection," or RDAs as they are commonly known, are forbidden on campus. But a freshman at Christendom would be hard-pressed to find any specific guidelines on this issue. The college handbook explains why they are prohibited but does not define them. "Over the years, there has been a natural ebb-and-flow controversy over this issue," says one student. "The administration has been asked to identify RDAs. But it's difficult to do, a lot harder than writing up a dress code. There are so many things that can fall under the RDA heading." At Christendom, one of those things is hand-holding, for which violators are each fined five dollars. The young man usually pays for both himself and his girl. "Fining students for hand-holding isn't unreasonable," says one student. "A couple who want to hold hands can do so in town, or in the woods near campus. If they choose to hold hands on campus, they're deliberately flouting the rules. That is, if they know what the rules are!"

Rather than damming up desire, such rules actually seem to channel it: there have been approximately 200 alumnus-to-alumna marriages to date. According to one professor, these students "are our great successes, because they are the restoration of all things in Christ, person by person, child by child, neighbor by neighbor."

To assist his fellow students in cultivating gentlemanly behavior, Christendom alumnus Thomas Cole wrote a "Guide to Etiquette" while still a student at the college. Copies of his guide are provided to all men at Christendom. The book contains quaint advice on how to seat a lady at table, when to lift one's hat, and how to greet a lady. (One must never say "hi" or "hello," but "good afternoon" and "good evening.") "I believe it's kind of silly," says one sophomore. "The book becomes inflammatory when it is forced on the students from upperclassmen instead of the administration. Its tone is preachy, and when you receive something like this in your mailbox it makes you feel inadequate and picked on, like some anonymous person leaving fashion tips in your mailbox." Other students disagree. "I think it's charming," says one female student. "Sure, lots of its advice is dated, but enough of it still applies. Politeness never goes out of style." According to the student handbook, the discipline fostered by the student code of conduct "makes possible the joy of living in a Christian community." Students who would not find this a joy have many other colleges to choose from.

Off-campus amusements include trips to Washington, D.C., about seventy-five miles away, where students can attend an occasional play or concert or visit one of the national museums. A group of students from Christendom travels to D.C. every week to pray the rosary at its area abortion clinics. On January 22 each year, classes are cancelled so that students may participate in the March for Life. Almost the entire student body chooses to take part.

Homeschooled students are welcome at Christendom. A full 40 percent of its freshman class is comprised of homeschoolers, a figure nearing 50 percent for the entire student body. Non-Catholic students probably won't feel very comfortable at the school, where references to papal pronouncements are commonly the clinching argument in everyday discussions.

At Christendom, devotion and diversion are often linked. A favorite Friday night activity, known simply as "the river," is kicked off with a rosary procession through a nearby wood. The rosary is followed by traditional Irish music played by students around a bonfire. When cold weather makes "the river" impractical, students may warm up in the new John Paul II the Great Student Center, dedicated in April 2006. The center will have a café, a stage for live entertainment, and a recreation center for ping-pong, air hockey, pool, foosball, and a full-sized basketball court.

The proposed name of the new student center has caused a bit of a stir. According to one source, "since John Paul II has not been officially declared 'Great' by the [Catholic] Church, the name is controversial in certain circles." Regardless, Christendom students are united in their admiration for the late pontiff. For his part, John Paul had a high regard for Christendom College, which he praised for "doing a great work for the Church."

Tuition, fees, and room and board for the 2005–6 academic year totaled $21,144. Christendom offers its students both need-based and merit-based financial aid. Need-based financial aid is given in the form of work-study grants and loans. Eligible students may receive merit-based aid through scholarships. Fifty-one percent of students entering Christendom in 2005 received need-based financial aid. The average loan debt of students graduating in 2004 was $11,240.

THE CITADEL

CHARLESTON, SOUTH CAROLINA • WWW.CITADEL.EDU

In the popular mind, military academies are all engineering schools. While that is true of those run by the federal government, schools in the hands of states or private foundations follow different rules and offer another sort of education. Whereas the three federal service academies are intended to turn out full-time active-duty officers for the three branches of the military, their four "civilian" counterparts were founded in the nineteenth century to produce all-around leaders, in times of war commanders of their native state's militia, and in times of peace responsible statesmen. So these schools aim to shape every graduate into a mentally and physically fit "whole man," a gentleman, a scholar, and above all, a leader. That demands, as it always has, a thorough background in the liberal arts. And the Citadel is one of the finest places in America at which to acquire it.

Academic Life: Educating "whole cadets"

The South Carolina legislature chartered the Citadel in 1842, when the decade-old state militia barrack in Charleston (called the Citadel) was transformed into the South Carolina Military Academy. The school took its place in history on January 9, 1861, when Citadel cadets fired on Fort Sumter. This must have seemed like a good idea at the time—but the war which resulted would close the school until 1882. The school had another run-in with centralized authority in the early 1990s, when it became the target of litigious feminists—and outright enemies of military education—who began a series of lawsuits designed to force the school to admit female cadets. The school fought valiantly but was forced to submit in 1996. Despite the many disruptions and anomalies that forced coeducation introduced into life at the Citadel (about which students and faculty are privately candid), the school carries on its venerable mission—to create a class of leaders endowed with mental and physical fitness, gentility, scholarship, and leadership.

Such a mission—which might sound anachronistic elsewhere—makes sense in Charleston, South Carolina, arguably our most aristocratic city. The Citadel retains deep connections to local groups like the St. Cecilia

Society and the Charleston Cotillion Club, where scions of families which have lived there for centuries speak of Charleston as the place "where the Ashley and Cooper rivers join to form the Atlantic Ocean."

The Citadel's administration attributes the school's academic success to the core curriculum, which the school website describes as "the major instrument by which an institution whose purpose is to provide a liberal education passes along to the rising generation the intellectual heritage of all people. This large treasury includes not only valuable knowledge acquired over the centuries but also the modes of thought by which that knowledge has been acquired." The goal of this education is to prepare "not only professional scholars but also leaders of society in all walks of life."

The Citadel's reasons for insisting on this curriculum might sound as antique to the ears of modern academics as a Confederate battle cry: "The core courses examine the foundations of particular, central disciplines in the perspective of the whole academic enterprise, the search for truth. These courses, therefore, have a decidedly philosophical cast, and for this reason they rightly emphasize the ultimate bases of the discipline, the validity of its method, its essential elements, and its distinctive character." All students must complete the following:

- four courses in English: English 101 (basic composition), English 102 (an introduction to various literary forms), "Major British Writers I," and then either "Major British Writers II," "Masterpieces of American Literature," "Masterpieces of World Literature I," or "Masterpieces of World Literature II";
- two courses in mathematics;
- two courses in the history of Western civilization or two courses in the history of world civilization;
- two sequences of two courses each in biology, chemistry, or physics, with no more than one sequence in any single science;
- one course in the social sciences ("Cultural Anthropology," "Honors Social Science Project," "American National Government," "General Psychology," or "Introduction to Sociology");
- four courses of French, German, or Spanish (students may test out, and some majors are exempt); and
- two courses in physical education, "Contemporary Health Foundations" and "Foundations of Fitness and Exercise," plus two different activity courses.

The school self-consciously presents these courses as valuable not only for their own sake, but as part of a holistic education. The academy asserts, for example, that "English studies are central to a college education because they are a forum where the rival and complementary claims of philosophy, practicality, science, ethics, politics, and religion come alive in concrete situations. The primary benefits in studying English come when a student engages in dialogue with the works of great authors, listening to their words receptively and responding to them critically." Wedded to this theoretical basis, however, is a demand for proficiency in the basic skills of grammar, writing, and literary analysis rare today among institutions of higher education.

Of course, the Citadel has its own blind spots. Classics of any kind are missing from the curriculum, and, as one faculty member says, "Students whose primary interest is in the humanities might find that the core is tilted a bit too heavily towards math and science." Still, the unique nature of the core curriculum certainly has an impact; one teacher says, "many students who would never have taken a history or an English class if they hadn't been made to by the core end up being excited by what they are studying."

The liberal arts majors offered by the Citadel are education, English, French, German, history, political science, psychology, and Spanish. Not surprisingly, one professor comments, "The Citadel is especially strong in modern languages, psychology, and history. The modern languages department has taken a great interest in grooming students for advanced study abroad. The record of their faculty in helping develop Fulbright scholars is nothing short of spectacular. Psychology has a strong focus on clinical practice, so undergraduates have numerous opportunities to become involved in community service. History has some of the finest scholars and teachers on campus." Undergraduate and graduate degrees in the humanities, business, math, science, engineering, and education are also offered.

Among the most highly respected teachers are Al Gurganus in German, who is called "demanding but particularly effective"; Jane Bishop, a "brilliant and universally beloved teacher" in ancient and medieval history; Kyle Sinisi in American and Michael Barrett in European history; Mark Bebensee in business administration; and Tom Jerse in electrical engineering. Not every department is equally strong. One professor complains that education "has never been able to attract many capable undergraduate students." Throughout the school, classes are small, and all are taught by faculty rather than graduate teaching assistants. Six cadets have received Fulbright scholarships to study abroad since 2001, more than at any other college or university in South Carolina.

"The Department of English has traditionally been one of the strongest on campus," says one professor, "strongest in American literature and in medieval and Renaissance studies. It is, however, going through a significant generational change with many established people retiring and many new people coming in," which might signal a shift in emphasis—and not for the better.

In keeping with the American military tradition, there is little political activism, either conservative or liberal, on the part of faculty and students. According to one

VITAL STATISTICS

Religious affiliation: none
Total enrollment: 3,351
Total undergraduates: 2,177
ACT midrange: 18–23
Applicants: 2,173
Applicants accepted: 1,725
Accepted applicants who enrolled: 28%
Tuition: $6,500 (instate), $16,225 (out of state)
Room and board: $5,100
Freshman retention rate: 78%
Graduation rate: 62% (4 yrs.)
Courses with fewer than 20 students: 47%
Student-faculty ratio: 15:1
Courses taught by graduate students: none
Most popular majors: engineering, business, English
Students living on campus: 100%
Guaranteed housing for four years? yes
Students in fraternities or sororities: none

cadet, "Most students at the Citadel are politically conservative. There are probably more liberals on the faculty than there are in the Corps of Cadets. But I would say that, on the whole, faculty and students treat each other with a great deal of respect."

While faculty are required to do some research in order to be tenured, one professor reports that "the tenure decision is primarily based on the quality of a faculty member's work in the classroom. We do a 4/4 teaching load, which is heavy. But most classes are pretty small, so an average semester would find a teacher with around eighty-five students total." This in turn builds a strong teacher-student relationship. "The Honors Program run by Professor Jack Rhodes is extremely popular with bright students. The Leadership Studies Minor is just getting off the ground, but it has a lot of promise," says another professor.

Of course, none of this demanding academic work takes place in a vacuum: cadets also follow a demanding schedule. "Citadel cadets are challenged physically all of the time by the rigors of cadet life, so they are often very tired," a teacher says.

As alumnus Pat Conroy discovered, "the institution offers a classic military education for young men and women who seek a college experience that is intense, meaningful, and academically strong."

"[E]ducating principled leaders through its Corps of Cadets and College of Graduate and Professional Studies programs" remains the Citadel's stated mission. Military life and training lies at the heart of the Citadel's ethos. Numbering more than 1,900, the Corps of Cadets is "the nation's largest military college program outside the service academies. All cadets are educated within a classic military system and about 40 percent of the graduating seniors earn military commissions." According to the school, the remaining graduates attend graduate school or enter the job market. *U.S. News & World Report* ranks the Citadel as number two in public colleges granting master's degrees in the South.

As best-selling author and controversial alumnus Pat Conroy discovered, "the institution offers a classic military education for young men and women who seek a college experience that is intense, meaningful, and academically strong. Most Citadel graduates say that the disciplined lifestyle and friendships they forged here have a profoundly positive effect on their lives."

Military science, the subject which aspiring officers must take, is the business of the whole Corps of Cadets—even if only about 35 percent end up as military or naval officers. Some 850 graduates have served or are serving in the present conflicts in Iraq and Afghanistan.

Student Life: Honor and Brother Knob

The basis of most students' lives at the Citadel is the Corps of Cadets, which is organized as a regiment of four battalions, within which the cadet will spend his four years. A self-run group (under supervision by the staff), the Corps' chain of command offers cadets who excel the chance to rise as far as their talents, abilities, and personalities will allow them. This learning of leadership through actual performance is a unique feature of military colleges and is particularly strong at the Citadel.

It is within the Corps, and particularly within its companies, that the cadet eats, sleeps, and socializes. Housing is in barracks, by company. The Corps has its own customs and traditions, which are imparted to the entering cadet through the "Knob" system. In addition to basic information, like the complexities of various uniforms (some of which require a great deal of maintenance), the first-year knob learns "Knob Knowledge," which is defined as "a collection of Citadel lore and trivia gathered by Citadel librarians over the years. It grew out of the tradition of upper classmen asking knobs (freshmen or fourth classmen) questions to enhance their knowledge of the Citadel and its history, and to build esprit de corps. Although this collection has been called Knob Knowledge for more than thirty years, it has evolved into a veritable encyclopedia of the Citadel," according to the school.

The first year is a difficult period, similar to the "Plebe" or "Rat" year at other military academies. But while it is physically, mentally, and emotionally demanding, the Knob system produces cadets who are tough enough to hold their own in most eventualities. Among other things, it teaches teamwork, since its requirements cannot be carried out without help from fellow knobs. The friendships forged in this crucible often endure for a lifetime.

Of course, this system has been altered somewhat in recent years due to the admission of women in 1996. The school's leadership in the decade since has worked hard, as good soldiers will do, to execute this civilian order, no matter how misguided. Despite the best efforts of the school's staff and faculty, cases of sexual harassment and fraternization have occurred (although none have been reported since 2002). As any veteran could have told the Supreme Court justices, close confinement of both sexes in a high-pressure environment like the military could and does lead to all sorts of problems.

While his novel *The Lords of Discipline* painted a searing portrait of the Citadel experience, author Pat Conroy has said of the school, "In this time of strange corruption of ethics and values and standards, I think the Citadel is the best place in the country for a young man or woman to be. It is tough and structured and Spartan and wonderful. It requires lion-hearted, fearless young men and women with great inner strength and unshakable resolve. By entering the long gray line, they turn their backs on what is soft and absurd and decadent about college life in America. By becoming

> **SUGGESTED CORE**
>
> The school's Honors Freshman sequence, HONR 100-104, should be supplemented with the following courses to complete the core curriculum: English 212: The Bible as Literature; English 303/304: Shakespeare; and History 201: Survey of American History I.

ALL-AMERICAN COLLEGES

65

cadets and not just students, they are trained by the Citadel in the art of becoming citizen-soldiers in a society that desperately needs more of them." In 1999, Conroy said to the *Charleston Post & Courier*, "I tell other writers that I meet in America that I received the best education for a novelist in the history of our republic. In the barracks I learned everything about the world I would need to know."

Another important aspect of cadet life is the Honor Code, which states that "a cadet will neither lie, cheat, nor steal, nor tolerate anyone who does." The Honor Code is defined in the Honor Manual, and a cadet-manned Honor Board administers the system. "It is each cadet's duty upon enrollment to be familiar with the honor system as set forth in this Honor Manual and to abide by the Honor Code," the school says. Service on the Honor Board is a great formative experience, the more so since alleged offenses against the code are dealt with in a quasi-judicial manner.

Periodic inspections of the barracks ensure that inhabitants keep each room clean. Both alcohol and tobacco are forbidden on campus. Campus life follows a set schedule that begins with reveille in the morning and ends with taps at night.

But it's not all work at the Citadel. All cadets are required to participate in intramural sports as a way of ensuring their physical development. State-of-the-art gymnastics equipment is available to everyone. Seven publications are produced by cadets, with names such as *El Cid*, *The Brigadier*, and *The Art of Good Taste*. These journals are all produced at Mark Clark Hall, a three-story building that also boasts the Citadel Gift Shop, a reception room, barbershop, game room, post office, billiard room, and large auditorium.

The religious life of the Citadel continues, despite the efforts of activist judges, who in 2003 forced the school to end its venerable tradition of saying grace before meals. (It was replaced by a moment of silence.) The updated 1892 prayer which gave such offense—and which many cadets still say privately—runs as follows:

> Almighty God, the source of light and strength, we implore Thy blessing on this our beloved institution, that it may continue true to its high purposes.
>
> Guide and strengthen those upon whom rests the authority of government; enlighten with wisdom those who teach and those who learn; and grant to all of us that through sound learning and firm leadership, we may prove ourselves worthy citizens of our country, devoted to truth, given to unselfish service, loyal to every obligation of life and above all to Thee.
>
> Preserve us faithful to the ideals of The Citadel, sincere in fellowship, unswerving in duty, finding joy in purity, and confidence through a steadfast faith.
>
> Grant to each one of us, in his (her) own life, a humble heart, a steadfast purpose, and a joyful hope, with a readiness to endure hardship and suffer if need be, that truth may prevail among us and that Thy will may be done on earth.

It concluded with a phrase that non-Christians were invited to omit: "Through Jesus Christ, Our Lord. Amen."

Such religious organizations as the African Methodist Episcopal, Bible Study, Baptist Student Union, Campus Crusade for Christ, Knights of Columbus, Fellowship of Christian Athletes, Gospel Choir, Full Gospel Business Men's Fellowship, Hillel Foundation, Lutheran Student Association, Muslim Student Association, Navigators, Officers' Christian Fellowship, St. Photios Orthodox Christian Fellowship, Wesley Foundation, and Westminster Fellowship provide outlets for members of their respective faiths. There are two chapels on campus. One is the nonsectarian Summerall Chapel, built in Gothic style during 1936–37. Every Sunday morning at 9:00 there is a general Protestant service, followed by a Catholic Mass at 6:30 p.m. Students with particularly traditional religious interests may find a Latin Mass at Stella Maris Catholic Church on nearby Sullivan's Island, and high-church Anglican services at Charleston's Church of the Holy Communion—which hosted the funeral, a few years ago, of the recovered crew of the *Hunley*, one of the few Confederate submarines.

Every Advent, the Corps of Cadets offers its Christmas Candlelight Service, during which "cadets from the Protestant, Catholic, and Gospel Choirs, Chorale, and members of the Citadel Regimental Band take part in the annual celebration of the birth of Christ, observing the events of the Advent, the Annunciation, the Birth of the King, and Epiphany through Scripture lessons and carols. Traditional and international favorites are sung, and special highlights include the Procession of Lights," according to the school's chaplaincy. The service is one of the highlights not only of the Citadel but of the Charleston social calendar.

Although a wide number of religious, professional, athletic, honor, and hobby clubs exist, there is only a single political club—the Society of Citadel Republicans. Moreover, there are no fraternities or sororities; such organizations would be considered divisive, and in such a tight-knit environment, superfluous.

As far as campus security goes, it would be hard to find a safer campus anywhere. Between the Citadel's own police force and self-enforcement of the Honor Code, there is little room for criminal activity, either homegrown or from beyond the gates. The most serious infractions of the law reported in 2005-6 were six thefts of "unsecured property."

The Citadel is a particularly good deal if you come from South Carolina. Tuition and fees are $6,500 for local residents and $16,225 for nonresidents, while room and board is $5,100. Add to this $5,800 for books and uniforms. Charges decrease about $2,700 after the first year. To offset the costs, the Citadel's financial aid office is very helpful in arranging scholarships, grants, loans, and work programs. Twenty-five full academic grants are awarded each year. Approximately 68 percent of aid comes in scholarships, with the rest consisting of loans and campus jobs.

ALL-AMERICAN COLLEGES

UNIVERSITY OF DALLAS

IRVING, TEXAS • WWW.UDALLAS.EDU

One of the very best schools for a liberal arts education in America lies in one of the grimmest suburbs of Dallas, a strip-mall burg halfway to Fort Worth called Irving, Texas. Founded in 1956, the school is just a baby compared to, say, William and Mary, but by Dallas standards it might as well be 500 years old. (To put this in perspective, fifty years ago Fort Worth was more ranch than city; realtors in the area consider a house built in 1995 to be "an older home"; and residents can still remember the days when pigs were herded down the street right into the bacon plants.) Dallas is now a sparkly new city with lots of big glass boxes and shopping centers, world-class museums, and a serious symphony orchestra. The University of Dallas campus sits right across a multilane highway from Texas Stadium, home of the Dallas Cowboys. A more important neighbor is the beautiful Cistercian abbey whose monks help staff the school and maintain its dogged fidelity to the Catholic traditions of educational excellence and doctrinal integrity. Students looking to learn the best of the Western tradition—from the Great Books to the great ideas—seen through the eyes of faith seeking understanding could not find a more congenial school. But they'd better bring a car.

Academic Life: Preventing Mental Chaos

The University of Dallas hired a new president, Dr. Francis Lazarus, in the summer of 2004—in part to undo the sometimes damaging work of his predecessor, who'd attempted to expand the school by watering down its liberal arts emphasis and boosting its ties to Dallas's business community. That costly experiment left the school in financial straits, and it has struggled ever since to put itself back in the black. As one professor put it, "That UD survived this eight-year test of its liberal arts program is testimony to the convictions of faculty, alumni, and supporters." Faculty and friends of the university report that UD is back on track and has reinvigorated the programs upon which its sterling academic reputation was built.

The school leans heavily on the traditional Great Books program for the shape of its core curriculum. The result is an admirable list of requirements that better known schools would do well to emulate. Most of a student's first two years will be occupied with completing the following:

- "The Literary Tradition" I and II. Readings range from Homer to Wallace Stevens and emphasize great works from Europe and America;

- "The Literary Tradition" III and IV. Here students enter the tradition in greater depth, studying Aeschylus, Sophocles, Aristophanes, Aristotle, Marlowe, Austen, Melville, Dostoevsky, and Faulkner;

- "American Civilization" I and II. These classes go through the writings of the founders, the abolitionists, and major twentieth-century documents through the writings of Martin Luther King Jr.;
- "Western Civilization" I and II. In the first course, students read the book of Job, Thucydides, Livy, Boethius, and Thomas More. In the second they cover Calvin, Kant, Diderot, Burke, Marx, Pope Leo XIII, and Elie Wiesel;
- "Philosophy and the Ethical Life." Course readings include Plato, Aristotle, Aquinas, Kant, and Nietzsche;
- "Philosophy of Man." Students read more Plato, Aristotle, and Aquinas, along with Augustine, Descartes, and Hegel;
- "Philosophy of Being." Readings include Parmenides, Aristotle, Aquinas, Kant, and Heidegger;
- "Understanding the Bible";
- "The Western Theological Tradition." This course goes from Augustine and Aquinas through the Reformation;
- "Fundamentals of Economics." The texts come from Adam Smith and Pope John Paul II;
- "Principles of American Politics." Original documents studied include the Declaration of Independence, the U.S. Constitution, *The Federalist*, Tocqueville's *Democracy in America*, and the speeches of Lincoln;
- two lab science courses. One must be in biological sciences and the other in the physical sciences;
- math and fine art (three courses, combined);
- coursework demonstrating an intermediate understanding of a foreign language, modern or classical;
- one additionalc ourse in philosophy; and
- a senior thesis.

As one history major states, "Some might complain that a UD education neglects non-Western civilizations, and there is some truth to that; however, I would argue that a UD education focuses on understanding one particular tradition—our own—through an intensive program of study. Many universities provide a salad bar sampling of various civilizations which leaves their students with an insufficient knowledge of all of them; UD's approach may be a narrow one, but it succeeds in what it sets out to do." (As this book goes to press, the core curriculum is under revision. There is talk of eliminating one introductory science course for nonscience majors—which means that many undergrads would have to bone up on their math. Interested students would do well to keep an eye on developments.)

The university insists that the lessons learned from its liberal arts program can be applied to every area of life, including the practice of leadership and business. As one faculty member notes, "Some mention should be made about UD's innovative approach for those interested in business. These students take UD's full core and their program is focused on business leadership." Warren Bennis and James O'Toole remarked in the May 2005 *Harvard Business Review*: "We are impressed with the University of Dallas's recognition that an overly narrow approach to business education may have been a factor in the Tyco, Arthur Andersen, WorldCom, and Enron scandals." And as Thomas Lindsay, the university's former provost, said while addressing the latter scandal (which was even bigger news in Texas):

> Business education in this country is devoted overwhelmingly to technical training. This is ironic, because even before Enron studies showed that executives who fail—financially as well as morally—rarely do so from a lack of expertise. Rather, they fail because they lack personal skills and practical wisdom; what Aristotle called prudence. Aristotle taught that genuine leadership consisted in the ability to identify and serve the common good. To do so requires much more than technical training. It requires an education in moral reasoning, which must include history, philosophy, literature, theology, and logic. . . .

One student lauds the school's emphasis on holistic learning: "I think the single greatest debt I have to UD is for an integrated intellectual life. The world as a whole is very specialized, and this specialization often leads to fragmentation because it is not coherent, ordered, related, structured. The education I have received at UD has kept my own pursuits in order and balance and prevented what would have been mental chaos."

The school offers a wide range of preprofessional programs, including architecture, dentistry, engineering, law, medicine, veterinary medicine, and business leadership. The university's student-faculty ratio is a reasonable 12 to 1, and all classes are taught by professors, not grad students.

Students and faculty alike recommend in particular the following teachers: Brian Murray in business leadership, Grace West and David Sweet in classics, David Andrews in mathematics, and Susan Hanssen, Thomas Jodziewicz, William Otto, and John R. Sommerfeldt (founder of the International Medieval Congress) in history. Also in history, students praise Francis Swietek, "a furious lecturer who, in ages past, might have been a great orator." Students speak highly of Thomas West and Richard Dougherty of the politics department. (Dr. Dougherty is an expert in St. Augustine and modern American case law. His classes are called both "entertaining and insightful.") In theology, students suggest seeking out William Brownsberger, Mark Lowery, and Christopher Malloy. In English, recommendations include John Alvis, David Davies, Fr. Robert Maguire, and Gerard Wegemer—who's said to have an impressive ability "to bring Thomas More to life." Also highly rated are Frank Doe in biology, Richard Olenick in physics, Alexandra Wilhelmsen in Spanish, William Frank and Fr. James Lehrberger in philosophy, and William Doyle in economics.

In music, students praise Fr. Ralph March, O.Cist. (Getting rather advanced in years now, Fr. Ralph began his life as a young monk in Hungary, but was forced to flee the country when the Communists took over the monastery. He served as the Cologne Cathedral Kappelmeister for two decades and now teaches Gregorian chant and tells stories about everything under the sun.) Other students rave about Scott Crider, the English department's "greatest lover of Aristotle's *Poetics*." As one student put it, "Considered a UD 'liberal,' Dr. Crider is in fact a moderate and complements the more conservative school. Though one of the few non-Catholic professors at the university—he is in fact of an eastern philosophic persuasion—Dr. Crider calls himself a guest of Christianity, and in his case that's not just a fluffy term he cooked up. Dr. Crider is deeply respectful of the Christian tradition and is deeply imbued with Western literature. He provides a fresh perspective and demands that his students think carefully about their arguments."

One of the highlights of the UD experience is the trip to Rome, generally taken in the sophomore year by students who fulfill certain academic requirements. Some 80 percent of the student body participates. The program is meant to bring theoretical knowledge to life in the very heart of what used to be Christendom. While in Rome, students reside on a twelve-acre property owned by the school that includes a pool, tennis courts, a working vineyard, and an olive grove—even as they take a full load of fifteen credits. The semester fittingly includes a ten-day trip to Greece.

VITAL STATISTICS
Religious affiliation: Roman Catholic
Total enrollment: 3,021
Total undergraduates: 1,166
SAT/ACT midranges: SAT V: 580–700, M: 540–650; ACT: 24–29
Applicants: 817
Applicants accepted: 81%
Accepted applicants who enrolled: 39%
Tuition: $19,604
Room and board: $7,026
Freshman retention rate: 85%
Graduation rate: 61% (4 yrs.), 66% (6 yrs.)
Courses with fewer than 20 students: 49%
Student-faculty ratio: 12:1
Courses taught by graduate students: none
Most popular majors: English, business leadership, biology
Students living on campus: 61%
Guaranteed housing for four years? no
Students in fraternities or sororities: none

Campus Life: Glass Towers, Chant, and Barbeque

Founded by nuns and heavily assisted by the Cistercians across the street, UD has a solidly Catholic identity; but the school doesn't feel like a cloister. Non-Catholics, about 30 percent of the student population, do not feel out of place. That might not be true for outspokenly liberal students—but that's thanks mostly to the school's location. In a part of Texas that's one part Bible Belt and two parts cosmetic surgery, Democrats are as thin on the ground as Republicans at a Garrison Keillor house party. The Princeton Review listed UD as among the top ten places where "students pray on a regular basis" and are "most nostalgic for Ronald Reagan" (though they're too young to remember him).

The campus church, the Church of the Incarnation, is modern but reverent; it seats about 500. (Since this is Dallas, the city has plenty of Protestant churches as well.) Campus chaplains are said to be low-key but reliably orthodox. The same can't really be said for the Institute for Religious and Pastoral Studies, a graduate program on campus that showcases dissenting Catholics such as Margaret O'Brien Steinfels, former editor of *Commonweal*.

Most of the other graduate programs are solidly traditional in their approach, attracting erudite older students who mix well with the undergrads. Many students of every age take advantage of the Cistercian monastery nearby. "Large numbers of UD students and professors attend Mass at the abbey, both on Sundays and weekdays, and many receive spiritual direction there. Six of the monks are currently members of the UD faculty, teaching theology, philosophy, literature, and music, and all of the monks have either taught or attended classes at UD at some point," one student says.

The school describes its 1,000-acre campus as set among "rolling hills," but unless you are coming from Kansas, it looks pretty darn flat. In fact, one of the architectural highlights of the campus is the 200-foot Braniff Memorial Tower, which was built in the 1980s and is just a few feet shorter than the control tower at the Dallas–Fort Worth Airport. (There's a rumor that you can see the Braniff Tower from Lubbock.) And bring a car: if you're looking for something as simple as a Starbucks, you'll need to drive to get it. Dallas is totally dependent on highways, so there's no easy alternative transport to get downtown.

> *"I think the single greatest debt I have to UD is for an integrated intellectual life. . . .UD has kept my own pursuits in order and balance and prevented what would have been mental chaos."*

The school tries to fill in some of this by planning trips to various cultural sites, of which there are many.

The campus is active enough to engage students who have many and diverse interests. The *University News* is the campus newspaper; its quality is described as "varying." UD Radio offers classic rock, news, and sports. Students of the arts will find that both the college and the city provide abundant attractions. UD has recently completed the Haggerty Arts Village, a five-building complex of studios, galleries, and classrooms. One student notes, "The music department is small, but the quality is quite high; the chamber recitals every semester are amazing and the school choirs are second to none." Fans of a capella will be delighted by the Collegium Cantorum, a group that focuses on sacred Latin polyphony.

Students augment their coursework with off-semester offerings during winter break, May term, and summer break. While the selection is not wide, courses are offered for an intensive three weeks, at a discounted price, during winter break and May term.

For high school students interested in exploring the University of Dallas, the school offers the Odyssey Days program. This two-day program is essentially an open house that gives an excellent overview of the school. High school students with three years of Latin can apply for the Latin in Rome program, which studies classic texts from the university's core curriculum during July. Participants read passages from Cicero, Pliny, Virgil, and Horace that are relevant to their travels.

The University of Dallas is not known for its athletics, but it does offer thirteen intercollegiate sports programs for men and women. Those include lacrosse, soccer, volleyball, cross-country, basketball, softball, and track and field for women, and soccer, cross-country, basketball, baseball, track and field, and golf for men. Various intramural teams and clubs also exist, such as Tae Kwon Do, ultimate Frisbee, hacky sack, sailing, and rugby. For the more sedate, clubs such as the Freeze Frame photography club, the Chesterton Society, Crusaders for Life, and the Lady American Sewing Circle and Talking Society may be of interest.

Students who want single-sex dorms can live in one; other dorms are segregated by floor, with very restricted visitation hours for the opposite sex. During such visits, students must keep their doors "bolted"—that is, kept ajar by extending the deadbolt with the door open. Approximately 60 percent of students live on campus; others find off-campus housing across the street or in adjoining neighborhoods.

Crime is low on campus if you exclude alcohol-related incidents—which have been on the rise in recent years. No violent crimes were reported in 2004–5, though there was a single burglary.

The tuition, fees, room and board for the 2005–6 academic year ran to almost $27,000. The semester abroad in Rome works out to be about $4,000 more. Some 61 percent of students receive need-based financial aid. The average student loan debt in a recent graduating class was $21,700.

ALL-AMERICAN COLLEGES

73

DEEP SPRINGS COLLEGE

BISHOP, CALIFORNIA • WWW.DEEPSPRINGS.EDU

It's a little misleading to say that this school is "in" Bishop, California. In fact, it's about an hour's drive away, situated in the midst of the pristine desert that joins New Mexico and California. To put it in perspective, the nearest major airports (Los Angeles and Reno, Nevada) are four to five hours away by car, and the closest tourist attractions are Death Valley and UFO landing strip Area 51. The neighboring counties of Nevada offer little except legal brothels, some of which double as gas stations and the last place where a driver can buy water for the next one hundred miles.

An oasis in these austere surroundings, Deep Springs is one of the most high-minded colleges in the country—still animated to a startling degree by the mission of its founder, L. L. Nunn. Mr. Nunn was a pioneer in the electrification of the American West—an endeavor that made him wealthy, but left him worried. When he was working with the scientists and engineers who laid the infrastructure that transformed California, Nunn was profoundly impressed with their technical competence, but appalled at their ignorance of the humanities. He decided to use some of his wealth to endow one or more schools which would combine an emphasis on serving mankind with a rich, humane education.

Himself a "Social Gospel" Christian, Nunn created in Deep Springs a unique institution that would carry on his vision: A two-year "working college" in the desert where some thirty young men would isolate themselves from the world to study the humanities while helping to support the school by operating a farm and cattle ranch. Nearly all decisions would be made by student vote, the better to prepare responsible citizens of a republic. Attendance at the school would be free.

Despite all the changes that have swept universities and colleges in this century—and despite its eventual secularization—Deep Springs remains remarkably true to its

founder's intent. It offers a unique educational opportunity for the young men who meet its demanding admissions standards and are willing to spend their first two college years studying Greek, roping cattle, and running a college. As one teacher said, "This is a school for students who want to share deeply in a community, think deep thoughts, and get their hands dirty."

Academic Life: Greek by Popular Demand

In the past thirty years, academic curricula at schools from the Ivy League to the Southeastern Conference have been dumbed-down and gutted, supposedly in answer to student demands for greater "relevance," turning what had once been carefully thought-out programs of liberal education into take-out menus. At Deep Springs, something close to the opposite has happened. The school, by its founding statutes, is not permitted to impose a set curriculum; Nunn was a convinced "small-d" democrat. The only requirements are a single writing course, a public speaking class, and an introductory, late-summer survey in Great Books and humanities to prepare newcomers for college-level work. (By all accounts these courses are excellent; they differ in focus each year as the faculty varies.) Most of the students, however, arrrive more than prepared. The selection process for new admissions—conducted entirely by students—is rigorous and requires a series of seven searching essays, high test scores, and a campus visit and interview. Indeed, the process itself scares off many aspiring students who don't share the Deep Springs ethos. Those who are admitted are typically, according to one professor, "students who have been heavily involved in volunteer or service activities during high school. The admissions committee is very interested in finding students who are committed to the school's ideal of service to mankind, and have demonstrated that before they apply. Of course, they also must have excellent academics."

VITAL STATISTICS

Religious affiliation: none
Total enrollment: 26
Total undergraduates: 26
SAT midranges: V: 750–800, M: 710–780
Applicants: 169
Applicants accepted: 8%
Accepted applicants who enrolled: 92%
Tuition: free
Room and board: free
Freshman retention rate: 92%
Graduation rate: 92% (4 yrs.)
Courses with fewer than 20 students: 95%
Student-faculty ratio: 3:1
Courses taught by graduate students: none
Most popular majors: n/a
Students living on campus: 100%
Guaranteed housing for two years? yes
Students in fraternities or sororities: none

The students at Deep Springs themselves decide through their curriculum committee which courses are offered every year. These decisions, like all others, are hashed out by the student body (SB) at one of the contentious, high-minded meetings that take up every Friday night of the school year, attendance at which is mandatory. The type of students attracted to Deep Springs are usually infused with a kind of intellectual curiosity and academic seriousness that prevents them from asking for trivial, ideologically blinkered, or hopelessly arcane courses. In fact, in recent years, the most frequently requested and heavily subscribed courses, according to students and teachers, were in classical Greek, ancient philosophy, Nietzsche, Heidegger, and (alas) Lacan.

In lieu of a core curriculum—and this school, unlike most, seems to be doing just fine without one—here is a listing of some of the courses recently chosen by the student committee:

- "The Problem of Historical Knowledge," with readings ranging from Giordano Bruno to Nietzsche
- "Greek Tragedy"
- "What is Justice?"

- "Accelerated Ancient Greek"
- "Advanced Latin Poetry"
- "Poetry Workshop"
- "Emily Dickinson"
- "The History of Religion in America"
- "Myths, Fables, and History"
- "African-American History"
- "Appalachian History"
- "Poetry and the Uses of History"
- "Plato"
- "Ecology"
- "Tropical Biology"
- "Evolutionary Theory"
- "Piano Performance"
- "Painting"

These students are not asking for fluff. The classes we observed were small, intellectually intense, and conducted more like graduate school seminars than freshman and sophomore humanities classes. Students display a high level of responsibility in completing assigned readings, and they frequently make polite interruptions to question particular interpretations of a text—or to ask for details of its translation from the Latin or Greek.

There are no majors. Students treat their time at Deep Springs as a replacement for the first two years at another college. Nearly all transfer to top-notch schools, where they complete standard courses of study. Typical destinations for Deep Springs grads in recent years have been the University of Chicago, Brown, and Harvard. In fact, Harvard has a long-standing relationship with Deep Springs and works to accommodate transfers.

Deep Springs is much stronger in the humanities than in mathematics or the hard sciences, faculty report. Its laboratory facilities will not impress graduates of a prosperous public high school, and the general consensus on campus is that "students aren't interested in real science, and don't request many courses in it. When the courses are offered, few of them sign up." The most popular recent class in science was taught by a philosophy professor. The course, called The Copernican Revolution, immersed students in Ptolemy and other ancient astronomers and included observing the sky using the same primitive measuring devices that were available before Galileo; then they moved on to Copernicus and the use of a telescope. (Since it's located in the desert, Deep Springs offers a stunning view of the constellations.) Deep Springs is a place for would-be philosophers of science or medical ethicists—not those who aspire to work as surgeons, researchers, or science teachers (though a few graduates have gone on to enter such fields). Most mathematics classes are conducted as independent studies.

The students and faculty we talked to reported that the prevailing attitude in Deep Springs toward the Western civic, cultural, and religious heritage is "extremely respectful, but searchingly critical." One student said, "We haven't gotten that many devoutly religious students lately, but that changes with every class. A few years ago, we had a committed Catholic, and he requested and got a seminar on the thought of Maritain, which the other students enjoyed very much. People who come here with strong beliefs will feel quite welcome, but they'll have to be prepared to defend whatever assertions they make in class." Another student agreed: "Several of the professors and staff members go to church every week, and take along whichever students want to go. It's a mostly secular but definitely tolerant environment."

Most of the faculty to whom we spoke seem to be either moderates or what we term "old-fashioned liberals"—that is, people committed, regardless of their political preferences, to high standards in traditional liberal arts, the Great Books, great ideas, and close scrutiny both of Western and non-Western cultures. These civilizations are viewed through a prism of academic rigor, not political correctness or postmodern theoretical dogma.

Another distinctive facet of Deep Springs is the relatively ephemeral nature of its faculty. Most teachers are employed as "short-term," which means they are on year-to-year contracts renewed according to the desire of the students on the curriculum committee. A smaller group signs on for longer periods. Most short-term faculty members seem to be recent Ph.D.'s from leading universities who are still searching for tenure-track positions. The long-term faculty tend to be Great Books aficionados happy to find an environment where the students are clamoring for—rather than reluctantly taking or outright avoiding—their classes.

Deep Springs offers a unique educational opportunity for the young men who meet its demanding admissions standards and are willing to spend their first two college years studying Greek, roping cattle, and running a college. As one teacher said, "This is a school for students who want to share deeply in a community, think deep thoughts, and get their hands dirty."

There is no such thing as tenure at Deep Springs, and even the president and dean of the college must remain closely attentive to the expectations and standards of the student body. One teacher pointed out that "this means that there is virtually no institutional memory at the place. However earnest and hard-working are the students who make decisions, they tend to repeat the same mistakes as others made a few years before, and it's impossible to make long-term changes for the better. Apart from the ranch staff, there has been no one here longer than seven years."

But few at Deep Springs seem to think that much about the school needs changing. It has been growing even more selective over the past fifteen years, with average SAT scores rising. The median student GPA has risen too, leading some to worry about grade inflation. However, in a self-study published by the school, it appears that SAT scores have increased in tandem with, or faster than, the average grade. So the school isn't becoming lax—it's just attracting even smarter students.

Since many of the teachers at Deep Springs stay for only a year or two, it might be misleading to print a list of favorites; several could be gone by the time you read this. But as of publication, highly recommended teachers include David Neidorf in philosophy, Matthew Fox in comparative literature and classics, G. C. Waldrep in history and poetry, Ross Peterson (also college president) in history, Justin Kim in art, and Frederick Will, whom one student called "an amazing polymath," in classics, philosophy, and theology.

Students have no trouble at all getting private time with teachers, who live on campus and are used to intense, one-on-one consultation. Indeed, a fair percentage of coursework is often done via independent study on subjects ranging from "Jazz Theory and Composition" to "The Vedic, Hindu, and Buddhist Traditions."

One of the few mandatory classes at Deep Springs is public speaking. Professors work on topics and techniques in class, and students stand up in front of the student body once a week to offer orations—sometimes rather elaborate compositions in verse or dramatic performances. Their skill level is typically high. For example, one recent performance, titled Liberty vs. Love, wove together ideas from a dialogue of Plato, a poem of John Donne, and Nietzsche's aphorisms. Later the same night, a professor read aloud from an epic poem he was composing on physics and the creation of the universe.

Well-known graduates of this school include novelists William Vollman, Benjamin Kunkel, Peter Rock, journalist Walter Isaacson, anthropologist Julian Steward, and computer programmer Silas Warner—founder of Muse Software and developer of the pioneering PC game *Castle Wolfenstein*.

Student Life: Brook Farm Hands

The first thing you notice about the students at Deep Springs is that they are all male, all physically fit, and all tired. Not harried, bored, or dissatisfied—just bone-tired from the thousand little tasks that go into running the college. Students maintain and do most routine repairs on buildings, dig trenches, build fences, fertilize and harvest a working alfalfa farm, cook all the food, and do all the cleaning. But that's not all. "We have to keep down the gopher population," one student said. The rodents are prone to dig through and destroy the farm's vital irrigation system. "That means dynamite and flamethrowers. It's a little bit like *Caddyshack*. It's fun." Another didn't have such a romantic attitude. "Gopher-hunting gets real old after a few days."

What's more interesting for most young men considering the school is that the students also operate a beef cattle ranch. That means feeding, tending, birthing, slaughtering, and butchering cows every year, as well as rising at 4:00 a.m. to milk a small dairy herd, which provides the school with plenty of raw milk and several varieties of homemade cheese. Each year, at least one student is trained as a cowboy and charged with moving the herd as needed from horseback. Prominently visible on the campus between a classroom and the lab is a practice cow for students to lasso, and the cafeteria usually smells of fresh, organic beef.

The strenuous physical work in which every student engages—campus labor details are mandatory for all students—leaves them healthy but often sleepy, particularly after the hours of reading and writing demanded by every course. "Sometimes it's hard to stay awake to finish that last Greek translation," one student said. But working all these different jobs "really helps you understand your relationship towards work, authority, and personal responsibility," one student said.

The students have a strict policy against alcohol and drugs on campus, which they've tightened in recent years. "A few years back, things got a little lax on this score," one student said, "but we've tightened up." The curious thing about the rules at Deep Springs is that they're virtually all chosen by student committees and majority vote—with the result that youthful idealism tends to trump hedonistic impulses. "Since we make the rules ourselves, we take ownership of them," a student said. "There's really no satisfaction in trying to get around the rules you yourself helped hammer out."

All such decisions are made in Friday night's student body (SB) meeting, which can last between three and seven hours, dragging into the night as students speechify about the mission of the school, drawing on the readings in their courses, citing Plato and Aristotle alongside Deep Springs' founding Constitution and Deed of Trust and other writings of founder L. L. Nunn. For instance, Nunn decreed that students should remain "isolated" from the world at large for most of their two years at Deep Springs in order to fully immerse themselves in the experience of learning, work, and service. To implement this, students have voted that no one is permitted to leave the campus during a class term except to run vital errands in nearby Bishop, or to go to church. Similarly, students have limited their own access to the Internet to a few hours per week—though this is a subject of perennial debate, with some advocating no Internet at all. (That prospect seems unlikely, given the sheer size of book shipments from Amazon.com which arrive every week at this school of avid readers.) Another frequent subject of debate is the idea of admitting women—which provokes intense arguments pro and con but is essentially moot, since the school's all-male status is written into its charter.

Attendance at SB meetings really is mandatory: one student reports that he was late to a meeting because he had a girlfriend visiting—so the entire student body showed up at his room to remind him. Likewise, professors have been known to lead a seminar class to the room of a student who has overslept and hold the class in his bedroom. The atmosphere at Deep Springs is something of a cross between a small Swiss village (sans women!), and a never-ending New England town hall meeting.

The dorms are comfortable, clean, and of recent construction. One student called them "luxurious." But don't expect any privacy. Many students sleep in bunks, and locked doors (not even in the bathrooms) are not allowed on campus. Faculty members keep the front doors of their homes unlocked, and students feel free to drop by at any reasonable hour to talk about classwork, career aspirations, or life in general.

ALL-AMERICAN COLLEGES

One member of the admissions committee admitted that he was "disappointed" at the relative social homogeneity of recent admits. "We used to have more students from working-class families, but it seems to happen that the students on our committee are impressed by students from similar educational backgrounds as themselves—often from the same schools they attended." Admissions committee members currently hope to broaden Deep Springs' appeal to a wider range of applicants. There are usually students of different races (and sometimes from different continents) in each class, and typically one or two who self-identify as gay. "But that's not a big issue here," a student said.

Students at Deep Springs tend to be idealistic and spiritual, but not particularly religious. However, Christian students will find several co-religionists among the faculty, who are happy to drive them to church on Sundays (there are several Protestant churches and a Catholic parish in Bishop), or to join them at a weekly Bible study conducted Sunday nights at the home of the ranch manager.

Crime is simply "not an issue" on campus, students report. "Pretty much everything students have is treated as community property," one student said, "so the only problem is sometimes aggressive borrowing."

After two years at Deep Springs, most students apply for transfer status at leading universities. There is a downside here: these schools accept most but not all transfer credits, so students may have to take extra classes after they transfer. Furthermore, financial aid for transfer students is usually much stingier than for new admits, one faculty member points out. As it happens, most Deep Springs students are from relatively prosperous backgrounds—many are the more public-spirited graduates of elite prep schools—so this issue is less important to them than it might be to public or parochial school graduates. This is rather a shame, since one of the most attractive aspects of Deep Springs is the fact that attendance is free: each student admitted receives a full scholarship valued at $50,000 per year.

EASTERN MENNONITE UNIVERSITY

HARRISONBURG, VIRGINIA • WWW.EMU.EDU

Eastern Mennonite College was founded by its mother church in 1917. The Mennonites have kept tight control over Eastern, which in 1994 became a university, with the addition of graduate departments of business, education, counseling, and conflict transformation. A recent graduate admitted that the campus is probably "a little more relaxed than it was during World War I," but insisted that it remains faithful to its Anabaptist principles—nicely laid out in EMU's statement of purpose: "The educational task of Eastern Mennonite University is rooted in the Christian faith and its scriptures as they have been interpreted and lived out in a unique 476-year Anabaptist-Mennonite tradition. This tradition embraces God's gift of reconciliation through the cross and the power of the resurrection to create new life in conformity to the teaching and spirit of Jesus."

This faith is seen as an invitation, not an imposition: "Students are encouraged to embrace this faith heritage while their own convictions and experiences and those of other religious heritages are respected. EMU seeks to deepen students' faith and life in Christ, while also encouraging them to critique their own faith tradition in wholesome ways." If this vision appeals to you, this academically impressive school is a choice worth taking seriously.

Academic Life: A Core Curriculum for the Global Village

The core curriculum at EMU is extensive, taking up more than a quarter of the credits required for graduation, and extending throughout the four years of undergraduate study. Each student must complete a first-year seminar designed to nurture "an understanding of world views and the student's place in relation to God, self and others." The course centers on applying a biblical verse which EMU considers the keystone of its educational approach, Micah 6:8 ("He hath shewed thee, O man, what is good; and what doth the Lord require of thee, but to do justly, and to love mercy, and to walk humbly with thy God?") The rest of the core requirements are as follows:

- a freshman writing course, with level determined by a student's SAT score;

- one class in speech communication;
- three "writing intensive courses," chosen by the student;
- a mathematics proficiency exam;
- a "highly experiential" wellness course drawing on faculty from theater, nursing, physical education, and psychology and focusing on "stewardship of the body in relation to doing justice, loving mercy, and walking humbly with God";
- two interdisciplinary colloquia that "explore a particular theme through the lenses of several disciplines," helping students "to learn and experience the interconnectedness of the world through exposure to the arts/humanities, natural and social sciences, and Bible/theology." In 2004–5, the themes of these classes were "Gold" and "The City";
- one class in Anabaptist biblical perspectives, chosen from "Introduction to the Bible," "Becoming God's People: Old Testament Themes," "Following Jesus Christ: New Testament Themes," "Living Faith: The Way of Jesus in the World," and "Ethics in the Way of Jesus";
- one course in Christian identity and witness, with choices ranging from "Spiritual Formation" to "Contemporary Culture" to "Topics in Theology" to "Ancient Philosophy";
- three courses in cross-cultural studies, requiring participation in a semester-long crosscultural program, a three- to six-week summer seminar, or participation in the Community Scholars' Center in Washington—which EMU students share with those from other Mennonite schools. Other courses are offered in the Middle East, Guatemala, Austria, France, Benin, New Zealand, Lithuania, Lesotho, China, Peru, Greece, India, and Costa Rica;
- three more courses with a community learning component, each involving at least fifteen hours of service to the surrounding community; and
- a senior seminar "designed to broaden from the major to integration within an interdisciplinary world and to revisit Micah 6:8 prior to graduation."

Eastern Mennonite considers itself a university for students who are "called to serve" the church, the family, or the community at large. Education and nursing are the most popular majors. Business, which comes in third, stresses the biblical "servant leader" model, according to which the successful businessman not only serves his family and his community, but also his employees in their common mission to fulfill a corporate vision which is for the good of the larger society.

The humanities and social sciences are taught from the same perspective, as part of the Christian vocation, rather than as platforms for shrill attacks on (or knee-jerk defenses of) Christendom, America, and the West. The spirit at Eastern Mennonite might make conservatives and evangelicals nervous—at first glance these people look like liberal Quakers—but it flows straight out of the authentic Anabaptist tradition. Teachers and students treasure simplicity of living and the voluntary sharing of goods and services. At EMU there is little respect for jingoism, and much regret at the coercive nature of much of America's involvement with the rest of the world. Most students at Eastern Mennonites would not consider themselves conservatives in the current American context—seeing the term as tainted by what they might consider greed and militarism. But nearly all would describe themselves as pro-life, pro-family Bible Christians. More than others who'd claim these titles, Mennonites might qualify as "old-fashioned liberals," especially in their emphasis on brotherhood among the races.

At EMU, the authority of the professor rests on three pillars, of which intellectual commitment is only one, and, indeed, the last named: "Faculty are expected to practice what they teach, demonstrating the creative possibilities of devout faith combined with serious reflection. The spiritual, moral and intellectual persuasiveness of faculty comes from significant engagement in congregational life, Christian service, and a demonstrated love for learning." The student-faculty ratio at EMU is outstanding at 9 to 1, and no classes are taught by graduate students. Sixty-two percent of courses have fewer than twenty students.

Student comments emphasize the great informality of the teaching, with material that would elsewhere be covered in large lecture sections conveyed in the manner of a conversation between personal friends. They also speak of the meticulous patience of the instructors of more technical subjects such as organic chemistry, making sure that everyone who makes an effort gets the point. Eastern Mennonite students particularly recommend professors Ken Nafziger in music, Mark Sawin in history, Jerry Holsopple in communications, and Herm Weaver in psychology.

The Mennonites have always emphasized foreign missions, and many EMU faculty served and continue to serve as missionaries. The Mennonite heritage as a Peace Church gives the missions a special character. Missionaries go to places in the world suffering violent conflict and preach the Gospel of peace to those in the midst of war. Indeed, as of publication, members of the Mennonite-sponsored organization Christian Peacemaker Teams (CPT) are being held hostage by terrorists in Iraq. Perhaps most impressively, they have trained Moslem Peacemaker Teams to go where Christians aren't welcome. The Mennonite message goes beyond preaching individual salvation and involves teaching ways of changing hurt into forgiveness and hostility into reconciliation. Students report that one great advantage of an Eastern Mennonite education is to be taught by men and women who have been to places and involved in situations that the rest of the world only reads about, not as tourists or even as reporters, but as active participants.

VITAL STATISTICS
Religious affiliation: Mennonite
Total enrollment: 1,302
Total undergraduates: 1,012
SAT/ACT midrange: SAT V: 480–630, M: 480–630; ACT: 22–28
Applicants: 636
Applicants accepted: 77%
Accepted applicants who enrolled: 41%
Tuition: $20,612
Room and board: $6,550
Freshman retention rate: 74%
Graduation rate: 55% (4 yrs.), 57% (6 yrs.)
Courses with fewer than 20 students: 62%
Student-faculty ratio: 9:1
Courses taught by graduate students: none
Most popular majors: education, nursing, business
Students living on campus: 56%
Guaranteed housing for four years? yes
Students in fraternities or sororities: none

ALL-AMERICAN COLLEGES

In March 2006, the body of Christian peacekeeper Tom Fox—taken hostage in November—was discovered in Iraq. After his training at Eastern Mennonite, Fox wrote, "It seems easier somehow to confront anger within my heart than it is to confront fear. . . . Does that mean I walk the streets of Baghdad with a sign saying 'American for the Taking?' No. . . . But if Jesus and Gandhi are right, then I am asked to risk my life, and, if I lose it, to be as forgiving as they were when murdered by the forces of Satan."

It's no exaggeration to say that the graduate program in conflict transformation epitomizes the mission of EMU as a whole. Through its summer institutes, this program reaches out to professionals who have their degrees. For instance, the Greek Orthodox Archdiocese of North and South America sent a priest from New York's East Village to Eastern Mennonite to learn how to minister better to the special needs of families affected by the events of September 11, 2001. Although representing a religious tradition far removed from the Anabaptist, he speaks of his weeks on campus with warmth and gratitude, saying that any awkwardness was dissolved by "southern graciousness."

The business school also draws on the missionary enterprise in a way that affects the whole university. A student team affiliated with Sam Walton's Students in Free Enterprise (SIFE) organizes entrepreneurial activities in aid of local charities and offers assistance to entrepreneurs, sometimes through the Mennonite chain of native crafts stores, Ten Thousand Villages. Through their involvement with such endeavors, EMU students learn first-hand the real obstacles that hinder economic development in poor countries.

"Creative teaching and learning affect the mind and character of the student. At its best, education engenders in students a sense of idealism and responsibility, as well as a reverent humility before the awesome complexities and ambiguities of life."

Like many other Christian schools, EMU believes that education is intended to nurture the whole person, not just the mind: "Creative teaching and learning affect the mind and character of the student. At its best, education engenders in students a sense of idealism and responsibility, as well as a reverent humility before the awesome complexities and ambiguities of life." Eastern Mennonite University doesn't pretend that it has all the answers. The last word is humility. It is a good one.

Student Life: Commitment to Community

The Eastern Mennonite campus consists of forty-four buildings on ninety-three acres in Harrisonburg, a city of just under 45,000, which is also home to James Madison University. A branch campus in Lancaster, Pennsylvania, offers graduate and adult degree completion programs.

There is always something to do, either at EMU or at nearby James Madison, and there is a movie house in Harrisonburg. A recent weekend at Eastern Mennonite featured an Anabaptist colloquium in the library, bread-making in the science center, two concerts, two films, a stage play and a dance on Friday, public student presentations, a YPCA work day, a trip to Six Flags, an outing to local farmers' markets, varsity competitions in baseball, tennis, and softball, a gallery opening, the same two films and stage play and a barn dance on Saturday, a half dozen music recitals, varsity softball, a USA vs. Rest of the World (i.e., international students) soccer match, and a foreign film on Sunday—an impressive selection of activities for a school this size. EMU students could also have attended a chamber concert on Saturday or a percussion ensemble concert on Sunday at James Madison, but there was quite enough going on in their own end of town.

SUGGESTED CORE
1. English 341: World Literature I
2. Philosophy 302: Ancient Philosophy
3. Biblical Studies 111-2/121-2: Old Testament Studies / New Testament Studies
4. Church Studies 382: Church History (*closest match*)
5. Philosophy 361: Modern Philosophy
6. English 361: Shakespeare
7. History 131: American History to 1865
8. History 192: The Global Past II (*closest match*)

Many campus activities are religious in nature. Three campus ministers, two Mennonite and one United Methodist, are assisted by eight student pastoral assistants and thirty student ministry assistants in the dormitories. The Young People's Christian Association offers various activities on and off campus, and students are encouraged to organize Bible studies and other small groups. University chapel is held on Wednesdays and Fridays, and there are student-led worship services on Sunday and Wednesday nights—the latter often featuring chants from the ecumenical monastery Taizé. Neighborhood parishioners volunteer to drive Catholic students to Mass in town, and there is also a small Jewish congregation in Harrisonburg.

Eastern Mennonite requires that all members make a personal commitment to live according to the Mennonite vision of the Christian faith:

> As a member of the EMU community, I will strive to practice steward-ship of mind, time, abilities and finances. I will pursue opportunities for intellectual and spiritual growth and demonstrate care for my body. I also will exercise social responsibility in my standard of living and use of economic resources. Realizing the destructive character of an unfor-giving spirit and harmful discrimination based on prejudice, I will seek to demonstrate unselfish love in my actions, attitudes and relation-ships. I will be honest and show respect for the rights and property of others.

Some expectations are recognized as binding at all times, on campus and off. Students agree "to refrain from sexual relationships outside of marriage, sexual harass-ment and abuse, pornography, acts of violence, abusive or demeaning language and the use of illegal drugs." EMU acknowledges that it has discharged faculty for homosexual activity and will continue to do so. Adultery and drug use are similarly forbidden. The

ALL-AMERICAN COLLEGES

prohibition of alcohol and tobacco is limited to university property and events, though drunkenness, even off campus, is not allowed: "Recognizing that EMU supports non-use of alcohol and tobacco, I will respect and abide by the university policy that prohibits the use of alcohol and tobacco on campus or at university functions and the misuse of alcohol off campus."

Eastern Mennonite rejects the idea of set penalties for specified actions, except for visiting hours infractions: "The purposes of discipline at Eastern Mennonite University are to create an opportunity for change and growth in the individual and to maintain an environment that furthers the educational purposes of the academic community. For these reasons a punitive list of actions and punishments is not kept. Instead, a model of restorative justice, taking into account the persons and context for a particular incident, is upheld." The basis of all disciplinary action is biblical: "Matthew 18:12–17 outlines the principles of this approach to behavior and relationships. Thus, growth is not entirely an individual process but involves the entire Christian community as we seek to share our own concerns and at the same time respect the convictions of other Christians," the school declares.

In 2004 a board member strongly objected to the programming of WEMC, the college radio station, which was airing Amy Goodman's "Democracy Now!" Monday through Friday from five to six. This program, produced by radical Pacifica Radio, was considered too "polarizing," and the station cut it back to the 6:00 Friday evening hour, despite some signs of support, and replaced it in the weekday rush-hour slot with the BBC. Some were unhappy with this resolution, but it didn't become the flashpoint it might have elsewhere.

Six small dormitories, three apartment complexes, and a theme house offer accommodations on campus. Men and women are housed in separate residences, or in separate floors or wings of the same building. The residences are modern or modernized, and the architecture is characteristically Anabaptist—functional but not ugly. Visiting hours for members of the opposite sex are limited, and remaining past the cutoff time incurs a fine of a dollar a minute for both guest and host.

Clubs and organizations include the Alpha Omega Steppers for Christ, Black Student Union, Campus Activities Council, Celebration, Chess Club, Committee on Peer Education, Cycling Club, Earth Keepers, Eastern Mennonite Student Women's Association, Future Leaders of Equality and Diversity, German Club, Gospel Choir, Inklings, International Student Organization, Latino Student Alliance, Math Club, Peace Fellowship, Peer Review Board, Pre-Professional Health Society, Recreational Sports (intramurals), Royal Ambassadors, the *Shenandoah* (the yearbook), Social Work Is People, Student Education Association, Student Government Association, Student Health Advisory Council, Students in Free Enterprise, Student Nurses' Association, Table Tennis Club, Ultimate Frisbee Club, the *Weather Vane* (the student newspaper), Young Democrats, and the Young People's Christian Association.

While Mennonite babies may not emerge from the womb proficient at singing four-part harmony a capella, by the time they get to college they are good enough to be the envy of the Russian Orthodox. When—outside church, of course—they are permitted the use of instruments, the results are remarkable. One result of this is the Shenandoah Valley Bach Festival, which brings Eastern Mennonite annual national attention. More importantly, it is said that the spirit of music pervades the campus.

Eastern Mennonite is a safe campus. Burglaries are the only crimes reported for the last three years. There were five in 2004, only one of them in a residence.

For 2006–7 undergraduates, tuition was set at $20,612, and room and board was $6,550. Fifty-eight percent of students receive need-based financial aid, and the average student loan debt of a recent graduate is $17,680.

EMORY AND HENRY COLLEGE

EMORY, VIRGINIA • WWW.EHC.EDU

Emory and Henry College is bursting at the seams now that its student body numbers over a thousand students, a benchmark reached in 2005. The school has only eighty-eight professors—one for each key on a piano—and yet, when in 2005 historian John Herbert "Jack" Roper was named Virginia Professor of the Year by the Carnegie Foundation, he was the sixth Emory and Henry Professor to be so honored in seventeen years. In spite of its humble size, the college must be doing something right. Students seeking a small school, a liberal education, personal attention, and moderate politics will find them all here—and in a beautiful southern setting.

Emory and Henry was founded in 1836 and enrolled its first students in 1838, with Wesleyan graduate Ephraim Emerson Wiley serving as its first and only full-time professor. The dual name of Emory and Henry goes back to revolutionary governor Patrick Henry, whose family settled in the region, and to Bishop John Emory, an early Methodist evangelist with a love of learning. James Ewell Brown "Jeb" Stuart attended Emory and Henry from 1848 to 1850. After being appointed to West Point, he went on to lead Confederate cavalry in a long series of heroic engagements. His alma mater isn't too fond of remembering him, though the village of Emory's website boasts that he's an alumnus.

The college served as a Confederate military hospital in the Civil War. In October 1864, after the nearby Battle of Saltville, Confederate soldiers shot two wounded Federal troopers of the Fifth Kentucky Colored Cavalry, prisoners of war at the local hospital, where the medics made it a point of honor to treat all the wounded, Federal and Confederate as well as black and white. General Lee personally ordered the capture and court martial of the main perpetrator, but justice had to await the end of the war. The victims are buried in the college cemetery.

Emory and Henry continues to celebrate its dual heritage of piety and involvement in the world, even as the world has changed around it. In 2006, Douglas Covington, an African American, was appointed to administer the school during its search for a new president.

Academic Life: The Little College That Could

The college's mission statement affirms that the Christian faith is "our spiritual and moral heritage" and encourages "all our members to grow in faith as they grow in knowledge." This encouragement involves a curious and attractive blend of pluralism and regionalism: "We believe in the worth of each person's religious and cultural heritage, inasmuch as that heritage leads to service to others in our region and the larger world." Note the "inasmuch as" clause: Emory and Henry is not going to "believe in the worth" of anything and everything a student might take into his head to claim for a "religious and cultural heritage." Service is the criterion, not just service to the world (too easily defined as worldly success) but to the region. You must honor your roots and give back to your community. True to its regional vocation, the college, small as it is, offers a minor in Appalachian Studies.

While the Wesleyan version of the Christian faith may be the College's particular spiritual and moral heritage, the educational bedrock goes deeper: "We affirm the liberal arts as our intellectual foundation and believe that excellence results from active participation by all involved in the educational process. We challenge all persons to confront historical and contemporary ideas and issues and to develop the ability to apply critical thought to all areas of human experience." What this means in practice is a core curriculum that extends over four years. Students must complete the following:

- "The Western Tradition," an admirable two-semester survey of our civilization;
- "Great Books," one class which covers major works, such as (recently) *The Odyssey, The Inferno, Twelfth Night, Pride and Prejudice, Pere Goriot, Things Fall Apart,* and *Song of Solomon;*
- "Ethical Inquiry";
- "Global Studies";
- two courses in Christianity, chosen from among "Old Testament Survey," "New Testament Survey," and "Introduction to the Christian Faith";
- "Freshman English" (students may test out);
- one course in the humanities, with options ranging from "History of Ancient and Medieval Philosophy" to "Beginning Spanish";
- one course in the natural sciences;
- one course in the social sciences, with choices such as "American Civilization I" and "Mass Media and Society";

VITAL STATISTICS

Religious affiliation:
United Methodist
Total enrollment: 1,101
Total undergraduates: 1,027
SAT/ACT midranges: SAT V:
470–590, M: 460–580;
ACT: 20–26
Applicants: 1,329
Applicants accepted: 76%
*Accepted applicants who
enrolled*: 34%
Tuition: $19,530
Room and board: $7,040
Freshman retention rate: 72%
Graduation rate: 43% (4 yrs.),
54% (6 yrs.)
*Courses with fewer than 20
students*: 72%
Student-faculty ratio: 14:1
*Courses taught by graduate
students*: none
Most popular majors: business, biology, education
Students living on campus:
66%
*Guaranteed housing for four
years?* yes
Students in fraternities: 11%
sororities: 26%

- a computing class;
- a spoken rhetoric course, taken from one of several departments, including theater, political science, speech, or philosophy; and
- attendance at five arts events per semester through the college's Lyceum program.

Each major has its own mathematics requirement, and some have a foreign language mandate. The liberal arts curriculum has more than twenty-five programs of study, including interdisciplinary programs, which permit students to combine classes from more than one subject area to create a more specialized major.

Emory and Henry balances its strong regional identity with a distinguished program in international studies. In 2006, the college planned study tours of China, India, Germany, Italy, Bulgaria, Eastern Europe, Egypt, Jordan, Lebanon, Morocco, Mexico, and Costa Rica.

"We affirm the liberal arts as our intellectual foundation and believe that excellence results from active participation by all involved in the educational process. . . ." What this means in practice is a core curriculum that extends over four years.

As noted above, six members of the Emory and Henry faculty have been named Virginia Professor of the Year. The only higher Carnegie/CASE honor is United States Professor of the Year, and Stephen L. Fisher of Emory and Henry won that in 1999. Professor Fisher considers himself a spokesman for the Appalachian region. He is proud of the fact that a third of Emory and Henry students are the first of their families to attend college—as he himself was. His voice, and that of the faculty as a whole, is a powerful defender of so-called "poor whites" so universally demonized by the culture of political correctness. It is significant that the college has chosen Fisher to draft a new version of its mission statement.

The other faculty at Emory and Henry who have been named Virginia Professor of the Year are Ed Damer (philosophy, 1989), Kathleen Chamberlain (English, 1993), David Copeland (mass communications, 1997) and Teresa Keller (mass communications, 2003). Damer is well known for his widely assigned book, *Attacking Faulty Reasoning: A Practical Guide to Fallacy-Free Arguments*. Chamberlain has been quoted in the *New Yorker* as an expert on and admirer of the Three Stooges, whom she compares to the Commedia del' Arte. In addition, Emory and Henry students recommend Scott Boltwood, James Harrison, John Lang, Robin Reid, and Meighan Sharp in English; Mark Davis, Matthew Frederick, Trevor Smith, and Lisa Withers in music; Mike Duffy, Gregory McConnell, Melissa Taverner, and George Treadwell in science; Celeste Gaia, James Hamilton, and Chris Qualls in psychology; James Dawsey, Fred Kellogg, and Joe Reiff in theology; Ed Davis and John Morgan in geography; Thomas Little and Jack Roper in history; Joseph Lane and Ali Nizamuddin in political science; Xiangyun Zhang in languages; Denise Stanley in accounting; Mark Hainsworth in mathematics; Linda Dobkins in economics; and Ben Letson in philosophy.

The student-faculty ratio at Emory and Henry is a middling 14 to 1, and over a third of classes have fewer than ten students.

Student Life: www.Mayberry.edu

In addition to the college, the municipality of Emory, which describes itself as a "quaint village," boasts Addison's restaurant, the Emory Mercantile and Deli, the Emory Depot and 1912 Gallery, a post office, a modest number of homes and, not to be missed, a reputedly haunted graveyard. No wonder it calls itself quaint. The only church in town (United Methodist), with a congregation of around 200, is on the campus, and the entire campus is listed in the National Register of Historical Places. The town grew up around the college, which opened its doors in 1838; the railroad didn't arrive until 1856.

Emory sits in that little corner of Virginia that extends out to the southwest between Kentucky and Tennessee. It is a half mile from the interstate and about forty minutes from the Tri Cities Regional Airport in Blountville, Tennessee, which offers flights to and from Atlanta, Charlotte, and Memphis, as well as such exotic destinations as Orlando, Cincinnati, and Detroit. Nine exits away down the interstate from Emory is historic Abingdon, the oldest town beyond the Blue Ridge and home to the Barter Theater—where Gregory Peck, Ernest Borgnine, and Patricia Neal got their starts. It is still a regional center for the arts, and people come from many miles around just to go to the movies. The Virginia Creeper National Trail, named for the steam trains that once chugged over its route, connects Abingdon with the Mount Rogers National Recreational Area. A little further away are the "Tri Cities" of Bristol, Virginia, where the Bristol Caverns are located; Johnson City, Tennessee, which the college website recommends for clubbing and shopping; and Kingsport, Tennessee, with its charming park and planetarium.

The student who needs or merely craves the excitement of a fast-paced urban location would probably not be greatly impressed with the attractions of Bristol, Johnson City, and Kingsport, even if they were closer to campus. Most Emory and Henry students have family and friends nearby. But the urban or suburban students from out of state might find the initial transition something of a challenge. The southern Appalachians constitute a distinct American region with a culture all its own, and the college has not turned its back on its roots. Even students from the Virginia tidewater or those parts of Tennessee that run along the Mississippi might feel a certain invigorating culture shock here. The Greek system, which is a bit of an anachronism elsewhere, here has served a real purpose, helping students adjust to campus life and creating small

SUGGESTED CORE

The college's general education requirements should be supplemented by the following courses to complete a core curriculum: Philosophy 201: History of Ancient and Medieval Philosophy; Religion 311: Early Christianity; Political Science 340: History of Political Philosophy; English 360: Shakespeare; and History 211: American Civilization to 1861

ALL-AMERICAN COLLEGES

quasi-familial groups. Emory and Henry has a dozen Greek letter fraternities and sororities.

All full-time students under the age of twenty-two are required to live on campus and participate in the meal plan unless living with a parent, guardian, or spouse, or documented as having special needs. Older, part-time, and special students are accommodated as space permits. Most first-year students are housed in Hillman Hall for men and Wiley Jackson Hall for women. For upperclassmen there is Stuart for men and Weaver Hall for women. Both feature rooms for two.

Emory and Henry competes in baseball, basketball, cross-country, football, golf, soccer, and tennis for men, and basketball, cross-country, soccer, softball, swimming, and volleyball for women (NCAA Division III, Old Dominion Athletic Conference). Among a surprisingly large number of student organizations are the literary magazine *Ampersand*; the college radio station, WEHC-FM; the newspaper, the *Whitetopper*; the Mathematics Association; Outdoor Leadership Program; and many others. Religious groups include the Campus Christian Fellowship, Covenant Disciples Group, Fellowship of Christian Athletes, Habitat for Humanity, and Kerygma. No pagan, Jewish, Catholic, or Orthodox Christian groups are listed, so churchgoing students of the non-Protestant variety will need a car to drive to services in neighboring towns. Bible study groups meet on Monday, Tuesday, and Thursday. In the fall of 2005 these included "The Spiritual Realm: Angels, Demons, and God" on "the character and nature of spiritual beings and their role in the physical and spiritual realms," led by the dean of faculty.

Emory and Henry students are forbidden the use or even possession (on campus), of "fireworks, firearms, ammunition and other weapons or materials which endanger student health or safety." Such an offense "is sufficient cause for disciplinary action." There are, however, more serious matters: "Students are prohibited, on penalty of dismissal, from going into the college duck pond or creek or causing others to do so." Students have evidently tried to find places to hide from busybodies. The college helpfully reminds students that "the Code of Virginia includes a state law making it a misdemeanor to enter a cemetery at night."

The campus is safe. In 2004, one forcible sex offense was reported in a residence hall, as was one burglary, with another five burglaries outside the residences.

In 2004–5 tuition and fees were $19,530, and room and board was $7,040. Approximately 74 percent of students received need-based financial aid. The average grant and scholarship award to incoming freshmen was $11,400. Emory and Henry alumni are unusually generous; the school is ranked in the top 5 percent in the nation for annual alumni donations.

EUREKA COLLEGE

EUREKA, ILLINOIS • WWW.EUREKA.EDU

"If I had to do it all over again," said Ronald Reagan, fortieth president of the United States, "I'd go to Eureka College." Of course, that is where Reagan really went, along with his brother Neil, in the 1930s. It was here, during a student uproar over the administration's decision to eliminate certain programs, that Ronald Reagan stepped into leadership. As a freshman he made his first public speech—which resulted in a student strike and the resignation of the college president. The future president was a starter on the Red Devils' offensive line and swam for the college team. He began his acting career as a member of the Drama Club. "The institution is publicly proud of Ronald W. Reagan," says a Eureka student; the college's Reagan Exhibit draws thousands of visitors each year. The presidential connection means that Eureka has a strong institutional stake in remaining friendly to conservatives. But it also offers a serious education in a traditional college environment.

Academic Life: Morning in America

February 6 is a big day for Eureka—being both Ronald Reagan's birthday and the date Eureka was founded in 1855 by abolitionists affiliated with the Christian Church (Disciples of Christ). Eureka was one of the first colleges in the nation to admit men and women on an equal basis. Some 150 years later, Eureka College continues to produce leaders through its solid curriculum and unique programs, such as the Reagan fellowships and Sandifer mentorships (more on which below).

"Not only does Eureka College emphasize liberal learning, but it also takes seriously its original foundations in faith and service. Public and community service, responsible citizenship, and the commitment to putting higher ideals into action are cultivated," says a former student. "Whether graduates become company, college, or even U.S. presidents, Eureka has discovered the secret of educating leaders through transforming young lives and building community through service," says college president J. David Arnold. Recent graduates have been accepted into graduate programs at Stanford, Yale, George Washington University, Tulane, the University of Chicago, and Johns Hopkins.

According to the catalog, Eureka's general education program seeks to "engage students in the exploration and acquisition of the knowledge, skills, and values that provide a foundation for lifelong excellence in learning, service, and leadership." Though not a true core, the distribution requirements ensure exposure to the colleges' five

ALL-AMERICAN COLLEGES

divisions: Education, Fine and Performing Arts, Humanities, Science and Mathematics, and Social Sciences and Business. "The faculty as a whole remains committed to the ideals of a liberal education and this is reflected in the general education requirements," says a student.

The following is required of every student, regardless of major:

- "Interdisciplinary Studies 101," an orientation course emphasizing service and writing, taken in the first semester;
- "Western Civilization and Culture" I and II;
- "Composition" I and II, plus a total of twelve additional writing-intensive courses (they're not *that* intensive; these classes require "at least twelve to fifteen pages of writing" per semester);
- one mathematics course at the pre-calculus level or higher;
- one course in laboratory science chosen from biology, chemistry, physical science, or physics (e.g., "Field Biology," "Chemistry I," "Introduction to Astronomy," or "Methods of Science and Critical Thinking");
- one literature course from the English, French, Spanish, or theater department, as well as one course in philosophy or religion (such as "Ancient Philosophy," "Metaphysics," "Western Religious Traditions," or "The History of Religion in America");
- one theory course and one applied course from different disciplines in the fine and performing arts—options include "Painting," "Survey of Music," and "Introduction to Acting" (these courses can be replaced by participation in chorale or chamber singers, or by taking private lessons in voice, piano, or organ);
- either "General Psychology" or "Principles of Sociology," plus one course chosen from the following: "Principles of Macroeconomics," "Principles of Microeconomics," American government (either state or local), or any history course in the social sciences;
- a single health course, "Wellness," which includes an individual health assessment and physical activity component such as yoga, jogging, or tennis;
- a Global Awareness course, which can be in Greek, French, or Spanish through the 225 level; participation in an approved international study/cultural study program; or two courses from a list that includes "International Business," "Non-Western Literature," "World Geography," and "Minority Peoples in the United States"; and
- a senior capstone course that explores "the great issues which have confronted humankind, issues with both historical roots and contemporary relevance."

Thus, every student must take a yearlong course in Western civilization. The team-taught course considers "cultural questions that speak to present Western culture and have animated Western civilization from its beginning." Students speak enthusiastically about the course; one says it provided him with "a greater awareness of where [we] live and how it came to be." The college has produced its own reader for the course, and students read excerpts from a wide range of original sources. The first semester focuses on politics, economics, and social issues with the help of Plato, Aristotle, Machiavelli, Hobbes, Locke, Rousseau, Augustine, Marx, Swift, Huxley, and others. During the second semester, students study religion, aesthetics, and intellectual issues with readings from Luther, Gandhi, Plato, Darwin, and the like.

Eureka offers thirty undergraduate majors and preprofessional training in art or music therapy, engineering, ministry, law, medicine, dentistry, and veterinary medicine. Nearly 40 percent of Eureka students participate in the arts. The college's small size, about 550 students, and student-faculty ratio of 13 to 1 means plenty of personal attention. Classes are kept small, usually about fifteen students.

Although most of Eureka's departments are small and have limited offerings, the courses are solid and most teachers are exceptional. "Many of the resources found at medium to larger private colleges will not be found at Eureka College simply because of its size," says a graduate. "This deficiency is more than overcome by the quality of the faculty and their instruction." One of the strongest departments is political science and history, a combined major with course requirements from both disciplines. Students take basic courses in American history and government, European history from 1660 to the present, comparative government, and political philosophy. Business administration, another strong program, emphasizes internship experiences. Majors intern at nearby corporations such as Caterpillar and State Farm Insurance. Sometimes they go further afield: nearly 20 percent of internships have been international. Enrollment in the education department is also high.

Professors and students alike see teaching as the college's greatest strength. "Teaching is central to who we are as an institution and a family. It is what we do. It is what we are all about," says a professor. Scott Wolland, a Eureka graduate, says: "The amount of time the teachers make for students, the genuine concern they have for the minds and souls of their students, their willingness to take on the role of mentor, these are what

VITAL STATISTICS
Religious affiliation: Christian Church (Disciples of Christ)
Total enrollment: 538
Total undergraduates: 538
ACT median: 22
Applicants: 1,100
Applicants accepted: 73%
Accepted applicants who enrolled: 28%
Tuition: $13,760
Room and board: $6,200
Freshman retention rate: 67%
Graduation rate: 46% (4 yrs.), 52% (6 yrs.)
Courses with fewer than 20 students: 90%
Student-faculty ratio: 13:1
Courses taught by graduate students: none
Most popular majors: education, business, history
Students living on campus: 91%
Guaranteed housing for four years? yes
Students in fraternities: 30% sororities: 31%

ALL-AMERICAN COLLEGES

make Eureka College such a wonderful place to learn and live." Wolland was student body president from 1995 to 1996 and is currently on the alumni board of directors. He is a security specialist for the Department of Homeland Security in Washington, D.C., and serves as a lieutenant in the U.S. Coast Guard Reserve. "It's hard for me to think about whom I would be today if I had not taken that first honors seminar on Plato's *Statesman* with Dr. Scott Hemmenway," says Wolland. "Professor Hemmenway took my interest in ideas and the past and turned them into a love for the truth about the noble and the beautiful and the good. It was through Scott that I confronted the eternal questions and the possible answers to those questions as presented in the greatest thinkers of the Western tradition," he says.

Students highly recommend Hemmenway in philosophy as a true scholar and committed teacher. One describes him as "*the* defender of the liberal arts at Eureka."

> *"The amount of time the teachers make for students, the genuine concern they have for the minds and souls of their students, their willingness to take on the role of mentor, these are what make Eureka College such a wonderful place to learn and live."*

Wesley Phelan is the "brilliant and dedicated" one-man political science department. An expert in constitutional law, Phelan teaches an independent-study course on the LSAT—which may explain Eureka's 90 percent success rate in placing students who apply to law schools. Junius Rodriguez in history is another favorite, recommended by students and faculty alike. One student describes John Halpin as "the best and most inspirational teacher I have ever had." Other excellent professors include Richard Sanders in history, Harry Fisher and Paul Lister in business, Bill Davis and Brian Sajko in theater, Paul Small and Mike Tolliver in biology, Loren Logsden in English, and Karen Bartelt in chemistry.

Most students feel the campus is friendly toward conservative or religious students. While professors are predominantly liberal, "Eureka College is all about free and open debate," says one teacher. Wolland says, "Eureka's location in a small midwestern town lends itself towards an apolitical atmosphere, and it's my experience that the student body is generally conservative in temperament. But there is true political diversity and tolerance at the institution. It was never my experience that campus politics intruded into the classroom nor did I know of conservative or religious students feeling unwelcome in any class." Another student agrees: "Eureka's professors and students surprisingly keep a very open mind about almost everything. The religious community of Eureka is very diverse and very respectful."

Each year the college selects five incoming freshmen to receive the Reagan fellowship, a full-tuition scholarship for four years. Reagan fellows participate in special activities focused around leadership training and serve two summer "monitorships," paid for by the program, with selected leaders in their chosen fields. Past mentors have included a U.S. ambassador and a former U.S. secretary of state. Approximately seventy-five candidates visit campus in February to compete for the fellowships through a series of interviews and group activities. Most of the faculty participate in selecting the fellows who best demonstrate academic, service, and leadership achievement and potential.

While the Reagan fellowship is highly competitive, Eureka's Sandifer mentorship is available to any student who maintains a 3.5 cumulative GPA through the end of their sophomore year and has an established record of leadership and service while at Eureka. The college will pay expenses up to $2,500 for mentorships anywhere in the world. The mentorships are usually four to eight weeks long and involve significant elements of research, study, or work.

Student Life: Ten Miles from the Movies

Eureka (population 5,000), is located in the heart of Illinois, thirty miles from Peoria, forty miles from Bloomington–Normal, and two and a half hours from Chicago. Locally, students can shop at Dollar General or walk to the bowling alley. There is a nearby lake and park with walking and biking trails. The nearest movie theater is in Washington, a city of 13,000, about ten miles away. The town of Eureka ended its dry status in April 2004, but local establishments have yet to sell alcohol.

SUGGESTED CORE
1. English 310: Classical Literature
2. Philosophy 250: Ancient Philosophy
3. Religion 217/219: Introduction to the Hebrew Scriptures / Introduction to the New Testament
4. Religion 321: Seminar on Classical Christian Thought
5. Political Science 320: Political and Social Philosophy (*closest match*)
6. English 330: Seminar in British Literature (*may focus on Shakespeare once in a while, but is only offered in alternate years*)
7. History 250: History of the United States to 1865
8. No suitable course.

In spite of, or perhaps because of, its remote location, Eureka students manage to have fun, and campus life is steeped in tradition. "Eureka is more than a college. It is a community, very close-knit; with a rich history of traditions that binds its members together," says a former student. Another student reports that "Eureka College has a way of attracting all the right people and keeping them there with its charm and warmth and homey atmosphere."

Freshman begin their tenure at Eureka during the opening convocation's "Ivy Ceremony." Each freshman places a sprig of ivy into a basket, a symbol of their entry into the Eureka community. At graduation, seniors form a circle holding an ivy chain. Each graduate is cut loose from the circle, signifying his departure from the community and entry into the world. Both Homecoming and Founder's Day are formally celebrated with parades, competitions, and processions. "Homecoming is huge," says one student. At Christmas time, students gather in front of the chapel for the annual Christmas tree lighting followed by carol singing and hot chocolate at the college president's house. Each semester students are freed from classes for Term Study Day. At 9 a.m., the cafeteria opens for breakfast, which is served up by faculty members.

Lincoln Rock marks the place on Eureka's historic campus where, in 1856, Abraham Lincoln gave a ninety-minute speech on behalf of Republican presidential nominee John C. Fremont. Suffragette Susan B. Anthony and educational reformer Horace Mann also once spoke on campus. Two campus buildings, the Chapel and Burruss Dickinson Hall, are listed in the National Register of Historic Places. Throughout its 150-year history, the 112-acre campus has grown to include twenty-four academic and residential buildings, an open-air theater, an arboretum, and athletic facilities. The Reagan Exhibit, housed in the Cerf Center, features the largest collection of Reagan memorabilia outside of the Reagan Library in California. More than 10,000 visitors come to campus each year to visit the exhibit and the Reagan Peace Garden.

Student participation in extracurriculars is highly encouraged, and the small student body takes advantage of the ample opportunities to get involved in service organizations, governing councils, the arts, and athletics. The Eureka Red Devils compete in Division III NCAA athletics in men's football, basketball, swimming, tennis, golf, track, and baseball, and in women's volleyball, basketball, swimming, tennis, golf, track, and softball. Men's and women's soccer and men's and women's cross-country will be offered as club sports in the fall of 2006, moving to Division III competition status the following year. There is also an extensive program of intramural sports such as flag football, badminton, and bowling. The student-run Campus Activities Board plans entertainment events throughout the year, bringing a wide range of activities to campus, including movies, concerts, demonstrations by professional pool players, and, yes, hypnotists.

The college website lists a variety of official student organizations, including academic and honor societies, sororities and fraternities, service and religious organizations such as Habitat for Humanity, and special-interest groups such as the College Republicans. The CRs have a strong presence on campus and have brought in speakers such as Ann Coulter, Gary Aldrich, Ed Meese, and Star Parker. There are active Campus Crusade and Disciples of Christ organizations on campus and weekly on-campus chapel services.

All full-time students are required to live in one of Eureka's seven residence halls. Greek students typically live in their Greek houses, of which Eureka has six (including Tau Kappa Epsilon, whose membership included Ronald Reagan); there are three sorority houses and three fraternity houses, two of which are off campus. Langston Hall, the newest residence hall on campus, houses upperclassmen in suite-style living. Students each have their own room and share a bathroom with one other student of the same sex. All other residences are single-sex. Residence halls and Greek houses maintain the same visitation policy, whereby members of the opposite sex are permitted in student rooms at any time with the roommate's approval. The campus is a very safe one, with only a few minor liquor and drug violations reported in 2004. Eureka Police patrol the campus between 7 p.m. and 3 a.m., and officers will escort students at night if requested.

The college has tried to make its education affordable through the "Eureka Idea," a pricing strategy implemented in 2004 that lowered tuition by 30 percent. The program eliminated the practice of "discounting," instead combining a low flat-rate tuition of $14,000 per year with merit scholarships. State and federal educational grants reduce tuition even more, making Eureka one of the most affordable private educations in the country. Designed to increase enrollment, the strategy seems to be working: enrollment jumped 28 percent the first year it was implemented. With room, board, and fees estimated at another $6,000, the total cost of a Eureka education is about $19,000. More than 90 percent of Eureka students receive some kind of financial aid. The average student loan debt of a recent graduate is $13,277.

GEORGE FOX UNIVERSITY

NEWBERG, OREGON • WWW.GEORGEFOX.EDU

"The university from which you earn an academic degree is part of you for the rest of your life," announces George Fox University. "You are 'branded' with your diploma and transcript. Each graduate school or future employer will know your educational identity." The distinctive brand of George Fox is Christian: "Our faculty, staff, and administration are committed to the purpose and person of Jesus Christ. They are ready to be your friends, teachers, role models, and mentors." Students and alumni agree that this lofty aspiration is true to a remarkable extent at GFU, a theologically conservative school in the tradition of the Society of Friends.

Notice the distinctively Quaker language here: the "purpose and person" of Jesus Christ. According to the Quakers, Jesus is alive today as an Inner Light to accomplish his divine purpose in and through us. That is why education is so important to Quakers of all sects. George Fox University's first objective is to "teach all truth as God's truth, integrating all fields of learning around the person and work of Jesus Christ, bringing the divine revelations through sense, reason, and intuition to the confirming test of Scripture."

A further objective of the university is to "maintain a program of varied activities that directs the student to a commitment to Christ as Lord and Savior, encourages attitudes of reverence and devotion toward God, leads to recognition that the revealed commandments of God are the supreme criteria of the good life, enables the student to mirror the example of Christ in human relationships, and develops a greater desire to serve humanity in a spirit of Christian love." If you are a lifestyle conservative tired of the culture wars, an evangelical Christian looking for a first-class education, or a Quaker or Mennonite uncomfortable with the theological modernism some of your churchmates take for granted, take a good look at George Fox University. It's an inspiring place.

Academic Life:
Following the Inner Light

A humorist once defined the "Quaker" faith of the Religious Society of Friends as pertaining to the fatherhood of God, the brotherhood of Man, and the neighborhood of Philadelphia; indeed, the three flagship Quaker colleges, Haverford, Bryn Mawr, and Swarthmore, are located in the western suburbs of Philly. The Friends-sponsored Earlham College is further away, in Richmond, Indiana, but Oregon's George Fox University is, in many, many ways, about as far away from all of them as you can get in America—which is all to the good.

Eastern Quakers tend to distance themselves from the Christian faith, often condemning traditional statements of belief as "Christocentric" and therefore "exclusive" and wicked. For many of them, religion—beyond the silent-group meditation of their Meetings for Worship—consists of political action directed against war and capitalism and in favor of legal abortion, homosexual rights, and environmentalism. From them you would never know that George Fox, who founded the Society of Friends around 1650, was an evangelical Christian. He rejected the services and sacraments of the Church of England because he believed that in doing so he was turning directly to Christ—whom he believed dwelt within every man and woman as an Inner Light.

George Fox University unabashedly follows the Christocentric teaching of Fox and other early Quakers. Today it maintains the Quaker "witness" for peace, justice, and the environment, but without the ideologically motivated anti-American slant of all too many eastern Friends. George Fox University is a ministry of the Northwest Yearly Meeting of Friends, which is part of Evangelical Friends International and not affiliated with either of the two major American Quaker denominations.

The school's solid connection to its roots shows up in its core curriculum. Students must complete the following:

- "Freshman Composition" (students may test out);
- "Freshman Seminar," a "small seminar-style topical course for the first five weeks of fall semester, meeting weekly with an advisor and a returning student peer advisor";
- either "Bible Survey" or a two-course sequence, "Literature of the Old Testament" and "Literature of the New Testament";
- "Christian Foundations," a church history and theology course;
- "History and Doctrine of Friends" (for Quaker students; others may substitute one of several solid theology electives);
- four humanities courses, including one (but not more than two) in fine arts,

VITAL STATISTICS

Religious affiliation: Society of Friends (Quaker)
Total enrollment: 3,210
Total undergraduates: 1,865
SAT/ACT midranges: SAT V: 470–600, M: 480–600; ACT: 26 (median)
Applicants: 1,522
Applicants accepted: 82%
Accepted applicants who enrolled: 47%
Tuition: $21,400
Room and board: $6,780
Freshman retention rate: 79%
Graduation rate: 58% (4 yrs.), 63% (6 yrs.)
Courses with fewer than 20 students: 63%
Student-faculty ratio: 12:1
Courses taught by graduate students: none
Most popular majors: business administration, biology, elementary education
Students living on campus: 65%
Guaranteed housing for four years? yes
Students in fraternities or sororities: none

history, and literature, and not more than one in philosophy—all solid choices, consisting of surveys of Western art, writing, music, and history;
- one course in mathematics;
- two courses in natural science;
- two courses in social science (e.g., "Principles of Microeconomics" "Principles of Macroeconomics," "Introduction to Political Science," "General Psychology," and "Principles of Sociology");
- one course in oral communication, acting, or oral interpretation of literature;
- "Lifelong Fitness" and an additional credit of physical fitness;
- one course involving global studies (foreign language courses count);
- one course involving either global studies or "domestic cross-cultural" (i.e., minority) studies; and
- a senior capstone course, "Faith, Liberal Arts, and the World."

According to the college, the senior capstone course is designed to "encourage students to integrate their specialized knowledge and general education with Christian faith, in the context of addressing a public issue of current significance. . . . Students will participate in groups to research the chosen public issue and formulate an action proposal."

This core seems focused, fittingly, on faith rather than culture; indeed, the school's strong theological focus gives unity to studies which at other schools might remain diffuse. At George Fox, "interdisciplinary" study does not mean a vague, bland survey of things the student doesn't intend to pursue seriously, but a dialogue among students who have mastered particular disciplines on matters of common concern—leading to a plan of action, as formulated in the senior capstone class. The school's demand that the graduating student reformulate his faith commitment in the light of what he has learned, and relate it to his sense of vocation in the world, shows how serious the university remains about its mission.

Fox offers sixty undergraduate (B.A. and B.S.) majors and concentrations, from religion and philosophy to church recreation and fashion merchandising/interior design. The school offers advanced degrees in such fields as business, counseling, education, leadership, psychology, and seminary.

If at other colleges and universities the teaching is often politicized, at Fox it is "theologized"—but that theology is not politically neutral. A student with strong libertarian or neoconservative beliefs will find them challenged regularly by the firm witness of the evangelical Quaker faith, which bears superficial resemblances to "progressive" politics. However, students soon see the difference for themselves.

"Attending George Fox has been an amazing experience for me," one student reports:

> The Christian atmosphere is wonderful, as there are people all around who truly care about your well-being. For me, coming from California, a very liberal state, there have been several instances here where I have been amazed by religion in the classroom, something absolutely pro-

hibited in my home state. My first class was "Introduction to Political Science" with Professor Mark Hall. Before he began class, he asked that we pray. He said a short, twenty-second prayer, and then continued. I had another class with him later that day, and he did the same thing. I assumed it was just a first-day-of-school ritual. However, for the rest of semester he always began his classes with prayer. Mark went beyond that as well. He also incorporated the Christian faith into his analysis of political events. Everything we studied in his class was viewed through a Christian lens. This has enabled me to spread my faith into all facets of my life, even school work. This is one of many examples of how George Fox can help a person grow in faith.

Faculty devote their time and attention to help students grow; the student-faculty ratio at George Fox is a fine 12 to 1, with no courses taught by graduate students—despite the four doctoral programs offered by the school. Some 63 percent of all courses have fewer than twenty students.

Another professor praised by students is the chair of religious studies. One student says, "Paul Anderson's compassion for the world and love for his students, coupled with his excellent teaching, make him one of the best teachers I've ever had. He challenges me to think outside of the box, both in my faith and intellectually." Other faculty recommendations include the aforementioned Mark Hall in political science, Corey Beals and Phil Smith in philosophy, and Caitlin Corning in history. One student says, "These four professors have been integral in my development as a student, both in the intellectual realm as well as in the spiritual realm. They have been palpable examples that you can be a thinking person as well as a Christian. I very much admire these professors and am privileged and honored to take classes from them and with them." Another student praises Bill Joliff in English as "one of the most challenging professors intellectually that I've ever had," who "challenges the core of students' existences, asking us to step outside our upbringings and to discover what truth is." In French, one student points to Sylvette Norre, who "expands students' worldviews by asking us to look at the world from a non-American perspective. She is not only a wonderful French teacher, but cares about our spiritual formation. She continuously asks us to be concerned with the state of the world and to make a difference in it."

> *"The Christian atmosphere is wonderful. . . . My political science professor always began his classes with prayer, and incorporated the Christian faith into his analysis of political events. Everything we studied in his class was viewed through a Christian lens. This has enabled me to spread my faith into all facets of my life, even school work."*

1. No suitable course.
2. Philosophy 380: History of Philosophy Survey (*closest match*)
3. Biblical Studies 101/102: Literature of the Old Testament / New Testament
4. Religion/History 401: Christianity in History I
5. Political Science 280: Introduction to Political Philosophy
6. Literature 379: Shakespeare
7. History 457/458: The Colonial Experience / The Making of the American Republic
8. No suitable course.

H. David Brandt, who has served as president since 1998, was raised in the Evangelical Mennonite Brethren Church, attended Wheaton College, and taught physics there before earning his doctorate. He served for over a decade as dean and vice president for academic affairs at Messiah College before his appointment at George Fox.

Student Life: Brotherhood, Yes. Fraternities, No.

George Fox's main campus of over one hundred acres is surrounded on three sides by Newberg, Oregon, with Hess Creek flowing along the fourth. Newberg, a community of just over 20,000, is located between Portland and the state capital, Salem, although not on the main highway. About a third of the student body lives off campus, many others live at home, and the rest are able to visit home on the weekends. Because of the kind of student Fox attracts, there isn't the kind of estrangement from family that seems to be the norm elsewhere. The school's atmosphere of brotherhood reflects its Friends heritage.

Some 18 percent of the freshmen entering in 2004 described themselves as nondenominational Christians, 14 percent as Baptists of different varieties, and only 8 percent as Quakers. Although Fox boasts students from twenty-seven states and twenty-two countries, the student body has a strong regional character, with 82 percent coming from Oregon and Washington.

The school expects students to conduct themselves in accord with Christian morality (as traditionally understood) both on campus and off. No alcohol, tobacco, illicit drugs, or pornography are to be indulged in on or off campus—and no clothing or decor advertising any such products are to be displayed on campus (e.g., no Cuervo hats). "Immodest attire" is forbidden on campus.

George Fox offers varsity volleyball, soccer, cross-country, basketball, softball, tennis, and outdoor track and field for women, and soccer, cross-country, basketball, baseball, tennis, and outdoor track and field for men. The college boasts that "the values of athletics are integrated with the goals of Christian higher education in a process that includes physical conditioning, managing emotions, courage, teamwork, cooperation, and being gracious in winning and losing." There are no athletic scholarships.

The Associated Student Community sponsors international, outdoors, multicultural, emergency relief, and social work clubs, the College Republicans, and Sigma Zeta, an honor society for science and mathematics. If there are any Democrats at the college, they are unorganized or unofficial. Urban Services volunteers at soup kitchens for the homeless in Portland and Salem; a men's ministry and an international coffee shop offer fellowship; there is student-led worship every Friday and Sunday morning and Tuesday evening. There are no fraternities or sororities.

Most resident students who don't go home for the weekend find their worship needs met on campus. For others, there are several Protestant churches and a Roman Catholic church in Newberg. In addition, nearby Portland offers a great variety of religious resources, and Salem is home to the Mount Angel Abbey of the Swiss Benedictine Congregation.

The abbey is one of the great attractions in the region, featuring a world famous library designed by Alvar Aalto, pipe organs built by Martin Ott, and a small museum. The museum holds collections of photographs and icons of the Russian Orthodox Old Believer community that settled in the area shortly after the Communist revolution, along with what is reputed to be the largest hairball ever retrieved, two and a half pounds, from a hog's stomach. (Monks, like Quakers, have an odd sense of humor at times.) The abbey is also host to a world-famous Bach festival in late July. For a more boisterous celebration at the beginning of the academic year, the town of Mount Angel features an annual Oktoberfest with a plethora of German food and drink and dancing in the streets. The 2006 festival will feature Nashville accordionist LynnMarie of the Boxhounds, the first woman ever nominated for a Best Polka Grammy.

The dorms on campus are of recent vintage (not so long ago, GFU only had around one hundred students) and are more functional than quaint. Men and women are segregated by building or wing, and bathrooms are not shared. Intervisitation between the sexes is restricted and must be conducted with open doors. Twelve dormitory burglaries were reported on the Newberg campus in 2004, and three cars were stolen, but no violent crime has been reported in recent years.

Tuition at George Fox was last reported as $21,400, with room and board costing an additional $6,780. However, some 81 percent of students receive need-based financial aid. The average student loan debt of recent Fox graduates is $15,026.

GORDON COLLEGE

WENHAM, MASSACHUSETTS • WWW.GORDON.EDU

Gordon College was founded in Boston in 1889 as a missionary training institute. It was named for its founder, the Rev. Dr. A. J. Gordon, a then-famous Boston preacher. In 1955, Gordon moved to its Wenham, Massachusetts campus, and in 1985, it merged with another Christian institution, Barrington College. The end result was the only nondenominational Christian college in this section of the Blue States. Gordon describes itself as a traditional New England liberal arts college—one which is committed to teaching the latest in science, philosophy, literature, and so forth, while working with the student's faith in Christ, not against it. (Believe it or not, such was the original spirit and mission of almost all the Ivy League schools.) The school maintains a rigorous scholastic atmosphere, small classes, and a moderately strong core curriculum that guarantees students a broad-based (as well as a faith-based) education. Its academic quality was recognized by the John Templeton Foundation's *Colleges That Encourage Character Development*. For intellectually serious evangelical students who wish to study in the snowy northeast, Gordon is the first place to apply.

Academic Life: Freedom within a Framework

Gordon College says up front that its outlook is based on the Bible, but it is not a "Bible college." One faculty member says, "Christian colleges come in all shapes and sizes. Please don't confuse us with places that are rather deliberately constructed to escape the challenges and responsibilities of contemporary life. Such rules as there are—no alcohol on campus—are in place to keep us focused on why we are here, not as remnants of traditional morality. We read the authors we choose to read, and live, nude models are used in the art classes, et cetera. There is a great sense of trust among the faculty and between faculty and administration." In other words, Gordon does not wish to be known as a comfortable place for true-blue fundamentalists.

The school says that its goal is not indoctrination, but education based on the Word of God. Gordon offers thirty-six majors across five academic divisions: Education, Fine Arts, Humanities, Natural Sciences, and Social Sciences. The most popular majors are English, psychology, and business administration. The school also has the distinction of conferring three separate undergraduate degrees: Bachelor of Science, Bachelor of Arts, and Bachelor of Music.

The core curriculum is substantive—though it could and probably should be a little stricter. Students must complete the following:

- "Christianity, Character, and Culture," a small-group, yearlong interdisciplinary course which focuses on character development and the role of the Christian within society;
- two semesters in pursuit of "an understanding of the Old and New Testaments within their historical, geographical, literary, and cultural contexts";
- a humanities requirement, which allows students (rather too much) freedom to choose between a philosophy course, such as "The Great Ideas: Antiquity" and a literature course, such as "Women's Literature: International";
- a fine arts course, such as "Survey of Musical Masterworks" or "Arts in the City," or a study-abroad program in Orvieto, Italy;
- a history course, such as "Western Civilization in World Context" or "Modern Civilization," and one other social science course, such as "Microeconomics" or "Psychological Perspectives on Reality";
- two semesters in the natural sciences, mathematics or computer science, including one lab;
- two semesters of a foreign language; choices include French, Spanish, German, Greek, and Hebrew;
- at least one semester in a writing or writing-intensive class; and
- a noncredit wellness/physical education class.

One professor says that "the core is under revision, but the aim is to improve it, not to gut it. It's not four years of Great Books, but it's light years from an undirected, cafeteria-style approach."

For those who want more focused fare, we recommend the Jerusalem-Athens Forum, a new interdisciplinary honors program consisting primarily of a Great Books course in the history of Christian thought and literature. The program helps students reflect on the relationship between faith and reason, deepen their own sense of voca-

VITAL STATISTICS

Religious affiliation:
  Nondenominational
  Christian
Total enrollment: 1,672
Total undergraduates: 1,617
SAT/ACT midranges: SAT V:
  550–660, M: 540–650;
  ACT: 23–28
Applicants: 1,222
Applicants accepted: 83%
*Accepted applicants who
  enrolled:* 47%
Tuition: $21,930
Room and board: $6,270
Freshman retention rate: 88%
Graduation rate: 60% (4 yrs.),
  73% (6 yrs.)
*Courses with fewer than 20
  students:* 65%
Student-faculty ratio: 14:1
*Courses taught by graduate
  students:* none
Most popular majors:
  English, psychology,
  business administration
Students living on campus:
  88%
*Guaranteed housing for four
  years?* yes
*Students in fraternities or
  sororities:* none

tion, and stimulate their capacities for intellectual and moral leadership. For participation in the program students receive twelve hours of elective course credits—including core credits, if needed, for history (four credits), philosophy (two credits), and literature (two credits). The program covers all costs and also provides students with a stipend to help them subscribe to a scholarly periodical and pursue vocational exploration and career development. As one professor describes it, "The Jerusalem-Athens Forum for fifteen sophomores combines selectivity, a close look at the Western tradition, and high-powered guest lecturers."

The school's admissions committee says it is more interested in an integrated person than a rigorous academic profile. A faculty member reports, "The faculty, as well as the students, must profess Christian orthodoxy *and* a commitment to a vibrant intellectual life. What Harry Blamires [formerly of Wheaton] called the 'Christian mind' is overtly encouraged in both students and faculty." The teacher continues, "Our best students match up with anyone, something we've discovered from our sixteen-year experience in sending people to Oxford. Our students tend to be serious, earnest and diligent without a lot of flash and dash. It may not attract headlines, but it's very satisfying in a classroom setting."

> *"The faculty, as well as the students, must profess Christian orthodoxy* and *a commitment to a vibrant intellectual life. . . . The 'Christian mind' is overtly encouraged in both students and faculty. Our best students match up with anyone, something we've discovered from our sixteen-year experience in sending people to Oxford."*

Teaching at Gordon is said to be strong—although some departments such as history, music, languages, and literature rely heavily on part-time faculty. In fact, 36 percent of courses are taught by part-timers, which limits the availability of some professors to their students. The English department (one of the most popular) and communications department are said to be a bit weak, due to aging teachers and the school's reported problems in attracting full-time (as opposed to adjunct) faculty.

But quite a number of teachers come highly recommended by students. Gordon sources speak highly of Thomas Howard in history (also director of the Jerusalem-Athens Forum), William Harper and Timothy Sherratt in political science, Bert Hodges in psychology, Malcolm Reid in philosophy, Steve Smith and Bruce Webb in economics, Bruce Herman in art, Dorothy Boorse in biology, and Thomas Brooks and David Rox in music. Dr. Marvin Wilson, professor of biblical and theological studies, is an expert on Jewish and Semitic studies. Jennifer Hevelone-Harper is chair of the history department and holds a Ph.D. from Princeton, where she studied under Augustine scholar Peter Brown.

No description of Gordon would be complete without a nod to its noteworthy music department. At this relatively small school of fewer than 1,700 students, one can earn a Bachelor of Arts in Music, a Bachelor of Music in Performance, or a Masters in Music Education. The school also hosts a nonprofit organization, Christians in the Visual Arts.

By working with the Council of Christian Colleges and Universities, Gordon offers some impressive off-campus opportunities for students interested in experiential learning. Unsurprisingly, as Gordon students can attest, such programs go well beyond drinking beer in another country. The options include semester-long programs in Uganda, Russia, the Middle East, and China. The Gordon-in-Oxford program is available to qualified juniors and seniors. Art students have access to the Gordon in Orvieto program, which allows them to spend a semester in this ancient Italian hill town between Rome and Florence. There, they are introduced to the Italian language through an interdisciplinary course in the cultural history of the Renaissance, plus two classes in studio, history, or theory. For students who are not busy earning next semester's tuition, the school also offers brief international seminars during academic breaks.

Some programs don't require students to go so far away. The Gordon-in-Boston program uses the city as its classroom, exposing students to various parts of the city in order to discuss poverty, urban renewal, and the role of art in the city. The Lynn Initiative takes students to Lynn, Massachusetts, to participate in various outreach programs. Another program offers a comprehensive look at the Christian music industry. This program offers students a chance to use a recording studio, research song writing, develop a marketing plan, design a performance, and bring it all together with a capstone event that involves a ten-day trip to Nashville, Tennessee.

Student Life: Birdwatching and the Bible

Gordon's location enjoys the benefits of both an urban and a rural setting. There's enough countryside for students who like to hike, but the setting is not so bucolic that a quick trip to Boston's Museum of Fine Arts is out of the question. The school buildings, eight of which are residential, are located on several hundred acres of woodlands. The campus is only two miles away from the Atlantic coast and many affluent, beachfront communities. Just down the road is Gloucester, the quaint fishing town featured in the movie *A Perfect Storm*. North of campus is Plum Island, home to the Parker River National Wildlife Refuge, a 4,662-acre site best known for its birdwatching and endless

SUGGESTED CORE
1. English 262: Classical Literature
2. Philosophy 112: The Great Ideas: Antiquity
3. Biblical Studies 101/103: Old Testament History, Literature, and Theology / New Testament History, Literature, and Theology
4. Biblical Studies 305: Development of Christian Thought
5. Political Studies 323: Theories of Politics
6. English 372: Shakespeare
7. History 232: America 1492–1846
8. History 230: Revolutionary Europe 1789–1914 (*closest match*)

ALL-AMERICAN COLLEGES

beaches. In the colder weather, students can head up to New England's major ski areas, which are only a few hours away. Boston is accessible by train in the nearby town of Manchester-by-the-Sea. For access right from the school, students can take the recently launched weekend shuttle bus, which will take them to the "orange line," an arm of the Boston subway—or the "T," as locals call it.

The "Quad" lies at the center of campus. It formerly served as the polo field of the Prince family, from whom the property was originally purchased. Of the 1,600 students, 88 percent live in one of eight dorm buildings. They are required to live on campus unless they are married, live nearby, or are over twenty-three years of age. Apartment-style buildings are reserved for upperclassmen, while the traditional dorms, usually triples, are for freshmen and sophomores. The dorms are not strictly segregated by sex, but male and female quarters are usually separated by a common area and the school is very clear that visitation has its limits. Gordon requires members of the opposite sex to remain in the common area of the dorm they are visiting and to keep the doors open. Resident assistants enforce visiting hours and monitor interactions to prevent any violations. There are also restrictions on drinking alcohol and smoking. In addition, the student handbook states that pranks must be respectful and courteous. (Are there any other kind?)

The school places a healthy emphasis on athletics. The school's athletes, known as the "Fighting Scots," compete in basketball, baseball, track and field, lacrosse, softball, field hockey, tennis, swimming, volleyball, and golf. Facilities include the Bennett Recreational Center, a 72,000-square-foot teaching and sporting venue with an outdoor rock gym and an indoor pool. The Brigham Athletic Complex has a new artificial turf field for lacrosse and field hockey and is surrounded by an NCAA- (Division III) caliber all-weather track. Intramural sports are encouraged. For the more military-minded students, ROTC is on campus to provide leadership, team-building, and decision-making skills to qualified candidates.

While reason dominates in the classroom, faith formation is the ribbon that weaves through the texture of life at Gordon. The school requires all students to earn thirty Christian Life and Worship credits each semester regardless of their work schedule. (Married students and parents of young children can apply to have this reduced to fifteen.) Students earn credits by attending chapel services, attending the various convocations held each week, attending the annual college symposium, or attending the Provost's Film Series. The school does not deny admission to people of other faiths; its ideal is to "agree on the basics and show charity on the peripherals." Despite this irenicist attitude, students from a more liturgical church may find it difficult to fulfill both their own and the school's Sunday obligations. For those willing to travel, nearby Boston offers every kind of worship service imaginable.

The Student Ministry Office has a vast array of opportunities for students to put their faith into action on campus and off. The Community Outreach programs include Adopt-a-Grandparent, Deaf Ministry, Habitat for Humanity, and REALITY Abstinence Educators. The SMO's discipleship opportunities allow for students to engage in prayer, Bible study, mentoring, discussion, and fellowship. Some of those ministries include Campus Crusade for Christ, Companions on the Journey (a mentoring program), the Disaster Relief Organization, International Justice Mission, and Orthodox Christian Fellowship. All of these practices lead up to the missions that the school runs during academic holidays, such as the spring-break trip to Mexico.

The school reports that the cost of discipleship is about $29,000 if you are a "light eater." If you are an "above average" eater—we assume they are referring to *quantity*—add $400. Above and beyond tuition costs, the school raises about $1,500 per student each year to help defray expenses. Several scholarship programs are available, but most students take out government loans. Some 87 percent of students receive need-based financial aid, but the average student loan debt of a recent graduate is rather hefty at $28,039.

GROVE CITY COLLEGE

GROVE CITY, PENNSYLVANIA • WWW.GCC.EDU

Grove City College was founded, in 1876, upon a vision of Christian society that, according to the school, values "free enterprise, civil and religious liberty, representative government, arts and letters, and science and technology." Although historically and informally affiliated with the Presbyterian Church of the United States, the college has never been officially sectarian. Instead of undertaking to spread Calvinism across Pennsylvania, the college took on the broader mission of "fostering intellectual, moral, spiritual, and social development consistent with a commitment to Christian truth, morals, and freedom." Grove City College continues to uphold its founding commitment to a vision of objective truth and liberal learning, and it strives to remain committed to Christian principles while seeking "to provide liberal and professional education of the highest quality that is within the reach of families with modest means who desire a college that will strengthen their children's spiritual and moral character." In other words, it's deeply Christian, quite conservative, and relatively cheap. Grove City is also tightly focused on teaching, offering exciting classes led by dedicated professors. It is one of a small number of schools in the United States that still reflect the once-dominant Protestant ethic that helped shape American culture and society.

The school is quite explicit about its academic and religious agenda, and how these work in tandem (and occasionally in tension) with its embrace of the classical liberal arts:

> The core of the curriculum, particularly in the humanities, consists of books, thinkers, and ideas proven across the ages to be of value in the quest for knowledge. Intellectual inquiry remains open to the questions religion raises and affirms the answers Christianity offers. The ethical absolutes of the Ten Commandments and Christ's moral teachings guide the effort to develop intellect and character in the classroom, chapel, and co-curricular activities. And while many points of view are examined, the College unapologetically advocates preservation of

America's religious, political, and economic heritage of individual freedom and responsibility.

Grove City's presentation of the Western tradition is not of the value-neutral variety to be found, for instance, at St. John's College in Maryland and New Mexico, where the authors of the Great Books—from Plato and Augustine to Hobbes and Marx—tussle for dominance in the minds of students, and where teachers serve as learned, impartial referees. The school is openly committed to defending traditional Christianity and the American political and economic systems. Grove City strives to foster not only the intellectual but also the moral and spiritual, development of its 2,300 students.

Academic Life: Defending the West

Although Grove City offers degrees in business, science, and engineering as well as in the humanities, the school requires all students to complete its extensive core curriculum, so that "Grove City College graduates have the marks of educated persons, whatever their profession." Of the minimum 128 credits needed to graduate, thirty-eight to fifty hours (science majors are exempt from studying a foreign language) go to satisfying the general education requirement.

Within this core, we are happy to note that the largest segment is the Civilization Series, or Humanities Core, a sequence of six classes that examine the "origins, merit, and influence of history's most decisive ideas, literary works, and artistic products." To graduate, all students must take the following:

- "Civilization," an introduction to the principles of the core curriculum;
- "Civilization and the Biblical Revelation," which examines the influence of Christian revelation on Western civilization;
- "Civilization and the Speculative Mind," an analysis and defense of the Christian worldview in comparison with other modern perspectives;
- "Civilization and Literature," a survey of classic literature in light of Christian truth;
- "Civilization and the Arts," which examines works of art and music through the eyes of faith;
- "Modern Civilization in International Perspective," which examines the major events and ideas following the French and American revolutions;

VITAL STATISTICS

Religious affiliation: Presbyterian

Total enrollment: 2,318

Total undergraduates: 2,318

SAT/ACT midranges: SAT V: 575–696, M: 578–688; ACT: 25–30

Applicants: 2,091

Applicants accepted: 47%

Accepted applicants who enrolled: 29%

Tuition: $10,962

Room and board: $5,766

Freshman retention rate: 92%

Graduation rate: 75% (4 yrs.), 86% (6 yrs.)

Courses with fewer than 20 students: 36%

Student-faculty ratio: 16:1

Courses taught by graduate students: none

Most popular majors: elementary education, English, mechanical engineering

Students living on campus: 92%

Guaranteed housing for four years? yes

Students in fraternities: 15% *sororities*: 19%

- "Science, Faith, and Technology," "Science and Religion," or "Foundations of Science";
- one basic social science course in economics, education, political science, psychology, or sociology;
- two courses in statistics, mathematics, or computer science;
- two courses, with labs, in the natural sciences;
- two classes in physical education; and
- courses or tests to demonstrate proficiency to the intermediate level in a foreign language (including French, German, and Spanish, with Greek as an option for students studying religion).

The experience that students have with the humanities component of the general education requirement can vary according to the sections they take. "For some [professors] it is a religious history course, while others teach it in other ways," comments one faculty member. One professor characterizes the Grove City core this way: "Six hours of the core curriculum are devoted to more or less traditional 'Western Civilizations' matters, with enough 'world' perspective tossed in to keep the accreditation authorities at bay. The rest cover topics like 'Biblical Revelation,' et cetera. In Humanities 101 and 302, when it is not taught as a religion course, students will come away with what they might have gotten in two courses in Western Civilizations or World History taught elsewhere." Another criticism some have voiced about the core concerns the readings assigned to students: the quality is high, but the quantity low. Instead of reading entire great works, students read mostly excerpts (and sometimes snippets) compiled into readers. This means they are rarely challenged by encountering important ideas in their original contexts, or by being required to work their way through foundational, if difficult, texts.

> *"Grove City's presentation of the Western tradition is not of the value-neutral variety. . . . The school is openly committed to defending traditional Christianity and the American political and economic systems."*

Grove City College encourages entering freshmen to declare a major at the time of admission, in order to balance the number of students in each program, but it does offer them the chance to wait until the end of their sophomore year by allowing them to choose "Undecided—Liberal Arts" or "Undecided—Science and Engineering." This may present a problem later, however; as one student reports, it can be difficult to get into particular majors for those who do not declare them upon entering.

The college comprises two schools, the School of Arts and Letters and the School of Science and Engineering. The former is larger, with education and English two of the most popular majors, but the School of Science and Engineering is also strong, and the Department of Engineering is particularly recommended by both faculty and students. The education major at Grove City is said to be quite solid and intellectually serious—a fact which in itself makes the school unique. Aspiring high school teachers therefore ought to consider closely what Grove City has to offer.

Students have the opportunity to pursue liberal studies and a professional program at the same time. This offers the advantage of allowing students to gain a humane education and still prepare for specialized professions. One student, double-majoring in biochemistry and Christian thought, says that she appreciates the fact that "the science professors are all very focused on our future, and getting us into good jobs" after school, and finds the Christian thought major "very useful for life." However, some students bite off more than they can chew. Some Grove City undergrads report that the large number of required classes can make it challenging to fulfill all the gen ed requirements while pursuing a single (much less a double) major. Also, while the school is large enough to offer a wide variety of majors, every incoming student must take the same core classes, thus making some of the liberal arts sections much larger than they ought to be. This fact is mirrored in Grove City's 16 to 1 student-faculty ratio—which one might expect to find at a massive state university, rather than a small liberal arts college. Each faculty member teaches four courses (and upwards of 150 students) per semester. Since these are typically four different courses, this means preparing four lectures each week—a burden some teachers call "crushing." "There are dedicated professors, but many are overworked, and classes can be too large," says one professor.

Unsurprisingly, some at the school believe that Grove City has not achieved the proper balance of catechesis and inquiry. One professor says, "There are some very bright students, but the tendency for most is to focus on grades." And apparently a few professors do not always challenge students to question their presuppositions, especially religious and political presuppositions. In some cases, one faculty member suggests, this is attributable to an anti-intellectual prejudice that "questioning faith is wrong," or in some cases, to a super-conservative belief "that anyone left of Reagan is wrong." This professor adds, "There are other faculty, however, who are much more independently minded and critical."

Grove City College is a teaching college and proud of it. As the school advertises to prospective students, "At Grove City College, you'll find professors who like to teach—they don't cloister themselves to work on research while leaving classroom instruction to assistants." All courses are taught by regular faculty, rather than by teaching assistants; 88 percent of the professors have their doctorates. One professor remarks, "Excellence in teaching is a hallmark of Grove City College, and most of the faculty are good teachers." Students appreciate the high quality of classroom instruction and report that faculty make themselves very available. "They are very effective teachers, and they really care about their students," one student remarks.

Despite the primary focus on teaching, the college does urge its faculty to conduct research—in what time they can find. "In recent years, an effort has been made to encourage more scholarship and publication," one professor notes. The college recently awarded several of its faculty one-semester research sabbaticals, marking the second time in the history of the college that sabbaticals were granted. Particularly recommended faculty in the humanities include T. David Gordon, Paul Kemeny, and Paul R. Shaefer in religion and philosophy; Gillis Harp and Gary Smith in history; Michael Coulter, Paul Kengor, and Marvin J. Folkertsma Jr. in political science; James G. Dixon III and Eric Potter in English; Jefferey M. Herbener in economics; and Paul Munson in music. Excellent faculty are also found in the vocational and science programs, including Timothy C. Homan in chemistry; Roger Mackey and John A. Stephens in education; and Linda Christie, Andrew Markley, and John A. Sparks in business.

One worthy resource at the school is the Center for Vision and Values, opened in April 2005. The purpose of the center is "to encourage and to support Grove City College faculty and kindred scholars in faith and freedom scholarship and to teach their ideals and ideas to our students, our nation and the world beyond." In order to do this, the center provides a forum through which students and faculty can conduct and disseminate research and scholarship on the meaning of freedom. One professor explains that "within the Center several 'study groups' have been established to address areas like American culture and terrorism. Students and faculty can affiliate with these study groups to work on special projects or bring in speakers." The Center also hosts conferences and seminars, which include students and scholars from across the country.

The college is led by President Richard G. Jewell, an alumnus. He has been politically active as chairman of the Republican Committee of Allegheny County, and as such has brought many politicians to speak at the college. He remains cochair of the ongoing capital campaign at the college and holds faculty rank as professor of business law and public policy.

Student Life: Observing Standards

Grove City College is located in Grove City, Pennsylvania (pop. 8,000), approximately sixty miles north (and hence an hour away) from cosmopolitan, artsy Pittsburgh. The 150 acres of the college grounds are divided into the Lower and Upper Campus by Wolf Creek. The two campus sections are connected by a footbridge and city streets. Many of the athletic fields and facilities are located on the Lower Campus, while the Upper Campus includes administrative buildings, classrooms, laboratories, the library, chapel, and fine arts center, among other facilities.

The Henry Buhl Library houses 139,000 volumes and offers interlibrary loan services to students and faculty. Other educational resources on campus include a Technological Learning Center, which holds equipment used for computer-assisted instruction; the Rockwell Hall of Science, which contains multimedia classroom and teaching laboratories; and the J. Howard Pew Fine Arts Center, which includes a small theater, a large auditorium, studios, practice rooms, exhibition halls, and an art collection donated by Pew, who was once chairman of the school's board. The college has also recently opened the Hall of Arts and Letters, a state-of-the-art facility which houses the School of Arts and Letters.

The nearly 150 student organizations include a variety of honor societies in academic subjects, professional and academic organizations, service organizations, and the student government association. Religious groups on campus include a Newman Club for Catholics, as well as many nondenominational Protestant groups. There are also a number of special interest organizations, such as the ornithology club, and many political student organizations. The College Libertarians, College Republicans, and College Democrats are all represented on campus. In addition to the college newspaper and yearbook, Grove City College students also produce two other publications: the *Echo*, a creative magazine featuring fiction, photography, and artwork; and the *Entrepreneur*, which is supported by outside funding and features articles by both students and faculty promoting the free market economy (are you catching the theme here?). There are also a number of musical organizations on campus, ranging from a chapel choir to several jazz bands, a stage band, woodwind and brass ensembles, and the college orchestra. Particularly remarkable is the college marching band, which with some 200 members is one of the largest bands for a college of Grove City's modest size.

College athletics plays a modest role at Grove City— the students are pretty busy completing the core requirements and trying to finish a major—but a wide variety of sports are played at both the intercollegiate (NCAA Division III) and intramural levels. The campus has a number of outdoor playing fields, and students enjoy the use of the Physical Learning Center, which houses two swimming pools, eight bowling lanes, a dance studio, and basketball and racquetball courts.

Grove City College offers a number of cultural opportunities on campus through lecture series and its Guest Artist program, which features accomplished performers in music, dance, and drama. Recent visiting artists have included jazz musician Ellis Marsalis, Ballet Magnificat! ("America's premier Christian ballet company"), a youth chorus from the Czech Republic, and a variety of musical groups.

Beyond the opportunities available on campus, Grove City College offers several study-abroad options. Various two-week courses are offered in Europe, China, and Canada during the early January and late-May intersessions. The college also allows students to participate in external programs, from which academic credit can be transferred.

In keeping with the college's mission to "promote spiritual and moral development," Grove City College emphasizes that its charges are "expected to observe Christian moral standards." And we're not talking about the "social gospel" here. Students have been disciplined, even expelled, for breaches of school policy regarding drugs, alcohol, or extramarital sex. Full-time students are required to live on campus. The college provides separate residential facilities for men and women, with "limited inter-

SUGGESTED CORE

1. English 302: Classical Literature in Translation
2. Philosophy 334: Plato and Aristotle
3. Religion 211/212: Old Testament Literature and History / New Testament Literature and History
4. Religion 341: Church History I
5. Political Science 256: Modern Political Thought
6. English 351/352: Shakespeare
7. History 251: United States Survey
8. The required "Civilization" courses cover this area.

ALL-AMERICAN COLLEGES

visitation privileges for students who desire them." In practice, students report that visitation is allowed on Friday and Saturday nights and on Saturday and Sunday afternoons.

Grove City College remains open to students of any or no religious background. It does, however, require chapel attendance. The college catalogue states, "Chapel services are the common expressions of our Christian faith as members of the campus community. Thus, chapel/convocation attendance is a core component of the student's experience at Grove City College. There are many chapel options available to students, and each student is free to select from among these options according to his/her own interests as long as the student meets the college graduate requirement of attending sixteen (16) chapels per semester."

While the campus employs security personnel, it enjoys a reputation for safety. In 2003, the most recent year for which statistics are available, there were no violent crimes or robberies on campus, and only ten acts of theft and two instances of vandalism.

In keeping with its original mission to provide an education "within the reach of families with modest means," Grove City College charges very little for a private college—tuition is just $10,962, with room and board averaging $5,766. These figures include a laptop computer, which students keep upon graduating. The tuition rate at Grove City is especially remarkable because the school does not accept any government funding. Since government aid opens the way for federal micromanagement, Grove City has resolved to accept no federal aid. This means that students at Grove City cannot accept Stafford loans or Pell grants, but the college does offer scholarships based both on need and merit, and because of the general policy of maintaining low tuition and boarding fees, the cost of an education here remains affordable. Some 36 percent of students receive need-based financial aid. The college boasts that it operates "virtually debt-free," but despite its generosity many of its students can't say the same. The average recent graduate has emerged with a student loan debt of $22,035.

HANOVER COLLEGE

HANOVER, INDIANA • WWW.HANOVER.EDU

Hanover College is the oldest private four-year liberal arts college in Indiana. In the last 122 years, the college has had only five presidents, an impressive example of consistent leadership that has served the college well. The current president, Russell Nichols, was inaugurated in 1987. During his tenure, the college has increased its faculty and student body and improved its financial stability. Nichols has doubled the college's endowment, and Hanover now ranks in the top 10 percent of American colleges on an endowment-per-student basis, with over $200 million in investments.

The class of 2008 is the largest incoming class in the college's history. It is also the first to enter under the college's new Academic Vision Plan, a revamped set of inter-disciplinary liberal arts requirements. Despite the changes, the school's curricular requirements are reasonably strict, the classes are small, and the professors are deeply involved in the lives of students. Set in a lovely rural environment, Hanover is a solid choice for students looking for a fine education and an old-fashioned college experience.

Academic Life: Learning to Make Connections

In 2002, Hanover adopted what it calls the Academic Vision Plan, reaffirming the college's commitment to providing a liberal arts education through "disciplined and morally concerned inquiry." The First-Year Experience includes extensive academic counseling, as well as a series of courses introducing students to various disciplines. Along the way, each student must fulfill Hanover's Liberal Arts Degree Requirements (LADRs). To do so, students must complete:

- "Human Nature." This course is taken during the spring term freshman year and focuses on "the essential, defining qualities of being human";
- two "Great Works" courses, in sequence, both taken during the freshman year. Students in these classes analyze and interpret great works of literature and/or visual and performing arts from diverse cultures and reflect on "the enduring questions they raise." Students choose from among ten topics, including "Great Works of the British Empire," "Great Works of Times of Revolution," "Beauty," and "The Quest Archetype";

ALL-AMERICAN COLLEGES

119

- "The Examined Life," a two-course sequence designed to "confront foundational questions essential to the examined life." Students may choose from one of six sequences on the human condition, including "Philosophy and the Human Condition," "Theology and the Arts," and "Philosophical Issues and Classic Texts";
- "Modern Society," a two-course sequence in which students choose from eleven topics, such as "Foundations of Economics and Democracy," "The Family and the Modern West," "Psychology of the Family," "Africa and the Americas," and "The Economic Implications of Property";
- a two-course sequence on the natural sciences, including a lab. Students choose from linked courses such as "General Physics I," "Introduction to Physical Geology," and "Global Environmental Change," or "Heredity and Evolution" and "Environmental Geology," among others;
- "Other Cultures." Options include "The World of Islam," "History of Eastern Art," "Latin American History," "Odyssey to the Holy Land," and "Philosophy and the Martial Arts," among others;
- one course that emphasizes formal abstract reasoning and its application. Choices include "Introduction to Computer Science," "The Structure of the English Language," "Formal Logic," and math courses such as "Calculus" and "Statistics";
- two semesters in a foreign language. Choices include French, German, Greek, Latin, and Spanish;
- "Lifetime Wellness," a health course, plus two physical education activity classes; and
- one interdisciplinary capstone course on "Great Issues," to be taken during the senior year.

A distinguishing feature of the curriculum is the integrative and collaborative nature of its courses. "I had many classes that seemed unrelated in which I was able to connect and use material from one class to the next," a student says. "I think the vast knowledge that I have taken from introductory courses has definitely benefited me throughout my college career and will continue throughout my life. I have had to think about things that I had never thought about before and to consider how they fit into the grand scheme of my life. I have come to the conclusion that all education is interrelated." Another student says, "I think everyone at Hanover becomes a deeper learner. Most of the students come in as good students, but unprepared for the challenges of Hanover. We are forced to think critically about the classes we take and the world around us."

One weakness of the new system is that students are no longer required to take a course focused solely on Western civilization. They must, however, complete a Great Works sequence—most of which still focus on great works of Western culture. The Modern Societies sequence also leans towards the study of Western cultures, though it includes courses on non-Western ones as well. To fulfill the Other Cultures requirement, students must take at least one course on non-Western cultures—although it might surprise Latin Americans to learn that their culture falls outside the West.

One student characterizes the approach to studying Europe and America at Hanover this way: "We often question the institutions of Western heritage and American institutions, but we do so for the purpose of understanding them better. We take a deep look into understanding why a person would think the way he does, and are able to develop our own minds about things. Therefore, I think by studying hard and looking into the content as it relates to Western heritage and American institutions, we are paying them the ultimate respect." A faculty member adds, "The introductory classes in Western civilization strike the right balance between respect and criticism. Our students walk away with a healthy respect for both Western and Eastern traditions, as well as a strong understanding of the rationales behind the Constitution."

For good or ill, acceptance seems to be a guiding principle on campus. "I think in nearly every department, professors are mostly concerned with the well-being of the student and would never make him feel uncomfortable or unwelcome. With that said, conservative and religious students will be challenged to defend what they believe, and understand why they believe the way they do," says a student. "People who consider themselves conservative or religious and are willing to understand and develop their beliefs against others will be more than welcome at Hanover. Hanover College is a place that does not encourage blind allegiance to anything. It does, however, encourage thought and allows people to make their own personal choices. At Hanover, we breed acceptance and if that means we need to be more politically correct, then we are going to do that," he adds.

A professor says, "The administration has a generally socially conservative outlook, but it does not intrude into the classroom. Top administrators were not happy about the first campus production of *The Vagina Monologues* or the creation of a gay and lesbian club, but registered no more than a measure of caution." Interpret that "caution" however you wish. Hanover certainly backs away from its Christian identity. "None of the academic departments nor the administration push religious issues on students. Even the required theology classes are exploratory and not intrusive at all," says a student. "Our Christian affiliation would definitely be termed 'loose' and does not affect campus life unless desired by the individual student," he says. A teacher adds, "Students tell me there are a handful of professors who might make a conservative or religious student feel uncomfortable (though they aren't concentrated in any one depart-

VITAL STATISTICS

Religious affiliation: Presbyterian

Total enrollment: 1,008

Total undergraduates: 1,008

SAT/ACT midranges: SAT V: 540–650, M: 550–650; ACT: 23–29

Applicants: 1,680

Applicants accepted: 70%

Accepted applicants who enrolled: 23%

Tuition: $21,150

Room and board: $6,500

Freshman retention rate: 77%

Graduation rate: 68% (4 yrs.), 70% (6 yrs.)

Courses with fewer than 20 students: 84%

Student-faculty ratio: 10:1

Courses taught by graduate students: none

Most popular majors: public administration, business, psychology

Students living on campus: 94%

Guaranteed housing for four years? yes

Students in fraternities: 35% sororities: 38%

ment.). However, my impression is that the percentage of those professors is much lower at Hanover than at other schools. The war in Iraq has heightened some of these tensions, and there is probably more politics intruding into classrooms than there would normally be."

Students and professors report a close relationship between faculty members and undergraduates. "Hanover's biggest strength, and the reason I came here, is the faculty relationship with the students," says a professor. "Classes of eight to ten students are common in my department. I've been able to work closely with many students and form satisfying personal relationships," he concludes. A student agrees: "Every professor that I have had and known (which is most) is very accessible and helpful. They are always willing to work with students in and out of the classroom. They are readily available for tutoring and other help. Most importantly, however, they are more than willing and desire to form personal relationships with the students." One professor declares, "Teaching is the primary focus." It helps that the school's student-faculty ratio is an enviable 10 to 1.

The theological studies department at Hanover is blessed with many good professors. "Dr. Philip Barlow and R. David Cassel (both in theological studies) are known as two of the best professors on campus," says a theology major. "Our faculty are always more than willing to talk and interact with me and other students outside the classroom. That goes for not only the theology professors, but pretty much across the board." For this student, Dr. Mike Duffy in theological studies has been an influential professor. "He has done many things for me personally and I consider his willingness to chat and interact with students outside of the classroom as one thing that I cherish most about my experience at Hanover," he says. Michelle Bartel, who serves as the college chaplain in addition to teaching in the department, has an "amazing connection with students and is available for assistance personally, professionally, socially, and civically," says a former student. David Yeager, also in the department, is "very dedicated to his students."

Married couple Kate Johnson (philosophy) and Don Carrell (classics) are frequently mentioned as campus favorites. "Carrell has been one of the best professors I have had," says a student. A colleague says, "All three members of the classics department are outstanding teachers and scholars. David Banta by himself has revived the study of Latin at Hanover and is prominent in a movement to reintroduce it in secondary schools." To which we can only say "Bravo!"

The biology and chemistry departments are rigorous and prepare many students well for continuing education in medical and graduate school. Mike Worrell, a relative newcomer to campus, teaches in both the biology department and the new exercise science program. Paul Austin in chemistry and Walter Bruyninckx and Darrin Rubino in biology are also department favorites. Anthropology professor David Buchman is "one of the smartest people I have ever met. I have yet to meet a student who did not like one of his classes—even though he is very difficult," says a student. Buchman's work on Sufism in Yemen "represents probably the best research on campus," says a colleague. In geology, Heyo Van Iten's work in paleontology and hydrology has built him a strong reputation in the discipline. One colleague describes him as "an out-standing teacher."

"The history department holds a highly cohesive vision of a common Western tradition," says a faculty member. "Larry Thorton stands out as an excellent classroom professor in his classes on modern Europe," he adds. Jeff Brautigam and G. M. Curtis in history are also highly recommended. Other favorite professors include Bill Altermatt and Ellen Altermatt in psychology, Celia Dollmeyer in Spanish, John Martin in art history, and Jim Stark in theater.

Unique to Hanover is the Rivers Institute. Established in 2004 and funded by an $11.4 million grant from the Lilly Endowment, it is the first academic program in the world to use the liberal arts for the interdisciplinary and collaborative study of rivers. The mission of the Rivers Institute is to "enhance understanding of the culture, economics, and science of river systems around the world" through research, teaching, special programs, and outreach, as well as to provide scholarships and grants for faculty and students. Students have the opportunity to study land and water issues relating to any river ecosystem, not just the nearby Ohio River.

In 2006, the college launched the Center for Church Leadership, also funded by a Lilly Endowment grant. The center will "strengthen [the school's] historic relationship with the Presbyterian Church by providing mutual benefit to the church, the college, and its students." Specifically, it will provide continuing education for church leaders as well as vocational and preministry programs for students.

"The vast knowledge that I have taken from introductory courses has definitely benefited me. . . . I have had to think about things that I had never thought about before and to consider how they fit into the grand scheme of my life. I have come to the conclusion that all education is interrelated."

Hanover's Center for Business Preparation, which is modeled after MBA programs, provides real-world experience through internships and consulting projects with corporations, nonprofit organizations, and government offices. Students in the program must fulfill both curricular and cocurricular requirements, including a Career Portfolio that contains examples of their work, such as class presentations, internship projects, job-related projects, and a résumé.

The college strongly encourages off-campus study and has added ten approved programs during the current presidency. In fact, 90 percent of Hanover's students participate in some kind of off-campus study. The Hanover Plan, a 4-4-1 academic calendar, consists of two fourteen-week terms and a four-week Spring Term, during which most students study off campus. "The off-campus opportunities are exceptional," says a professor. "When a student goes abroad the college will send a professor to his location to evaluate the program to make sure it is up to Hanover standards." A student says, "I was able to take two courses in Greece and Italy, participate on two service

1. Classics 231: Ancient Epic
2. Philosophy 225: Classical Greek Philosophy
3. Theology 353: People of the Covenant *and* Theology 355: Jesus of Nazareth
4. Philosophy 226: Medieval Philosophy
5. Poli Sci 235: History of Political Thought (*closest match*)
6. English 334: Shakespeare
7. History 333, 334: American Colonial Period, 1600–1750 *and* The New American Nation, 1750–1815
8. History 213: History of Western Civilization, 1750–1914 (*closest match*)

learning trips to Jamaica, and informally study in Washington, D.C., for a week during my four years." Many departments offer Spring Term courses in locations around the country and abroad.

Student Life: A Red-Brick Idyll

Hanover College is situated on 650 of the country's most beautiful acres along the Ohio River in southeastern Indiana. The tree-lined paths and the red-brick Georgian-style architecture create an idyllic setting for the 94 percent of Hanover's 1,100 students who live on campus. The scenic beauty of the area is made accessible by a network of hiking trails. Weather permitting, commencement exercises are held outdoors at "The Point," which boasts a breathtaking view of the Ohio River valley. Historic Madison, population 13,000, is just minutes away and has over 133 blocks of quaint buildings listed in the National Register of Historic Places. The nearest metropolitan area is Louisville, Kentucky, some forty-five miles away.

In 1974, a tornado damaged thirty-two of the college's thirty-three buildings. The college community rallied together and quickly rebuilt, improving the campus—without the help of federal disaster aid—and continuing the college's tradition of financial independence. More recently, Hanover has invested over $45 million in new construction and facilities, including a $32 million Science Center completed in 2000, and the $11 million Horner Health and Recreation Center, one of the finest athletic facilities in the region. The college also recently completed the "Shoebox," an on-campus pub for students that serves beer and wine. Students may choose from among 132 cocurricular activities, including academic and preprofessional organizations, honor societies, intramurals, religious organizations, study-abroad programs, and special-interest groups.

In case it hasn't yet become clear, Hanover is a liberal place—and not always "old-fashionedly" liberal, either. The college recently acquired a chapter of Love Out Loud, a gay advocacy group. The group sponsors a National Coming Out Day celebration and other campus awareness activities such as a recent mock wedding ceremony for gay, lesbian, and straight couples, held in the lobby of the Brown Campus Center. We're not sure John Calvin would approve.

The Hanover Panthers compete in NCAA Division III athletics and the Heartland Collegiate Athletic Conference in men's and women's basketball, cross-country, golf, soccer, tennis, and track; men's football and baseball; and women's softball and volleyball. Hanover's Wayne Perry became the most successful coach in Indiana collegiate football history during the 2005 season.

Five fraternities and four sororities are located on campus. The college just completed a yearlong examination of Greek life at Hanover that addressed concerns about declining numbers of Hanover students choosing sororities and fraternities (a refreshing change from the usual persecution of such organizations). The Greek system, though shrinking, is still a strong presence on campus and includes more than one-third of the student body. Every spring, Hanover's chapter of Lambda Chi Alpha hosts a wiffleball tournament in which much of the student body participates to raise money for the Salvation Army. The tournament, a campus favorite, lasts about two and a half weeks and "is one of the greatest things ever!" says a student.

The college has seven traditional residential halls and two suite-style units, including the Greenwood Suites for upperclassmen, which were completed in 2002. Three residences are designated as theme houses for upperclassmen. Visitation policy varies among residences. Typically, members of each residence vote to determine visiting hours for the coming year. Men are restricted to the common areas of all sorority houses. Fraternity houses' visitation policies vary from house to house.

"The record for personal safety on the Hanover campus is excellent," says the college's security website. A student concurs, "I think that I live on one of the safest campuses. I rarely lock my door because I trust the people around me. The college is pretty well secluded from the outside world, so other people coming in is not too much of a problem," he says. The most common crime on campus is burglary, with four incidents in 2004. The school recently did make public a series of twenty-one reported rapes on campus, but cast doubt upon whether they actually happened—since all but two of them were reported by a second-hand source, which asserted that they'd occurred over a five-year period.

Tuition for the 2005-6 year was $21,150, plus $3,100 for room and $3,400 for board and another $500 in fees. The college offers a number of merit-based scholarships ranging from $2,500 to $5,000 per year. More than 90 percent of students receive some form of financial assistance. The average student loan indebtedness for 2004-5 seniors was $16,514.

HILLSDALE COLLEGE

HILLSDALE, MICHIGAN • WWW.HILLSDALE.EDU

Hillsdale's Statement on Academic Freedom, drafted by conservative political thinker Russell Kirk, states that the primary function of the college is to transmit to its students "some measure of wisdom and virtue." The college takes seriously its identity as "a trustee of modern man's intellectual and spiritual inheritance from the Judeo-Christian faith and Greco-Roman culture," and boldly endeavors to form the hearts and minds of its students through a liberal arts core. "The Western heritage and American institutions that have given us our liberties today are held in highest regard," says a history major. As a sign of this respect, the Pledge of Allegiance is recited before most college-sponsored events.

Hillsdale College's motto is "Educating for Liberty"—a mission the school has pursued since it was founded by abolitionist Freewill Baptists in 1844. The school's devotion to liberal education is evidenced by its rigorous core curriculum, dedication to intellectual inquiry, devoted faculty, and fierce independence. After a series of ham-fisted attempts by federal regulators in the 1970s to tinker with the school's athletic program—under the provisions of the infamous Title IX—Hillsdale decided henceforth to refuse all federal funds and student aid. Hillsdale was one of the first colleges in the United States to be founded on principles of equality, from the start admitting women, former black slaves, and students of every religion. Not coincidentally, the leaders of the college regard contemporary multiculturalism as a "dehumanizing, discriminatory

trend." True freedom, according to Hillsdale, "is dependent upon the maintenance of a moral order" and "attachment to a body of truth"—principles the college strives to transmit.

The school also passes along the principles of "movement" conservatism—a fusion of American Protestant morality and free-market, small-government principles. The school has become, among many other things, a hotbed of future writers, lobbyists, and think-tank officials promoting the ideals that motivated the Goldwater and Reagan presidential campaigns. For students committed to such principles, Hillsdale is a first-rate place in which to acquire an intellectual foundation; for others, it remains a stimulating and worthy liberal arts institution.

Academic Life: Dead White Men Are Cool

A Hillsdale education is built around one of the country's most solid and impressive core curricula. Students must take the following:

- "Rhetoric and the Great Books" I and II. Students in these courses study the principles of rhetoric and their applications. Readings include Homer, the Bible, Sophocles, Plato, Aristotle, Virgil, Dante, Shakespeare, Cervantes, Goethe, Tolstoy, Dostoevsky, Kafka, and Sartre, among others;
- "The Western Heritage to 1600." This course is meant to "acquaint students with the historical roots of the Western heritage and, in particular, to explore the ways in which modern man is indebted to Greco-Roman culture and the Judeo-Christian tradition." Beginning with a study of Mesopotamian and Hebrew civilizations, the course culminates in a survey of early-modern Europe;
- "The American Heritage." Picking up where "Western Heritage to 1600" leaves off, this course examines "the American experiment of liberty under law" from the founding to the modern Western world;
- "The U.S. Constitution." Students examine in detail the Constitution of the United States as the fundamental document of the "American experiment of self-government under law";
- "Physical Science." A lecture and lab course designed to introduce students to physics and chemistry. Topics include Newtonian mechanics, atoms, nuclear physics, chemical reactions, and organic chemistry;
- "Biological Science." This course introduces students to molecular, cellular, genetic, organismal, ecological, and population biology;
- one course in literature/classical studies. Options include classes in Greek or Roman civilization, "Colonial and Early American Literature," and "Anglo-Saxon and Medieval British Literature";
- one of five courses offered in the fine arts, including art, music, theater, and speech;
- one course in philosophy/religion. The two choices offered are "Introduction to Philosophy" and "Introduction to Western Religion";
- one social science course. Students choose from among the following: "Introduction to Political Economy," "Principles of Economics I," "Introduction to Psychology," and "Understanding Society and Culture";

VITAL STATISTICS

Religious affiliation: none
Total enrollment: 1,273
Total undergraduates: 1,273
SAT/ACT medians: SAT V: 600, M: 610; ACT: 27
Applicants: 1,060
Applicants accepted: 82%
Accepted applicants who enrolled: 42%
Tuition: $17,000
Room and board: $6,700
Freshman retention rate: 88%
Graduation rate: 65% (4 yrs.), 72% (6 yrs.)
Average class size: 21
Student-faculty ratio: 10:1
Courses taught by graduate students: none
Most popular majors: business, history, English
Students living on campus: 85%
Guaranteed housing for four years? yes
Students in fraternities: 15% *sororities*: 20%

ALL-AMERICAN COLLEGES

127

- three semesters of a foreign language. Choices include French, German, Spanish, Latin, and Greek, and students may *not* test out;
- two credit hours in physical education; and
- two credit hours of lectures offered through the Center for Constructive Alternatives (see below).

Students seem to appreciate being exposed to so many disciplines. A marketing major says, "I have been forced to take classes from all areas of study—from the universe to the atom, from Plato to President Bush. My education truly runs the gamut." Another student says, "Hillsdale has taught me that an education is not something one undertakes between the ages of eighteen and twenty-two, only to be replaced by a career. Rather, a good education continually molds one's heart, mind, and soul." "As liberty and responsibility in a liberal arts context are legacies hard-wired into the purposes of the college, the institution as a whole reflects them," says one professor.

Lofty ideals charge the atmosphere at Hillsdale. One student describes the college as "a community of people pursuing the highest things." Another student says, "My desire for the pursuit of liberal learning would probably not have been awakened had I not attended Hillsdale College. Being presented with ideas that have shaped the Western world and being forced to think about these higher things causes many people to dig deeply into the subject of who they are and how they ought to live."

Not surprisingly, Hillsdale's strongest departments are those which provide the bulk of the core requirements: English and history. The history department, whose honorary T-shirt proclaims "Dead White Men Are Cool," relies on readings from original sources such as the Bible, the writings of Cato, the Mayflower Compact, the Federalist papers, and the Constitution. History as taught at Hillsdale is designed to "draw students into the great conversation about those things that Matthew Arnold called 'the best that has been thought and said,'" reports a Hillsdale veteran. Students concentrating in history, one of the most popular majors on campus, must take at least nine hours in Western civilization courses, six hours in American history, and twelve hours of electives in addition to the freshman core. "Almost any history professor at Hillsdale provides a dynamic, interesting look at his or her chosen specialty," says one student. The department's popularity may be its only weakness. With more students enrolling in history courses, classes are growing to include as many as twenty-five to thirty students. "Having larger classes of this size does not allow for the sort of discussion that may be had with a class size closer to fifteen or twenty," says one history major.

The English department, according to the catalog, "seeks to develop in its students the skills of intelligent reading and effective writing, a deepened love for literature, an appreciation for certain seminal works in the Western literary tradition, and—in its majors—a solid grounding in English and American literature." Of the department's fifteen course listings, not one focuses on non-Western literature—which may be taking the Euro-American focus a little too far, but is still a welcome departure from the anti-European and anti-American biases that dominate English departments elsewhere.

The kind of students who end up at Hillsdale are not afraid to question—but one might be surprised to hear *what* some of them question. Evolution, for instance. A number of students are critical of the natural science and social science departments from a philosophical perspective. "My qualm is with their tendency to view the natural sciences as standing apart from the other disciplines—as standing on a separate and higher plane of truth because of their reliance on empirical data . . . and their stubborn adherence to evolution and refusal to consider the Intelligent Design Theory," says one history major. Another student agrees, calling biology her "only uncomfortable class as a Christian." Of course, sometimes it's healthy to be made a *little* uncomfortable.

Students consistently report that the teachers are what make Hillsdale exceptional. According to one student, "They are highly intelligent, eloquent, hardworking, honest, and always eager to interact with students. Moreover, many are devout Christians, which adds a deeper significance and validity to their lectures and conversations." Professors are extremely accessible, whether in the classroom, their offices, or just around campus. Students report being invited to dinner at a professor's home and having in-depth discussions with faculty about wide-ranging topics in and out of the classroom. Teaching, rather than research or writing, is the primary focus for professors. "Recently," says one professor, "a number of departments have moved to a three-course load . . . a move designed to improve teaching, not research. So, I think the priority is clear."

> *"Hillsdale has taught me that an education is not something one undertakes between the ages of eighteen and twenty-two, only to be replaced by a career. Rather, a good education continually molds one's heart, mind, and soul."*

Students find many faculty to praise. In history, favorite professors include Brad Birzer, Tom "Doc" Conner, Burt Folsom, Mark Kalthoff, and David Stewart. (Richard Gamble, a recent hire, will start teaching at Hillsdale in fall 2006 and was highly thought of at his previous institution, Palm Beach Atlantic University.) John Somerville in English is gifted, difficult, and demanding, as are Debra Belt, Andrew Cuneo, Michael Jordan, Stephen Smith, and David Whalen, who "pushes students to a level they didn't know they could achieve." In other departments, students laud in particular Ivan Pongracic and Gary Wolfram in economics; David Bobb, Mickey Craig, Will Morrisey, and Nathan Schlueter in political science; Tony Swinehart and Dan York in biology; James Stephens in philosophy; James Brandon in speech and theater; Tony Frudakis and Sam Knecht in art; Joseph Garnjobst in classics; Ken Hayes in physics; Tom Burke and Don Westblade in religion; and Lee Baron and Chris VanOrman in chemistry, the latter described as a "great professor who likes to blow things up." (We're glad he's not teaching political philosophy.) Even president Larry Arnn is said to be extremely accessible. He often eats lunch with students and knows many of them by name.

Hillsdale's campus is unquestionably conservative. For most students, it is this political homogeneity which attracted them in the first place. While the administration is extremely conservative, students believe that professors do a good job keeping politics out of the classroom. "When liberal education is understood in the terms identified in the Mission, then disciplines are free to be themselves without having to conform to the whims of contemporary ideological fashion," says one professor. The college officially "emphasizes the importance of the common moral truths that bind all Americans, while recognizing the importance of religion for the maintenance of a free society." "One can taste conservatism and religion in every classroom; it is the air we breathe," says one student.

Nevertheless, there is also an atmosphere of healthy debate on campus. The Fairfield Society, a student club, hosts a weekly forum in which students may present a topic of discussion, usually pertaining to (though not limited to) theology and philosophy, followed by an hour of questions. "There is constant debate—but all very civil—on campus on many issues," says one student, "But it's not typically a liberal versus conservative debate. There are frequent conservative versus libertarian debates and much discussion about different points of Christian doctrine. A criticism of Hillsdale from the outside is that it's a haven for conservatives who agree on everything; this is not the case, for debate is frequent among students. The professors challenge the students to read and think outside the liberal mainstream in order to find that which is good, true, and beautiful. On the down side, one faculty member claims that Catholic students are not particularly comfortable at Hillsdale, and that they speak of feeling "somewhat besieged." Some students even have complained (on a dissident website) that the school is moving in the direction of neoconservative globalism and away from its moorings in the traditional conservative politics of prudence—but others dispute this.

The Center for Constructive Alternatives offers seminars four times a year and one of the largest college lecture series in the nation. Topics vary widely from year to year and the lectures are published in Hillsdale's monthly newsletter, *Imprimis*, a brilliant fundraising circular that reaches over 1.2 million subscribers. In 2005-6 the center featured speakers such as film director Peter Bogdanovich (on screwball comedies); *Forbes* editor Steve Forbes; and David Brooks of the *New York Times*. Past presenters have included Ronald Reagan, Margaret Thatcher, Jeanne Kirkpatrick, Malcolm Muggeridge, and Peggy Fleming.

The honors program comes highly recommended by participants and is "much beloved and enthusiastically embraced," says one professor. According to the college catalog, the program exists to encourage students "in becoming broadly and deeply versed in the contents and methods of inquiry of the liberal arts, especially as conveyed by the great thinkers of the Western tradition. . . ." Honor students generally have a high school GPA of at least 3.7 and a combined SAT score of 1300 or an ACT over 30. Participation in the program is by invitation only. The curricular portion of the honors program consists of three components—core honors courses, special seminars, and a senior thesis. Honors students also participate in extracurricular opportunities such as trips to cultural attractions, lectures from guest speakers, dinners, service projects, and an annual spring trip to a major city. Honors students meet weekly to discuss readings from their courses or to talk to faculty from various departments on campus.

Hillsdale offers over twenty-five majors, nine preprofessional programs, and six interdisciplinary majors. Off-campus programs include journalism internships in Washington D.C., and study in Spain, England, Germany, France, and Scotland.

Student Life: Inside the Mitten

Hillsdale College, located on 200 rolling acres at the bottom of Michigan's "mitten," is home to nearly 1,250 students. The campus sits atop the highest point of the small town of Hillsdale, population 8,500, where Michael Sessions, a high school senior, was recently elected mayor. Yes, the local shopping hot spot is Wal-Mart, but intrepid students can escape to Detroit (one hundred miles), Toledo (eighty-five miles), or Ann Arbor (seventy miles). Central Hall, constructed in 1875, is the oldest building on an evolving campus that boasts the 32,500-square-foot Dow Science Building, a state-of-the-art science facility; the Sage Center for the Arts (which includes studios, a graphic design lab, photography lab, gallery, and 353-seat amphitheater); the 350,000 volume Mossey Library; and a Health Education and Sports Complex that has everything from racquetball to a 7,000-seat stadium. Plans are underway for a $32 million project that will house a new student union. Recently, the Kendall and Lane classroom building added forty new classrooms and faculty offices.

A residential campus, Hillsdale has eleven dorms and six Greek houses. Freshmen are required to live on campus, sophomores may move into a Greek house, and upperclassmen may apply for off-campus housing. All dorms are single-sex, with the exception of the newly constructed dorms, "The Suites," which are for upperclassmen only and have male and female wings separated by lobbies. "I am disappointed that Hillsdale recently opened a partially coed dorm," says one student, "It's a fairly innocuous change, but I believe it to be a step in the wrong direction." The new dorms resemble apartments, which some students feel hinders the spirit of community created by more traditional dorm life. Hillsdale's visitation policy permits men and women to visit each other in their rooms during limited hours.

Nearly half of the student body participates in athletics at Hillsdale. There are eleven varsity sports (NCAA Division II; five sports for men and six for women), plus a full program of intramurals. Student clubs include several religious groups, such as the Fellowship of Christian Athletes, and InterVarsity Fellowship, Equestrian Club, Debate Club, Swing Club, and PRAXIS, a political economy club.

SUGGESTED CORE
1. Classical Studies 313: The Ancient Epic
2. Philosophy 211: Ancient Philosophy
3. Religion 211/212: Old Testament History and Literature / New Testament History and Literature
4. Religion 213: History of Christian Thought I
5. Political Science 314: Modern Political Philosophy
6. English 471/472: Shakespeare
7. History 105: The American Heritage
8. Philosophy 217: Nineteenth-Century Philosophy (*closest match*)

ALL-AMERICAN COLLEGES

131

In 1854 Hillsdale's president, Edmund Fairfield, was a leading founder of the Republican Party. It's no accident that the College Republicans is one of the largest and most active groups on campus today. There is also a College Libertarians group and, refreshingly, a newly formed College Democrats. According to a recent article in the school's paper, the *Collegian*, the president of the College Democrats club has faced negative feedback, including hate mail, from fellow students for starting the club, with some students claiming it is impossible to be at once a Democrat and a Christian.

Nevertheless, most students feel comfortable on campus. One student says, "Most of us have never been in such a close community of like-minded people before. We revere what is old and true and pause before embracing the new. The conversations in the cafeteria often last for hours—everything from natural rights, natural law, supply-side economics, transubstantiation, the Civil War, Locke, Plato and Aristotle are discussed there; the great thing is that these conversations are not uncommon at Hillsdale. . . . The environment at Hillsdale is unlike any other place I have ever experienced." Another says, "I like Hillsdale's small student body—it feels like family. I like that I can talk politics and life with people who understand logic and reason. I like that most of the students are Christians and good people."

Crime is not a concern on campus. Students do not lock doors and they leave their laptops unattended. "Everyone leaves backpacks on the floor outside of the cafeteria and I have never heard of any problems," says one student. A young woman says, "The best testimony that I can give is that I feel safe." Campus security regularly patrols the campus at night and will escort students upon request.

Basic expenses for the 2005–6 school year at Hillsdale were $17,000 for tuition, $6,700 for room and board, and $410 in fees, for a total of $24,110. Since 1984, Hillsdale has avoided the imposition of racial quotas and other micromanagement by the federal government by refusing federal aid for scholarships. Instead, the college secures over $5.5 million dollars annually in privately funded loans, grants, and scholarships. In fact, the college catalog lists over 300 scholarships in addition to private-loan funds, merit-based awards, and other aid. Hillsdale arranges for students who receive merit-based aid to meet with their donors each semester. "The donors witness the direct effect of their money, and the students feel a deeper appreciation, gratitude, and responsibility for the scholarships. Many students, myself included, become friends with their donors, corresponding even after graduation," says one student. The average aid package per student is $10,000. Some 75 percent of students get need-based aid, and the average student loan debt of a recent graduate is a modest $15,500.

HOPE COLLEGE

HOLLAND, MICHIGAN • WWW.HOPE.EDU

One of three colleges nationwide with ties to the Reformed Church in America, Hope College was founded as a "Pioneer School" by Dutch settlers in 1851. Twenty years later, a massive fire wiped out much of the city of Holland, Michigan, leaving only Pillar Church and Van Vleek Hall, an impressive three-story stone and brick building that is today the oldest building on Hope's campus and a symbol of the school's enduring legacy. The college's name and its seal, an anchor, originated with its founder, Reverend A. C. Van Raalte, who wanted to provide a Christian education for the colony's children. Van Raalte said the school was an "anchor of hope for this people in the future."

Fortune did not cheat his hope—or Hope's—which still "challenges students to develop an understanding of the Christian faith as a basis for academic excellence and the fulfillment of human potential," in the college's own words. The students and faculty we spoke with confirm that the school walks its talk; Hope College is both academically serious and theologically earnest. It ought to appear on the short list of any evangelical student seeking to choose the right college.

Academic Life: The Sacred and the Secular

Hope's general education program promises a "liberal education within the Christian tradition." Its mandates are not quite strict enough for our taste, but they are nevertheless substantial. Students must take the following:
- "First Year Seminar," a two-credit course to be taken during the fall semester of a student's first year. This interdisciplinary course introduces the liberal arts and college-level learning, and it employs as primary texts a few of the Great Books;
- "Expository Writing I," a four-credit course on how to think critically and write clearly. The course is taught topically, with the subject of the course left up to the discretion of the instructor. The subjects offered in 2006 ranged from the promising "Conscience in Question" and "The Will to Survive" to the tedious "The Third Wave: Feminism for the New Millennium";

- "Cultural Heritage" I and II, an "introduction to some of the central events, questions, and concerns of Western culture." Students may choose to substitute one interdisciplinary course and one course from English, history, and philosophy, or three courses, one each in English, history, and philosophy;
- "Social Sciences" I and II, introductory courses with a lab in psychology, sociology, communication studies, economics, or political science;
- one introductory course in the arts and a studio or performance course in art, dance, music, theater, or creative writing;
- ten credits in math and the sciences, including a lab, with at least two courses in math, or from the General Education Math and Science (GEMS) courses;
- four credits in a foreign language. Students are expected to achieve at least a freshman-level competency. Choices include classical languages, French, German, Japanese, Spanish, and Russian;
- four credits in "cultural diversity." Choices range from the broadly useful "Geography of Developing Countries" to the overly specific "Black Women in the Diaspora";
- "Health Dynamics," a two-credit course on health, diet, and exercise; and
- "Senior Seminar," a four-credit capstone course in the student's major.

"A major goal of this portion of the curriculum is that students will come to understand the Western cultural inheritance, its chronological development, its strengths and weaknesses," says one professor. Another says, "Intellectual curiosity is highly encouraged through themes of critical thinking which permeate our General Education program and on into student research achievements, some of which are very impressive."

One recent graduate reports, "I have always loved the intellectual life; attending Hope College served to confirm that and enrich it. While a student there I learned not to be ashamed of my passion for learning, that learning is an expression of faith, and that learning takes place every day in a variety of different ways—not just through books." Another student, who became a Christian at Hope, says: "My investment of time and energy seems miniscule compared to the faith I have found, knowledge I have gained, and relationships I have made, which I am confident would not be as strong if I were anywhere else. I know these things will serve me well after I leave this place."

Hope offers eighty-three majors and eleven preprofessional programs granting Bachelor of Arts, Bachelor of Music, Bachelor of Science, and Bachelor of Science in Nursing degrees to its 3,100 students. The most popular programs are education, business, and psychology. The natural sciences at Hope are especially strong. According to the National Science Foundation, Hope ranks in the top twenty-five baccalaureate schools nationwide as a source of future Ph.D.'s in the sciences and engineering. One of the reasons Hope excels in the sciences is its emphasis on faculty-student cooperative research. According to the college website, Hope has held more "Research Experiences for Undergraduates" grants from the National Science Foundation than any other liberal arts college in the nation—more even than most research institutions. Hope's General Education Mathematics and Science (GEMS) courses for nonscience majors have been nationally recognized by the American Association of Colleges and Universities and have been funded by the National Science Foundation. Other strong programs include political science and history.

Hope believes in active learning. Collaborative research, internships, off-campus programs, and study-abroad programs abound. There are yearlong and semester programs offered on five continents and short-term study programs during the summer, such as the popular Hope College Vienna Summer School.

Hope is the only private, four-year liberal arts college in the country with national accreditation in art, dance, music, and theater. The college provides students ample opportunities for performance, as well as internships such as the Arts Program in New York, where students can spend a semester apprenticing with producing artists or arts organizations. The college gives up to sixty $2,500 Distinguished Artist Award scholarships each year to students in art, dance, music, theater, and creative writing, and it further supports the arts through programs such as the Visiting Writers Series, the Knickerbocker Film Series, and the Great Performances Series.

Closer to home, the Chicago Semester gives students a chance to intern in Chicago in fields related to their majors or career interests. The Oak Ridge Science Semester offers natural science majors the opportunity to do research at the Oak Ridge National Laboratory in Tennessee. Hope is one of only thirty-three colleges in the country selected to offer the Baker Scholars Program, which gives business majors special enrichment opportunities and real-world experience. The Washington Honors Semester Program in Washington, D.C., is for top juniors and seniors from all disciplines. This internship includes participation in seminars and interviews with government officials, and is capped off by a research paper. If none of the existing programs fit, students may propose their own internships.

Hope also offers several programs designed to help students discern their vocations, most notably the CrossRoads Project, whose mission is "thinking theologically about career, calling and life," and which was funded by a $2 million grant from the Lilly Endowment. The program helps students "explore how their work can be of service to the wider world" through its courses, workshops, seminars, speakers, and support for internships.

VITAL STATISTICS

Religious affiliation: Reformed Church in America

Total enrollment: 3,112

Total undergraduates: 3,112

SAT/ACT midranges: SAT V: 550–680, M: 560–680; ACT: 23–29

Applicants: 2,674

Applicants accepted: 77 %

Accepted applicants who enrolled: 37%

Tuition: $21,420

Room and board: $6,600

Freshman retention rate: 88%

Graduation rate: 62% (4 yrs.), 75% (6 yrs.)

Courses with fewer than 20 students: 54%

Student-faculty ratio: 13:1

Courses taught by graduate students: none

Most popular majors: management, psychology, education

Students living on campus: 80%

Guaranteed housing for four years? yes

Students in fraternities: 8% *sororities*: 13%

The Hope campus is characterized by its Christian commitment, intellectual curiosity, and as one professor puts it, "openness and dialogue." Though affiliated with the Reformed Church of America, Hope is clearly ecumenical. "Just as Hope College is intentional about providing a dynamic, supportive Christian atmosphere, it also strives to respect deeply the perspectives brought to campus by students from a wide range of denominational/church backgrounds," says the college website. "Our college does not try to create cookie-cutter Christians, or indeed to pressure students to accept a particular faith walk," says a professor. "Students at Hope College learn rather quickly that the faculty are deeply engaged in faith walks also," she adds. The college's Christian heritage "infuses education with purpose and direction, providing a framework for self-understanding, moral values, and social concern, without restricting inquiry," says another professor. "We see a liberal education within the Christian tradition as fully compatible with critical reflection."

For the most part, politics stays out of the classroom, and the administration is careful about balancing academic freedom with the historical identity of the college. "We have an ideologically diverse faculty and student body," says a professor. Nevertheless "the tension of different perspectives, opinions, and beliefs plays itself out in a very unique way," says a current senior. "There is respect from all sides and people oftentimes agree to disagree. It is this healthy balance that makes Hope such a unique place, and continues to sharpen its students and faculty into one of the finest Christian liberal arts colleges in the nation," he adds. A recent graduate concurs. "Of course, so many disparate worlds living together under one roof often makes for tension. There is often tension between more socially progressive faculty and more evangelical interests in the Office of the Chaplain, the Board of Regents, and a somewhat more conservative student body, many of whom are from Michigan," he says. "When it works," he adds, "Hope strikes a beautiful, dynamic, and very unique atmosphere of holistic, classical learning." "Many of our students come from conservative backgrounds," says a professor, "and many of our students are strongly Christian, but I have rarely heard of instances where any student felt uncomfortable in a class or department."

"While a student at Hope I learned not to be ashamed of my passion for learning, that learning is an expression of faith, and that learning takes place every day in a variety of different ways—not just through books."

Hope's faculty is noted for its high caliber of scholarship combined with teaching excellence. "No faculty member at Hope College succeeds in remaining on the faculty without a vibrant teaching record, compiled both through the evidence of course materials and student outcomes, corroboration of faculty colleagues, and student evaluations. Consequently, the quality and energy that most faculty devote to teaching is extraordinary," says a professor. Research and teaching are not mutually exclusive, but rather "are intimately related and enhance one another," argues another. Hope professors publish as many books and articles as their counterparts at research universities while maintaining teaching as a high priority, faculty report.

One professor says, "Probably the one aspect of the college that students remember for the rest of their lives is how they were changed by their professors, and how their professors took extra time with them, one on one, to get to know them and to help them succeed. Our campus is highly relational, and the faculty here believe very strongly in knowing each other, and knowing the students." Students agree. "The small class sizes enable students and professors the opportunity to engage in deep discussion and learning any day of the week. So rather than a student-professor relationship, it tends to look more like a mentoring relationship," says a student. A recent graduate says, "Many of the faculty could teach elsewhere at top research schools in their field, but choose Hope because they are paid to teach and be human, and because of Hope's unique mix of the sacred and secular."

SUGGESTED CORE
1. No suitable course.
2. Philosophy 230: Ancient Philosophy
3. Religion 220: Introduction to Biblical Literature
4. Religion 344: Christianity in the Middle Ages
5. Poli Sci 342: Modern Political Thought
6. English 373: Shakespeare's Plays
7. History 160: U.S. History to 1877
8. History 240: Enlightenment and Nationalism in Europe, 1688–1914 (*closest match*)

Favorite professors include Marc Baer in history, of whom one student says, "His passion lies in pointing out the connection between faith and learning, both yesterday and today, in and out of the classroom." Fred Johnson, also in history, is highly recommended. "The best teacher at Hope College is a philosophy professor named Jim Allis," says a Hope graduate. "Jim challenges students' worldviews with modern and ancient philosophers, but is there with students wrestling in the trenches for understanding and meaning." Ion Agheana, professor of Spanish, is a "wise, humble, wonderful scholar" whose classes are filled with rich discourses on philosophy, religion, culture, politics, and literature. Carol Simon, professor of philosophy, is described as "a great leader of the institution." Other favorite professors include Joel Toppen in political science; Steve Bouma-Prediger and Jeff Tyler in religion; John Shaughnessy in psychology; Jack Mulder in philosophy; and Ray Smith, the athletic director. Hope has many award-winning teachers on its faculty, including Susan Cherup in education, Donald Cronkite in biology, Maxine DeBruyn in dance, Stephen Hemenway and Jack Ridl in English, Lynne Hendrix in accounting, Huw Lewis in music, Thomas Ludwig in psychology, William Polik in chemistry, and Richard Ray in kinesiology.

Student Life: Tulips, Pickles, and Exceptional People

Holland, Michigan, is an idyllic resort town of 40,000 on Lake Macatawa, five miles from Lake Michigan, two and a half hours from Chicago, and three hours from Detroit. The town is home to the world's largest pickle factory, where over one million pounds of pickles are processed per day during peak season. But pickles aren't its only claim to fame. There is a $50 fine for picking one of Holland's six million tulips, which bloom each spring for the Tulip Time festival in May.

Hope's seventy-seven-acre campus is located two blocks from downtown Holland—close enough for students to walk to Lemonjello's, a favorite coffee hangout, or various restaurants in the quaint shopping district. Students report that one is better off without a car, as the campus is short on parking. At the heart of campus is the Pine Grove, a popular location for concerts and other gatherings. The Gothic Dimnent Memorial Chapel is a campus landmark. Bells from its 120-foot tower chime the Westminster peal across campus every fifteen minutes. "One of the nice things about Hope is its location and architecture," says a professor.

The college recently completed a $140 million campaign, the largest single fundraising effort in Hope's history. The result was major support for projects such as the Richard and Helen DeVos Fieldhouse, which opened in 2005. The 102,000-square-foot building seats 3,100 fans and houses the Department of Kinesiology and the college's athletic training program. The $12 million Martha Miller Center for Global Communication, which houses the departments of communication and languages, also opened for the 2005-6 school year. A recent $36 million building and renovation project doubled the size of the existing science facilities. The Van Wylen Library has been ranked as the top undergraduate library in the country, receiving the national "Excellence in Academic Libraries Award" for 2004.

Even though the campus facilities are exceptional, for most students it is the people that make the Hope experience so valuable. "From fellow students to professors, to lunch ladies, to librarians, to physical plant workers, to coaches, to administrators, there are special people with a significant commitment to making Hope both excellent academically while maintaining its vibrant Christian character—a tough but fruitful balance," says a student.

Virtually every student we talked to spoke enthusiastically of the 108-year-old tradition called the Pull, an annual tug-of-rope competition between freshman and sophomore classes over the Black River. Teams practice for three weeks before the event, which is usually held in the first month of the school year. The Nykerk Cup, another favorite tradition which started in 1935, is an annual competition between freshman and sophomore women in singing, oration, and drama. The yearly Dance Marathon is a twenty-four-hour, student-run fundraiser for the DeVos Children's Hospital in Grand Rapids.

Hope's eighteen sports teams participate in the Michigan Intercollegiate Athletic Association (MIAA), which consists of NCAA Division III schools. In 2004–5 Hope athletes and/or teams qualified for ten NCAA championships. Over sixty student organizations provide extracurricular opportunities for every interest from knitting to German.

Although Hope is affiliated with the Reformed Church of America, it is "ecumenical in character" and offers a variety of opportunities for Christian fellowship, including InterVarsity Christian Fellowship, Fellowship of Christian Athletes, Union of Catholic Students, Gospel Choir, and more. The Campus Ministries website provides links to twenty-five local churches in addition to three weekly on-campus chapel services, which one professor estimates about a third of the students attend, plus a Sunday evening service.

Many students also participate in spring-break mission and service trips. Says one, "Even for people that have had exposure to the Christian faith during their childhood or adolescence, it is common to hear many testimonies about their faith being taken to a whole new level during their time at Hope. The chapel services and campus ministries staff do a good job of reaching out to all students, regardless of their faith tradition or previous exposure."

Believing that residential life is an important part of a liberal arts education, Hope College requires full-time students to live in campus housing. Students live in one of eleven residence halls, fifteen apartments, or sixty-three cottages. The cottages are single-sex residences divided into neighborhoods of nine to eleven houses and headed by a neighborhood coordinator who plans activities for residents. Apartments are only available to upperclassmen. Visitation by the opposite sex is permitted until midnight Sunday through Thursday and until 2:00 a.m. on Friday and Saturday evenings.

The campus is quite safe. In 2004, the school reported one sex offense, five burglaries, and one arson. The college's Department of Campus Safety patrols the campus twenty-four-hours a day, providing escort and shuttle services and emergency phones around campus. Alcohol is prohibited on campus and in all campus housing. However, in 2004 there were eighty-seven liquor-law violations.

Most Hope students come from a middle-income background, and 58 percent receive need-based financial aid. Overall, 89 percent of Hope students receive some kind of financial assistance. Tuition for the 2005–6 school year was $21,420, while the room and board bill came to about $6,600, depending on the type of residence and food plan chosen.

HOUGHTON COLLEGE

HOUGHTON, NEW YORK • WWW.HOUGHTON.EDU

Houghton College sits about sixty-five miles southeast of Buffalo, New York, in rural Allegany County. Founded in 1883 by Willard J. Houghton as a high school called Houghton Seminary, the institution began offering college-level courses in 1899. It has grown into a full liberal arts college since then, offering baccalaureate degrees in forty-eight fields from accounting to psychology, plus master of music and master of arts in music degrees. Houghton is still operated by the Wesleyan Church and retains a strong Christian character as a member of the Christian College Consortium. Its Christian mission is well articulated, permeates every program of study, and shapes its student life. If you're seeking a rich and rigorous liberal education within a deeply Christian social milieu, here you will find it—situated in some of the most picturesque country of rural New York State. The school offers everything you'd find at other eastern liberal arts colleges—academic excellence, a community of scholarship, natural beauty, and a sense of discovery—without the intellectual and moral hazards found at comparable secular schools.

Academic Life: Forming the Whole Person

Houghton provides a comprehensive Christian education in the liberal arts—beginning with a core curriculum that reflects the school's commitment to Western civilization. As a school, Houghton professes some wonderfully old-fashioned ideas. According to its literature, "Maintaining a civilization requires that each generation transmit their knowledge of all these things to the next generation: this is what a liberal arts education is intended to do. To receive liberal arts education, therefore, is to receive a great inheritance—an intellectual inheritance derived from the accumulated learning of the ages." Well said, indeed. But this vision of education is now quite rare.

Houghton insists upon an extensive set of core requirements. Students must take the following:
• "Biblical Literature";

- "First-Year Introduction," an orientation course that prepares students for college-level academic work;
- an English composition course and a noncredit course in library research methods;
- "Western Civilization" I and II;
- a foreign language through the intermediate level, chosen from French, German, Latin, Greek, and Spanish;
- a college mathematics class;
- a course in public speaking;
- "Introduction to Christianity" and an advanced biblical studies course;
- "Literature of the Western World" and another humanities class, chosen from a long list of art, literature, music, and philosophy courses;
- three philosophy courses: "Knowledge and Reality" plus two more chosen from among "Ethics, Community, Ideology, and Environment," "Metaphysics, Morality, and Mind," and "History of Philosophy" I and II;
- one fine arts course, either a studio or history class in musical, graphic, or film arts;
- one social science course in microeconomics, macroeconomics, political science, sociology, or anthropology;
- one physical science course with lab; and
- one physical education class, e.g., "Backpacking/Canoeing" or "Ecotour in Honduras";

Students report that "the Western Civilization courses take students from the ancient world through the Reformation to today. The professors are respectful of the material and try to teach the history of ideas as it is." Some wonder aloud if Houghton's governing Christian worldview gets in the way of faithfully interpreting the material, but one sophomore says that "the Wesleyan tradition is a starting point, a frame of reference. In my intro courses the professors try as much as possible to let the text 'teach itself' and then they help provide a context where there are gaps in our knowledge." Another senior says, "They just present the material as fairly as possible. Of course professors offer their own interpretations where appropriate but they don't force a reading against the spirit of the text on us."

Overall, the requirements for a liberal education at Houghton total nearly sixty credit hours. "It's a lot of work," says one junior, "and the first thing you feel is relief when you complete the requirements. But now I can put my discipline into a much larger vision of the world." Other students amplify these sentiments. "The process of completing the requirements can be frustrating. But having that diverse of a background will make you a better person. It's definitely worth it." Students from several majors praised the "well-rounded" education they received.

The core program goes much further than the history of ideas. Houghton believes that the liberal arts are meant to do more than train an intellect; they are meant to form the whole person. "The liberal arts are surprisingly practical. Studies consistently show that graduates of liberal arts colleges excel professionally in a wide variety

Religious affiliation:
  Wesleyan
Total enrollment: 1,411
Total undergraduates: 1,398
SAT/ACT medians: SAT V:
  598, M: 580; ACT: 26
Applicants: 1,009
Applicants accepted: 90%
*Accepted applicants who
  enrolled:* 36%
Tuition: $19,420
Room and board: $6,560
Freshman retention rate: 84%
Graduation rate: 56% (4 yrs.),
  65% (6 yrs.)
*Courses with fewer than 20
  students:* 64%
Student-faculty ratio: 13:1
*Courses taught by graduate
  students:* 1%
Most popular majors: educa-
  tion, biology, music
Students living on campus:
  82%
*Guaranteed housing for four
  years?* yes
*Students in fraternities or
  sororities:* none

of fields, whether or not those fields are directly related to the major field of academic study. A liberal arts education stands in contrast to narrow, career-based education, as well as to the academic trendiness that overtakes so much of higher education," the school asserts. We agree.

Some exceptional professors often sought out by students include Jonathan Arensen in anthropology, Cameron Airhart and Meic Pearse in history, Blaine David Benedict and Peter Meilaender in political science, and Heather Armstrong and William John Newborough in music.

One course that several students recall fondly is the Highlander Wilderness Adventure program. Offered at the end of every summer to incoming freshmen and transfer students, the Highlander program is said to be "a lot more than ten days in the woods behind the college." One freshman reports, "It was great to know sixty students so well when classes started. . . . I not only knew their names but had accomplished something with them. It sets a great tone for the whole year." Houghton says that this program "combines problem-solving tasks and skills training in God's creation with group interaction and personal reflection, for an experience that will stretch the total person." The school lays out these goals for the HWA:

1. The student will experience joy after hardship.
2. The student will find adventure and satisfaction from doing hard work.
3. The student will learn skills that build confidence.
4. The student will learn to look inward to self, outward to others, and upward to God.

Philosophy professor Carlton Fisher, a dean at Houghton, says that this creed characterizes the Houghton experience. By contrast, he says, "the secular college/university campus—whether public or private—is no friend to grace. The Christian story is not held in high esteem, the virtues of chastity and temperance are not prized, and truth is often not much more than personal opinion. And Christian college students, with good home and church backgrounds, on Christian and on secular campus, are beginning to ask new questions about their faith. After all, they are in transition from childhood to adulthood. No matter how Christian their childhood, becoming a mature Christian adult remains a true 'becoming.'" In one senior's words, Houghton "strives to form Christians who can answer God's call to serve the world and to serve Him with their faith and reason working together." One student reports that "professors integrate their faith into the lectures and curriculum in general."

Music students in particular thrive at Houghton. The Greatbatch School of Music has been accredited since 1946, and in fall 2004 it received a $15 million grant to develop graduate programs. The school's religious worldview informs the music programs as much as it does the theology courses. The music program seeks to develop "Christian Scholar Musicians" who are committed to "the highest artistic values." But musical excellence doesn't take a backseat to piety. One junior stated that when he was looking at Christian schools he looked for the best music program he could find. "I definitely think I am in the right one. Houghton has a tremendous faculty. I really think it is an act of God that so much talent is on one campus." Many of the teachers are accomplished professional musicians who have competed internationally, and several sit in local orchestras and bands. Professor Lin He commutes to Cleveland to play in their symphony orchestra, while others play with the Rochester Philharmonic. Teachers are said to exhibit "great musicality, professionalism, and a real desire to see students succeed."

Houghton offers forty-eight majors and a variety of preprofessional degrees grounded in the notion of "Christian servanthood." Houghton students can obtain degrees in premed, prephysical therapy, and preveterinary medicine. Previous graduates have gone on to a variety of top graduate schools, including Tufts, Dartmouth, Columbia, and the Eastman School of Music. Alumni report that the "Christ-centered" view of the world they gained at Houghton helped keep them grounded when they went on to study at secular graduate schools.

"The liberal arts are surprisingly practical. Studies consistently show that those graduates excel professionally in a wide variety of fields. . . . A liberal arts education stands in contrast to narrow, career-based education, as well as to the academic trendiness that overtakes so much of higher education," the school asserts.

Most departments are said to be focused on disciplinary fundamentals. In political science, much attention is given to classical political theory and American political history. Philosophy courses are divided along traditional lines with introductions to ethics, epistemology, metaphysics, and morality—rather than eclectic classes focused on single thinkers, as is the case at many schools.

There are some more exotic programs of study which might be unique to Houghton. In the recreation and leisure studies major, students can focus on equestrian studies and learn classical horsemanship on the 386-acre farm adjoining the college. Many students receive certification through the Certified Horsemanship Association and go on to secure employment as riding instructors or trainers. A family studies minor combines the disciplines of anthropology, sociology, religion, and psychology—which sounds like it could be a recent invention for training "culture warriors."

Houghton also offers two very special first-year honors programs at no additional cost to students selected through an on-campus interview process: "Honors Study in London," and "Honors: East Meets West." Approximately twenty-five students are admitted to each program. In the former, students spend the spring semester with several Houghton professors in London, where they study Western culture, literature, philosophy, and the fine arts. The second honors course meets on campus during the spring semester and then spends May term traveling through Croatia, with side trips to neighboring countries. As its name implies, "East Meets West" studies Western and Eastern European cultures, and "the relationship between . . . Eastern Europe, the Middle East, and the West." Program director Meic Pearse has advised members of Congress on the same topic.

Student Life: Cream Rises to the Top

Houghton is located in the hamlet of the same name in Allegany County, New York. According to students, "the college is the town." The scenic beauty surrounding the campus makes for an idyllic setting. The campus is unobtrusively tucked into the encircling hardwood forests, with which students become acquainted on their Highlander Wilderness Adventure. Fifteen miles to the north are the Genesee's magnificent Portage Falls and Letchworth State Park. Houghton lies sixty-five miles southeast of Buffalo, making it much closer to Canada than to New York City, which is 330 miles from campus. Hikers will love the trails in Angelica, New York, about a twenty-minute ride south of the school.

Student life is often built from the ground up. The dozens of clubs started by students include Allegheny County Outreach, the Campus Activities Board, the Cheerleading Club, College Republicans, a webcast radio station, the Inter-Cultural Student Organization, the Shakespeare Club, a student newspaper called the *Star*, the Ultimate Frisbee Club, and the Ski Club. If there is a hot topic being discussed by students, groups often come together to organize a forum at which professors can shed light on it from the perspective of their own academic disciplines and engage outside scholars and commentators. Theological debates that started privately over lunch sometimes spill over into a public forum. "You can be constantly engaged as a thinking Christian at Houghton."

There are three chapel services held on campus each week (Mondays, Wednesdays, and Fridays at 11:00 a.m.). Students agree to attend two out of three. This makes for an especially pious campus, but not all students are Wesleyan. Sixty different Christian denominations are represented by the student body. According to one senior, "The diversity of Christians is amazing! Assemblies of God, Episcopalian, and Reformed Christians are all accepted on campus. . . . And at chapel service we witness an incredible Christian unity." Chapel services alternate between traditional and contemporary evangelical worship styles. Students are encouraged to find a local church within their own Protestant traditions to attend on Sunday mornings, but this sometimes requires having a car on campus. The chapel services are said to "create tremendous unity."

Prayer is a major part of life at Houghton. The dean's office maintains an intercessory prayer list and students can e-mail prayers of petition or thanksgiving to be added to the list. One astonished senior reports that he recently discovered that several professors had been praying for him for years. "It was a real surprise and a real comfort. I was touched to know they cared so personally." Petitions can be posted on a website to allow students to pray for each other, and if a particular concern is frequently expressed, chaplains will discuss them during communal worship. One student says that the religiosity on campus might seem "just a little short of cultish, just a little short." However, the diversity of Christian views also leads to frequent campus debates. At lunch, it is not uncommon to hear students taking sides in contemporary evangelical controversy. "Should women preach? Or, what is the best Bible translation? There are even groups representing certain views," an undergrad reports.

Even with this diversity of student views, Houghton maintains its Wesleyan identity. Drinking, smoking, and social dancing are forbidden. Students do report that there is "some dissent, particularly over dancing," among the student body. The school's policies on alcohol are strict. The first offense leads to disciplinary probation and the second can lead to dismissal from the college. The rules governing residential life are aimed at creating a peaceful and wholesome living space. Only movies rated G or PG can be played in common lounges, though students can make their own decisions about playing PG-13 or R-rated movies in their own rooms. Students are expected to conform to modest norms of dress and to eschew provocative dorm posters and foul language.

Surprisingly, campus politics are far from uniform. One graduate student reports, "I really mean it when I say the student body is diverse—not just in their religious denominations but in their politics. There are lots of Republicans of course, but also plenty of Democrats, Greens, and Independents. The political debate is open." Another student says that there is a small but strong antiwar voice, though it is generally not what you might expect. "It's not so much a liberal sentiment as a pacifist one. We have some Mennonites here." One student says he thinks "fully half of the student body are probably Republicans and another quarter have very little interest in either political party. There are some vocal Democrat professors but the professors are generally conservative."

While every student gives Houghton's academic, spiritual, and student life high marks, a number of students say that the way the administration communicates with students can be problematic. "They make budget cuts, for instance, and it is never explained why this is happening, what is expected, or in what direction they are trying to take a particular program." Another issue for some students is Houghton's isolation. "I love it here and wouldn't have chosen another school, but there isn't much else around. It creates a close community, but in the middle of the semester I wish there were more

---

SUGGESTED CORE

1. English 201: Literature of the Western World (*closest match*)
2. Philosophy 241: History of Philosophy I: Ancient and Medieval
3. Bible 101: Biblical Literature
4. Theology 453: History of Christianity
5. Political Science 260: Introduction to Political Thought (*closest match*)
6. English 350: Shakespeare
7. History 359, 360: Colonial America, 1600–1788 and Early National Period, 1788–1850
8. History 325: Europe in the Nineteenth Century (*closest match*)

places for an escape." On the whole, not many students complain about the school. One reports, "They do most things in a way that makes sense and it just works."

Students living on campus reside in single-sex dormitories or townhouses. Dorms are open to visitation between 7 p.m. and 11 p.m. Friday through Saturday and on one night during the week. The buildings have a stone facade that resembles the traditional style of colleges throughout New England. Dorms are equipped with wireless Internet access, generous kitchens, and cable television lounges. A few rooms in Gillette Hall, a women's dorm, are on the small side—but "not unbearable," according to one junior. Upperclassmen may live in campus apartments or townhouses built in the last ten years that have similar amenities. Upperclassman apartments set their own visitation hours.

The level of safety on campus matches the school's bucolic setting; no crimes have been reported there in several years.

The 2005–6 tuition, room, and board totaled $26,000, making Houghton competitive with other New York liberal arts schools, but by no means cheap. Houghton provides each student with a laptop computer and offers generous financial aid. Some 91 percent of students receive need-based financial aid, and 51 percent qualify for aid from the state or federal government. Merit-based scholarships are available and over 40 percent of students receive them.

THE KING'S COLLEGE

NEW YORK, NEW YORK • WWW.TKC.EDU

In the past thirty years, academic traditionalists and religious conservatives have launched a number of small colleges meant to counter those broad, destructive trends in higher education which have seemed impervious to reform: the dismantling of core curricula, the shock-secularization of church-founded schools, and the advent of what Roger Kimball has called "tenured radicals." A few such schools went bust, while others have become institutions with subcultures all their own, elaborate traditions, and distinctive interpretations of culture—where the children of alumni who met and married at the school now take the same courses, sometimes from the same professors. Perhaps because they were founded as acts of secession from "mainstream" institutions that had become corrupt or decadent—or maybe because the real estate was cheaper—such small schools were usually founded in rural areas, far from the nearest city of any size. This "splendid isolation" no doubt helps such colleges focus inwardly on their mission, but it also keeps away certain types of students. Until recently, none of the small, conservative start-up colleges in America had been situated in a major city.

Enter the King's College, which is not simply located in New York City but in midtown Manhattan. In fact, it's inside the Empire State Building. If this suggests that the school intends to engage the culture, well, that's true. In fact, the tiny school (only 250 students so far, and around a dozen permanent faculty) was founded to serve the following mission:

> Through its commitment to the truths of Christianity and a Biblical worldview, The King's College seeks to prepare students for careers in which they will help to shape and eventually to lead strategic public and private institutions: to improve government, commerce, law, the media, civil society, education, the arts and the church.

In practice, this means taking a body of largely evangelical Christian students—many of them homeschooled, and most from the Midwest—and introducing them to a level of scholarship and intellectual engagement that most have never before encountered.

The King's College was essentially re-founded in 1999 by the Campus Crusade for Christ, carrying on the name and heritage of a defunct Christian college that had once operated in the Hudson Valley. Since then, the King's College has had to fight against a host of regulators who have seemed intent on harassing the school, apparently because of its religious mission. Several bureaucrats among the New York State Board of Regents accused the school of attempting to confuse prospective students by taking the name (King's College) used by the present Columbia University before 1776. (The Regents were perhaps a tad optimistic about the level of historical knowledge possessed by high school students.) Eventually, this line of argument embarrassed even the Regents, and the school won accreditation. While what one professor calls "procedural harassment" continues, TKC seems to have weathered the storm. It will continue in its small, dogged way to pursue its lofty mission. Intellectually serious students who want a genuinely formative Christian education would do well to take a look at this high-minded little college in one of the world's tallest buildings.

Academic Life: Art Deco Oxford

At the King's College, students are exposed to a serious, integrated core curriculum such as used to prevail at most elite American colleges until the 1970s—when Harvard shoved its core over a cliff, and hundreds of lemmings followed. At TKC, students must take:

- "Foundations of American Politics";
- "College Writing" I and II;
- "American Civilization" I and II;
- "Introduction to Old Testament Literature" and "Introduction to New Testament Literature";
- "Foundations of Judeo-Christian Thought";
- "Philosophical Apologetics";
- "Western Civilization I";
- "Enlightenment and Liberal Democracy";
- "Culture and Aesthetics";
- "Theories of Human Nature";
- "Mathematical Ideas and Practice";
- "Fundamentals of Economics";
- "History of Economic Thought";
- "Logic"; and
- "Stewardship" (an economics course).

A professor at TKC says of the courses in this core, "Our introductory classes in Western civilization and American history and politics are deeply respectful of the heritage they present. Among the distinctive features of Western civilization we emphasize are the dignity of the individual; the capacity of Western civilization to reform itself (it alone abolished slavery); and its quest for scientific knowledge. We teach the American founding as one of the signal events in Western history, and pay particular attention to the rule of law, the separation of powers, freedom of religion and speech, and the protection of property rights. These are not courses on the West or the United States as perfected. The struggle to form a 'more perfect union' rightly implies the limitations of any human order."

One student calls the classes on Western culture "for the most part very elementary. The classwork is basically a lot of information [that] attempts to grasp our civilization's past. Unfortunately, there seems to be limited flexibility in avoiding the survey-course feel, while still trying to teach all of Western civilization in a two-semester block. There is only so much that you can teach." But the school's provost, Professor Peter Wood, writes in the *American Conservative*, "Because the curriculum is mostly a 'core,' with most of the students taking the same classes in the same sequence, they know each other's views, opinions, and intellectual styles as familiarly as the village elders might in a nineteenth-century New England town."

Beyond its wide-ranging core, the King's College limits its mission, offering just two majors: a B.S. in business, and a B.A. in a program called Politics, Philosophy, and Economics (PPE)—the latter modeled on those famous programs at several Oxford colleges which trained numerous generations of British cabinet ministers. The school has rather a hankering fondness for statesmen (and stateswomen); several of its student residential groups are named for politicians—Margaret Thatcher, Ronald Reagan, Winston Churchill, and Queen Elizabeth I. If this seems mildly incongruous, it is at least in keeping with the founders' aspiration to train young Christians for positions of leadership.

Says one student of the PPE major, "Very few schools offer this unique degree, but I believe it to be valuable because it speaks to the three most influential areas of human interaction with God, money, and power." Another says that "the strongest aspect of this major is the philosophy portion, and in particular, political philosophy. You come away from this course being able to think very critically about issues and also (hopefully) being able to write well. The economics portion is somewhat weak in my opinion, but I know that the school is working to develop this end of the major." According to a faculty member, "The emphasis in economics had been very free-market. It could have been described as all-Hayek all the time, but that's changing." Two new economics professors have recently been hired to bolster this program, the school reports. In one economics class, a professor integrates his free-market approach with the school's biblical inspiration—for instance, by using the parable of the prodigal son to illustrate the U.S. trade deficit and the dangers of profligate federal spending.

VITAL STATISTICS

Religious affiliation: Nondenominational Christian

Total enrollment: 250

Total undergraduates: 250

SAT/ACT midranges: SAT V: 570–670, M: 520–640; ACT: 23–27

Applicants: 348

Applicants accepted: 56%

Accepted applicants who enrolled: 40%

Tuition: $18,590

Room and board: $7,980 (room only)

Freshman retention rate: 77%

Graduation rate: not provided

Courses with fewer than 20 students: 60%

Student-faculty ratio: 13:1

Courses taught by graduate students: none

Most popular majors: business; philosophy, politics and economics (PPE)

Students living on campus: 90%

Guaranteed housing for four years? yes

Students in fraternities or sororities: none

The political science program at TKC bears a heavily philosophical stamp, in part because the school's current president, J. Stanley Oakes, and several of its faculty were trained by the followers of Harry Jaffa, an influential constitutional theorist among many neoconservatives. However, the atmosphere at the school "is by no means monolithic," one teacher insists. As one student says, "People often joke that King's is a cookie-cutter school of right-wing Republicans from Middle America. The student body is actually quite diverse—King's has many international students and students from all over the country. Divergent opinions are well tolerated." Another agrees, saying, "Debate is quite vigorous on campus, especially on issues such as Teri Schiavo or gay rights. A big campus-wide debate concerns to what degree religious morality should enter the American political arena. As TKC is a Christian college, religious students are quite welcome, and on the flip side, more liberal, less religious students are also very welcome. Non-Christians have come to King's and loved it. They said they didn't feel oppressed by religion in the classroom."

The King's College "is a magnet for a very ambitious sort of self-consciously Christian student who loves the intense focus of the curriculum and who thrives on the tight-knit face-to-face community," writes provost Wood. However, many of these students "aren't aware of the powerful intellectual tradition within evangelical Christianity," another professor laments. "I have to remind them that C. S. Lewis was a literary scholar at Oxford—and that most of America's great universities were founded by devout Christians. That helps them understand that developing intellectually is part of the walk of faith."

This reminder is important because "the evangelical world in which these students were raised isn't known for pushing hard on intellectual rigor," Wood writes. "Keeping true to the faith, reading the Bible every day, and treating others with heartfelt sincerity count a lot more in these communities than sharp elbows and a manic work style. And evangelicals tend to be forgiving when it comes to things like crisp writing, precise diction, and an agile grasp of political theory. . . . [However,] I expect them to develop an ethic of unrelenting excellence in their writing, speaking, and analysis. That's the only way they will succeed in the elite institutions that they aspire to join."

Students seem to appreciate being held to such a high standard. According to one, "in a recent student satisfaction survey conducted at King's, the aspect of the school most valued by students is academic rigor. King's students work hard for their grades, and most are, of necessity, 'awakened' intellectually."

At the King's College, faculty foster such awakenings through small classes with an emphasis on Great Books and great ideas, trips to the innumerable artistic and cultural treasures of one of the world's great cities, and work in local soup kitchens as part of theology class. Since the school's emphasis is on that "mere Christianity" shared by most broadly "orthodox" believers, it attracts as students and faculty both Catholics and Protestants—although the latter, unsurprisingly, predominate. Renowned Catholic writer Peter Kreeft has for several years come down from Boston College weekly to teach philosophy classes, while other distinguished professors come in from points much further south and west. However, the school is building its permanent faculty, and will probably soon diminish its reliance on visiting professors.

By all accounts, members of the permanent faculty work closely with students outside of class time—and even visiting professors make sure to schedule extensive office hours. "King's professors are for the most part extremely accessible," a student says. All classes are taught by professors, rather than grad students. Furthermore, "many professors are involved as faculty advisors in the House system. Through this channel and others, professors get very involved in students' lives. From frequent meals or coffees in between classes to home-cooked meals to just walking about the city discussing the pressing issues our country and world face, the professors go out of their way to extend the education experience beyond the classroom," reports the student.

Favorite teachers include visiting professors Peter Kreeft in philosophy and Paul Cleveland in economics—who is praised for his "energetic lectures." Permanent faculty praised by students include David Tubbs in politics and Robert Jackson in English. One undergrad singles out for notice Steve Salyers in communications, praising him for the care he shows students: "He spends almost all of his time on campus, has students to his home for dinners or parties frequently, and really extends the process of learning beyond the classroom." Theology teacher Robert Carle is said to be "incredibly knowledgeable, [with an] incredible grasp of the material he teaches—whether it's civil rights, church history, writing, or comparative religions." Also in theology, Darian Lockett is called "inspiring and passionate. . . . His

"I expect [TKC students] to develop an ethic of unrelenting excellence in their writing, speaking, and analysis. That's the only way they will succeed in the elite institutions that they aspire to join."

love for learning and pursuit of excellence is contagious. He is fired up in the classroom, and is so dedicated as to have additional seminars at his home." Another says of Lockett that he "has inspired me through his class on biblical interpretation to look far beyond the surface levels of my faith and dig deep into the Bible as bedrock for my life."

The school has a smallish library full of conservative and religious classics and texts used in class. However, TKC stands only one block from the Science, Business, and Industry division (and ten blocks from the main branch) of the New York Public Library—so nearly any text that a teacher or student could possibly need is easily accessible.

Some of the acknowledged weak points at TKC comprise those areas which the school has not yet found time to address. The school teaches only two mathematics courses and no hard sciences or foreign languages, although sources say TKC hopes to address these subject matters in the future. The college hopes to roll out a number of study-abroad options in the future, but only offers one at present: students interested in international business or law can spend a year at Handong Global University in

South Korea. Students from King's have also done summer mission projects in Peru, Asia, and the Middle East, and they have often joined ministry teams led by TKC's organization, Campus Crusade for Christ. No doubt, for many of the students at TKC, living in polyglot, postmodern New York feels like they are already studying abroad.

Student Life: Jonah in Nineveh

If you visit the King's College, don't expect a panoramic view; the classrooms, library, and student lounge are in the basement of the Empire State Building, not the seventieth floor, and all entering must pass through strict security checkpoints. One student reports that "it's really cool to flash your Empire State Building security pass and skip the lines." Administrative offices are on the fifteenth floor. The facilities are clean and have a slightly corporate feel, although the students have made the lounge their own; it looks like a trendy "alternative" coffeeshop such as one would find near any college.

As one might expect of a Christian school that locates itself at what many believers might consider the heart of Mammon, the King's College takes a more laissez-faire approach toward student life than do many religious colleges. The school is not "value-neutral," of course, and it maintains a reasonable set of rules for a Christian college. But rather than build up an elaborate structure for discipline, TKC has emulated American military academies and older religious schools in crafting an honor code, which students adopt and enforce themselves. "We see that as more suited to young adults living in a major city," says an administrator. "We want the students to take ownership of these values and internalize them—not look at a list of imposed, detailed rules which they're immediately tempted to try to circumvent. That's just (fallen) human nature," he observes.

One student reports, "The school's location in New York City is a huge boon. King's students are not in a 'Christian bubble,' but in an extremely worldly city that is 'the center of the universe.' The school's location is strategic to cultivating leadership in the secular national institutions of government, business, media, education, et cetera."

There are no dorms per se, but blocks of apartments in two nearby buildings; these are arranged into "Houses." According to TKC, "a House consists of twenty to twenty-five students who live, study, and work together. A TKC faculty member serves as an honorary member of the House, acting as a link between students and the college administration. Each House is named after a great historic leader who left his/her mark on our world . . . and carries with it the values and traditions particular to that House." As students are wont to do, they have already begun to come up with their own such traditions, sources report, in the hope that they will eventually become venerable. The student houses compete in debates, contests, sports, and projects for missionary outreach.

Says one a student, "The men live at one building, the Vogue, and the women at another, Herald Towers—although there is talk of moving all students to one building. It's an interesting environment for college life because we share those buildings with hundreds of other tenants. Our rooms are spread throughout the buildings, so we're not really clumped into one big party hall. Students spend a lot of time studying with each other in the various apartments. Because they all have kitchens, group meals are also a frequent part of 'dorm life.' Every apartment has four students (typically), and each apartment has its own bathroom." Says another, "The residence director lives with his family in the girls' building. There are eight or so 'chamberlains,' who share RA responsibilities among themselves, on a scheduled rotating basis. All visitors are announced by the buildings (they check in at the desks and are buzzed up). All overnight guests must be reported to a chamberlain. Guys cannot be in girls' rooms and vice versa past 1 a.m."

"Housing rules are actually very limited," reports one student. "King's wants to treat its students as adults and let them make their own decisions. You can smoke or drink, if you are of age, but not in the apartments themselves—out of respect for your roommates (and New York laws). And there are 'privacy hours.' This is not so much a curfew but a way to make sure two or three roommates don't dominate the apartment over the others." Infractions of rules are handled by student committees, in accord with the school's honor code. "Dorms are dry, and most students don't drink. But if students come back to the dorm [short of] really drunk, they're likely at most just to be questioned," another student says.

SUGGESTED CORE
1. History 217: Western Civilization I (*closest match*)
2. Philosophy 367: Plato and Aristotle
3. Religion 157/167: Introduction to the New Testament / Introduction to the Old Testament
4. Biblical Studies 380: Church History (*closest match*)
5. Politics 387: Enlightenment and Liberal Democracy
6. English 410: Renaissance Literature (*closest match*)
7. History 117: American Civilization I
8. History 227: Western Civilization II (*closest match*)

Student groups have already begun to proliferate. "Anyone can start a student group or club. These allow for leadership development," remarks one student. "Personally I've started two—the C. S. Lewis Society, which is a philosophical debate society in the tradition of Lewis and Tolkien's group, The Inklings, and a Christian worship organization called The Tent, which has involved over forty people in leadership roles, learning how to run an organization and lead other people and teams. We also have an annual Fall Retreat out of the city which is designed to help integrate the new students with the upperclassmen."

Students seem enthusiastic about their location, and manage to get their work done despite the many distractions offered by a many-splendored city—which offers every possible variety of theater, popular and classical music, arts performance, and ethnic cuisine, along with dozens of museums and hundreds of historic buildings. Churches of every denomination are a short walk or a safe subway ride away. Best of all, says one TKC student, "The King's College is in the Empire State Building—what could be cooler than that? It's impressive to watch the Macy's Thanksgiving parade walk past your front door, and to walk to New York's largest building every day and think 'That's my school building.'" Conversely, "Sometimes I go uptown to Columbia University to study or relax and think that it would be nice to have a campus."

ALL-AMERICAN COLLEGES

Crime is not an issue inside the heavily patrolled Empire State Building, or in the nearby dorms, while the midtown area has one of the lowest crime rates of New York—itself now one of America's safest major cities.

As private colleges go, TKC's costs are midrange, with tuition $18,590 and room fees averaging $7,980. No board plan is offered; students have kitchens, and there are literally hundreds of eateries within walking distance. The school works hard to help students financially; some 79 percent get need-based aid, and the average student loan debt of a recent grad is an outstandingly low $2,857.

LEE UNIVERSITY

CLEVELAND, TENNESSEE • WWW.LEEUNIVERSITY.EDU

Although this school named Lee is in the South, it's not named for the general, but for a minister—the school's second president, Rev. F. J. Lee. Begun in 1918 by the Church of God, it was renamed in 1947 and added graduate programs a half century later. In the past twenty years, Lee has experienced phenomenal growth, nearly tripling its student body, which now approaches 4,000. But through all this growth, Lee has retained a strong Christian identity, as well as its affiliation with the Church of God, a Pentecostal Christian church in the Holiness tradition. In the words of the school's mission statement, Lee "seeks to provide an education that integrates biblical truth as revealed in the Holy Scriptures with truth discovered through the study of arts and sciences and in the practice of various professions. A personal commitment to Jesus Christ as Savior is the controlling perspective from which the educational enterprise is carried out." The stated goal of Lee's educational programs is "to develop within students knowledge, appreciation, understanding, ability and skills which will prepare them for responsible Christian living in a complex world."

Academic Life: The Early Church and the Great Books

Lee is serious about building a solid foundation in biblical education and theology for all its students. The theology department in the School of Religion conducts a required eighteen-credit-hour program—which adds up to a minor in the Bible for every student. In general, the curriculum required of every undergraduate covers an impressive range of learning. Lee students must complete the following:

- "Gateway to University Success," an introduction to college-level work;
- "Foundations of Western Culture";
- two more classes in the humanities, chosen from among "Rise of Europe," "Foundations of the Modern World," "Twentieth-Century Western Culture," "Western Civilization II," "Masterpieces of the Western World I," and "Masterpieces of the Western World II";

- "The Message of the Old Testament" and "The Message of the New Testament";
- "Introduction to Theology";
- "Introduction to Christian Ethics";
- eight units of community service;
- "Computer Literacy and Applications" or "Introduction to Computer-based Systems";
- "Contemporary Mathematics," "College Algebra," or a class in higher mathematics;
- one or two composition classes (depending on test scores);
- "Art History II," "Survey of Drama Literature," "Music Survey," or "Introduction to Philosophy";
- "Recent American History and Government" or "Understanding Contemporary Politics";
- two courses out of the following three: "Understanding Human Behavior," "Understanding Contemporary Society," and "Understanding Economic Issues";
- one science course with a lab; recommendations for nonscience majors include "Andean Biogeography," "Australian Wildlife Biology," and "Ornamental Horticulture";
- a "Global Perspectives" seminar and a "Cross-Cultural Experience"; and
- an integrative capstone course in the student's major or a religion elective chosen by the student's major department.

In addition, B.A. students are required to take coursework or pass a test showing intermediate mastery of a foreign language (French, German, Spanish, or New Testament Greek); B.S. students require a lesser level of mastery or completion of the "Language and Culture" course.

The students we consulted were overwhelmingly grateful for these core classes, which they said gave them a greater appreciation for history, literature, and the Bible. "The courses were very respectful of our American heritage and the institutions that America has created. Students who take these courses (and take them seriously) will leave with both a better understanding of the world and a deeper respect for the Western heritage," says one communications major. Another student reports that these courses helped her develop a new respect for the life of the mind. "I have always been smart, but in high school I just went through the motions because I had to—I wasn't really interested in what I was learning. However, since my first semester at Lee, I have built up a great desire to learn as much as I can. I enjoy going to classes; I enjoy writing papers, because I know I'm going to learn; I enjoy interacting with my professors, because I know they have so much to share. I'm sure a part of it is growing up, but I think a huge part of it is the atmosphere at Lee." Lee's approach, claims another student, "flipped a switch in me, intellectually."

As befits a school in the Holiness tradition, special attention is paid to the formation of the early church in the New Testament. Almost all the professors in the religion department get high marks from students—and from faculty in other disciplines, one of whom says that this department consists "almost entirely of world-class teachers." Andi Blackmon is praised especially for the personal attention he pays to his students' questions—often going out of his way to help them find answers. According to one former student, he is "a guru for future youth ministers." Terry Cross, who also teaches philosophy, is also recommended. One junior says, "Take anything you can with him."

Another strong department is music. This is no surprise, as the Church of God Publishing House is one of the leaders in religious music publishing. "The piano performance and music education programs are up there with the best schools in the country," says one junior music education major.

In general, students say, "professors are very accessible and helpful—even the deans of the colleges who teach. Professors (not assistants) teach their own classes 99.9 percent of the time." Some faculty members whom students should seek out include Steve Swindle in political science; Bill Estes, chairman of the education department; Matthew Melton, dean of arts and sciences, whom one colleague describes as an "old-fashioned humanist who loves the Western tradition"; and Jeri Veenstra in natural sciences—who is known for winning over nonscience majors with her enthusiasm and high expectations.

Some may wonder whether a school so closely associated with one Christian denomination creates an oppressive atmosphere in the classroom for students of other churches and faiths. To this concern, one senior responds, "I think our school does an excellent job of allowing students to express their thoughts freely and without feeling ostracized, while still maintaining the school's doctrine of belief. Political correctness or unwarranted 'orthodoxy' does not intrude into the classroom—I would say the classroom is one of the best places for a student to express his or her beliefs, even if they go against the school's official doctrine."

The one glaring weakness in Lee's core is the absence of philosophy requirements. Students may study music, art, or drama instead—as if those disciplines were interchangeable. (This suggestion would have confounded early Christian thinkers such as Justin Martyr, Augustine, and Irenaeus.) The core does a good job of covering the West's cultural history, and of helping students develop a "biblical worldview and lifestyle," but it does not necessarily impart to students a rigorous understanding of competing worldviews outside the Christian tradition, teachers say. There is no independent phi-

VITAL STATISTICS

Religious affiliation:
 Church of God
Total enrollment: 3,930
Total undergraduates: 3,648
SAT/ACT midranges: SAT V:
 480–610, M: 450–600;
 ACT: 19–26
Applicants: 1,465
Applicants accepted: 61%
*Accepted applicants who
 enrolled*: 84%
Tuition: $9,888
Room and board: $5,024
Freshman retention rate: 73%
Graduation rate: 28% (4 yrs.),
 47% (6 yrs.)
*Courses with fewer than 20
 students*: 52%
Student-faculty ratio: 18:1
*Courses taught by graduate
 students*: none
Most popular majors:
 religion, communica-
 tion, psychology
Students living on campus:
 48%
*Guaranteed housing for four
 years?* yes
Students in fraternities: 12%
 sororities: 10%

losophy department, although Lee does offer, through its religion department, such courses as "The Philosophy of Human Nature," "The Philosophy of Freedom," "Philosophical Ethics," and "Philosophy of Religion." Other electives include "Major Thinkers of Western Christianity" and "Major Thinkers in Modern Continental Philosophy," both of which have solid reading lists.

The political science major requires courses in American government and international relations. Poli-sci majors must also choose from a number of courses in ancient and American political theory. Electives include courses on constitutional law, foreign policy, and "Morality and Politics." The major's capstone is a comprehensive course, "Christianity and Politics."

Lee requires English majors to complete courses in English and American literature, literary criticism, and Shakespeare. The electives in this major seem quite solid, including classes on Chaucer, Milton, and Victorian literature.

Almost all the professors in the religion department get high marks from students—and from faculty in other disciplines, one of whom says that this department consists "almost entirely of world-class teachers."

Some faculty describe the history courses in the core as "uneven," but students who major in the subject face serious requirements. History majors must take classes in American and modern European history, plus survey courses on Western civilization that include a heavy emphasis on ancient Greece. Electives stress both American history and church history. There is also a course on the history of the South.

One mildly troubling development at the school is Lee's decision to add a women's studies department. While it is too early to say what direction that program will take, what has happened at virtually every other university that has allowed such a department to be formed is not encouraging. While we don't expect that Lee will soon have a lesbian theologian preaching Wicca, just that has happened at other Christian (or at least formerly Christian) colleges.

Lee is particularly well known for its study-abroad programs. It is ranked number one in *U.S. News and World Report* for the number of students studying in other countries, including China, Japan, Italy, Russia, Germany, Britain, Chile, and Mexico. The school says that "numbers aside, it would be hard to overestimate the influence that the Global Perspectives Program exerts in students' academic, social, and spiritual lives." The program serves to take students out of a sometimes otherworldly social environment on campus. As one senior says, "We need to connect with people who are not going to chapel three and four times a week."

Student Life: Power in Christ

Prospective students unfamiliar with the Church of God ought to consider their theology before enrolling, since most students at Lee belong to that church. The denomination traces its history to the Barney Creek Meeting House on the border of Tennessee and North Carolina. Although the Church of God is historically "Wesleyan/Arminian," believing in the conditional security of believers, there is a growing contingent of Calvinist-minded members in the church. The Church of God operates within the Holiness and Full Gospel Pentecostalist tradition—meaning that members believe that the baptism and gifts of the Holy Spirit recorded in the New Testament are still available to believers today. To learn more, one student recommends a history of the church titled *Like a Mighty Arm,* by Charles W. Conn. Attitudes at Lee concerning particular tenets of the church vary. One student, referring to the gifts of the Holy Spirit (which

SUGGESTED CORE
1. and 2. Humanities 201: Foundations of Western Culture
3. Bible 101/102: Old Testament Survey / New Testament Survey
4. Theology 323: History of Christianity I
5. Political Science 472: Modern Political Theory
6. English 410: Shakespeare
7. History 301: History of Colonial America
8. Humanities 302: Modern Western Culture

include speaking in tongues, prophecy, and healing), insists that "a Christian without power in Christ is no Christian." But other students adopt a more easygoing, pan-evangelical stance: "A Christian believes that Christ is his personal savior, and holds that the Bible is the Word of God."

Chapel services are held regularly on Sundays, Tuesdays, Wednesdays, and Thursdays. A professor observes that attendance at so many "chapel services throughout the week makes for a pious student body." Students are permitted to express respectful disagreement with certain tenets espoused by the Church of God, but overt questioning of basic Christian doctrine would not find a welcome here. Members of "high-church" traditions would also experience an enduring culture shock.

Politics at Lee are generally very conservative, but dissenting views are increasingly expressed on campus. "There is not a completely free atmosphere for debate, but the school has definitely been working to improve on this—recently the school has sponsored guest politicians to speak on campus from both political parties, allows freedom of speech from anyone in the campus newspaper's Op/Ed section, has hosted debate sessions during election times, et cetera," a professor said.

Unlike many Christian schools, Lee University has a Greek club system of ten organizations that are not affiliated with national fraternities or sororities. "They are Christian-based social service organizations whose purpose is to serve the faculty, administration, and student body of Lee," says a student. "The clubs are quick to help out with campus events, put on events for the student body, and do numerous service projects throughout the community," she continues. "The Greek community is very close and is built on strong traditions that go back far in Lee history. Many of the professors and administrators were members of these institutional clubs, which forms a bond between them and students." In addition to these Greek groups, there are student-run organizations dealing with spiritual life and discipleship, art, and academics.

Academic groups include the ecology-minded Conservancy Club and the Sociology Club. Other groups include Amnesty International, Circle K, College Democrats, College Republicans, International Justice Mission, and the Philosophy Club.

Freshmen and sophomores are required to live in dorms, which one undergrad describes as "very nice, clean, and new, for the most part." In keeping with Lee's Christian vision of education strict rules govern dorm life; extensive, unsupervised visits between the sexes are not permitted. "The dorms are very community-based. . . . RAs and RDs are a big part of residents' lives. Lee also has dorm chaplains," a student reports. Lee also forbids the drinking of alcohol and smoking on campus. Scott Stapp, who went on to become the lead singer of Creed, famously ran afoul of these rules and was expelled. In a minor concession to vice, the residence halls have common TV lounges—with cable.

Lee is set on over one hundred acres in beautiful Bradley County, Tennessee. Its facilities are mostly attractive Georgian-style buildings. Nearby Chattanooga offers pleasant diversions, including the Tennessee Aquarium and a minor league baseball team, the Chattanooga Lookouts. Crime has not been a big concern at Lee. Students feel entirely safe as long as they conduct themselves sensibly. The school did report thirteen burglaries on campus in 2004.

Tuition at Lee is an astonishingly affordable $9,888, with room and board $5,024. Some 55 percent of students receive need-based financial aid. Despite the reasonable price tag, the average student graduates owing approximately $26,500.

MESSIAH COLLEGE

GRANTHAM, PENNSYLVANIA • WWW.MESSIAH.EDU

Messiah College was founded in 1909 as the Messiah Bible School and Missionary Training Home of the Brethren in Christ Church (MBSMTHBCC). Quite a mouthful. Fortunately, the school was renamed Messiah College in 1951. In 1967, Messiah merged with Upland College, and in 1972 it became independent of its founding church, with a self-perpetuating board of trustees. Messiah is still bound to the Brethren by a covenant, and the church exerts significant denominational control.

The school endorses a "faith statement" that begins with the Apostles' Creed and expands on it in telling ways. For instance, Messiah asserts that "God creates each of us in the very image of God to live in loving relationships: free, responsible and accountable to God and each other for our decisions and our actions." The school also explains that "God instructs us to pursue the kingdom of peace, righteousness and justice which ultimately will prevail with the return of Christ. . . . " These official statements nicely suggest the flavor of a school where evangelical Christianity and a certain peace-loving, Anabaptist spirit coexist amicably.

The Brethren in Christ is a small church with a unique heritage. It emerged in the 1770s, when some Pennsylvania Mennonite congregations became influenced by the more mystical approach of the neighboring German Pietists and the Holiness teachings of the early Methodists. The Brethren are more engaged with the world than are the Old Order Amish, but they maintain the traditional Anabaptist witness for peace and reconciliation. They believe in fervent prayer and cherish the Bible as a communication from God without embracing literalism. Though once inclined to view worldly learning as a temptation to the sin of pride, the Brethren in Christ now pursue it avidly as a means of preparing themselves to do God's work in the world. Messiah always was a good Bible school; today, it has evolved into an excellent liberal arts college with a Christian orientation. For this reason, it has been listed for more than ten consecutive years on the Templeton Foundation's "Honor Roll of Character-building Colleges."

Academic Life: Engaging the World

While Messiah has no real core curriculum, the robust general education requirements take up fifty-six of students' 123 required credits. Students must complete:

- a "First-Year Seminar." This introduces each student to college-level work and promotes "a positive integration of Christian faith and the intellectual life." Many options are offered in an array of topics which change every year;
- a class in speech;
- three classes in mathematical and natural sciences;
- two classes in social sciences and history. Choices range from "American Government" to "Principles of Sociology";
- three classes in humanities and the arts. Options include "Writings of the Inklings," "Introduction to Shakespeare," and "Multi-Ethnic Literature";
- one class in philosophy—either "History of Philosophy" or "Problems of Philosophy";
- one art class. Choices range from the foundational ("Introduction to Drawing") to the discouraging ("Guitar for the Church Musician"—maybe they mean *classical* guitar . . .);
- foreign language and culture classes—either three semesters of the same language, reaching the intermediate level, or two semesters of the same language plus an approved cross-cultural study. Students may choose French, German, Spanish, Greek, Latin, or Hebrew;
- two courses in the Bible—"Introduction to Biblical Studies" plus an elective;
- one course in Protestant theology;
- two courses in "Interdisciplinary Perspectives." Options range widely, from "Christian Perspectives on Patriotism, Terrorism, and Politics" to "Environmental Ethics";
- one course in the category called "World Views/Pluralism," with options including "The Holocaust" and "Immigrant America"; and
- one health course—"Life Fitness"—plus a sports elective.

Messiah College also offers an impressive honors program presided over by Professor Dean Curry, a man revered by his students. The program selects up to eighty-five incoming freshmen for full and partial tuition scholarships, rigorous interdisciplinary courses, and a senior research project.

Students seem mostly satisfied with their education at Messiah. "While some courses have been less than rigorous," one reports on the college website, "overall, Messiah College has provided an excellent education. From the science to the humanities to faith issues, I feel that I am a well-rounded and educated person." While professors and students of the liberal arts are in a minority at Messiah—many more focus on business and education—they display a distinctive awareness of scholarship as a Christian calling, which is manifestly superior to the academic careerism one finds elsewhere. The student-faculty ratio is a middling 14 to 1.

Messiah faculty singled out by students as outstanding include Daniel Finch and Ted Prescott in art; Charles Jantzi and Winston Seebogin in psychology; Anita Voelker in education; Stephen Cobb in sociology; Bernardo Michael in history; Henry Venema in philosophy; Lareta Finger in biblical studies; Crystal Downing in English; Kathleen Quimby in communications; Marti Byers in nursing; Jack Cole and Scott Kieffer in health and fitness; Erik Lindquist in biology; Terry Earhart and Robert Kilmer in business; Douglas Phillippy in mathematics; Dean Curry and John Harles in political science; and Vince La France in business.

While the faculty mostly focus on teaching, they also publish. In 2004–5, Messiah professors generated seventy-five academic presentations, twenty-four essays, articles, poems, and images, nineteen books and chapters in books, eleven book reviews, six performances, exhibitions, and readings, and two external grants. Per capita, that's a pretty impressive level of production. According to the school, among the faculty one will find a "Rhodes scholar, Marshall scholar, Truman scholar, and several Fulbright fellowships and awards."

In 2004, Oxford University Press published *Scholarship and Christian Faith: Enlarging the Conversation*, edited by Messiah professors Douglas and Rhonda Jacobsen, and including essays by other members of the faculty. This book, which set the agenda for a major conference on campus, critiques the Reformed model of the Christian academy (as represented by Calvin College) and argues for a more ecumenical approach, including Catholic and Pentecostal perspectives among others in a widened dialogue. The book proposes going beyond the "apologetics model" of defending Christian faith against secular learning in order to explore the manifold ways faith, knowledge, and reason interact and interpenetrate in the life of the individual, church and society. One professor at the school writes, "Messiah offers on one campus what many Christian faculty members find only at occasional conferences: an ecumenically zesty mix of Anabaptists, Wesleyans, Catholics, Evangelicals, Episcopalians, Pentecostals, and persons from the Reformed tradition who talk with one another daily about teaching, scholarship, and the purpose of Christian higher education."

Opportunity to study off campus is offered through Brethren Colleges Abroad, Daystar University, Jerusalem University College, AuSable Institute of Environmental Studies, Oregon Extension, and the Coalition of Christian Colleges and Universities. There is also an extension campus in Philadelphia operated in cooperation with Temple University—a unique public/religious relationship.

VITAL STATISTICS

Religious affiliation:
  Brethren in Christ
Total enrollment: 2,916
Total undergraduates: 2,916
SAT/ACT midranges: SAT V:
  550–660, M: 540–650;
  ACT: 23–28
Applicants: 2,730
Applicants accepted: 75%
*Accepted applicants who
  enrolled*: 35%
Tuition: $21,420
Room and board: $6,800
Freshman retention rate: 85%
Graduation rate: 69% (4 yrs.),
  75% (6 yrs.)
*Courses with fewer than 20
  students*: 43%
Student-faculty ratio: 14:1
*Courses taught by graduate
  students*: none
Most popular majors: elementary education, nursing,
  biology
Students living on campus:
  84%
*Guaranteed housing for four
  years?* yes
*Students in fraternities or
  sororities*: none

Student Life: People of the Covenant

The students and teachers of Messiah College are expected to acknowledge the immediate and absolute lordship of Christ—which extends to the smallest details of everyday life. While as Christians they bear with each others' sins and imperfections, a student with the secular notion that people should mind their own business will not fit in well here. What this means in practice is carefully spelled out in a lengthy and rather impressive document called the Community Covenant. While containing prohibitions some would find irksome, it puts these in the context of the college's core values. The college explains thusly:

"As people created in God's image we are to follow Christ's example in preaching the good news to the poor, binding the brokenhearted, proclaiming freedom to the captives, and restoring sight to the blind. As those committed to living out the teachings of Scripture, we are to act justly, love mercy, and walk humbly. We are to bring peace and unity where there is conflict and discrimination. We are to respect people and to value life above material wealth. Because we see people as having intrinsic worth, we avoid gossip, manipulative behavior, and sexist or racist attitudes or behaviors, stressing instead integrity, commitment, and compassion in relationships with others."

The school describes its mission in this way: "God creates each of us in the very image of God to live in loving relationships: free, responsible, and accountable to God and each other for our decisions and our actions."

In practice, the school goes on, "prohibitions about the use of alcoholic beverages, tobacco products, and the abuse or unauthorized use of prescription or non-prescription drugs relate most clearly to concerns about personal well-being and the scriptural mandate to care for our bodies. Gambling is prohibited because we want to be wise stewards of the resources entrusted to us by God. As a community we believe that certain scriptural teachings apply to us as they have to all people in all cultures. Our lives are to be characterized by love, joy, peace, patience, kindness, goodness, faithfulness, gentleness, and self-control. We are to use our gifts in doing such things as serving, teaching, encouraging, giving, leading, and showing mercy. In contrast, we are to avoid such sinful practices as drunkenness, stealing, dishonesty, profanity, occult practices, sexual intercourse outside of marriage, homosexual behavior, and sexually exploitative or abusive behavior. Although wrong attitudes such as greed, jealousy, pride, lust, prejudice, and factiousness are harder to detect than wrong behaviors, both are prohibited as sinful and destructive of community life and of the body of Christ."

A cynic might well ask what is left of the traditional college experience. One recent graduate throws some light on the question. He remembers that, as the product of private Christian academies, he had pretty much decided on a secular higher education, considering Messiah only because of the excellence of its athletic programs. He reports that on visiting the place he found such joie de vivre that he was entirely won over. He now looks back to his years at Messiah with profound gratitude.

Even those students who cannot accept the Covenant without reservation acknowledge the community's positive aspects. Another recent graduate, a homosexual who served as president of his class, writes that "even in my anger and bitterness in regards to my experience at Messiah, there are whispers of joy too. There were things and people that I absolutely loved. I learned lessons from amazing individuals and professors. I am sure one day, as I grow, those memories will become far more dominant!"

To be sure, most students are neither devout covenanters nor decided rebels. Brethren in Christ form a tiny minority of the student body; indeed, as far as church affiliation goes, only the Baptists (13 percent) outnumber the nondenominational (11 percent), with the Methodists coming in third (8 percent). "Messiah College has sometimes been criticized as not [being] very Anabaptist by some of its constituencies, and as too Anabaptist by others," historian David Weaver-Zercher notes. "Indeed, the college has consciously chosen a middle way, underscoring in concrete ways its unique Brethren in Christ–rooted theological heritage and, at the same time, choosing to be inclusive of students and faculty from other Christian traditions."

Messiah may be religious, but it's not stuffy. A recent issue of the student newspaper laments the lack of imagination displayed by that year's Halloween costumes; it also celebrates the tradition of food fights (marshmallows) between Messiah and Elizabethtown fans at athletic contests.

Long Islander Kim Phipps took over the presidency of Messiah in 2004 after six years as academic dean at Malone College, an evangelical Quaker school in Ohio; Anna Quindlen gave the inaugural guest lecture. President Phipps expresses a personal and professional concern for the continuing education of educators in "anti-racism," and may be an important influence in steering legitimate concerns with the evils of racial prejudice away from the multiculturalist crusade against America, Christendom, and the West. Call us intractable optimists.

Although it is just twelve miles from the state capital at Harrisburg, Grantham is almost as rural as it is suburban. Indeed, the college is pretty much all there is to the town, and the college itself is, from a worldly point of view, pretty much a monastery. The campus consists of twenty-three buildings, only four of which date from before 1964, sitting among 484 acres on the banks of the Yellow Breeches Creek—which is crossed by a covered bridge and a swinging bridge on either end of the college. Over 80 percent of the nearly 3,000 students live in the eight dorms and two apartment complexes, freshmen in their own dorms.

SUGGESTED CORE
1. No suitable course
2. Philosophy 247: Ancient and Medieval Philosophy
3. Biblical and Religious Studies 213, 214: Old Testament Literature and New Testament Literature
4. History 343: Medieval Europe (*closest match*)
5. Poli Sci 204: History of Political Thought (*closest match*)
6. English 364: Shakespeare
7. History 103: U.S. Survey to 1865
8. History 352: Modern Europe, 1799–1918 (*closest match*)

Messiah believes in educating the whole person, and in this respect campus life outside the classroom is regarded as a "co-curriculum" rather than "extracurricular activity." Apart from studies, time is to be spent in worship, wholesome recreation, and rest. Messiah boasts a cocurricular staff of thirty; their work is supplemented by students called to various forms of formal and informal campus ministry.

The college is home to twenty NCAA Division III athletic teams. There are also numerous club sports, recreational sports, leadership opportunities, outreach teams, music ministry teams, Bible studies/discipleship groups, and experiential learning opportunities. Political groups include College Democrats and College Republicans. There are dozens of special-interest student organizations; a very incomplete list includes the Swing (Dance) Club, the *Swinging Bridge* (a student newspaper), the Ultimate Frisbee Organization (UFO), and WVMM (Messiah College Radio Station—90.7 FM). In 2005, Messiah made NCAA history by being the first school to have its men's and women's soccer teams win national titles in the same year. Soccer coach David Brandt exemplifies for many the Messiah attitude toward sports. He reminds his charges that athletic prowess diminishes with time; it is the discipline of character and humility of a servant-leader that remain—and that make the competition valuable for life.

The sense of community at Messiah College is established by mandatory chapel twice a week. Common Chapel is held for all students on Tuesdays and some Thursday mornings, a variety of Elective Chapel held on the other Thursdays, and Alternative Chapel at various times and places. Attendance is taken with the electronic student ID card. Students must attend chapel twenty-four times a semester, and twelve of these occasions must be Common Chapel. Upperclassmen may fulfill up to two semesters of chapel through community service.

There are no Greek organizations, but there are lots of student ministries, including Abba's Place, Amnesty International, Bethesda Mission, Big Brother/Big Sister, CATRA, Chapel Worship Band, Deaf Ministry, Habitat for Humanity, Harrisburg Tutoring, Music Ministry Teams, Special Olympics, the South Central PA Foodbank, and a dozen others.

Messiah students tend to be quiet, hardworking, socially and culturally conservative young folks who want to make decent lives for themselves and their families as businessmen, schoolteachers, or nurses. Most come from Pennsylvania and the neighboring states and remain in the region after graduation. Their campus is commensurately calm: in 2004, the only crimes on campus were six burglaries, none in residences, and six arsons, two of them in residences.

Messiah is in the middle price range for private schools, with annual tuition at $21,420, and room and board $6,800. Almost every first-year student, the school reports, receives some need-based financial aid, but the average graduate still emerges owing $27,322.

NEW SAINT ANDREWS COLLEGE

MOSCOW, IDAHO • WWW.NSA.EDU

In historic downtown Moscow, Idaho, some 130 students and their professors are building an institution that takes as its inspiration the famed St. Andrews University of Scotland. Founded to offer a classical education that is both intellectually rigorous and
firmly grounded in the Christian tradition, New Saint Andrews College immerses students in reading the great works of Western civilization, as viewed through the distinctive lens of Calvinist theology. And unlike some other small liberal arts schools, this
college is situated within a historic town, a meeting place for farmers and tradesmen
who might—like traditional liberal education itself—seem to belong to an older, almost
vanished America.

Academic Life: Calvin in Moscow

New Saint Andrews College officially began with the
1994–95 academic year, but the idea for the college
came from a reading list compiled in the early 1980s
by a group of men at Christ Church, a Reformed congregation in Moscow, Idaho. This reading list developed in the mid-1980s into a series of evening courses
on classical subjects, offered to adults. Elders of Christ
Church later undertook formal oversight of these
courses and organized a degree-granting, four-year
college. New Saint Andrews officially opened its doors

to its first matriculating class in 1994. Although it became an independent, self-sus-
taining institution in 2001, the school has continued to be closely associated with Christ
Church, a "reformational body of believers committed to the historic confessions of the
Reformation . . . [which is] a member of the Confederation of Reformed Evangelicals."
That's the Geneva, not the Wittenberg, Reformation.

New Saint Andrews is firmly committed to the traditional idea that the liberal
arts are formative of the whole person—not just the intellect. While the school is only
twelve years old, the faculty and students see themselves within the continuum of the
great Western tradition; the curriculum upon which they focus is one that has its roots
in the Middle Ages and the early Christian church. New Saint Andrews offers only two
degrees, a two-year associate of arts and a four-year bachelor of arts, both in Liberal
Arts and Culture. For the B.A., students must complete the following impressive core
curriculum:

Religious affiliation: Confederation of Reformed Evangelical Churches
Total enrollment: 126
Total undergraduates: 126
SAT/ACT midranges: SAT V: 620–690, M: 530–640; ACT: 22–30
Applicants: not provided
Applicants accepted: 88%
Accepted applicants who enrolled: 90%
Tuition: $7,200
Room and board: n/a
Freshman retention rate: 83%
Graduation rate: 70% (4 yrs.)
Courses with fewer than 20 students: not provided
Student-faculty ratio: 9:1
Courses taught by graduate students: none
Most popular majors: n/a
Students living on campus: none
Guaranteed housing for four years? no
Students in fraternities or sororities: none

- "Lordship Colloquium," a yearlong, double-credit class "which introduces the worldview of historic, creedal Protestantism";
- "Principia Theologiae," likewise yearlong and double credit, which focuses on "biblical, historic, and systematic theology";
- "Classical Rhetoric Colloquium," a course in oratory, composition, and logic;
- "Natural Philosophy Colloquium," which introduces mathematics and science, the "deductive and empirical disciplines that have always been important to Western cultural vitality";
- "Classical Culture and History Colloquium," a systematic introduction to the Western heritage "from Near-Eastern antecedents up through modern times";
- "Traditio Occidentis Colloquia," a two-year sequence covering Greek, Roman, and medieval texts in the junior year, and modern texts in the senior year, focusing on "themes in Literature, Philosophy, Law and Politics, Art, and Architecture";
- a year and a half of Latin;
- a year and a half of Greek;
- "Music Colloquium," a class applying "Christian approaches to aesthetics," which focuses on choral singing;
- "Thesis Research Seminar," which prepares students for writing their final project; and
- a senior thesis of approximately 20,000 words.

Although students may choose from several electives during their third and fourth years, the vast majority of their classes come from this core. Because New Saint Andrews offers only one major and its classes are interdisciplinary, the faculty work together without the distraction of departmental politics. As one professor explains, "We are all focused on making our one degree exceptional; because of this, I think it is an incredibly strong program."

Despite the fact that the curriculum is very structured, leaving room for few electives, the program still allows scope for individual interests. Professors report a high level of creativity and intellectual curiosity among students, which the school actively fosters. The weekly Disputatio, a public discussion of controversial topics attended by the entire faculty and student body, encourages questioning and debate. During their senior year, students are given the opportunity to explore subjects of individual interest within the framework of a senior thesis, a yearlong project directed by a faculty committee. In addition, students frequently take advantage of directed studies in order to pursue interests not addressed directly by the set curriculum.

Classes at New Saint Andrews are rigorous in terms of both material and teaching style. The reading list for the bachelor's degree includes about one hundred texts that might be called Western "classics," taken from various periods. Because of the college's commitment to Christianity, and because the Western heritage is in large part a Christian one, much of the curriculum consists of the study of that heritage. The two-year course Traditio Occidentalis focuses most clearly on the literature, art, and philosophy of the Western world, but all the courses are concerned to some extent with these topics. The faculty strive to engage students in critical thinking rather than mindless hagiography, while reinforcing a basic allegiance to the Western tradition. One student reports, "The history colloquium was very critical and very respectful of both the Western heritage and American history. We were taught to ask why certain events happened, what the historian who wrote about them was saying (about himself and the times) by what he chose to narrate, and what relevance the past has to us today."

As at most liberal arts colleges, the reading and writing requirements of the courses are heavy; more unusual, perhaps, is the emphasis New Saint Andrews places on rhetoric. In the first-year colloquium "Classical Rhetoric," students study and practice persuasive writing and speaking—both prepared and impromptu. Discussion of the readings, of course, is essential to a liberal arts program, but in addition to this, New Saint Andrews students often make declamations, oral presentations given before faculty and other students. Throughout their time at the school, they are also required to give weekly speeches. The emphasis on oral expression is also evident in the practice of oral examinations; with the exception of some language tests, all students meet with their instructors for an oral exam at the end of each academic term.

The education is based on both faith and reason. "The classes I've taken so far have all intensively encouraged and improved my ability to think critically . . . and to identify the presuppositions and worldviews that lie behind the surface facts, stories, or assignments," says one student.

The education at New Saint Andrews may be based on faith, but it works via reason. "The classes I've taken so far have all intensively encouraged and improved my ability to think critically—to analyze books, lectures, conversations, movies, newspaper articles, everything, really; and to identify the presuppositions and worldviews that lie behind the surface facts, stories, or assignments," says one student. "We are taught to ask why and how and what is the religious or political or psychological position or agenda behind something."

Although New Saint Andrews has grown significantly since its first graduating class of two students in 1998, it remains small, accepting only about fifty applicants each year. Administrators say they prefer to keep the school its present size, in order to ensure that each student becomes part of a genuine community, rather than a face in the crowd. Both faculty and students see the school's size and sense of community as an asset, with graduates often recalling this as one of the school's best features. As one professor says, "New Saint Andrews is a very small school and Moscow is a very small town. Because of this we are fairly close to our students, and half the education that we give is at the dinner table rather than in the classroom."

Classes are taught in the tutorial style, and professors have the opportunity to know their students as individuals. Students see this as a privilege, and appreciate it: "Our teachers all are wonderful people who thoroughly know their subjects, [and are] role models who care about us and wish to help us learn. The students truly love them," one student comments. Although the faculty do remain involved in research and publishing, and some professors have published widely, New Saint Andrews is very much a teaching college. Particularly notable faculty include Peter Leithart, a theology professor; Nathan Wilson, who gives weekly feedback to his students; and Douglas Wilson, who teaches electives. It should be noted, however, that many faculty do not have terminal degrees in their field.

The school now operates under the direction of a five-member board of trustees that appoints administration, faculty, and staff. The current president of the college is Dr. Roy Alden Atwood, who came to the position in 2004 after serving as dean of the college for several years.

The structure of the academic year and the classes at New Saint Andrews is somewhat different than at most colleges. The academic year is divided into four eight-week terms, each named after major doctrinal gatherings in church history: the Jerusalem and Nicea terms make up the fall semester, while the spring semester is divided into the Chalcedon and Westminster terms. A fifth term, the Dordrecht term, takes place during the summer, when additional classes, such as the refresher courses in Latin, are offered. Many of the classes at New Saint Andrews are a year rather than a semester in length, although electives are often one-term classes.

The dedication of the faculty and administration to providing an education that is Christian as well as classical goes much deeper than the monikers of the academic terms. In addition to the required courses in theology, all classes are grounded in a traditional Christian perspective of the world. The school does not require a particular denominational commitment of its students beyond asking that they "should refrain from actively promoting doctrines contrary to the Reformed mission and goals of the College," but the spirit of Calvin walks abroad at New Saint Andrews. "Though students do not have to subscribe to anything other than the most basic orthodox Christianity," states a professor, "the faculty are all dedicated to a very high octane Reformed Christianity, which pervades everything we do and is really the motivation for the entire education."

Student Life: Vast Quiet Fields of Wheat

New Saint Andrews sits in downtown Moscow, Idaho (pop. 20,000), some ninety miles from Spokane, Washington. The area surrounding the town is agricultural, but the town has a wide variety of cultural amenities. As the school's website boasts, "The local symphony performs just minutes from vast, quiet fields of wheat." The school's location on the city's Friendship Square puts it near a weekly farmer's market and a small park that features open-air concerts and other outdoor activities.

> SUGGESTED CORE
>
> The school's required core curriculum suffices.

New Saint Andrews places a high value on integration, whether that integration be between the Christian and classical traditions, within interdisciplinary classes, or between the academic world and daily life. The school encourages students to take a lively part in the local community, and to mix both with the townsfolk and the students of nearby University of Idaho and Washington State University. To foster community engagement, and to keep costs down, the college provides no student housing. Instead, students rent apartments or houses or arrange to board with families who reside near the school.

The tiny school is entirely contained within a historic (late-nineteenth-century) building on the Skattaboe block of downtown Moscow. Facilities include a newly renovated student common room, the Augustine and Calvin classrooms, the college bookstore, administrative and faculty offices, a conference room, and the Tyndale library—which contains a small collection, supplemented by the libraries at the University of Idaho and Washington State University. New Saint Andrews students have borrowing privileges at those schools, giving them access to almost six million books.

The school celebrates a number of festivals, including the Feast of St. Andrew and the anniversary of the Reformation—in honor of which it holds a banquet every year. The school also holds a ball, known as a "Windy," several times a year. While the college has no intercollegiate athletic teams, students have organized various intramural sports and club activities, and the college also maintains a choir, in which all students participate at least during their second year, when they take the colloquium on music.

The Code of Student Conduct reflects the Reformed Christian background of the school. Students are required to "pledge in writing their commitment to personal holiness, sound doctrine, cultural reformation, and academic integrity." This means, in practice, that everyone at the school belongs to some variety of Protestant church and tries to live by the tenets of traditional Christian morality. The college catalog gets pretty specific about the school's expectations:

> Students should exercise their Christian liberties not as an occasion to indulge the flesh, but to serve others out of love through the wise and moderate exercise of their liberty (Gal. 5:13–14; 1 Peter 2:13–16). By God's grace and through the church's instruction and discipline, students should abstain from the works of the flesh, such as sexual immorality, idolatry, hatred, discord, jealousy, wrath, selfish ambition, drunkenness, or debauchery, and to flee all temptations to those sins (Gal. 5:19–21, 24, 26; Eph. 5:3–7).

ALL-AMERICAN COLLEGES

Furthermore, students are expected "to participate cautiously and critically in our predominantly pagan popular culture, and to avoid and to repudiate the culturally destructive (but often 'socially acceptable') glorification of sin found in contemporary films, music, video games, websites, and so forth."

The school also requires that students "neither embrace nor promote, formally or informally, historic or contemporary doctrinal errors, such as Arianism, Socinianism, Pelagianism, Skepticism, Feminism," or several other heresies so obscure that the editors of this guide had to Google them.

Attendance at all seminars, recitations, and Disputatios is required, and modest, semi-formal dress is expected at all classes and school activities. Despite the school's close relationship to Christ Church, students are not required to attend services there, although they are expected to attend a local church on Sundays.

Founded to serve a niche audience of intellectually serious Protestants, this is clearly not the school for everyone. But those students who embrace its traditions and high aspirations will find New Saint Andrews invigorating and challenging. As one staff member expressed it, "Joy and cheer in general come out [at New Saint Andrews]. The community is really exuberant, a place where serious academic rigor is combined with rich camaraderie and fellowship."

The town of Moscow—and hence the campus—is a remarkably safe environment, reporting annual instances of violent activities and thefts in the single digits.

Like several other schools in this guide, such as Hillsdale College and Grove City College, New Saint Andrews maintains it freedom from federal micromanagement by refusing government aid—either for the school or for students. Nevertheless, the school strives to keep the cost of a private college education manageable; tuition is a modest $7,200, and rooming arrangements in Moscow, Idaho, are rather inexpensive. The college also offers both need-based and merit-based scholarships.

COLLEGE OF THE OZARKS

POINT LOOKOUT, MISSOURI • WWW.COFO.EDU

Students at College of the Ozarks roll up their sleeves for a college education. In exchange for tuition-free classes, they work on the school's cattle and pig farm, bake and sell fruitcakes, and staff the radio station and lodge—among the more than eighty available jobs at the school. About 90 percent of students are from low-income backgrounds, and many are first-generation college students. "Other schools may talk about the American dream (though I suspect far too few actually do); we *are* the American dream," says one professor. The mountain campus is like a town—with its own airport, hospital, fire department, farm, greenhouses, grain mill, meat processing plant, museums, motel, bakery, and restaurant—all manned by student workers.

Since its founding in 1906 by John Forsythe, a Presbyterian missionary, this institution has transformed itself from a high school into a two-year junior college and, in 1965, a full liberal arts college. Forsythe wanted the school to be "a self-sustaining 'family,'" according to the college. Students "without sufficient means" working for an education is a continuing tradition at C of O. The school is governed by a board of trustees made up of business and professional leaders and has a "covenant relationship" with the Presbyterian Church. President Jerry C. Davis has been at its helm since 1988.

Dubbed "Hardwork U" by the *Wall Street Journal*, the school draws tourists who visit its historic sites, dine on country-style cooking, and shop for products bearing the label "Hardwork U." Hand-in-hand with an excellent liberal arts education, students learn lessons about the worth and dignity of work, personal responsibility, and free enterprise at this impressive, blue-collar academy.

Academic Life: A Character Curriculum

C of O provides students with the foundations of a liberal arts education and a familiarity with the Western tradition through its general education requirements. Students must complete the following:

- "The American Experience," covering our history from pre-colonial times to the present;
- "Exploration of the Arts";

- an American, Western, or classical literature class;
- a Western civilization survey class;
- a philosophy or fine arts class;
- "The Changing Universe of Science";
- one course in social science (for example "The American Economy" or "Introduction to Psychology");
- a laboratory science course;
- one college mathematics class;
- one semester of French, German, Spanish, Greek, or Hebrew;
- a two-course sequence in English composition;
- "Biblical Survey" and "Biblical Theology and Ethics";
- a two-course sequence on "Citizenship and Lifetime Wellness";
- a fitness-based activity class;
- a public-speaking class; and
- a capstone course in the junior or senior year.

In addition, Bachelor of Arts students must take an additional foreign language class and Bachelor of Science students must choose either an additional lab science, mathematics, or computer science course. An excellent way to enrich the solid educational experience at C of O is by taking courses in its optional Character Curriculum, a Great Books program. The Character Curriculum focuses on ideals of virtue from different eras. "Great authors from Homer to Sophocles, Virgil to Dante, Shakespeare to Milton present us with imaginative visions of the human condition, sweeping backgrounds against which we can see the significance of human decisions and the consequences of character," says the program description. Course selections include "Biblical Ideas of Character," "Medieval/Renaissance Ideals of Character," "Reformation/Modern Ideas of Character," and "Capstone: American Ideas of Character."

Along with academics and work, the college emphasizes spiritual growth and patriotism. "We seek to challenge students as they prepare for life, and we strive to develop citizens of Christ-like character who are also well-educated and patriotic," says the school bulletin. "Through our innovative work program, we prepare you to enter the workforce with the confidence and skills you need. We encourage a campus atmosphere of honor and respect for our country, and we believe that your relationship with Christ is another facet of your education. We care about developing the 'whole person' within each student at College of the Ozarks." The school is not shy about proclaiming its values—one needs to only drive through the "Gates of Opportunity" at the entry of the campus to encounter the core values of the school. The streets are named, charmingly, Academic Avenue, Vocational Way, Spiritual Street, Opportunity Avenue, and Cultural Street.

The college offers more than thirty majors in six divisions: education and health, human and social sciences, technical and applied sciences, humanities, performing and professional arts, and mathematical and natural sciences. In addition to traditional liberal arts disciplines, the school offers majors tied to the businesses on campus, including agriculture, conservation and wildlife management, criminal justice, dietetics, family and consumer sciences, hotel and restaurant management, aviation science, and horticulture.

Department requirements for English majors are impressive. The department requires thirteen courses: "Foundations of Literary Studies," "Introduction to Grammar," "History of the English Language," two "Survey of British Literature" and two "Survey of American Literature" classes, "Western Literature" (Greek, Roman, and medieval), three English electives, a creative writing class, and an ungraded portfolio class. Many work assignments in the school's work program reinforce an academic program in English, including positions in the Lyon's Memorial Library, KZOC radio station, *Outlook* student newspaper, tutoring services, and public relations and academic offices.

History majors at C of O are required to take two Western civilization survey classes and a historiography class. The department calls for seven courses at the 300–400 level with at least three courses in American history and two in modern European history; one course in either third world or non-Western history; and one elective. Students also complete a writing-intensive seminar focused on a period or topic in European, American, or third-world history and an ungraded portfolio class. Students say that while some of the history classes are taught from a liberal perspective, professors treat the Western heritage and American institutions with reasonable respect and welcome opposing viewpoints.

The philosophy and religion department, according to its website, seeks to enable students to "become familiar with the great philosophical traditions and representative thinkers of Western civilization" and to "understand and relate biblical teachings to contemporary society." Courses include "Biblical Survey," "History of the Christian Church," "Biblical Theology and Ethics," "History of Philosophy," "Grammar of the Greek New Testament I," and "Logic and Language." A philosophy and religion major has found that the department is more focused on religion than philosophy but says that professors are "more than willing" to create programs based on student interest and to research new topics for study side-by-side with students. The full-time faculty members are "extremely student-oriented" and mentor students inside and outside the classroom, he says. Another student praises the professor who "encouraged his class to look at Scripture in an objective manner, seeking only truth and right interpretation. His life is devoted to seeking truth, and this quality is apparent in his classes."

The college encourages faculty to enhance their course content through travel and will contribute funds to worthy proposals through the Citizens Abroad Program.

VITAL STATISTICS
Religious affiliation: Presbyterian
Total enrollment: 1,333
Total undergraduates: 1,333
ACT median: 22
Applicants: 2,666
Applicants accepted: 11%
Accepted applicants who enrolled: 90%
Tuition: free
Room and board: $4,100
Freshman retention rate: 86%
Graduation rate: 34% (4 yrs.), 52% (6 yrs.)
Courses with fewer than 20 students: 56%
Student-faculty ratio: 16:1
Courses taught by graduate students: none
Most popular majors: business administration, elementary education, agriculture
Students living on campus: 84%
Guaranteed housing for four years? yes
Students in fraternities or sororities: none

ALL-AMERICAN COLLEGES

175

History faculty and students have traveled to Europe to study the history of World War II, visited Civil War battlefields and national parks, civil rights historic sites in the South, and presidential libraries. They have also attended state and regional history conferences. The school supports a foreign exchange program with a Christian college in the Netherlands.

The agricultural programs preserve the agrarian tradition of the school and the region, while the military science programs foster character development, patriotism and physical fitness. The largest number of majors are in business administration, elementary education, and agriculture.

Among C of O's strongest departments are English, philosophy and religion, education, business, military science, and agriculture. Mass communication is considered by students to be the weakest department. They say that it suffers from a lack of leadership and too few teachers. (The head of the mass communication department is a member of the music faculty and also oversees the art, music, and theater departments.)

Noteworthy faculty members include Eric Bolger, Courtney Furman, and Mark Rapinchuk in philosophy and religion; David Bearden, Rex Mahlman, and Kevin Riley in business; Colonel Gary Herchenroeder and Major James Schreffler in military science; Danita Frazier and Dana McMahon in education; Andrew Staugaard in computer science; Herb Keith and Daniel Swearengen in agriculture; Hayden Head and Larry Isitt in English; Gary Hiebsch in speech communication; and David Dalton and David Ringer in history.

> *"The accessibility and the willingness to help of C of O professors is probably one of the institution's strongest traits. Every professor I had took a vested interest in me; each wanted me to succeed," says a graduate.*

The faculty at C of O do not have publishing requirements, teaching assistants, or tenure. Teaching loads are heavy—normally five courses in one semester, four in the other.

Students say that professors are actively involved in their lives and that most faculty participate in different organizations on campus. "I believe that the accessibility and the willingness to help of C of O professors is probably one of the institution's strongest traits. Every professor I had at C of O took a vested interest in me; each wanted me to succeed," says a graduate who now works at the college. One transfer student from a large state university says that before Thanksgiving he went to dinner with his class at a professor's home. "Upon leaving [the professor's] house that evening, he inquired about my Thanksgiving plans. I informed him that I was driving to my parents' home for the holiday, at which time he proceeded to ask me if I had enough money for gas. I assured him that I did, three times." Finally, the student says, the professor took his word for it. "This is just one example of how most professors from College of the Ozarks treat their students," he says.

Students agree that professors are open about their beliefs but don't try to discourage or stifle debate, nor do they pretend to be final authorities. A professor says, "We are freer to discuss controversial issues than the faculty and students at those campuses which are supposedly more open-minded."

Student Life: Two Miles from Branson

The College of the Ozarks sits forty miles from the city of Springfield and two miles from Branson, Missouri—which, we are reliably informed, is a popular vacation site. The area is known for its lakes, live performance theaters, theme parks, and historic downtown. The College of the Ozarks' thousand-acre campus provides a peaceful setting in Point Lookout, including a lovely view of Lake Taneycomo. Students take painstaking care of the landscaping, which includes walking paths, a pond, and fountains.

A focal center on campus is the Keeter Center, built in 2004. It houses Dobyns restaurant, a gourmet bakery, a gift shop, meeting and conference space, lodging rooms, an auditorium, and classrooms. The center is a re-creation of a vast log cabin displayed by the state of Maine at the 1904 World's Fair in St. Louis, then sold to the school along with 207 acres of land. The log cabin became one of C of O's original school buildings. It was lost in a fire in 1930.

The newly renovated neo-Gothic Williams Memorial Chapel was built by students in 1956 out of locally quarried limestone. The structure features a soaring eighty-foot-high vaulted ceiling and stained-glass windows depicting a chronological history of the Bible. Other notable buildings on campus include the Fruitcake and Jelly Kitchen, which makes and sells the school's famous fruitcakes (more than 40,000 cakes are baked each year) and a variety of jellies and apple butter.

Edwards Mill, built in the 1880s, is powered by a twelve-foot waterwheel turned by runoff water from nearby Lake Honor. Student workers grind whole-grain meal and flour. Upstairs is a weaving studio, where students design and produce rugs, shawls, placemats, and other items on traditional looms. Downstairs, students hand-weave baskets.

The Ralph Foster Museum is dedicated to the history of the Ozarks region. Called the "Smithsonian Institution of the Ozarks," the museum houses thousands of objects, including an extensive collection of Western and Native American artifacts. One of the less scholarly exhibits displays the original vehicle used in the television series *The Beverly Hillbillies.*

Each C of O student works fifteen hours during the week and two forty-hour work weeks over the course of the academic year. To cover their room and board, students have the option of paying cash or working in a summer program. The management of the work-study program is handled by the dean of work. Students are assigned workstations as they are available on the basis of interest, experience, and ability. Students have supervisors and grades are given for each work assignment.

Attendance at chapel and convocations is mandatory. Students with fewer than ninety-one hours are required to attend Sunday chapel a minimum of seven times dur-

SUGGESTED CORE

1. English 303: Western Literature I (*closest match*)
2. Philosophy 313: History of Philosophy
3. Religion 253/273: New Testament / Old Testament
4. Religion 223CC: Medieval/Renaissance Ideas of Character (*closest match*)
5. No suitable course.
6. English 403/423: Shakespeare Tragedies / Shakespeare Comedies and Histories
7. History 303/313: Colonial America / Early Republic
8. No suitable course.

ing each semester. "The Christian faith is stressed and no denominational emphasis is made. The college's idea is to receive students of different denominations and help them become more faithful members of their respective churches," says the student handbook. Students also will need to attend convocations until they have accrued ninety-one hours at the college. The convocations include the Gittinger Convocation Series, forums, artistic programs, general-interest, and Christian-themed lectures and events.

C of O's intention to enhance the development of character and good citizenship among its students is manifest in its rules and regulations concerning conduct between the sexes, appearance, and alcohol and drugs. Eighty-four percent of the student body lives on campus in one of the seven single-sex residence halls, where visits between the sexes are limited to the lounge areas. The RAs are "very friendly and the housing directors take a strong interest in students' well-being," a student says. Students follow a sensible, work-friendly dress code. Regarding alcohol and drugs, the school has adopted a "zero-tolerance policy." Students say that failure to comply leads to immediate expulsion.

The school accepted only 11 percent of applicants in 2005. Ninety percent of the students from each entering class must, by school policy, be from low-income backgrounds—while the other 10 percent consists of children of alumni, scholarship recipients, and some international students. About 70 percent of students are drawn from the largely rural and mountainous Ozarks region encompassing southern Missouri, northern Arkansas and small parts of Kansas, Oklahoma, and Illinois. The remaining students come to the school from forty-one states and fifteen countries.

A recent graduate says that he has gained from C of O a very large community of friends who are like family. It is a place where "healthy relationships" are the norm and where people "put others ahead of themselves," he says. "The work program weeds out the less than serious students," he notes. He added that the educational experience at C of O is "broad and deep," and that understanding the reasons and purpose of work gave him an edge when working on Capitol Hill. This former student has returned to rural Missouri to run for state representative.

One of the most active student groups on campus is the Student Senate. It organizes activities including the fall's Welcome Week, which involves skating or bowling, movies, and a dance; monthly coffeehouses; residence-hall open houses; campus debates; and the Spring Formal.

Other activities that students enjoy when they are taking a break from hard work include Homecoming Weekend and Lip Sync, an evening of faculty and student performances to favorite songs. The vignettes are held together by on-stage hosts and original video spots including creative, comedic commercials. It plays to a standing-room-only crowd every spring.

Students in Free Enterprise takes on many projects each year and travels internationally to pioneer other SIFE clubs. In addition to academic clubs, some of the other student groups on campus include the Student Alumni Association, Baptist Student Union, Bonner Scholars, Catholic Christian Newman Association, Handbell Choir, Horticulture Club, Hotel and Restaurant Society, International Student Club, InterVarsity Christian Fellowship, Jazz Band, Jones Theatre Company, Pep Band, Point Lookout Point Guard (Fencing Club), Wilderness Activities Club, College Democrats, and College Republicans.

Campus ministries programs include the Camp Koinonia retreat in the fall and the Christian Academy of Lifestyle Leadership program, which pairs up students with faculty for one semester to work on various service projects in order to teach life and leadership skills.

College of the Ozarks Bobcats participate in the NAIA (National Association of Intercollegiate Athletics) Division II. The school sponsors men's teams in basketball and baseball and has teams for women in volleyball and basketball. The school frequently hosts the Men's NAIA National Basketball Championship.

A student-administered intramural sports program includes basketball, flag football, soccer, volleyball, softball, tennis, and ultimate Frisbee. The college fieldhouse has three basketball courts, an Olympic-sized swimming pool, weight room, racquetball courts, dance studio, and volleyball, badminton, and table tennis facilities. Outdoor areas include an all-weather track, softball and baseball fields, and tennis courts.

C of O has to be one of the quietest campuses in the country. Students say that they leave residence hall doors unlocked. "The only crime of which I am aware is the occasional student who tries to hide alcohol in his or her dorm," says a student. "It is quite rare." There were no criminal offenses reported in 2004. Campus security provides twenty-four-hour patrols of the campus.

The college charges no full-time tuition and requires all students to work at an on-campus job. The college discourages student borrowing and does not participate in federal educational loan programs. Some 86 percent of students receive need-based financial aid, and the average student loan debt of a recent graduate is a piddling $4,648.

PEPPERDINE UNIVERSITY

MALIBU, CALIFORNIA • WWW.PEPPERDINE.EDU

Pepperdine University is rather famous in the secular world for being a strongly Christian school. This fame derives partly from its successful (and highly promoted) MBA program, and partly from its sheer size. The university's 830-acre campus overlooking the Pacific Ocean is home to five colleges and schools: Seaver College, the School of Law, the Graduate School of Education and Psychology, the Graziadio School of Business and Management, and the School of Public Policy. In addition, there are six Pepperdine graduate campuses sprinkled throughout southern California and international campuses in four foreign countries.

This impressive institution owes its 1937 origin to George Pepperdine, founder of the Western Auto Supply Company. Pepperdine was a devout member of the conservative Churches of Christ, and he "envisioned a college with the highest academic standards guided by the spiritual and ethical ideals of Christian faith." Getting there would be an uphill battle. Opening at Seventy-Ninth Street and Vermont Avenue in south-central Los Angeles, Pepperdine began as a small undergraduate school. The college soldiered on through the Watts riots, which chased out most of the area's middle-class population. In 1971, the school added its graduate and professional schools and became a university. When Mrs. Frank Roger Seaver donated more than 800 acres of prime Pacific Coast real estate in 1972, Pepperdine left the inner city and settled in Malibu.

To this day, Pepperdine University is officially affiliated with the Churches of Christ, although faculty, administrators, and members of the board of regents belong to many faiths, and students "of all races and faiths are welcomed." Nevertheless, the purpose of Pepperdine University remains "to pursue the very highest academic standards within a context that celebrates and extends the spiritual and ethical ideals of the Christian faith." According to the school's mission statement, "Pepperdine is a Christian university committed to the highest standards of academic excellence and Christian values, where students are strengthened for lives of purpose, service, and leadership."

Academic Life: Keeping the Vision

Although Pepperdine may well be known best for its legal and business graduate programs, the Seaver College of the Arts, Pepperdine's undergrad wing, offers a wide-ranging liberal arts curriculum with impressive General Studies requirements. Students must take:

- one "First-Year Seminar," which prepares students for college-level work and introduces "the Christian mission of the university." Many courses in various departments qualify;
- an "intensive writing workshop";
- three Christianity and Culture courses, which must be taken in sequence: "The History and Religion of Israel," "The History and Religion of Early Christianity," and "Christianity and Culture";
- three Western Heritage courses in sequence. These are "primarily history courses enriched by a study of the art, music, literature, and philosophy of the corresponding time periods." They are "Western Heritage I (30,000 BC to AD 1300)," "Western Heritage II (1300–1815)," and "Western Heritage III (1815–present)";
- one course in a non-Western culture. This may include "Sources of Asian Tradition," "Traditional Chinese Thought and Society to AD 1000," or "Intercultural Communication";
- "American People and Politics," and "History of the American Peoples," which "explores the diversity of the American Experience";
- two of the following three social science courses: "Economic Principles," "Introduction to Psychology," and "Introduction to Sociology";
- depending on the major, between one and three courses in Chinese, French, German, Greek, Biblical Hebrew, Italian, Japanese, Spanish, or Russian;
- one course in laboratory science;
- one course in mathematics;
- one course in speech and rhetoric, "Public Speaking and Rhetorical Analysis." This requires a minimum of four prepared speeches;
- one course in fine arts. Non-art majors may fulfill this by taking two units of any studio course in the fields of design, drawing, painting, crafts, sculpture, music, dance, or theater;
- one course in literature (either English or foreign);

VITAL STATISTICS

Religious affiliation: Churches of Christ
Total enrollment: 8,300
Total undergraduates: 3,000
ACT midrange: 24–29
Applicants: 6,024
Applicants accepted: 29%
Accepted applicants who enrolled: 44%
Tuition: $30,770
Room and board: $9,100
Freshman retention rate: 88%
Graduation rate: 68% (4 yrs.), 77% (6 yrs.)
Courses with fewer than 20 students: 63%
Student-faculty ratio: 12:1
Courses taught by graduate students: none
Most popular majors: business, communications, psychology
Students living on campus: 62%
Guaranteed housing for four years? no
Students in fraternities or sororities: 25%

- a "Junior Writing Portfolio" showcasing their compositional skills in several academic papers from various classes. If the work does not pass muster, students must take a special writing course; and
- one course in health and lifestyles.

The range of subjects that Pepperdine mandates is admirable. One teacher says that "the three-course humanities sequence is quite respectful of Western culture. Even the multicultural American history course is taught by faculty who are reluctant to turn it into an attack on Western culture." However, some faculty question how strong these courses really are. "We have lots of requirements, but somewhat thinly treated—a mile wide and an inch deep," a professor complains. "The school is increasingly committed to putting core courses in large lecture halls, without discussion sections, and without assigned papers—so that upper-division courses can remain small. This reduces the depth of exposure to the liberal arts." Students' attitudes toward these core subject matters are not uniformly promising. "Students do not come in particularly curious, and Pepperdine does not stimulate them to become more intellectual. The general education courses are easy classes that one has to 'get through' in order to get to the 'real' reason for being at Pepperdine—taking courses in one's major to get a job," an instructor laments.

This pragmatic attitude towards learning seems widespread at the school—and is reflected in the school's own materials. The liberal arts major, says the school, "is primarily designed for students who are seeking a multiple-subject credential, so two interdisciplinary education courses are included in the major." Along similar lines, it's unfortunate that Pepperdine offers no traditional classics education; the Greek taught is strictly New Testament, and there is not a single course in Latin.

Probably the best program at Pepperdine is its "Great Books Colloquium." Billed as a "four-course sequence on masterpieces of Western civilization," the colloquium promises to engage students in "close, critical reading and small group discussions of selected works from the time of the Greeks to the present day." Great Books students who finish the course will thereby fulfill five general education requirements. Some 15 to 20 percent of incoming students choose this worthwhile program. Not all are liberal arts students; according to the school, many go on to graduate schools and professional study in such fields as law and medicine.

What Great Books offers is summed up as "the opportunity to read celebrated, 'classic' works; rigorous training in close reading, writing, and discussion; a forum for sharing ideas; and a closely knit group of peers and professors in which to grow intellectually." A survey of the university's alumni discovered that "80 percent appreciated the help that the Great Books Colloquium had given them with their other courses; 85 percent credited it with developing their faculties of critical thought; and virtually every respondent praised its contribution to his or her college experience."

The colloquium uses the typical Great Books method of close reading of selected classic texts, followed by intense, guided discussion. The program favors reading entire works rather than excerpts. Dealing with the classical world, "Great Books I" features such works as Homer's *Iliad*, Plato's *Republic*, Aristotle's *Nicomachean Ethics*, and Virgil's

Aeneid. "Great Books II" goes on to consider the Middle Ages, Renaissance, and Reformation through works like Dante's *Divine Comedy*, Machiavelli's *Prince*, Shakespeare's *King Lear*, and Thomas More's *Utopia*. In "Great Books III," the Enlightenment and Romantic periods get their turn; readings include Milton's *Paradise Lost*, Kant's *Foundations of the Metaphysics of Morals*, Locke's *Second Treatise on Government*, Swift's *Gulliver's Travels*, and Austen's *Emma*. "Great Books IV" deals with the modern period; students read, among other works, Dostoevsky's *Brothers Karamazov*, Kierkegaard's *Fear and Trembling*, Freud's *Interpretation of Dreams*, Nietzsche's *Genealogy of Morals*, and Toni Morrison's *Beloved*. According to one instructor, "Great Books is the closest thing we have to a real community of inquiry at Pepperdine."

The school has several other strong programs, according to faculty. "Natural science is strong, with dedicated faculty, high standards, and a chance for students to conduct research as undergraduates. History has some fine young professors who for the most part respect the Western tradition," reports a teacher.

Highly recommended professors include Paul Contino and Don Marshall in Great Books; Stewart Davenport and Jeff Zalar in history; Joel Fetzer and Chris Soper in political science; David Holmes and Victoria Myers in English; Robert Lloyd in international relations; and David Gibson in philosophy. Students should also seek out highly respected scholars Ted McAllister in public policy and Douglas Kmiec in the Schoolf of Law.

Admirably, Pepperdine does not employ any of its legions of graduate students to teach undergrad courses—an expensive decision, but one which ensures that undergraduates' parents get their money's worth. On the other hand, "the classes in communications are not very rigorous, and what substance there is, is the worst sort of communications theory—impenetrable jargon, dubious distinctions," according to a faculty member. Even so, "The rhetoric people are quite good."

> *"[T]he three-course humanities sequence is quite respectful of Western culture; even the multicultural American history course is taught by faculty who are reluctant to turn it into an attack on Western culture. . . ."*

Unlike some schools, "Teaching is still central at Pepperdine" says a faculty member. "There is more emphasis on research than there was ten years ago, but a bad teacher, or a teacher who is not obviously devoted to teaching, will not get tenure. A good teacher can get by with a tad bit less research, but a good research record cannot make up for poor teaching. I think we teach just about the right amount (three courses per semester), although a course reduction is always welcome (five per year would be better)."

Many students report being drawn to Pepperdine by its many opportunities for overseas study; the school maintains campuses in Germany, England, Italy, and Argentina. Says a teacher, "There are tons of opportunities to study abroad here; I know the classes are not as rigorous overseas, but the full experience may be worth it."

As a rule, instructors do not impose their views on their pupils. "Students feel free to express their opinions here," says a professor. "There is some self-censorship, but mostly of the sort that students bring with them after a lifetime of programming: 'Women should achieve in the workplace,' 'Society is full of discrimination,' and so on. Although there are a few writing professors who let politics intrude too much, for the most part professors allow students to disagree without consequence to their grade."

One faculty member says, "You can get a fine education at Pepperdine, if you don't go along with the flow and get sucked into the 'I-need-a-job-so-I need-vocational-training' racket. Pepperdine has been hiring a generation of excellent, devout professors over the last decade. They are the real treasures in the curriculum."

Student Life: Sects on the Beach

Malibu, California, the seaside town where Pepperdine is located, has a reputation for hedonism. It is famous the world over as a surfer's paradise, and only slightly less so as a home for celebrities drawn by the beautiful beach and the town's proximity to Hollywood. Barbra Streisand is one of the many famous locals.

By way of contrast, Pepperdine bases its Code of Conduct firmly on its interpretation of Christianity: "In keeping with Pepperdine University's Christian mission and its heritage in Churches of Christ, all members of the University community are encouraged to consider and respect the teachings of Jesus and historic, biblical Christianity. It is expected that all students will adhere to biblical teaching regarding moral and ethical practices. Engaging in or promoting conduct or lifestyles inconsistent with biblical teaching is not permitted. It is expected that students will maintain the highest standards of personal honor, morality, and integrity. The University reserves the right to refuse admittance to or dismiss any person who violates these principles."

In keeping with these standards, the "promotion, distribution, sale, possession, or use of alcohol or narcotics or other controlled substances" is strictly forbidden. So too is "sexual activity outside a marriage between husband and wife including, but not limited to, premarital, extramarital, or homosexual conduct." Also taboo is "visitation" overnight in the dorm room of a member of the opposite sex. Pornography is not allowed on campus, nor is smoking, other than in "non-restricted outdoor areas." Hazing is not tolerated in any form, and "participation in student organizations not recognized by the University" is also banned.

Pepperdine students are required to take three religion classes as part of their general education curriculum. In addition, "Students are also required to attend events from the Convocation series. These events include weekly, student body–wide gatherings in the Firestone Fieldhouse, daily chapels in Stauffer Chapel, and various lecture programs throughout campus. The Convocation series is dedicated to help students build Christian faith, affirm Christian values, and address the moral and ethical dimensions of current issues." According to the school, "Students are strongly encouraged to become active in a local church. Worship services are held on campus each

Sunday morning and evening and on Wednesday night at the University Church of Christ." There is common worship at Thanksgiving and Easter, and many faculty pray before class. Spiritual Life advisors reside in dorms with the students, offering counsel and a watchful eye. While the school has a strong Protestant orientation, students of all faiths are said to feel welcome.

The university encourages students to live on campus—and given the gorgeous location, they don't require much prodding. Still, the school offers incentives other than natural beauty, enlivening dorm life with many social events, mentorship programs, peer counseling, and service and leadership opportunities. As one alumna says, "I think you make a lot of good friendships living on campus because you get to know people you might never get to know otherwise. It's an environment where it's easier to make more diverse friendships." On-campus services include some housekeeping, on-site barbeque grills, beach facilities, volleyball courts, and a number of dining options.

Undergraduate students are housed in the Suite residence halls, the Rockwell Tower Residence Hall, the Lovernich Residential Complex apartments, and the Honors Community apartments. Students also have an organized off-campus option: Oakwood Apartments, which is located in nearby Woodland Hills and caters to undergraduate students who want a feeling of community.

A twenty-four-hour student facility called the Howard A. White Center is located in the heart of the residential community and is equipped with a round-the-clock computer lab, billiards, table tennis, foosball, big-screen TV, and a coffeeshop.

In one sense, Greek life at Pepperdine is extremely alive and well, as evidenced by the brethren and sisters' very public involvement in Pepperdine activities. But those hoping for the drinking societies so well known at other schools will be disappointed. Instead of toga parties and bizarre initiations, Pepperdine fraternities and sororities are known for their "scholastic achievement, service to the Pepperdine community, and school spirit." As their literature says, "Pepperdine's Greek system and campus administration take the University commitment to being a dry campus very seriously, and as a result, stereotyped 'animal house' chapters do not exist here. Furthermore, the 'dry campus' policy extends to events hosted by student organizations off-campus, meaning groups cannot simply 'take the party elsewhere' without accountability and repercussions." Neither are there separate Greek residences.

The ambitious students at Pepperdine are active in a wide variety of organizations, particularly professional and ethnic-oriented clubs. Activity-based groups range from the Bridge Club and the Swashbuckler Society to the Debate Club. Political groups include the College Republicans, Young Democrats, and the Feminist Forum.

SUGGESTED CORE
1.-2. General Studies 121: Great Books Colloquium I
3. Religion 101/102: The History and Religion of Israel / The History and Religion of Early Christianity
4.-5. General Studies 122-123: Great Books Colloquium II-III
6. English 420: Major Writers, Shakespeare
7. History 520: Colonial and Revolutionary America
8. General Studies 324: Great Books Colloquium IV

ALL-AMERICAN COLLEGES

The school competes in NCAA Division I in the following sports: men's baseball, basketball, cross-country, golf, tennis, volleyball, and water polo; and women's basketball, cross-country, golf, soccer, swimming, tennis, track, and volleyball. Intramural sports are also popular, including dodgeball, flag football, tennis, volleyball, basketball, soccer, and beach volleyball.

Pepperdine's Malibu campus is reasonably safe. A twenty-four-hour campus patrol is provided, as well as Escort Program–Student Service officers, available between 8:00 p.m. and 2:30 a.m., seven days a week. In 2004, Pepperdine reported nineteen burglaries, fourteen illegal weapons violations, eighteen drug charges, and 107 liquor violations, but no violent crimes.

The surf, the sun, the fine education: what would you pay for all this? If you answered "upwards of $40,000," then step aboard. In 2005–6, Pepperdine's tuition was $30,770, with room and board another $9,100. Approximately 47 percent of Pepperdine students receive need-based financial aid. The school says that "university grant funds are limited, and priority for these funds is given to students who have the strongest academic records, as defined by the grade point average and college entrance exam scores."

PRINCETON UNIVERSITY

PRINCETON, NEW JERSEY • WWW.PRINCETON.EDU

In *This Side of Paradise*, alumnus F. Scott Fitzgerald wrote that Princeton is a place of bright colors, where "the quiet halls with an occasional late-burning scholastic light" held rapt his hero Amory Blaine's imagination. These days, too, Princeton is the undergraduate's Ivy. With a small graduate program and no professional schools, big-name professors actually teach. Most humanities courses are, mercifully, nonpolitical; professors display an affection as much as a reverence for learning, and most of them have little desire to spoil the fun by treating their disciplines as perverse, postmodern games. Couple these opportunities with a gorgeous campus and enough activities to satisfy any taste, and you can see why 17,478 worthies applied for just over 1,100 spots in the class of 2010.

While the school is by no means conservative, it is more tolerant of political diversity than most elite colleges—and it boasts a burgeoning subculture of traditionalist professors and students that is sufficient to worry the editors of the *Nation*. That hard-left journal recently published an "exposé" warning that Princeton's James Madison Program in American Ideals and Institutions, led by Professor Robert George, "functions in many ways as a vehicle for conservative interests, using funding from a shadowy, cultlike Catholic group [i.e., the harmless devotional organization Opus Dei] and right-wing foundations to support gatherings of movement activists, fellowships for ideologically correct visiting professors and a cadre of conservative students." In other words, there's a genuine contest of ideas on campus, and room for students who wish to explore them. Given the sheer intellectual rigor demanded by Princeton, it might well be the finest choice around for super-talented students of all religious and political stripes.

Academic Life: Choose Wisely

Princeton students earn either an A.B. (arts and sciences) or a Bachelor of Science in Engineering (B.E.S.) degree. As at most Ivies (except for Columbia), the school imposes no genuine core curriculum but rather a grab-bag of distribution requirements. At Princeton, however, one's choices are likely to be sound, serious classes taught in a fair, apolitical fashion by tolerant teachers. For the A.B. degree, all students must complete the following:

- a Freshman Writing Seminar. Subjects range widely from "American Politics and Culture after World War II" to "The Culture Wars in Philosophical Context";
- sufficient courses in a foreign language to show proficiency. Choices include Arabic, Chinese, French, German, Greek, Hebrew, Hindi, Italian, Japanese, Korean, Latin, Persian, Portuguese, Russian, Spanish, Swahili, and Turkish;
- one course in Epistemology and Cognition. Choices range from "Origins of Monotheism" to "Forensic Anthropology";
- a class in Ethical Thought and Moral Values. Options include "Ethics and Economics" and "The Media and Social Issues";
- just one course in Historical Analysis. Choices range from "Archaic and Classical Greece" to "Black Power and Its Theology of Liberation";
- two courses in Literature and the Arts. Choices here are extremely wide, embracing everything from "Introduction to the History of Art: Ancient to Medieval" to "Women's Speech: Literature, Gender and the Francophone African Women's Experience";
- one course in Quantitative Reasoning, such as "Molecular Structure and Property" or "Rivers and the Regional Environment";
- two classes in Science and Technology, with lab. Options include "Human Adaptation" and "Principles of Computing and Connectivity"; and
- two classes in Social Analysis, such as "Introduction to Microeconomics" or "The 1950s."

For B.S.E. (engineering) students, the school imposes these requirements:

- a Freshman Writing Seminar;
- four mathematics courses;
- two physics classes;
- one chemistry course;
- one computer science class; and
- seven courses in the humanities, including one course in four of the six areas mentioned above: Epistemology and Cognition, Ethical Thought and Moral Values, Foreign Language, Historical Analysis, Literature and the Arts, and Social Analysis.

The Freshman Writing Seminar is new to Princeton. The university implemented this requirement a few years ago to deal with the unfortunate fact that few high schools teach analytical writing skills ("I was like, what, my paper needs a thesis?" explains one recent grad). These small seminars give students the opportunity to learn compositional techniques through extensive and systematic revision. At least, that's the idea. The consensus among students we spoke with is that Princeton is still ironing out the details. The quality of seminars varies widely, and students do a lot of reading in addition to writing. Wise freshmen choose topics that fascinate them.

Academics at Princeton are rigorous; talk to a student for ten minutes and she'll bore you with how many papers she has to write, how many tests she has and so forth. Recent crackdowns on grade inflation have made the situation even tougher. One professor notes that "the physics, mathematics and philosophy departments are the best in the world, period." History, economics, politics, religion, classics, and the Woodrow Wilson School of Public and International Affairs (the only selective undergraduate major) are all exceptional. Serious Christian or conservative students should certainly look into the conferences and seminars offered by the James Madison Program and get to know its director, Robert George. On the other hand, students interested in the edgiest extremes of contemporary thought have the chance to study with "ethics" teacher Peter Singer—an animal rights activist who defends euthanasia for handicapped infants and, er, "intimacy" between man and beast. In other words, choose wisely.

Literary types should apply for seminars in the Creative Writing department, where luminaries such as best-selling writers John McPhee and Paul Muldoon critique your papers. Many students take Economics 101 and 102 with the excellent libertarian Elizabeth Bogan. James McPherson teaches a lively Civil War class, as lively as his popular books on the topic. Robert George's "Constitutional Interpretation" and "Civil Liberties" classes have a reputation for tough grading, but also for being worth the C on your transcript. John Fleming, the former chair of the English department, receives high marks from students for his classes on medieval literature.

Other highly recommended teachers include Peter Brown, Anthony Grafton, William Jordan, Stephen Kotkin, and Peter Lake in history; Stephen Macedo, Russell Nieli, Paul Sigmund, and Keith Whittington in politics; Miguel Centeno, Thomas Espenshade, Sara McLanahan, Paul Starr, Robert Wuthnow, and Viviana Zelizer in sociology; the provocative and controversial Cornel West (no, we're not kidding) in African American studies; Alan Blinder and Burton Malkiel in economics; Eric Gregory, Martha Himmelfarb, Leigh Schmidt, and Jeffrey Stout in religion; Oliver Arnold, James Richardson and D. Vance Smith in English; Ellen Chances in Slavic languages and literature; Michael Doran in Near Eastern studies; Robert Hollander in Romance languages and literatures; Joshua Katz and Josiah Ober in classics; and Bastiaan van Fraassen in philosophy.

The humanities department offers excellent courses on everything from classical mythology to the Bible in Western cultural tradition. Accessible and interesting courses on music and art history introduce students to the world of high culture.

Lectures at Princeton are never huge and are supplemented by "precepts"—small group discussion sections. Professors teach many of these sections themselves, offer-

VITAL STATISTICS

Religious affiliation: none
Total enrollment: 6,677
Total undergraduates: 4,678
SAT midranges: V: 700–780, M: 700–790
Applicants: 16,529
Applicants accepted: 11%
Accepted applicants who enrolled: 67%
Tuition: $33,050
Room and board: $9,130
Freshman retention rate: 98%
Graduation rate: 88% (4 yrs.), 97% (6 yrs.)
Courses with fewer than 20 students: 74%
Student-faculty ratio: 5:1
Courses taught by graduate students: none
Most popular majors: politics, history, economics
Students living on campus: 100%
Guaranteed housing for four years? yes
Students in fraternities or sororities: none

ALL-AMERICAN COLLEGES

ing a good way to get to know some beautiful minds one on one. Except for the occasional wild-card course (e.g., a ten-student seminar team-taught by Nobel laureates Toni Morrison and Gabriel García Márquez a few years ago) it's never difficult to get into the classes you want. Some of the precepts are taught by graduate students.

Unfortunately, Princeton's official academic advising system is hit or miss. You can't expect your advisor necessarily to steer you right. Fortunately, other people are helpful—professors, older students, residential college advisors. These folks can fill in the gaps, as can the student reviews of courses that Princeton makes available online.

All Princeton students finish off their academic careers with a senior thesis. Students select their majors during the sophomore year, do an independent research-oriented Junior Paper (JP) or two in this field during the junior year, then undertake the major research work known as a thesis before graduating. Students take these projects seriously. Many artistic undergrads write plays or novels or compose symphonies. Wendy Kopp's "Teach for America" project actually began as her senior thesis. Other people craft serious academic studies that might lead to dissertations someday. If you're interested in slacking off, Princeton is not the right choice.

"While the majority of students are certainly not religious, within the Ivy League I think Princeton is probably the most religion-friendly institution," one student tells us, noting "a lingering religiosity on campus that hasn't gone away as at many other elite schools."

For students tempted to cheat, Princeton is not the right choice either; the Princeton honor code is a long-standing university tradition. Exams are not proctored; students sign their tests saying, "I pledge my honor that I have not violated the honor code during this examination." They also sign papers with a note saying the writing represents their own work in accordance with university regulations. Students must accept the honor code to attend Princeton. Students found in violation of the honor code can be suspended or expelled. Few take the risk; why risk getting tossed out of what one student calls "the finest educational institution in the galaxy"?

Student Life: The Pleasantest Country Club in America

Princeton, a cozy Ivy League institution in central New Jersey, has two sides to her complex personality. These are shown best by two of her most famous sons, Bill Bradley and F. Scott Fitzgerald.

Long before his Senate days, Bradley led Princeton to the final rounds of the 1965 NCAA basketball tournament with his deadly aim and backdoor passes. After games, he hit the books hard enough to receive perfect marks on his senior thesis and win himself a Rhodes scholarship. Even if he was studying until 4 a.m. on a Saturday night, though, he'd show up Sunday morning to teach a Sunday school class at a local Presbyterian church.

A few decades earlier, F. Scott Fitzgerald, the effortlessly brilliant literary figure, had cut a gin-soaked swath through Princeton. Fitzgerald himself noted these two sides, that "Princeton was one part deadly Philistines and one part deadly grinds." It might be better to say that Princeton students work hard and play hard. They are brilliant. They have big ambitions. They amble through what Fitzgerald called the "pleasantest country club in America" with as much comfort as Bradley felt on the basketball court. As Bradley told his biographer, John McPhee, after years of success on the court you develop "a sense of where you are."

On a recent visit to this manicured Gothic campus, we asked students for "only at Princeton" moments. One told us of sitting at dinner, sandwiched between two physics majors, hearing them debate the best techniques for playing beer pong based on the laws of physics, aerodynamics, the properties of air, and the shape of the ball and cups. Another told us of packed noon Masses in the Catholic chapel, with attendance outstripping that of most parishes across the country. A different student spoke of taking a seminar on Jesus in Rabbinical literature with ten supportive classmates and three all-star faculty members—as a freshman. Then he praised the annual tradition of spring "houseparties" at Princeton's eating clubs. "Three days of elegant socializing, good music, and good food at the end of the semester at the Prospect Avenue clubs really make Princeton feel like F. Scott Fitzgerald Land," he said.

"There's something here for everyone," a student tells us, "and if not, the university will give you money to start it." A capella groups sing in the campus's Gothic arches. Publications abound. With thirty-eight varsity teams competing in NCAA Division I, a huge percentage of Princeton students play sports. Princeton always fields competitive teams in the "preppy" sports such as lacrosse and field hockey. Big-budget sports are sometimes less competitive; Princeton may be one of the few universities where the architecture of the football stadium (designed by Rafael Violy) is more exciting than the competition on the field. But even if the varsity teams in "big" sports aren't always up to par, Princeton students do love to stay fit. About half participate in intramural athletics, and many others take advantage of the student gyms. Princeton's Outdoor Action program leads troops of freshmen hiking into the wilderness as part of orientation every year. The Princeton ideal worships body and mind; despite heavy beer consumption, you rarely see out-of-shape students.

These svelte students are not particularly political. "The majority of students label themselves liberal-ish," one student notes. The only major protest of late was a "filibuster" in front of the Frist Student Center (named after the family of the Senate

> ## SUGGESTED CORE
>
> The four-semester humanities sequence (Humanities 216-219: Interdisciplinary Approaches to Western Culture: From Antiquity to the Middle Ages / From the Renaissance to the Modern Period) is recommended with the following supplements: Religion 230/251: Old Testament/ New Testament; Politics 303: Modern Political Theory; English 310/311: Shakespeare I/II; History 372/373: Revolutionary America / The New Nation.

majority leader) during the recent national controversy over judicial nominations. Students protested Senate Republicans' threats to dismantle the filibuster—currently abused by liberals eager to keep the courts in their hands. But even that high-concept protest was an exception. In general, when people disagree at Princeton, they do it calmly and reasonably. They don't take over the administration buildings. Conservative students on campus are in the minority, but they are organized and vocal. Some complain that the administration, led by President Shirley Tilghman, pushes the standard liberal social agenda and plenty of diversity programming, but such programming is easily (and widely) ignored. Classes are an intellectual proving ground; knee-jerk political opinions of any persuasion won't survive fellow students' quick minds. Says one student, "I find it difficult to argue my own points clearly and effectively unless I come well-read on the topic and well-equipped with facts. This is a testament to students' knowledge and debating skills." If your views are thought through, any perspective is welcome.

This includes devoutly religious perspectives. "While the majority of students are certainly not religious, within the Ivy League I think Princeton is probably the most-religion-friendly institution," one student tells us, noting "a lingering religiosity on campus that hasn't gone away as at many other elite schools." The university's Catholic chaplaincy is particularly active, according to its members; evangelical students tell us that about 250 students participate in major Christian groups on campus. Jewish students can find services (in the Reform, Conservative, and Orthodox traditions) at the Center for Jewish Life; the CJL also serves such tasty meals that many a non-Jewish student winds up keeping kosher by default. The Muslim Students Association has been growing in prominence in recent years. Secular students embrace these differences as they'd tolerate other ones; one student tells us that a devout Mormon in his hip-hop dance troupe was loved by the other members, and it bothered no one that he didn't dance in the numbers he found inappropriate.

In particular, very few students or professors take an interest in attacking people's faith. A classic *Princeton Tiger* magazine cartoon printed decades ago shows a WASPy young man returning home for fall break of his freshman year. When his parents ask what he's learned in college, he says, deadpan, that he no longer believes in God. The cartoon is funny, in part, because it's not true. "At Princeton, more than any other university community that I have ever heard of, students end their careers here much more strengthened in their faith," one evangelical student tells us. Students worship with those who share their faiths, then study their religions' theological and historical underpinnings with the best professors available. The devout often come out more devout. On the other hand, "students with slight religious leanings who do not actively seek out religious outlets will probably not find Princeton to be an environment that fosters and encourages their beliefs," another student tells us.

The biggest complaint religious students have is that Princeton's social life centers on the peculiarly Princeton institution of "eating clubs." These dozen mansions line Prospect Avenue, or "The Street." Every Thursday and Saturday students hit the Street in their club clothes; every Friday and Sunday morning the clubs reek of beer residue. Each club has its own character. About 80 percent of Princeton students join a club for meals and socializing during their junior and senior years. Half the clubs require a "bicker," an elaborate audition process. The other half are "sign in"—anyone who wants to join can if there's space. In general, bicker clubs are more selective about who they allow into their parties.

The clubs add another expense to Princeton's already staggering tuition. They are cliquish, and to play the game right, you need to come to Princeton knowing which ones are cool, and plan your platform for admission from day one. No wonder that minority students and students from lower socioeconomic backgrounds feel less welcome—and so are less likely to join. Many of these students then center their social lives around ethnic organizations. This is understandable, but it leads to further segregation on campus.

Because of this—and because of the binge drinking and "hook-ups" the clubs encourage—the university administration is implementing a new four-year residential college system in the fall of 2007. Currently, most students live in a residential college for two years (eating their meals in dining halls), then join a club for their last years. Under the new plan, students will have the option to join one of three four-year colleges. No one is sure how this will work with the eating clubs, or how it will work at all, but it will change the Princeton social scene.

Dorms are mostly coed; rooms and bathrooms are not. Almost all students live on campus; town-gown relations are pretty much nonexistent. Upperclassmen can elect to live in a few apartments with kitchens on campus, and a few join co-ops to sharpen their cooking skills. Crime is not a major concern; in 2004, the school reported three forcible sex offenses, one aggravated assault, fifty-eight burglaries, and thirteen stolen cars.

For 2006–7, Princeton's tuition was set at $33,050 and room and board cost another $9,130. Like all Ivy League institutions, Princeton does not offer merit scholarships; all students admitted are guaranteed the aid they need. Indeed, Princeton's financial aid package is the most generous in the Ivy League. Some 54 percent of students get need-based aid. Several years ago, Princeton made the decision to do away with student loans. All aid comes as grants or work-study jobs—which means that many students graduate debt-free. Princeton started this program specifically to lessen the sticker shock for families who didn't think they could afford Princeton. The proportion of Princeton students from lower- and middle-class backgrounds has risen since 2001. One reason the school can afford to be generous is that alumni are unusually giving. Most of them look back fondly on their time at this cozy campus. They sing at the annual carnival-like reunions of "Going back to Old Nassau . . . to the best damn place of all." There the deadly Philistines and deadly grinds come together for a debate or two, and to raise a glass in honor of having a sense of where they are.

PROVIDENCE COLLEGE

PROVIDENCE, RHODE ISLAND • WWW.PROVIDENCE.EDU

Providence College, located a mile from downtown Providence, is the only college in the nation operated by Dominican friars, a Catholic religious order. That order, steeped in intellectual and spiritual tradition, believes with its most famous member St. Thomas Aquinas that faith and reason are meant to be companions in the search for truth. Rev. Brian J. Shanley, the new president of the college, is quick to point out that divine providence was an important theological concept long before it was the name of a city or a college. He believes that it also reflects the school's primary mission: to provide an environment that allows each person to understand his or her identity and role in the plan of God. Shanley, a young president at forty-seven, comes to the office from his post as professor of philosophy at Catholic University. In his inaugural address of September 2005, he said, "Universities and their teachers should not treat students as consumers whose demands must be met for fear of losing market share. It is rather that professors need to teach students to want to know what they need to know so that they can come to see the truth for themselves and choose what is worthy of choice." An admirable creed for a worthy school. Though it has a much lower profile among American Catholics than Jesuit universities such as Georgetown and Boston College, Providence's intellectual seriousness and genuine fidelity to the church in fact put it head and shoulders above them.

Academic Life: Between the Acropolis and the Berlin Wall

Providence's new president has a solid foundation to work with. The school's core curriculum was initiated in the '70s when most other colleges were running in the opposite direction—toward consumerist choice and postmodern ideology. Providence provides an opportunity for students to struggle with the quest for truth, wrestling with historical facts, time-tested ideas, and great works of literature. For some students, the "light goes on" right away, while others simply come away with the sense that they have brushed shoulders with something big—our civilization. All benefit on some level.

    The school requires students to spend their first two years in the Development of Western Civilization program (known around campus as "Civ" or DWC). According to the school, the best definition of this program came about after a prospective student asked, "What is this thing called Civ?" In response, Dr. Rodney Delasanta, then Director of the Liberal Arts Honors Program, opened his desk drawer and pulled out two rocks. In one hand, he held a rock from the Acropolis in Greece; in the other, a rock chipped from the Berlin Wall. "Civ," he explained, "is everything between these two rocks." To learn what resides there, students must take the following core:

- a four-semester class, "Development of Western Civilization." This course is "team-taught by members of the departments of art, English, languages, history, philosophy, and theology" and deals "with major developments in the making of Western Civilization from the classical period to the present";
- two courses in social science. Students may choose any course from anthropology, economics, history, linguistics, political science, psychology, sociology, or women's studies. Examples range from "Microeconomics" to "Modern Italy";
- two courses in natural science. Students may pick biology, chemistry, or physics—or a special Natural Science Core I and II sequence that offers nonscience majors classes such as "Contemporary Chemistry" and "Genes and Gender";
- just one course in philosophy. Choices range from "Introduction to the Philosophy of St. Thomas" to "Contemporary Women Philosophers";
- one course in ethics. Options include "Business Ethics" and "Biomedical Ethics";
- two courses in theology. These could be "Theology of St. Thomas Aquinas" and "The Church in Today's World";
- one course in mathematics, such as "Introduction to Mathematical Methods" or "Calculus and Analytical Geometry";
- one class in fine arts, ranging from "History of Church Music" to "Analyzing Film"; and
- demonstration of English proficiency and writing skills.

The school's Civ program is the cornerstone of the curriculum. It offers Providence students a more coherent view of culture than they would get at almost any other college in the country—apart from some of the Great Books schools recommended

VITAL STATISTICS

Religious affiliation: Roman Catholic
Total enrollment: 5,468
Total undergraduates: 4,548
SAT/ACT medians: SAT V: 597, M: 606; ACT: 25
Applicants: 8,237
Applicants accepted: 55%
Accepted applicants who enrolled: 24%
Tuition: $24,800
Room and board: $9,270
Freshman retention rate: 93%
Graduation rate: 85% (4 yrs.), 87% (6 yrs.)
Courses with fewer than 20 students: 42%
Student-faculty ratio: 12:1
Courses taught by graduate students: none
Most popular majors: marketing, management, biology
Students living on campus: 88%
Guaranteed housing for four years? no
Students in fraternities or sororities: none

ALL-AMERICAN COLLEGES

elsewhere in this book. Four faculty members from key departments work as a team for each group of one hundred students, which moves through the program together for two semesters. As one professor puts it, "The course is designed to be interdisciplinary—that is, the literature professor will also talk about philosophy, theology, and history—everyone talks about all four fields, and they each attend the lectures of their three teammates."

Professors and students are passionate about the program. The faculty shows this by their regular efforts to improve the Civ core by making class sizes smaller and increasing instructional time. Students seem to enjoy, or at least make the most of, the camaraderie that results from working through the program together. As one former student puts it with a satirical grin, "PC pumps out great Jeopardy players." Another student notes that Civ offered "a chance to meet people outside of your major." The students, when they have finally completed the program, come together at midnight before the final exam for the "Civ Scream" in the courtyard. Sophomores design and print up T-shirts to mark the occasion.

While the sections are team-taught, a class size of one hundred students can put a damper on Socratic participation. Students interested in this program should be ready to take advantage of the weekly seminars, akin to "break-out" sessions, held with a faculty member. The average seminar size is currently at twenty-five and indications are that this number will hold steady into the future, though it is up a bit from the immediate past.

According to Providence's student newspaper, the *Cowl*, the quality of Civ classes can vary widely according to the faculty teaching particular sections. One parent of a former student complains that "there was an appalling lack of writing" in the Civ courses. And a faculty member admits, "You have to make allowances for the dreadful education that many receive at our 'best' public schools." Entering students should inquire from upperclassmen about the best sections to take.

Highly qualified students entering Providence College may be invited to enroll in the Liberal Arts Honors Program, which promises "more reading, more writing, and more seminar discussion." It provides the same general core curriculum but in a smaller setting and with a different team of faculty members. One faculty member claims that the program offers "a better education than I received at Princeton." The feeling that this is true crystallizes as one speaks to honors students.

All classes at Providence are taught by professors, not graduate students. The school's student-faculty ratio is 12 to 1. Highly recommended teachers include Brian Barbour, Rodney Delasanta, Anthony M. Esolen, and Steven Lynch in English; Mario DiNunzio, Richard Grace, John Lawless, Fr. Thomas McGonigle, and Raymond Sickinger in history; Matthew Cuddeback and Vance Morgan in philosophy; Joseph Cammarano in political science; and Paul Gondreau, James Keating, and Fr. David Stokes in theology.

By March of their sophomore year, students are required to pick a major area of study within a degree program. The school offers twenty-nine different majors (having recently eliminated Environmental Science) in the B.A. and eleven in the B.S. program.

The most heavily represented majors are in education, business, political science, biology, English, history, and psychology. Departments such as philosophy, English, theology, history, political science, and biology are said by faculty and students to be the strongest academically, alongside weaker sisters such as education and sociology. Even within the best departments, students advise shopping around for the best professors and classes. One faculty member warns, "The introductory course in political science, a course in American politics, is usually excellent, though listing heavily to the left. . . . Most introductory courses in the social sciences should be avoided at all costs. Students would do well to stick with the history and economics courses to fulfill this requirement." Students have complained long and hard about one professor in sociology, Jim Moorhead, who teaches courses such as "Sociology of the Family." Students note that what Moorhead calls his "sex classes" defend contemporary secular practices such as divorce and adultery, discussing sexual intimacy in coarse language. Students note that Moorhead describes religion generally, and Catholicism in particular, as "patriarchal bull—t." Nor does he welcome outside scrutiny; a *Cowl* piece described his refusal to allow their reporters to attend his classes. The new administration seems less inclined than previous ones to tolerate such behavior; however, the iron law of tenure has been known to shelter far worse.

Refreshingly, Providence requires its theology department members to sign the *Mandatum*—an oath of fidelity to church doctrine required by the Holy See, which most Catholic colleges in the United States have chosen to defy.

The school requires each student to spend their first two years in the Development of Western Civilization program ("Civ"). A student once asked, "What is this thing called Civ?" In response, the director pulled out two rocks: one from the Acropolis, the other chipped from the Berlin Wall. "Civ," he explained, "is everything between these two rocks."

In addition to a solid list of degree programs, the school offers some interesting special options. Even though Providence doesn't require the science course load of a typical premed major, its premed program allows early admission to the Brown Medical School. One faculty member comments, "Of course, if you're asking me, any student smart enough to be a medical doctor should be majoring in one of the liberal arts during his or her undergraduate years. We need medical practitioners who are first good human beings, with minds open to universal Truth."

Students can take a semester abroad or spend it in Washington, D.C., at American University. The Johnson C. Smith University semester program is open to any student who wishes to experience a predominantly historic, black liberal arts setting. For students interested in advanced degrees, the combined degree programs are attractive:

a 3+4 optometry program through the New England College of Optometry, a 3+2 engineering program, and a 4+1 MBA program. The school also offers a military science/ROTC program.

Student Life: Orderly, Not Preachy

Providence's attractive campus, home to most of the school's 4,000 or so students, has just undergone a building spree that included some significant cultural improvements. Historic buildings and open space give the campus a very traditional "college" feel. The campus is also just a mile down the road from one of the most vibrant cities in New England; free city buses stop on campus to make getting around easy.

One immediately notices that the campus is not a vast expanse of club notices and angry protests. The students appear to be speaking to each other, instead of listening to cell phones or iPods. Activists are rare—as if they could not escape the gravitational pull of the "other college" in town, Brown University.

But student life is far from inert. The school lists about sixty active clubs that include music, philosophy, politics, sports, spiritual, and preprofessional groups. Though the administration has the right to veto content, the student newspaper, the *Cowl*, is intelligent and occasionally critical.

One recent article was quite frank about the relationship between PC students and the adjacent community—which it described as strained but improving. In the past, the town had complained about noisy students living in nearby apartments. But since then new dorms have been built, and most students now live on campus. (There are no Greek organizations or houses.) As is the case with most colleges, the stream of students headed to off-campus bars can mean destruction and noise.

Some students prefer to save their energy for games. Of the nineteen Division I varsity sports played at Providence, fifteen participate in the Big East conference, including the basketball teams, whose games are held at the Civic Center in downtown Providence; tickets are in high demand. There are also plenty of intramural teams, most of which play in the giant Peterson Recreation Center. This indoor facility has a twenty-five-meter pool, five multi-purpose courts with a 200-meter perimeter track, racquetball courts, and dance studios. As part of the school's continuing expansion plan, a glassed-in fitness area is also in the works. Most recently, a new varsity level, multi-purpose artificial turf field has been constructed near the Peterson Center. Hockey fans, up to 3,000 of them, watch games in the nearby Schneider Arena.

For students devoted to the arts, the new Smith Center houses the Department of Music and the Department of Theater, Dance and Film. Inside, performers make use of the 283-seat Black Friars Theater stage, the 270-seat concert hall, and the 110-seat studio theater.

Dormitories, many of which are new, are divided into male and female living quarters. Visitation hours are restricted for members of the opposite sex, though some students say enforcement could be tighter. Upperclassmen may choose to live in Suites Hall, a new dorm with a kitchen and common space on each floor, or they may choose to live in a four- or six-person apartment building on campus.

One faculty member is happy to note that the school is in the process of reclaiming its Catholic identity. "Providence College is certainly becoming more, not less, faithful to its Roman Catholic heritage, and has welcomed a new president whose mission it is, I think, to make the college a fit place for Catholic scholars who want to engage the world such as we find it now." The St. Dominic Chapel, a beautiful free-standing edifice, was dedicated in 2001. With forty-five stained-glass windows and seating for 600, it is where most students attend Sunday afternoon Mass. St. Pius parish, right across the street from the school, offers more options. The campus has daily Mass and weekly Adoration for students who practice those devotions, but there is no pressure to do so.

SUGGESTED CORE

The college's twenty-credit interdisciplinary program, "Development of Western Civilization," suffices.

The move to restore the school's old Catholic identity will require confronting some entrenched opposition. The school lists some student groups at loggerheads with church teaching. For instance a feminist club, Women Will, has managed for several years running to bring the objectionable *Vagina Monologues* to the school, despite administrative disapproval. In January 2006, President Shanley announced the school would not be hosting the production again. In defense of his decision, he stated, among other things, that "any depiction of female sexuality that neglects its unitive and procreative dimensions diminishes its complexity, its mystery, and its dignity." Both the stand he took and the philosophical manner in which he expressed it—with reference to Paul VI's encyclical *Humanae Vitae*—are highly encouraging.

For the naïve student, the local area can be dangerous, since there are small pockets of trouble if one wanders down the wrong street. Generally speaking, though, most of the crime both on and off campus can be traced to alcohol: Providence is close to the downtown bar scene. In an attempt to give atmosphere-seeking students a place to kick back, the school has built an on-campus bar, McPhail's, which is open seven nights a week. It has a great sports atmosphere, big-screen televisions, and entertainment, but is very tough about serving only those students that are legally allowed to drink. As one parent puts it, "Of course you'd rather they didn't drink at all, but if a student is going to drink, on campus is safer than off campus." In 2004, the school reported three aggravated assaults, twenty burglaries, and two stolen cars on campus—quite a good record for an urban school. However, there were a whopping 527 arrests for liquor-related offenses.

A student can expect to pay $24,800 in tuition and $9,270 for room and board. Sixty-three percent of full-time students receive need-based aid, and the average student loan debt in a recent graduating class was $23,125.

RHODES COLLEGE

MEMPHIS, TENNESSEE • WWW.RHODES.EDU

Rhodes College began life as the Masonic University of Tennessee, but it has been more recently affiliated with a conservative Presbyterian denomination. Today, Rhodes is a uniquely Christian college: generally evangelical but not fundamentalist, broadly orthodox but not obscurantist, generally liberal without being modernist. While the spirit of Christendom pervades the lovely Gothic campus, there is no church on its grounds. It is understood that Christian students will wish to worship in a parish of their own denomination as members of the local community, though Christian study, prayer, and social groups abound. While the college bulletin states that the institution's affiliation with the Presbyterian Church (USA) is "more than assent to a set of vague values or sentimental emotions," one professor complains that "the symbolic and rhetorical trappings of church-relatedness have been gradually disappearing." One member of the Rhodes Christian Fellowship says, "As a Christian, my faith has grown tremendously since I arrived at Rhodes. The student body here has been very encouraging, and it is not unpopular for students to show interest in religious functions. I would say that Rhodes passively encourages spirituality by making resources readily available, but by no means does it force beliefs upon anyone."

For Christian students who don't feel the need to study at a school shaped by the particular traditions of their denominations, Rhodes is an appealing and ultimately worthy choice.

Academic Life: Athens and Jerusalem

One of the strongest features Rhodes has had to boast about is its core curriculum. Up through 2007, Rhodes will maintain the following requirements:
- "The Search for Values in the Light of Western History and Religion," a four-course sequence that covers the development of the West from "the Hebrews, the Greeks, the Romans, and the Early Christians" up through "the Middle Ages to the present," covering "fine arts, history, literature, philosophy, politics, and religious studies";
- "Life Then and Now," an alternative to the above sequence, which consists of a narrow range of courses in religious studies, "ethics, history of religions, or philosophy," to be chosen by the student with faculty approval;
- "First-Year Writing Seminar" (students with high test scores may opt out);

- coursework or tests to demonstrate proficiency in a foreign language at the third-semester level;
- three courses in humanities, "at least one in literature or film—English or foreign—and at least one in history or philosophy";
- three courses in natural science (with one lab) from at least two of five science areas: biology, mathematics/computer science, chemistry, physics/astronomy, or geology;
- three courses in social science from at least two of these areas: anthropology/sociology, political science and international studies, economics, and psychology (including one education course);
- two courses in fine arts from any two areas: art, music, or theater; and
- three seven-week noncredit units of physical education.

It is unclear whether these requirements will be kept beyond 2007; it appears that the school is in a state of flux—perhaps a battle between factions with different perspectives on the nature of liberal education, with the outcome impossible to predict. However, even if a student follows the looser "Life Then and Now" option to fulfill his requirements, he will face solid courses in real disciplines—not fluff. Indeed, one might say that Rhodes offers a virtually no-fluff catalog.

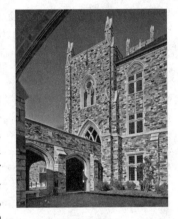

After this grounding in the fundamentals, students choose a major from among twenty-four traditional disciplines; the college does not offer many newfangled, ideologically slanted majors. The college also offers seven interdisciplinary majors, most of which combine this or that discipline with international studies. In consultation with faculty members and their academic advisors, students can also create a major by concentrating in two or three academic departments. Each entering freshman is assigned an academic advisor who helps him select courses and a major. Once he has declared a major, he is assigned a different faculty advisor within the major department.

"The Rhodes approach to a broad liberal arts education is as good as you are going to see," a professor says. "The college is committed to it, and so are most of the faculty." This person continues, "How well it works in practice varies widely from student to student. For those who want it, they can get it here. For those who are determined to remain narrow, they can succeed as well." But the latter may have to work at it. "As in any school there exists a minority of students who would rather get by with as little work as possible," one student admits, "but even the slackers will learn from their friends, if nothing else." Slackers appear to be a minority at Rhodes.

This fact points to something paradoxical about Rhodes. Experts in the field with diverse points of view highly respect it, but its admissions are not highly selective. Rhodes accepts almost half of its applicants (49 percent), and of these, fewer than a quarter (24 percent) choose to attend. These numbers may indicate that Rhodes is

Religious affiliation:
   Presbyterian
Total enrollment: 1,692
Total undergraduates: 1,677
SAT/ACT midranges: SAT V:
   580–680, M: 580–670;
   ACT: 25–30
Applicants: 3,695
Applicants accepted: 49%
*Accepted applicants who
   enrolled*: 24%
Tuition: $27,546
Room and board: $6,904
Freshman retention rate: 88%
Graduation rate: 76% (4 yrs.),
   79% (6 yrs.)
*Courses with fewer than 20
   students*: 74%
Student-faculty ratio: 11:1
*Courses taught by graduate
   students*: none
Most popular majors: social
   sciences, biology,
   business administration
Students living on campus:
   77%
*Guaranteed housing for four
   years?* no
Students in fraternities: 48%
   sororities: 53%

often selected as a "safety" school by many of the academically talented who shy away from the significant demands of the core curriculum, who do not wish to be a part of an academic community that still identifies itself as Christian, or who do not want to spend four years in the South. The students who do end up attending will face serious academic challenges in a supportive and serious environment—which is more than one can say for many more selective schools. And they won't have any trouble pursuing their studies; the admissions office says that 95 percent of Rhodes graduates who apply to business, divinity, and law schools are accepted.

There are some indications that the administration and faculty are not happy with Rhodes's image as a traditional school, and that they are trying to do something about it—the wrong thing. There is suspicion among the faculty that recent curricular reforms may have begun as an attempt to undermine one of the bases of Rhodes's excellence, its insistence on strong humanities requirements. If so, it was not successful. The core remains as strong as ever—and we hope it stays that way.

Rhodes students are predominantly white, Anglo-Saxon, and Protestant; not a popular profile for your school to have, if you are an administrator, and the school consequently reaches out to minority students. The Office of Multicultural Affairs was established in 1990 and employs a full-time director who sets up workshops, orientation programs, and mentoring programs matching minority freshmen with minority upperclassmen. The mandatory freshman orientation features a day dedicated to multiculturalism. The office also advises several cultural groups. "Multiculturalism" is often a code word for hatred and contempt for the Christian faith, the American nation, and Western civilization, of course, but at Rhodes it is at least partly about making our triple heritage more consciously present in the lives of certain students.

The student body is moderate to conservative in politics and culture, while most faculty members tend to be liberal but not radical. "The Rhodes community is more conservative than anything else," a student says. "It rarely influences course content in any noticeable way." Another student says that she took a course on the American presidency during an election year. Her professor invited the class over to watch the returns, but refused to reveal for whom he had voted. "He tried hard not to influence us politically," the student says. The academic disciplines themselves are straightforward. A major in English is a major in English, not in ethnic studies or gender studies or any other type of ideology. Even women's studies, an interdisciplinary minor, balances its courses on feminism and gender studies with reasonable fare such as "History of Southern Women" and "Women in U.S. History." Politics at Rhodes are not a matter of life or death. One student says, "It's usually a matter of, when discussing politics, more veer right than left, and afterwards, both parties go to the cafeteria to eat together." Says another, "Those who try to make politics a more public issue have trouble getting others to rally around them."

Rhodes is a community of scholars. Frequent, close faculty-student interaction is one of the college's primary selling points. Class size is small (averaging around fifteen students per class) and the student-faculty ratio is 11 to 1. The administration has never pressured professors to publish, and faculty members focus their attention on teaching; any writing they do is a labor of love. "The professors at Rhodes place teaching as their highest priority," a religious studies major says. "That is a huge advantage of a small school like Rhodes: professors know who you are and are interested in your academic success, even if you are not majoring in their departments." One professor says that at Rhodes today "there is no more pressure to publish" at the expense of good teaching than there was in the past; "I'm very confident that our primary mission is teaching."

Members of the community stress the importance of the college's Honor Code. "Nearly all of my tests last year were unproctored," a student says. "I can honestly say that in all of those exams I know of no instances of that trust being abused. Cheating is not an option at Rhodes."

Students name the following professors as particularly good teachers: Joseph Favazza, Luther Ivory, Steven McKenzie, and Bernadette McNary-Zak in religious studies; Marshall McMahon in economics; Kathleen Anne Doyle and Amanda L. Irwin in Spanish; and Patrick Shade in philosophy.

Particularly outstanding departments at Rhodes include biology, English, and political science. Some say that the measure of a good liberal arts college is the extent of its foreign language curriculum. If that is true, Rhodes is in good shape. Rhodes offers majors in French, German, Greek and Roman studies (including language studies in ancient Greek and Latin), Russian, and Spanish, as well as a minor in Chinese and intermediate course offerings in Hebrew and Italian.

To judge from the course catalog, one would think that the religious studies department's orientation was rather traditional, with an emphasis on biblical studies and Christian theology. Students choosing to major in religious studies must take "Introduction to the Biblical Tradition," "History of Christian Thought," courses on both

> *"The professors at Rhodes place teaching as their highest priority," one student says. "That is a huge advantage of a small school like Rhodes: professors know who you are and are interested in your academic success, even if you are not majoring in their departments."*

the Old and New Testament, and a course in the religions of Asia, among others. However, religious studies is one of the more politicized departments on campus, students report.

For the most academically gifted students, the honors program provides an opportunity to engage in a more intense academic experience. During their senior year, honors students work with faculty members by taking one to three honors tutorial courses, culminating in a "project of a scholarly and creative nature." The "directed inquiry" option allows students to work closely with faculty members in independent-study courses. One of college president William Troutt's initiatives has been to better integrate Rhodes College into the Memphis community, and one way this has been accomplished is through internships. While gaining practical experience with area companies like FedEx, International Paper, and Merrill Lynch, students can earn course credit in various departments.

Academic opportunities are not limited to the Memphis campus; about 30 percent of students study abroad. Rhodes students can study in several European locations through the University of the South at Sewanee, or transfer credit from programs at various American and international universities. Rhodes itself conducts two shorter foreign-study programs in Honduras, where participants study coral reef ecology and participate in service learning. Engineering students can earn a dual degree by taking three years of coursework at Rhodes and two at Washington University in St. Louis.

Student Life: Behind the Walls of Ivy

Rhodes is strictly traditional when it comes to architecture. Every building on campus is made of gray-orange stone, with slate roofs and stained-glass Gothic windows. With one hundred acres and only 1,566 students, there is plenty of room for studying outdoors, playing ultimate Frisbee, and other activities, as well as for expansion. Generous donations have allowed Rhodes to provide facilities that are uncommon for a school of its size. (A $198 million endowment—"more than it knows what to do with," says one professor—provides a great many amenities.) The Bryan Campus Life Center includes a large dining hall, a performance gymnasium, another three-court gym, a fitness center, an outdoor swimming pool, reception halls, and plenty of social areas for students and faculty.

Freshmen and sophomores are required to live on campus, freshmen for the most part in their own dorms. Half of the upperclassmen live on campus. Male and female students live separately in dorms, but there is no strict visitation policy. The dorm rooms are comfortable, some with private bathrooms and wood-burning fireplaces. The dormitories are located on the outer edges of campus, with the academic buildings and other campus facilities in the center. The East Village townhouses, each of which includes a living room, kitchen, bedrooms, and bathrooms, house 200 students. Although half of Rhodes students are members of fraternities or sororities, these provide social facilities only, not living accommodations. One recent alumna says that the fraternities and sororities "are not all that exclusive" and that independent students feel comfortable attending Greek parties.

Students spend most of their free time on campus, but Memphis also offers an attractive smorgasbord of restaurants, bars, shops, blues clubs, and other forms of entertainment. The center of the action, Beale Street, is a short drive from campus. Elvis's Graceland is nearby as well.

Although Rhodes has no campus church, many students have religious commitments and regularly attend services in the area; this prevents the college from interfering in the religious lives of their students, who are much more conservative in their spiritual lives than their teachers, especially in the religion department. Two small rooms in dormitories serve as on-campus chapels. One of the most active campus organizations is the Rhodes Christian Fellowship, which is affiliated with the evangelical InterVarsity Christian Fellowship; the group meets every Wednesday night to pray and listen to a speaker. Other religious groups include the Westminster Fellowship, Catholic Student Association, Fellowship of Christian Athletes, Interfaith Circle, and Jewish Student Union.

Community service is probably the most popular extracurricular activity; a full 80 percent of students volunteer for one cause or another. The Kinney Program, founded more than forty years ago, organizes opportunities on campus and in the Memphis area and recruits students to participate. Rhodes students independently run a downtown soup kitchen, lead a Habitat for Humanity group, volunteer countless hours as tutors in public schools and at Memphis's renowned St. Jude Children's Hospital, and help out at dozens of other places. Students active in community service can apply for a scholarship, take courses to supplement their hands-on learning, and even earn academic credit for service internships. A student affairs coordinator, also an alumna, says that this spirit of volunteerism is the one thing she is most proud of about Rhodes: "I bet you wouldn't find a more service-committed student body anywhere."

The $23 million Bryan Center, dedicated in 1997, has encouraged students to become more active in athletics. Around a quarter of the student body participates in at least one of the nineteen varsity sports. Club and intramural sports options abound. The Rhodes Lynxes compete in the Southern Collegiate Athletic Conference; the University of the South at Sewanee is their main rival.

Recent statistics show no crime other than seven residence hall burglaries in 2004, the last year for which we have data, and even the trend in burglary is down, from twelve in 2002 and ten in 2003. A stone wall surrounding the campus keeps strangers

---

SUGGESTED CORE

For courses 1.–3., see also Humanities 101-102: The Search for Values in the Light of Western History and Religion

1. Greek and Roman Studies 211: Myth and Community in Ancient Greece and Rome or English 831: Epic Poetry
2. Philosophy 201: Ancient Philosophy
3. Religious Studies 101: Introduction to Biblical Literature
4. Religious Studies 214: Early Christian Literature
5. Political Science 314: Modern Political Philosophy
6. English 230: Shakespeare's Major Plays
7. History 231: North American in the Colonial and Revolutionary Eras
8. History 326: Modern European Intellectual History

ALL-AMERICAN COLLEGES

205

out, if not by force, then by giving the appearance that the private property within is well guarded. A bicycle patrol of campus policemen covers the grounds, and the college offers a student escort service around the clock, as well as plenty of crime prevention workshops.

Rhodes is by no means inexpensive, with tuition at $27,546, and room and board at $6,904. About 34 percent of students receive some need-based aid, and the average debt of a recent graduate is $20,770.

ST. ANSELM COLLEGE

MANCHESTER, NEW HAMPSHIRE • WWW.ANSELM.EDU

Located high on a hill over Manchester, New Hampshire, this 400-acre college is one of the oldest Catholic schools in New England. It is run by the Order of St. Benedict, the most ancient Catholic religious order—the same group of monks that copied and transmitted most ancient texts of Western civilization during the Dark Ages. Father Jonathan DeFelice, OSB, president of St. Anselm College since 1989, graduated from St. Anselm in 1969 with a major in philosophy. His focus has been to provide an environment where students are civilly engaged and globally informed. Under his leadership, the school has strengthened its liberal arts core and developed programs that take advantage of New Hampshire's position as a hotbed of primary politics. The school hosts the New Hampshire Institute of Politics, a venue for dialogue hosting widely known speakers from across the political spectrum. St. Anselm also focuses on public service, working hard, through the school's Meelia Center, to connect students' theoretical education with practical action in order to solve social problems in the local (Rust Belt) community.

While the school is not well known enough to be particularly selective in its admissions, by all accounts it offers students an education in the old liberal arts tradition, dedicated and accessible professors, and a sound curriculum, all in a distinctively Catholic (indeed, a monastic) environment. The school stands out for requiring students to take a wide-ranging, two-year sequence in Western civilization. It also requires three substantial classes in philosophy—a central discipline most undergrads in the country, even at religious schools, are free to skip. Particularly for devout students who wish to study in New England—where serious curricula and serious Catholics are thin on the ground—St. Anselm deserves a look.

Academic Life:
A Core That Leads to Service

The educational philosophy that prevails at St. Anselm is an appealing combination of traditional high-mindedness with earnestness about serving the community. The school asserts, "We challenge our students to engage in the fullest experience of a liberal arts education, to free them-

selves from the strictures of ignorance, illiteracy, and indecision and to dedicate themselves to an active and enthusiastic pursuit of truth. It is through an appreciation of several kinds of truth—scientific, technical, poetic, philosophical, and theological—that our students may learn to challenge resourcefully both personal and social problems." To this end, students must complete the following core curriculum:

- "Freshman English" I and II. These writing courses take the student through the basics of composition and research methods;
- "Humanities" I and II, two semesters devoted to presenting a rough history of Western civilization and its governing values, both secular and religious. This course takes a unique approach to exploring culture, examining periods through the "great" men and women viewed as examples of the "Warrior," "Convert," "Philosopher," "Citizen," "Poet," and so on. The course covers the growth of our culture from ancient Greece through the Middle Ages;
- "Humanities" III and IV. These two semesters take a similar approach to the period from the Italian Renaissance to the present. Figures covered include Michelangelo, Martin Luther, Elizabeth I, Galileo, Thomas Jefferson, Ludwig Van Beethoven, Charles Darwin, Andrew Carnegie, Sigmund Freud, Pablo Picasso, Duke Ellington, and Albert Camus;
- "Philosophy of Nature and Man," an introductory course to the "traditional topics of speculative philosophy pertaining to nature, the human person, and God";
- a philosophy course in ethics;
- a philosophy elective. Options range from "Metaphysics" to "Existentialism";
- "Biblical Theology";
- two theology electives. Options range from "Medieval Theology" to "Liberation Theology";
- two semesters of a foreign language. Choices include Greek, Latin, French, German, Russian, and Spanish; and
- two semesters of a lab science. Choices range from "Physics" to (for the nonscience major) "Chemistry and Society."

Students at St. Anselm—many of whom come from middling high schools—appreciate the core's intensive approach to intellectual inquiry and the introduction it provides to cultural history. As one puts it, "Being required to take theology and philosophy courses has forced me to think more intellectually." And as one faculty member says of the humanities sequence, "The courses combine lectures for the entire freshman or sophomore class with seminar discussions (eighteen students each). The whole idea of the course is that there is such a thing as human greatness, that there are peaks of human experience that may serve as models for us, but those peaks are sometimes problematic. I don't think most freshmen arrive prepared for the course—curious about these ideas, or serious about them. But many, many times alumni have approached me to say that these courses are the ones that matter most to them later in life."

Students with high test scores and good high school grades are invited to join the school's honors program. One professor says that the program is "quite good, with smaller classes, a greater emphasis on writing, discussion, and research, and highly motivated students." Courses in the honors program generally have no more than fifteen students. One honors student told the school, "Life within the honors program has given me the capability to enjoy a close, personal relationship with my professors and classmates in and out of class. This program will have given me a greater feeling of accomplishment when I graduate."

The school also offers a "3-2" engineering program that combines a liberal arts core with a degree in engineering from Notre Dame, the University of Massachusetts–Lowell, or Catholic University. Also, any students interested in ROTC will find a recruiting office on campus.

Unlike some other Great Books–friendly schools, St. Anselm asserts that experiential learning deepens intellectual pursuit. Students here are expected to put down their books and get their hands dirty out in the "real world." The school's Meelia Center serves as the core of St. Anselm's service-learning operations. According to the college, the center "mobilizes student talent and energy to assist fourteen community partnerships and more than thirty other community service agencies throughout Greater Manchester." Recently, students working through the Meelia Center raised money to bring children with a rare genetic disorder from Tanzania to the United States for cancer prevention treatments. "Annually some 850 students, faculty, and staff volunteer more than 16,000 community service hours," the school reports. The Princeton Review recently listed St. Anselm as one of the "Best Colleges with a Conscience."

For the type of student who learns better by doing (educators call this the "kinetic model"), this curriculum is perfect. The average SAT score of an incoming student is relatively low, just below that of the University of New Hampshire, but most of the students are business majors and nursing majors, areas that demand hands-on learning. In other words, St. Anselm knows its students and serves them well.

For those who are more literary, a Great Books major is available, run by the philosophy department. Montague Brown, author of the book *The One Minute Philosopher*, heads it. The school describes the program as follows: "In addition to pursuing an integrated understanding of a great range of human wisdom, this course of study has two other significant features. The first is an emphasis on discussion seminars rather

---

VITAL STATISTICS

Religious affiliation:
  Roman Catholic
Total enrollment: 1,986
Total undergraduates: 1,986
SAT/ACT midranges: SAT V:
  510–600, M: 510–600;
  ACT: 21–26
Applicants: 3,258
Applicants accepted: 73%
*Accepted applicants who
  enrolled*: 22%
Tuition: $23,990
Room and board: $9,070
Freshman retention rate:
  not provided
Graduation rate: 74% (4 yrs.),
  77% (6 yrs.)
*Courses with fewer than 20
  students*: 52%
Student-faculty ratio: 13:1
*Courses taught by graduate
  students*: none
Most popular majors: :
  business/marketing,
  social sciences,
  psychology
Students living on campus:
  87%
*Guaranteed housing for four
  years?* yes
*Students in fraternities or
  sororities*: none

than lecture classes. The second is the use of primary rather than secondary sources or textbooks." The program is small and offers a rigorous academic experience. Another campus initiative, the Institute of Saint Anselm Studies, was inspired by Pope John Paul II, who, in his encyclical letter *Fides et Ratio*, spoke of the need for continuing philosophical speculation in order to come to an understanding of the Catholic faith. This institute is "an academic research center . . . established to promote and encourage the study of the life, thought, and spirituality of Saint Anselm of Canterbury, the patron of the College"—and one of the most important (if sometimes neglected) medieval philosophers.

Regarding the best teachers, students recommend Fr. John Fortin and Joseph Spoerl in philosophy, Kevin Staley in philosophy and humanities, and Max Latona in history. One student says, "Professor Dante Scala and Professor Dale Kuehne [both in the politics department] are probably two of the greatest professors I know." One teacher says, "In my view our history department is the strongest department on campus. The department is composed largely of serious young scholars who are deeply committed to teaching and to developing a pedagogy that encourages students to learn for themselves." As to the school's weaknesses, he notes, "There are some areas that we do not even cover. In part that's because we are a small school; but this may reflect something about the culture of the college. We do not have a performing arts department or an anthropology department, for example."

In 1999, St. Anselm founded the New Hampshire Institute of Politics. One politics major says the program "allows students to meet politicians of both parties and an assortment of interesting speakers. . . . This year I had the opportunity to hear from congressional insiders and had lunch with Senator Sam Brownback."

A newly organized program, aimed at creating active citizens, is the Learning Liberty Initiative, which over time will become a multiyear, small-group seminar for all students that is part of the core curriculum. According to the school, "Saint Anselm College seeks to provide an environment and an education for the development of engaged, active, and responsible citizens for a free and democratic community. Toward this end the College will emphasize the skills of the liberal arts (including reading, writing, speaking and thinking), will provide opportunities to practice moral obligations to self and community, and will offer an exploration of those obligations informed by the diversity within the Western tradition, by the American tradition and by the tradition of Catholic social thought." Of course, there is no easy consensus among Catholics as to what church social teaching really implies; its mantle is claimed by groups as disparate as Catholic Worker "distributists," market-loving libertarians, and New England Democratic party hacks. So it remains to be seen what shape the Learning Liberty Initiative will take.

While a bevy of habited Benedictines gives the campus a traditional feel, the rancid tide of modernity does wash over it as well. Students are as likely to read the spurious Gospel of Thomas and *The DaVinci Code* as they are Virgil and St. Thomas More. An enthusiastic tour guide told one parent, while attending a campus tour, that the entire school read *The DaVinci Code* together in 2004. Of course, theology professors might well have used this as a teaching moment that allowed them to point out the pulp novel's abundant absurdities. But this event does suggest that the school occasionally relaxes its adherence to orthodoxy.

Students insist that the school remains true to the church. "When most people talk about Catholic colleges, they focus upon colleges and universities like Holy Cross, Boston College, and Georgetown," one says. "However, these colleges have lost their Catholic identity, while Saint Anselm continues to maintain a strong religious identity despite pressure to move towards a more secularized college. Saint Anselm truly is a diamond in the rough in the world of colleges and is a positive environment for conservative and religious students."

One faculty member adds, "Having an active Benedictine monastery on campus gives the college a unique feeling. The monks are exemplary role models on how to live a religious life. As a Benedictine college, we emphasize that teaching is a moral and ethical activity and not one to be take lightly. This extends to our grading policy, which is fairly stringent. There is some grade inflation, I believe, but nothing like what I've seen at other schools. The dean's position—echoed by almost all the faculty—is that giving honest grades and not inflated ones is a moral duty."

> SUGGESTED CORE
>
> *Humanities I–IV, required of all students, should be supplemented with the following courses to complete the core curriculum:* Theology 10: Biblical Theology; Politics 9: Elements of Political Theory, Modern; English 51: Shakespeare; History 41: United States History.

Student Life: Out on the Hustings

At St. Anselm, all dorms are single-sex, and strict rules limit the hours that men and women can visit each other's rooms. One student says, "RAs are generally likeable and willing to help with any problems. Crime is not a major problem on campus. Due to the college's small size, most students feel safe and secure." Drinking does not seem more of a problem at St. Anselm than at most schools (which, admittedly, isn't saying much). All students are required to take an online course through AlcoholEdu before entering as freshmen (the school uses the feedback as a gauge of attitudes on drinking). Students make use of the numerous bars in Manchester, where they rub shoulders with denizens of nearby Thomas More College, also featured in this book.

According to the school, of the 87 percent of students who live on campus, only 60 percent remain on campus during the weekends. There are various opportunities for those who remain to get involved, with organized activities ranging from cheerleading to chess. The Dana Humanities Center is the hub of performing arts, classical concerts, and speakers. The Chapel Art Center presents various exhibits throughout the year and theater performances are regularly produced by the Abbey Players in the Koonz Theater. The student newspaper, the *Crier*, publishes on a semi-monthly basis. Another group, the Radio Flyers, is organizing a campus station. In addition to several politically oriented student groups, the Student Government Association gives students a chance to learn the art of politics. For students interested in the (genuinely) metaphysical, the philosophy club is said to be excellent, while religious clubs like the Organization for Life, Pax Christi, Knights of Columbus, and Campus Ministry provide opportunities to become active in organized events or to teach CCD at area parishes.

Sports are well represented at the school, both at the intramural level and in NCAA Division III. When the school recently decided to make a commitment to the football program, it built Grappone Stadium, and in 2003, St. Anselm completed construction of the Sullivan Arena, which hosts the hockey team. The school has several baseball fields, soccer and lacrosse fields, basketball, and a swimming pool. Although the school does not have its own programs at foreign schools, the college's Study Abroad office helps students find destinations where they can earn credit while broadening their horizons.

Sometimes it seems to outsiders that the state of New Hampshire exists solely for the sake of holding a primary every four years. Locals are not slow to take advantage of this cottage industry, turning the state from a rural hustings into a center for the practice of the electoral arts. In 1999, St. Anselm founded the New Hampshire Institute of Politics, which promotes civic engagement and provides a venue for hopeful candidates. This gives students a rare opportunity to hear from and meet some of the biggest names in politics. Recent speakers have included Ann Lewis, Senator Sam Brownback, Steve Forbes, and William Kristol. Students are invited to help organize these events, which allow them to network with and learn from top-notch political operatives (i.e., the candidates' staffers). One politics major says, "I would recommend the Kevin Harrington Student Ambassador program organized by the New Hampshire Institute of Politics. This program allows students to meet politicians of both parties and an assortment of interesting speakers." The student goes on to say, "The strongest point of my major is the ability of the professors to bring in guest speakers who have a tremendous amount of influence. This year I had the opportunity to hear from congressional insiders and had lunch with Senator Sam Brownback."

Of course, as is often the case, with opportunities come problems—for instance, many of the politicians who come to campus disagree with Catholic teaching, particularly on the sanctity of human life. The New Hampshire Institute hosted a debate during the 2004 presidential election that prompted protests from Catholic groups, outraged that a Catholic college would invite pro-abortion speakers, regardless of whether they were presidential candidates. On the other hand, no anti-life politicians are invited to speak at official college events, such as commencement. And it's impressive that a school as small as St. Anselm was able to hold an event of this magnitude. With its pragmatic bent, solid curriculum, and Capitol Hill connections, the school is certainly a good place for students with political aspirations.

The campus is relatively safe, given its location in a major city. In 2004, St. Anselm reported on campus one non-forcible and two forcible sex offenses, two aggravated assaults, three burglaries, one stolen car, and three arsons. The school employs seven full-time safety officers who patrol the campus twenty-four hours a day.

When it comes to cost, St. Anselm stands in the middle range of private colleges. Tuition is $23,990, room and board $9,070. Approximately 70 percent of students receive need-based grants or loans from the school or the government. The average graduate emerges with a student loan debt of $22,246.

ST. BONAVENTURE UNIVERSITY

OLEAN, NEW YORK • WWW.SBU.EDU

The heart of St. Bonaventure University is a place few campus visitors see, because it is on top of a mountain many miles away. The retreat center on Mount Irenaeus is a lasting monument to the troubles of the sixties and seventies, from which American higher education has never recovered, and the particular response of a unique institution. Like many colleges and universities in that period of on-campus protest and violence sparked

by U.S. intervention in Vietnam, St. Bonaventure held a series of off-campus retreats for administrators, professors, and student leaders, at which accommodations were reached to stabilize the situation on campus. Unlike other such academic retreats, St. Bonaventure's emphasized the spiritual vocation of a university embodying the Franciscan charism. The event not only helped pour oil on the waters; it also set the tone for a school that has remained strongly committed to its religious and educational mission.

While students don't come to St. Bonaventure to become friars or sisters, their education is permeated with the conviction that family life and worldly occupations are themselves religious vocations to be lived in the spirit of SS. Francis and Clare, and that these vocations require the intellectual formation exemplified by St. Bonaventure's *The Mind's Journey to God.* This belief explains the university's commitment to an impressive core curriculum that puts most elite liberal arts colleges to shame. St. Bonaventure clearly cares about forming its students into broadly educated adults. Today, it offers the kind of education to which all Catholic colleges once aspired.

In 2006, popular fantasy author P. K. Morrison returned to St. Bonaventure, her *alma mater,* and described the current crop of students in her blog: "I taxed one class with why their generation was so apathetic: the apathetic ones had of course nothing to say, but the other ones were eager to put forth any number of reasons, a few . . . with greatly reassuring intelligence and humor. . . . [M]ost of them were polite and genuinely interested, and I tried to give them a look at how what I learned at Bona has been of service to me my entire life." Since Morrison left the school, St. Bonaventure has reinvigorated its curriculum and once again embraced its religious identity—redefining its notion of service to more closely approximate that held by its founding friars.

Academic Life: The Journey of Vocation

St. Bonaventure maintains undergraduate schools of arts and sciences, education, journalism and mass communication, and business, but all undergraduates must take the core curriculum of Clare College, which is as follows:

- "The Intellectual Journey," an introduction to the life of rational inquiry based on themes from *The Mind's Journey to God*. Taught in small seminars, this course leads students "in reflective discussion, informed by the Bonaventurian spiritual vision, of substantive issues posed by the human community";

- "Inquiry in the Natural World," a course in the history of science;

- "Foundations of the Western World." The school calls this class an "introduction to the historical, intellectual, and religious roots of Western culture intended to serve as a basis for developing a comprehensive understanding of that culture and of other cultures";

- "The Good Life," a philosophy class meant to "introduce students to questions about the nature of morality, major ethical theories, Roman Catholic moral reflection, contemporary and classical ethical dilemmas, and models of moral behavior and character";

- "Inquiry in the Social World," an introductory course taught "from the points of view of several social sciences" that "unravels the assumptions and methods of study of each";

- "Foundational Religious Texts of the Western World." This theology class "introduces the foundational texts of the major Western religions, focusing largely upon the Hebrew and Christian Scriptures";

- "The Catholic-Franciscan Heritage," which presents "a critical reflection on the essential elements of the Catholic-Franciscan tradition";

- "World Views," an "interdisciplinary, team-taught introduction" to world geography;

- "Composition and Critical Thinking" I and II, a two-part course in writing that teaches core skills in English composition; and

- "The University Forum." This cross-disciplinary "capstone course of the Clare curriculum is a critical examination of a selected contemporary issue that may be studied by social and natural scientists, humanists, philosophers, and theologians."

Students in most undergraduate schools at the university also face foreign-language requirements.

There is a reason why St. Bonaventure has such a solid curriculum: it was forced to embrace academic seriousness in order to stay alive. In the 1990s the school faced bankruptcy, thanks in part to the competition of an aggressive State University of New York system. St. Bonaventure's leaders decided to embrace a more traditional core curriculum as a means of distinguishing the school from the herd. The Catholic and Franciscan heritage enabled it to embrace the Western intellectual tradition without the standard postmodern adversarial stance, and the university came up with the smart idea of putting the core courses and faculty in their own school—Clare College. Suddenly a university many had written off attained national recognition for its leadership and became a model for other schools seeking to reassert their Catholic and liberal arts identities.

St. Bonaventure's Franciscan Institute does not offer undergraduate majors, but its spirit suffuses the curriculum as a whole, much as Clare College assures that all undergraduates receive a traditional grounding in the classical liberal arts. Everyone who ever studied scholastic philosophy in English translation has reason to be grateful to the Franciscan Institute for its editions of such thinkers as Bonaventure, Duns Scotus, and even the razor-wielding slasher William of Occam. The business school is reliably conservative, with an active chapter of Sam Walton's Students in Free Enterprise (SIFE). On the other hand, the journalism faculty intends to imbue its students with a spirit of investigative reporting that tends to treat both business and government with salutary skepticism.

The university is committed to an impressive core curriculum that puts most elite liberal arts colleges to shame. This school clearly cares about forming its students into broadly educated adults.

The School of Arts and Sciences offers Greek and Latin in the classics department, Italian, Spanish, French, German, and Arabic in the modern languages department, and biblical Hebrew, New Testament Greek, and ecclesiastical Latin in the theology department. The English department teaches literature for its own sake—the great writers, such as Chaucer, Shakespeare, and Milton—and literary and critical theory for the sake of literature, not the other way around. Philosophy, too, is taught in the traditional manner, building on the core prerequisites. The history of philosophy courses include St. Thomas as well as his Franciscan rivals (such as, no surprise, St. Bonaventure), American philosophy, and poor old Nietzsche. In addition to the traditional major, the philosophy department also manages preprofessional programs in law and business. The history department offers reliable courses in world, European, and United States history; there is also a course in United States military history. An internship is offered in curatorship and archives management. The offerings in political science are similarly straightforward, but also include internships in local law offices (even in your hometown) to see how the law works in practice. Economics is taught in the business school from a market perspective.

The theology department emphasizes the spirituality of Thomas Merton, who served as an instructor in English at St. Bonaventure and attempted to join the Franciscans there before being accepted by the Trappists. The Franciscan masters, particularly St. Bonaventure himself, are studied as well. The charism of the university, like that of the Franciscan orders, is oriented to religious experience and Christian ethics rather than to the more abstract and intellectual aspects of dogma. Its ecumenical thrust is directed more toward other religions than to the other traditions of historic Christianity; the department more or less assumes that, as far as the Christian religion goes, the Roman Catholic Church is the only game in town, even though there are Maronite and Byzantine Catholic churches in Olean, and the university hosts the local meeting of the Religious Society of Friends. Certification in religious education is offered by the theology department, not by the School of Education, and only to theology majors or minors. Those who have observed the state of religious education in Catholic schools and parishes can only applaud St. Bonaventure's higher standards.

SUGGESTED CORE

1. Classics 105: The Heroic Greeks *or* Classics 205: Greek Literature in Translation
2. Philosophy 404: History of Ancient and Medieval Philosophy
3. Theology 470: Contemporary Biblical Interpretation (*closest match*)
4. Theology 460: History of Christianity (*closest match*)
5. Political Science 204: Political Thought (*closest match*)
6. English 423/424: Shakespeare I/II
7. History 201: United States History to 1865
8. No suitable course.

"We can talk about faith very freely in the classroom," said a teacher. "At least one management professor starts his courses with a prayer. Our School of Business tries to incorporate Franciscan thought into the curriculum. We now teach Francis's concept of 'fraternity,' building community, as a virtue of management." Since September 11, 2001, the university has taken particular pride in alumnus Mychal Judge, the first official casualty of the World Trade Center, who died while hearing the confessions of rescue workers.

Mount Irenaeus, the university retreat center, is located on 228 acres between Cuba and West Clarksville, New York, and has seven hermitages besides the retreat house proper, along with six miles of trails and a pond. St. Bonaventure has an agreement with Duquesne University Law School, to which students can be admitted after three years, receiving their B.A. from St. Bonaventure when they have completed the first year of law school. The university also offers a six-week, six- or seven-credit program in Perugia in the Umbrian hills of Italy in May and June.

Among the faculty, St. Bonaventure students speak highly of professors across a wide variety of departments. Outstanding teachers include Lauren Delavars, Charles Gannon, M. W. Jackson, Tracy Schrems, and Richard Simpson in English; Bob Amico, Barry Gan, Roderick Hughes, Adrienne McEvoy, and Russell Woodruff in philosophy; John Hanchette, Chris Mackowski, and Denny Wilkins in journalism; Adam Brown, Michael Lavin, and Charles Walker in psychology; David Matz and Philip Payne in history; Kevin Borgerson and Kathy Zawicki in sociology; Basil Valente and Pat Vecchio in communication; Joel Benington and David Dimattio in science; Frank Bianco and Guy Imhoff in languages; Mary Rose Kubal and James Moore in political science; Susan Anders and Darwin King in accounting; Susan Abraham and James Vacco in theology; Jeff White in classics; Charles Virga in education; Maureen Cox in mathematics; Bob Florence in economics; Steven Andrianoff in computer science; and Ted Georgian in biology.

St. Bonaventure recently stumbled, and stumbled badly, in relating the campus culture of athletic competition to the deeper spiritual values of its religious heritage. A 2003 scandal over a college athlete who had misled the university about his eligibility led to the firing of the president—whose son, an assistant coach, was allegedly complicit— and the subsequent suicide of the chairman of St. Bonaventure's board. This tragedy made the community more aware of the necessity of revitalizing its sense of living, faith-based tradition. The leadership of a number of Christian colleges and universities have attempted this in the past few years, with very limited success because of the opposition of faculty members whose hearts were in secular academe. If St. Bonaventure is more successful, it will be because there is a broad consensus about the urgent need for reform. Along these lines, in 2006 the university initiated a new First-Year Experience program to integrate academics, student life, spiritual formation, and vocational exploration.

Campus Life: Icy, Enchanted Mountains

St. Bonaventure University occupies 500 acres near the headwaters of the Allegheny River in the Enchanted Mountains of western New York. Buffalo and Jamestown are each about an hour away. From this spot, 200 years ago, intrepid boatmen would launch their rafts and barges and head out to the Ohio and the Mississippi. Olean, five miles away, was the location of the first discovery of petroleum in North America and was named for that precious substitute for whale oil. Olean Shepherd, the first child born in the community, received her unctuous appellation in 1807, and tiny oil wells can still be seen here and there in the landscape. The town, with a population of less than 20,000, houses Forness Family Fun Park with its "world-class" eighteen-hole miniature golf course, surely one of the last of its kind, and forty-four flavors of ice cream. Olean's better restaurants include the Century Manor, located in a former funeral home (which some like to say is haunted), as well as the Oh-Sta-Geh, and the Old Library. Beautiful as the Enchanted Mountains may be in spring, summer, and fall, the only word for the winter climate is "brutal," with the temperature ranging on the average from sixteen to thirty degrees—on the average. The record low was thirty-six below zero. But the snowy season is not without its advantages; nearby Ellicottville is an up-and-coming, some-what bohemian ski resort.

The campus itself is lovely, with an Italianate architecture better suited to the topography than collegiate Gothic would have been. There are unembarrassed shrines reflecting traditional Catholic piety, such as the Lourdes Grotto; and the occasional sight of a friar's habit, even if not as common as in years past, seems not at all out of place. The campus culture is friendly and welcoming to strangers—not that many strangers come. Athletics are still honored, though perhaps not as unreservedly as before the recent scandal.

Eight residence halls and a limited number of townhouses and apartments accommodate about 1,750 students. All students in the dorms are required to sign up for unlimited meals at Hickey Hall, even though the food served up there is universally deplored, ranked by several college guides as the worst in the United States. It is that as much as thirst that drives students to the Rathskeller, the social center of the campus, and to places in and around town.

Several campus subcultures coexist without undue friction. Some students imbibe liberally on the weekends and others profess themselves a bit shocked at this fact, Though there is not the extreme cult of drunkenness for its own sake that is found elsewhere in academe, it would be naïve to think that alcohol is not a problem for some; indeed, to describe a state of profound inebriation, some students use the term "Bonaventure drunk." "Apparently in the real world [if] you get Bonaventure drunk every weekend people will try and take you to AA meetings," one undergrad warned in an online forum.

There is an enormous range of student activities. St. Bonaventure boasts over twenty academic enrichment clubs, including Sigma Tau Delta (the national English fraternity), the Society of Physics Students, the Society of Professional Journalists, and Students in Money Management. For intramural athletics and recreation, there are aerobics, the Bonavoyagers (an outdoors club), chamber singers, cheerleading, chorus, concert band, Garret Theater, intramurals, jazz band, Legacy Dance Company, pep band, and performing arts such as small ensembles for trombone, saxophone, flute, clarinet, and other instruments.

Student advocacy groups include SBU for Life as well as Amnesty International, and such completely nonpolitical groups as the Security and Safety Committee and Students Against Destructive Decisions (SADD). Students may also get involved with the Academic Honesty Board, Campus Activities Board, Certified Mediators, Mock Trial Team, Residence Hall Council, Resident Assistants, Student Activities Council, Student Arbitration Council, Student Government, University Appeals Board, and University Judicial Board.

Student volunteers serve the university in MERT, the medical emergency response team; as new student mentors, orientation leaders, peer educators, student ambassadors, student assistant orientation coordinators, and at the Red Cross blood drives. It is worth noting that the university does not have the usual array of organizations hostile to Catholic doctrine.

The campus is relatively safe. In 2004, the only crimes reported were a single forcible sexual assault and nine burglaries.

In comparative terms, St. Bonaventure is not that expensive, with tuition at $22,515, and room and board $7,706. About 90 percent of students receive need-based financial aid, and the average student loan debt of a recent graduate is a moderate $18,500.

ST. JOHN'S COLLEGE

ANNAPOLIS, MARYLAND & SANTA FE, NEW MEXICO • WWW.SJCA.EDU

One of the most distinguished liberal arts colleges in the United States, St. John's College is unique in a number of ways. There are no academic majors or departments, no NCAA teams, and almost no careerists. The students are as high-minded as the professors, and often as conversant in classical languages. The courses focus exclusively on classic texts (the Great Books), and are taught entirely in the Socratic fashion—in small seminars, with a group of a dozen or so undergrads poring over Heraclitus,  Descartes, or Nietzsche, typically in the original languages, side-by-side with translations. You don't need to take the SATs to get in, and the school won't tell you your grades unless you ask for them. Tutors (i.e., professors) don't lecture, but ask provocative questions designed to help students explore the often hundreds of pages of assigned reading. In classic Oxford style, the lectures that are offered are open to all—and most of the time the whole student body gathers to hear them on Friday nights, with discussions afterward that often stretch into the wee hours. Topics of recent lectures have included "Aristotle's Investigation of the Citizen," "From Embryonic Stem Cells to End of Life Ethical Dilemmas in Medicine and Medical Research," and "Forgiveness."

Unlike most other Great Books schools in the United States, St. John's is entirely secular—and its politics skew somewhat to the left. But the atmosphere of open discussion and the intellectual rigor that characterizes the campus conversation prevent the rise of any cheap ideological consensus, such as afflicts too many colleges. Conservatives or religious believers will find themselves welcome—provided they are willing to read analytically and think searchingly about their convictions, and to defend them against the well-honed arguments of skeptics.

Academic Life: What's the Greek on That?

Chartered in 1784, St. John's College was founded by colonists as King William's School in 1696, making it the third-oldest college in the United States. After falling into tough financial times in the 1930s, the school decided to reinvent itself as a Great Books academy. In 1937, two Rhodes Scholars from the University of Chicago, Stringfellow Barr and Scott Buchanan, crafted a new plan for liberal education. The program centers on reading the seminal texts of the West, listening to great works of music, and reproducing historic experiments in natural science—and conducting this quest for knowledge entirely in small-group discussions. This innovative approach to education attracted attention worldwide and soon drew to campus a stream of distinguished visiting professors, including the philosopher Mortimer Adler. In 1964, the college decided to expand, opening a new campus in Santa Fe, New Mexico. The two campuses today operate under one governing board but with separate presidents and faculties, and students are able to transfer freely between them. At either one, they're liable to hear the same "Johnnie" jargon; a favorite question on each campus is (regarding a text), "What's the Greek on that?"

Here's how the school sums up its vision: "A genuine liberal arts education begins with a shared understanding of the ideas and questions that help define our intellectual heritage. The books that are at the heart of learning at St. John's are among the richest sources of that heritage. They are timeless and timely; they not only illuminate the persisting questions of human existence but also have great relevance to our contemporary problems. They change our minds, move our hearts, and touch our spirits."

The school puts this vision into practice through a rigorous curriculum. Students must complete the following requirements:

- "Freshman Seminar." Termed by the college the "Greek" year, this two-semester course "begins with *The Iliad* and *The Odyssey*, continues with the dramas of Aeschylus and Sophocles, allows much time for the works of Plato, and concludes with Aristotle";
- "Sophomore Seminar." This yearlong course carries students (perhaps too quickly) through the Bible, "classical Roman poetry and history," the Middle Ages, and the Reformation. "The seminar's diverse readings are thus unified by the common classical and biblical roots and by the accumulating record of responses to them," the catalog reports;
- "Junior Seminar." This year at St. John's focuses on the seventeenth and eighteenth centuries, including "the first encounter with American authors (Madison, Hamilton, Mark Twain) and a reflection upon our own way of life";
- "Senior Seminar." This year brings the student through the nineteenth and twentieth centuries nearly up to the present. Readings include *War and Peace*, *Faust*, and *The Brothers Karamazov*, as well as works by Hegel, Nietzsche,

VITAL STATISTICS

Religious affiliation: none
Total enrollment: 1,164
Total undergraduates: 931
SAT midranges: V: 660–760, M: 590–680
Applicants: 812
Applicants accepted: 80%
Accepted applicants who enrolled: 39%
Tuition: $34,306
Room and board: $8,270
Freshman retention rate: 76%
Graduation rate: 45% (4 yrs.), 54% (6 yrs.)
Courses with fewer than 20 students: 98%
Student-faculty ratio: 8:1
Courses taught by graduate students: none
Most popular majors: n/a
Students living on campus: 80%
Guaranteed housing for four years? no
Students in fraternities or sororities: none

ALL-AMERICAN COLLEGES

221

and Heidegger. According to the school, "In keeping with the college's mission to turn out educated citizens, the senior year also includes works central to American democracy, such as *The Federalist Papers,* the speeches of Lincoln, key Supreme Court decisions, and Tocqueville's commentary on the radical nature of the American experiment";

- four years of foreign languages. Note the plural: In freshman year, students examine ancient Greek grammar alongside English and learn to translate Plato. In their sophomore year, they translate Sophocles or Homer, segments from the Bible, and study Shakespeare and English lyric poems. In the junior and senior years, they study French language and literature;
- four years of math. Students follow the historical development of math from Euclid up through modern, non-Euclidean geometers;
- three years of laboratory science. Students gain hands-on experience in biology, chemistry, physics, and genetics; and
- one year of music. To fulfill this requirement students explore musical notation and theory and take listening classes in Bach, Beethoven, Mozart, Palestrina, Stravinsky, and Schoenberg—also gathering regularly to sing.

"Reading philosophy, literature, all these things, has helped shape my vision of what I want the rest of my life to look like, what matters to me, and who I want to be."

All students begin the St. John's program as freshmen and study the same core texts, even those who have begun or completed studies at other colleges. (Almost a fifth of a recent freshman class had switched to St. John's from another school in search of more serious academic inquiry.) This approach establishes common ground, so that everyone can argue (and argue, and argue) productively about the issues that have occupied thinkers for thousands of years. (Need it be said that the kind of college experience that St. John's offers is not for everyone and it is best for students to visit the campus before enrolling?)

The heart of the academic program is a twice-weekly seminar (which lasts all four years) in which philosophy, theology, political science, literature, history, economics, and psychology are all considered. The reading list for literature includes works by Aeschylus, Virgil, Aquinas, Dante, Chaucer, Luther, Shakespeare, Racine, Molière, Tolstoy, Rimbaud, Kafka, and Faulkner. The ground rules for discussion are basic. "Reason is the only recognized authority," the college explains. Some eighteen students and two tutors gather to consider an assigned reading. References to earlier readings can be made, but citing secondary sources is discouraged. Classrooms at St. John's do not contain clocks. Conversation spills from seminars out into the open air. "Discussions here take place—endlessly, it seems—beneath the quadrangle's trees, in the busy coffee shop, over meals," the *Chronicle of Higher Education* has noted. "I almost want to say that conversations outside of class are more significant than the conversations I've had in class," says a student. "The most interesting conversations I've had were with my friends and classmates outside of class or with tutors over lunch. I'm not sure why that would be, but it seems the seminars make possible a further inquiry into the works—a needed follow-up."

Johnnies must be willing to examine their preconceived notions and test their abilities. "It seems like the best part about it is the struggle," says a student. "I came here not mathematically inclined. I hated science. But just having taken freshman lab, I have the biggest appreciation for science now, because I was forced to be exposed to it. I was forced to see it as something besides memorizing a textbook."

As a reflection of the importance given to dialectical inquiry, few tests are given at St. John's. "But in an important sense every day is an exam because in such small classes whether you have prepared and how well you have prepared are very evident," a student says. "With Euclid, for example, in any class you might be asked to demonstrate at the board and from memory any proposition."

Unlike many other small liberal arts schools, St. John's takes science seriously—putting its bookish charges into the lab for four solid years so that they get a first-hand feel for the scientific enterprise. "They fit the great story," says a student, "of how things which were separate in antiquity—mathematics and physics—were united to become mathematical physics and conquer nature itself." The lab covers genetics at about the same time that students are reading Darwin in the seminar.

Finally, juniors and seniors choose from a list of twenty to thirty preceptorials offered by tutors each year. These are the only "electives" at St. John's. "The aim is to explore a book in greater detail than is possible in a seminar," says one alum. "My preceptorials on Dante's *Purgatorio*, Livy's *History of Rome*, and Machiavelli's *Discourses on Livy* were among the best classes I had at St. John's."

Other than the preceptorials, students pick and choose neither courses nor tutors. Tutors at St. John's tend to teach there for decades, and some can boast of having taught every class offered. "Teaching is all here," says a tutor. "Research plays no role at all in tenure decisions." The student-faculty ratio is a wonderful 8 to 1. Students frequently take advantage of the school's invitation, "Take Your Tutor to Lunch."

St. John's uses the inquiry and discussion approach to learning because it discourages the elevation of individual tutors' personalities over the texts. Nevertheless, students confess to having favorites, such as Michael Andrews, David Bolotin, Joshua Kates, and Edward Cary Stickney in Santa Fe; and Elizabeth Blettner, Mera Flaumenhaft, Anita Kronsberg, George Russell, Erik Sageng, and David Townsend in Annapolis.

Thanks in part to its venerable curriculum, the campus has not become scorched earth in the culture wars. Michael Dink, dean at Annapolis, explained in a convocation address recently that the college's intellectual tradition combines the best meanings of the words "liberal" and "conservative." "[O]ur intellectual tradition itself embodies an oxymoron: as a tradition, a handing down of previous ways of thinking, it is conservative, but as a tradition of radical questioning, in which what is handed down is constantly questioned, it is liberal."

Since tutors are supposed to function as participants in classroom discussions rather than as proponents for particular ideological viewpoints, there is little opportunity for political advocacy to seep into teaching. "St. John's is probably one of the few places in this country where you have the ability to study texts on their own terms—without a professor's bias (for the most part) and a certain 'accepted' interpretation of what the books say," one student says.

This fact sets St. John's apart from the Great Books schools with strong Christian characters. At this college, St. Augustine and sacred scriptures are treated as interesting texts—not authoritative or inspired documents. However, "tutors seem to have a basic respect for Christian beliefs, if dealt with in an intellectual rather than personal manner," a graduate says. She adds that students would be well advised to approach religious texts within the search for truth rather than as a "brief for certain points of theology." The Bible and several medieval and modern theologians are in the curriculum—although they're bunched together with secular Roman writings, and disposed of in a single year. That's not enough time to spend on the texts that created Christendom (the old, pre-PC name for the West), but at least these periods are treated with intellectual seriousness; at too many other schools they are simply skipped.

There is periodic discussion about whether the curriculum should be revised to include additional works by women and minorities. A black alumnus wrote an article in which he declared, "St. John's is what a college ought to be, and blacks, as well as all races, should not be put off by the general homogeneity of the curriculum." He added that the Great Books "lengthen our attention span, teach us to cultivate humanity, help us to fully appreciate what it means to be human and to exist."

Many students discover their calling as a result of their studies at St. John's. "I personally feel that reading the books has helped me decide what's important in my life and what I should be living my life for," says a student. "Reading philosophy, literature, all these things, has helped shape my vision of what I want the rest of my life to look like, what matters to me, and who I want to be."

After four years of great books and great conversations, where do St. John's graduates go? The answer is, mostly, to grad school. According to the college bulletin, nearly 75 percent of graduates go on to graduate or professional programs, and St. John's ranks in the top 10 percent among schools in the percentage of graduates who receive Ph.D.'s. A recent survey of the activities of graduates found that 20 percent go into law or teaching, with an equal percentage entering business careers.

One recent alumna has become a successful romance novelist. A 2004 graduate entered the formation program of the Dominican order. In the *College*, an alumni publication, an aspiring priest noted that reading, contemplation, and seminar discussions at the friary reminded him of his life at St. John's. Another alum, Ronald H. Fielding, found his calling in investments. In 2003 he gave his alma mater $10 million, saying, "At St. John's, you have to deal with things that are unfamiliar and difficult and work them out. If you have to grapple with the ideas of Kant and Nietzsche, and work out the mathematics of Einstein, you gain something very valuable for the long run." A 1995 graduate, after a seven year-stint in the United States Marine Corps, where she learned to fly helicopters, finds fulfillment as a pilot for a television news station and is studying for a master's degree in aviation.

In an effort to better prepare students for graduate studies and professional employment, St. John's has established summer internship programs on both campuses.

Student Life: Desert and Sea

The coastal Annapolis campus of St. John's College stands in stark contrast to the desert environs of the western Santa Fe campus, which lies in the foothills of the Sangre de Cristo Mountains. The campuses also have different reputations. Annapolis, with its colonial street names and brick buildings , takes its character from the legislators, naval officers, and affluent professionals who live there. Students who would chafe in such a starched atmosphere might prefer the Santa Fe campus, where things are a bit more hazy and nonconformist. Some students speculate that the importance given to rationality in classrooms encourages the bacchanalian excess that sometimes prevails among students on weekends and at social occasions. One alum, however, recalls that he was able to live Gustave Flaubert's famous dictum to artists: "Be regular and orderly in your life like a bourgeois, so that you may be violent and original in your work."

Freshman housing is guaranteed. Eight traditional dorms in Annapolis, coed by floor, house students, whereas the Santa Fe campus has constructed sixteen townhouse-style units for student lodging. The rooms are functional but not always spacious, and some of the Annapolis buildings show signs of aging. Both campuses offer students twenty-four-hour computer access and have libraries with collections—and furnishings—designed to aid serious readers. Students need to go off campus for religious services; there are many congregations of all denominations available in both cities.

As you might imagine, students frequently need a break from the intense academics. The school offers several club and intramural sports, but no varsity teams. The school hews to the Greek ideal of a "sound mind in a healthy body," and everyone is encouraged to participate in sports regardless of experience or ability. "Enthusiasm, fair competition and a sense of humor are more important than athletic skill," says the *Dialogue*, a school newsletter. In Annapolis, a boathouse hosts a crew team; students can also sign out college-owned sailboats and dinghies. An annual croquet match against neighboring Naval Academy midshipmen attracts spectators dressed in linen to munch on cucumber sandwiches while watching the competition (the Johnnies usually win). Santa Fe students go on rafting trips down the Rio Grande and on ski outings in Taos, which is a couple of hours away. A student search-and-rescue team also cooperates with New Mexico authorities in emergency operations. The Student Activities Center in Santa Fe includes a gymnasium, racquetball/squash courts, and a fitness room. The Annapolis campus houses gymnasium facilities, including a suspended running track, in Inglehart Hall. Fencing and soccer are popular at both campuses.

The theater group at the Annapolis campus is called the King William Players; Santa Fe's theater troupe is named Chrysostomos (derived from the "golden-mouthed" Saint John Chrysostom). Each performs works from the theatrical canon, ranging from Sophocles through Shakespeare to modern playwrights such as Beckett. The Annapolis student newspaper is the *Gadfly*; at Santa Fe, it's the *Moon*. Other activities include film clubs, madrigal, Sunday concerts, a Christian fellowship, and student government. Organized parties run the gamut from the Spring Cotillion (for which upperclassmen prepare newer students by teaching them to waltz) to the Reality Weekend festival, which features skits and parodies, picnicking, and athletic competition.

The Annapolis campus, with its proximity to both the state capitol and public housing, has experienced some muggings in recent years; campus security has offered safety tips and police whistles. In 2003 (the last year reported), that campus witnessed five burglaries and one case of arson. Santa Fe's adobe-style facilities are two miles from downtown and more isolated. In 2003, that campus witnessed one nonforcible sex offense and seven burglaries.

The educational experience at St. John's is heady but pricey; tuition is $34,306, and room and board adds $8,270. However, admissions are need-blind, and the school guarantees full aid to students who apply promptly (though aid packages may differ according to which campus one attends, an insider tells us). About 65 percent of students receive some kind of financial assistance. The average student loan debt of a St. John's graduate is around $20,000.

UNIVERSITY OF ST. THOMAS

HOUSTON, TEXAS • WWW.STTHOM.EDU

The University of St. Thomas was founded by a religious order that understands how to rebuild a tradition which has been under siege. Over 175 years ago in France, the Christian community was still reeling from the most comprehensive persecution experienced by the church since the Islamic seizure of North Africa. Churches had been closed, seized, or burned, clergy and religious massacred, and hundreds of thousands of ordinary people killed en masse for their faith— and a revolutionary government had attempted to impose by force a utopian secular cult, complete with its own ritual and creed. Once normalcy and the monarchy had been restored (i.e., after Waterloo), the Catholic Church began to

rebuild its educational institutions. To aid in this effort, a new religious order was founded: the Basilian Fathers. Devoted to higher education, the order flourished, and in 1947 the Basilians founded the University of St. Thomas in Houston (UST). That institution has weathered another revolution—the collapse of Catholic education in the 1960s and '70s—by staying true to its religious identity and to traditions of excellence in the liberal arts. Unlike most other Catholic schools in the United States, the University of St. Thomas has been faithful to the directives of Pope John Paul II's *Ex Corde Ecclesiae* by requiring its theology teachers to promise fidelity to official church teaching. The school has also maintained a serious curriculum that grants every student, regardless of major, a solid grounding in how to think (philosophy) and how to worship (theology), and in the history of the United States and Western civilization. The university also offers a wide variety of majors and graduate programs, many with fine reputations. All of this ought to be enough to attract the interest of any serious student who seeks a Catholic education. It has certainly gotten Rome's attention: the Vatican recently summoned former university president Archbishop Michael Miller to preside as Secretary of the Congregation of Catholic Education, a post he still holds.

ALL-AMERICAN COLLEGES

Academic Life: The Dialogue between Faith and Reason

An education at UST begins with the school's core curriculum, which centers on philosophy and theology. Students must complete these requirements:

- three courses in theology. Students take "Teachings of the Catholic Church," "Introduction to the Sacred Scriptures," and one elective, such as "Battle of the Sexes," which looks at modern feminism in the light of papal teaching;
- three classes in philosophy. Students may choose between two sequences, one thematic and one historical. The first consists of "Philosophy of the Human Person," "Ethics," and "Metaphysics"; the second "Ancient Philosophy," "Medieval Philosophy," and "Modern Philosophy";
- three more classes in either philosophy or theology;
- three classes in English. The only options here are "The Classical Tradition: Literature and Composition I," "The Middle Ages and Renaissance: Literature and Composition II," and "The Modern World: Literature and Composition III";
- two sequential courses in French, German, Greek, Latin, or Spanish;
- two courses in history. Students choose one of the following sequences: "World Community" I and II; "United States to 1877" and "United States since 1877"; "Europe: The Middle Ages" and "Europe: The Early Modern Age"; or "Age of Revolutions: Europe 1715–1870" and "Era of Great Wars: Europe 1870–1950";
- two courses in the social sciences. Students pick from a list of foundational courses in economics, geography, international studies, political science, psychology, and sociology;
- two courses in the natural sciences, with lab. Options include astronomy, biology, chemistry, environmental studies, geology, and physics;
- one class in mathematics;
- one course in speech, business communication, or homiletics (e.g., for seminarians); and
- one class in the fine arts. Options include "Introduction to the Visual Arts," "Screenwriting," and "Music and Western Civilization."

The university has no trouble explaining the rationale for these requirements: "Liberal education should include at least some appreciation of these areas of study. Unlike those attending many similar institutions, our students, regardless of their religion (and all are welcome), must also study both theology and philosophy. The first University catalog stated that 'the University of St. Thomas gives the place of honor to theology as queen of the sciences.' In so doing, the University is reaffirming the traditional practice of the church in her university program, since Pope Gregory IX issued the charter of the University of Paris in 1232, the first in the Christian West. According to that tradition, 'religious truth is not merely a portion of general knowledge, but its very condition.' Philosophy was, and is, viewed as complementing theology by responding to the deepest questions posed by our minds as we seek to understand our relation to God, nature, time and culture."

Fittingly, UST boasts a respected philosophy faculty, which students praise highly. Most philosophical study is grounded in the systematic approach of St. Thomas Aquinas, but students report that multiple perspectives are considered and disagreement is welcomed. Courses draw mostly upon primary documents, not textbooks. Majors may choose to follow either a thematic or historical path through the discipline, though all must take "Traditional Logic."

Another department that students praise is biology. The university is located close to the Texas Medical Center, where premed majors often secure internships and part-time employment. The history department at UST garners student plaudits for the quality of its teaching staff, among which are the former president of the university and the former vice president of academic affairs.

International studies offers both a strong program and an exceptional faculty; it is consequently one of the largest departments at UST. Teachers here are said to be more leftish than in other departments—but we have heard no complaints that this distorts classroom discussion, or that it rises to the level of dogmatism.

The English program takes a substantive, historical approach to the discipline, requiring students taking core classes to learn composition by studying classic texts from various centuries. English majors are required to study both Chaucer and Shakespeare, plus six more courses in literary history and a course in criticism.

Teaching is emphasized at the University of St. Thomas, and teachers regularly make themselves available to students. All classes are taught by professors, not graduate students. Faculty regarded highly at the school include Randall Smith in theology; Hans Stockton and Gustavo Wensjoe in international studies; Joseph McFadden and Lee Williams in history; Daryl Koehn, director of the school's Center for Business Ethics; and Sheila Waggoner in mathematics.

Students who want an even more thorough liberal arts education than UST guarantees for any undergraduate should explore the school's Honors Program, which provides students with a seven-course sequence meant to offer an integrated understanding of the humanities and their application in modern life: "The Tribe and the City," "From Empire to Christendom," "Church and Nation," "Revolution and the New Empires," "Community Service Project," "Independent Research Project," and "Contemporary Problems Seminar." Students interested in exploring the history, teaching, and literature of the Catholic Church more thoroughly ought to investigate the school's Catholic studies department.

VITAL STATISTICS

Religious affiliation: Roman Catholic
Total enrollment: 3,776
Total undergraduates: 1,884
SAT/ACT midranges: SAT V: 530–640, M: 520–640; ACT: 22–28
Applicants: 807
Applicants accepted: 92%
Accepted applicants who enrolled: 40%
Tuition: $16,950
Room and board: $6,700
Freshman retention rate: 69%
Graduation rate: 50% (4 yrs.), 50% (6 yrs.)
Average class size: 19
Student-faculty ratio: 14:1
Courses taught by graduate students: none
Most popular majors: biology (premed), international studies, business
Students living on campus: 12%
Guaranteed housing for four years? yes
Students in fraternities or sororities: none

Not everything is letter-perfect at UST, of course. Several departments provoke some complaints from students, though most of the issues raised did not appear to be especially serious. The psychology department is "in transition," meaning that there has been a major shift of faculty, and it consequently scores low with current students. The education program is . . . well, an education program, and is regarded by most students as less than challenging. Others complain of a liberal bias in justice and peace studies, where more conservative students are said to be reluctant to voice their opinions. One student reports that some campus students were upset over the visit of hard-right columnist and author Ann Coulter, who came at the invitation of a student group. With the encouragement of the local Catholic diocese, demonstrations frequently take place on campus in support of amnesty for illegal aliens.

Speaking of aliens, the most controversial veteran of the school is a former music professor, cult leader Marshall Applewhite, whom the school fired in 1970 for conducting a homosexual affair with a student. In 1997, Applewhite led thirty-nine followers in a mass suicide, hoping to meet an alien civilization aboard the Hale-Bopp Comet.

Unlike most other Catholic colleges in the U.S., the University of St. Thomas has been faithful to the directives of Pope John Paul II's Ex Corde Ecclesiae, *requiring its theology teachers to promise fidelity to official church teaching.*

In general, according to a teacher, the university "highly discourages any politicizing of the classroom," and religious students of any variety would "feel welcome anywhere" in the college. The university is described as "generally a fairly conservative campus."

The University of St. Thomas offers an array of special programs that are popular with students. There is a study-abroad program in Rome—particularly attractive to philosophy, theology, and Catholic studies majors, and opportunities to study in the Holy Land, Russia, and London. Preprofessional students have the option of five-year programs "combining undergraduate degrees in accounting, accounting and MIS, business administration, and international studies with graduate degrees in business administration (MBA) and international business (MIB)," reports the school. The school's business major is distinctive in offering a concentration in business ethics, sponsored by UST's Center for Business Ethics—nicely situated in the city that saw the birth and death of Enron Corporation.

Student Life: Houston, We've Got a Problem

Perhaps the worst thing about the University of St. Thomas in Houston is that it is, indeed, in Houston. That ultra-modern city, which lacks a downtown or public transit, often seems to offer little welcome to those human beings not traveling its streets in steel boxes. Students should bring cars and be prepared to drive everywhere they go.

The city also faces serious crime problems—made worse by an influx of refugees from Hurricane Katrina, some of whom brought along their abiding interest in street gangs.

The university does its best to provide a campus community. Many students live in independent and university-owned houses close to the college, while only around 12 percent of students reside on campus. Most of the residence buildings are single-sex, as are all floors and bathrooms. The new Vincent J. Guinan Residence Hall has been open to students under the age of twenty-one since 2004. Described as "state-of-the-art" by the university, it has 300 beds; laundries, computer rooms, and lounges are located on each floor, and the residence hall is located close to a cafeteria, coffeeshop, and bookstore.

Fans of ultra-minimalist religious art will be pleased at the proximity of the famous Rothko chapel, which offers nondenominational events in a nondescript environment. Speaking of modern sterility, the core of UST's campus was built by well-known modernist (and fascist) Philip Johnson. In other words, don't look for gargoyles, ivy, stained glass—or indeed, any evidence that these facilities were meant for use by flesh-and-blood men and women. (Perhaps this environment proved formative for Professor Applewhite.)

SUGGESTED CORE
1. English 1341: The Classical Tradition: Literature and Composition I
2. Philosophy 1315: Ancient Philosophy
3. Theology 2300: Introduction to the Sacred Scriptures
4. Theology 3363: Church History I
5. Political Science 4302: Political Theory: Hobbes to the Present
6. English 3316: Shakespeare
7. History 2333: United States to 1877
8. History 3331: Age of Revolutionary Europe: 1715–1870 (*closest match*)

Those University of St. Thomas students who choose to live on campus do so not for the architecture, but for the sake of a closer community—which includes a life of faith. Those who spoke with us highly praised the campus ministry. Hall chaplains are always available to talk, and students describe this to be the "highlight" of their relationship with the ministry (which they characterize as "vibrant"). The campus is welcoming to students of all faiths. Mass is said each Sunday at the Chapel of St. Basil, which also remains open throughout each day for private reflection and prayer. Occasionally celebrations are also given at the chapel in French and Spanish. The university chaplain, Fr. Daniel Callam, is called an "inspirational" speaker and is known for his thoughtful homilies. He is widely respected by students, who regularly seek his spiritual guidance. Since the chapel (see the photo on page 227) was also built by Johnson, it has rather less warmth and devotional imagery than the average NASA facility, and students with more traditional tastes might want to seek out other venues for liturgy. Annunciation Church on Texas Street offers a weekly Latin Mass in a beautiful Gothic building.

A variety of social events brighten students' lives when they're not poring over St. Thomas and wishing that their excellent school was located in Austin. Students speak fondly of Tuesday nights' (nonalcoholic) "party in the library"; an annual snowball fight between two of the dorms; and a pizza party to celebrate the completion of honors courses. Commuter students are given free bagels for breakfast once a month, a day celebrated as "bagel Wednesday." The school regularly provides free pizza—along with a professor, who eats with the students as he lectures, then conducts an impromptu seminar over the crusts. Another campus tradition is the annual "Neewollah" party (that's Halloween spelled backwards). Several hundred students appear in costume outside the Link-Lee Mansion to hear local bands and let off steam.

Houston boasts a lively arts scene, with sixteen nearby museums, a symphony orchestra, a Grand Opera and numerous dance companies, jazz concerts at Da Camera, and a variety of theaters. Other venues include Bayou Place, an indoor center housing nightclubs, theaters, concert halls, restaurants, and movie theaters showing "indie" titles. Locals recommend Ruggles Bistro Latino as a site for salsa dancing and Latino food. The Houston Astros play at a new stadium that is (alas!) no longer called Enron Field.

Back on campus, student-led organizations are many; they include Amnesty International, the Asian Students' Association, the Black Student Union, Campus Greens, the *Cauldron* (the student paper), the Chess Club, a religious fellowship called Chi Rho, College Republicans, Dodge Ball, El Club, the Filipino Students' Association, *Laurels* (a literary magazine), the Muslim Student Association, Pipe and Drum Corps, the Prelaw Club, University Democrats, University Speech and Debate Society, the Women's Interest Group, and VITA, a pro-life organization. There are no Greek organizations, however.

Football is followed closely, especially the seasonal game between St. Thomas and St. John's universities. Baseball and softball are also popular. Other physical activities include basketball, billiards, dodgeball, foosball, and Pilates. Most sporting activities are held at the Jerabeck Activity and Athletic Center, which contains a large gym, two tennis courts, a weight room, and swimming pool.

Crime seems to be a concern for some students, who have reported car break-ins, muggings, and one armed robbery in the locality. A few incidences of serious crime on the University of St. Thomas's main campus or between its north and south campuses are reported annually, according to one student, though the overwhelming majority of incidences appear to have taken place in the middle of the night. A small number of arrests were reported for drug- and liquor-law violations between 2002 and 2003, though none were reported for 2004. One student complains that security has been problematic in the past, though the university has recently made necessary safety upgrades. Pairs of student escorts are also available to attend fellow students as they travel across or between campuses regardless of the time of day or night.

The University of St. Thomas is less costly than many private colleges, with an annual tuition price of $16,950 and room and board costs of $6,700. About 65 percent of students receive need-based financial aid, and the average student loan debt of a recent grad is a modest $15,500.

ST. VINCENT COLLEGE

LATROBE, PENNSYLVANIA • WWW.STVINCENT.EDU

Founded in 1846 by the Bavarian monk Boniface Wimmer, St. Vincent College is firmly rooted in the Benedictine tradition of higher learning. Benedictine monks were the conservators of Western civilization after the fall of Rome, and they have been teaching the liberal arts for some 1,500 years. According to the *National Catholic Register*, this school, still run by the Order of Saint Benedict (OSB), is one of a small group of Catholic colleges that actually complies with official Vatican policy, requiring their Catholic theology professors to present church teaching faithfully. But while St. Vincent may be doctrinal, it is not doctrinaire; students report lively discussion and an atmosphere of open exchange at a high level of intellectual discourse. With one of the strongest political science programs of any Catholic college, St. Vincent is a choice worth considering for any bright and ambitious student.

Academic Life: Firm Foundations

St. Vincent says that it maintains its curriculum in accord with the vision of its founder, Archabbot Wimmer, who insisted that students must learn "first what is necessary, then what is useful, and finally what is beautiful and will contribute to their refinement." To accomplish this, the college requires that students take foundational courses in most of the disciplines of the liberal arts, chosen from narrow lists of substantial class offerings. Unfortunately, this doesn't constitute an entirely traditional core curriculum: For instance, students may choose to study either American history or ancient and medieval periods, when they ought to be made to study both. However, the curriculum shows more attention and care for students' formation than the average set of bland distribution requirements. Better still, students are required to study philosophy, the discipline of thinking. Specifically, students must take the following:

- a freshman seminar, which is designed to instill in students the habits of college-level work;
- two survey courses in history. Options include "Topics in U.S. History to 1865," "Western Civilization to 1300 I," and "East Asia I";

- two courses in philosophy. "First Philosophy" is an introductory class that explores central themes and major historical periods. Students then must choose an elective such as "Eastern Thought" or "Philos and Eros";
- three courses in religious studies. Students take "Exploring Religious Meaning," an overview course that covers multiple religious traditions, plus two electives. Options include both "Basics of Catholic Faith" and "The Faith Legacy of Jimmy Carter" (yes, we hear the snickers);
- three courses in English. These are "Language and Rhetoric," plus one literature course and one elective; options for these requirements range from "Major British and American Authors" to "Green Writing: Literature and the Environment";
- one course in art or music;
- two courses in a modern or classical language. Options are French, German, Italian, Latin, Greek, Chinese, or Spanish;
- three classes in the social sciences. Choices come from a wide range of disciplines: business administration, economics, political science, psychology, sociology/anthropology, and (for students seeking teacher certification) education. A maximum of two classes from any one discipline is allowed;
- two courses, with labs, in the natural sciences; and
- one course in mathematics.

Although it aims to foster self-reliance among its students, St. Vincent emphasizes teaching, allowing students and faculty to build healthy and mutually respectful relationships. Professors are generally available on campus, often staying longer than required and meeting with students in order to tackle any problems they may encounter in the curriculum. Small classes also provide an environment that is highly conducive to respectful intellectual debate, a hallmark of the school. Class sizes usually range from eight to twenty-five students.

Faculty say students are "curious" and "engaging," while tending to be politically conservative. This does not mean that St. Vincent is a hotbed of conservative ideology. Teaching remains largely unsullied by political correctness or dogma (except when dogma is the subject matter). Teachers expect students to take responsibility for their ideas, and say they encourage "free thinking."

Beyond the general requirements, students say that the curriculum is robust and challenging, providing a solid grounding for further study and widening their intellectual horizons. One student comments, for example, that when she later attended grad school she found that her education at St. Vincent had covered much of the graduate course curriculum.

For students who wish to take courses abroad, St. Vincent maintains a sister college relationship with Fu Jen Catholic University in Taiwan, offers summer study at Cuauhnahauc Institute of Language and Culture in Cuernavaca, Mexico, and sends students to other colleges in a wide array of countries through its study-abroad office. The college reports that "students have studied in such diversified places as Argentina, Australia, Canada, China, Costa Rica, Cuba, Egypt, England, France, Germany, Greece,

Ireland, India, Italy, Japan, Kenya, Mexico, Peru, Scotland, Spain, Taiwan, Wales, and the former Yugoslavia."

Among the strongest programs at St. Vincent are political science, economics, and business, all of which come under the umbrella of the Alex G. McKenna School of Economics and Government. The McKenna School also houses the respected educational and research organization, the Center for Political and Economic Thought, which brings many nationally and internationally recognized scholars to campus each year for conferences and lectures. Many of its graduates go on to receive graduate or law degrees. According to one professor, the political science program, which concentrates to a large extent on primary texts, "provides a strong philosophical grounding in Western philosophy and American political thought and institutions in an effort to produce civically literate, liberally educated citizens."

Students in the political science major do not spend their time (as at some schools) analyzing electoral trends and crunching numbers. Rather, the program has a strong emphasis on the principles of political philosophy. Those majoring in the subject must take courses such as "Principles of American Politics," "Western Political Thought," "American Political Thought," and "Constitutional Law," in addition to courses that deal with the particulars of political practice. This means that every major reads such pivotal thinkers as Plato, Aquinas, Hobbes, Locke, and Nietzsche, among others, in addition to the documents of America's founding.

The English department is regarded as having a well-rounded and compatible team of professors. All majors must take two survey courses that teach students the practice of literary criticism and include classics texts from the ancient, Renaissance, and modern periods.

Philosophy majors must take a single course in ancient and medieval philosophy, a logic course, an ethics class, one course in modern and one in contemporary philosophy, and write a senior thesis. Unfortunately, students report that philosophy classes at St. Vincent are "less challenging" than those in many other departments. One student complains that his courses did not adequately refer to primary texts, and that the teaching was somewhat unimaginative. Some communications majors have felt that the school did not devote enough resources to their department, though they report recent improvements. The students we consulted did not think highly of the sociology department.

As a Catholic college, St. Vincent does not hide its religious identity. The school offers a wide variety of religious studies courses. Prayer generally precedes formal meals,

VITAL STATISTICS
Religious affiliation: Roman Catholic
Total enrollment: 1,687
Total undergraduates: 1,576
SAT midranges: SAT V: 490–590, M: 490–590
Applicants: 1,458
Applicants accepted: 74%
Accepted applicants who enrolled: 33%
Tuition: $21,679
Room and board: $6,874
Freshman retention rate: 89%
Graduation rate: 61% (4 yrs.), 74% (6 yrs.)
Courses with fewer than 20 students: 83%
Student-faculty ratio: 15:1
Courses taught by graduate students: none
Most popular majors: biology, business, history
Students living on campus: 72%
Guaranteed housing for four years? yes
Students in fraternities or sororities: none

and monks make up a highly visible part of the administration and faculty. Nevertheless, those of different faiths are welcomed at St. Vincent. The school affirms the ecumenism embraced by Vatican II—and, like most institutions, perhaps even takes it further than the council fathers intended. St. Vincent's religious studies requirements are too weak for a Catholic school, allowing plenty of room for students to graduate without having taken a single course that explores church doctrine in any depth. The school's stated goal is rather that students "understand the relevance of the Judeo-Christian tradition to contemporary issues such as social justice, racism, and personal fulfillment." At least the courses that do focus on Catholic teaching are likely to present it accurately.

Students highly respect the St. Vincent faculty and speak about them with genuine enthusiasm and warmth. Teachers are often leading scholars in their subjects. Among those faculty which students commend are James Harrigan, Thomas Man, and Bradley C. Watson in political science; Fr. Wulfstan Clough, Beth Martinelli, Dennis McDaniel, and William Snyder in English; Andy Herr in economics; John Russell and Fr. Mark Wenzinger in philosophy; Fr. Patrick Cronauer and Fr. Thomas Hart in religious studies; and Doreen Blandino in Spanish.

According to one professor, the political science program, which concentrates to a large extent on primary texts, "provides a strong philosophical grounding in Western philosophy and American political thought and institutions in an effort to produce civically literate, liberally educated citizens.

Students seem to genuinely enjoy life at Saint Vincent College, which they describe as being a real community or family. As one student says, "My daily interactions with professors, other students, monks, and visitors have offered me some of the most uplifting experiences of my life." Another says that the college has proved "tremendously uplifting and transformative."

Student Life: Monks Putting Out Fires

Freshmen whose families reside more than fifty miles from St. Vincent College are required to live on campus. This helps new students settle into college life, as the first year on campus focuses on community and interaction among students. Dorms are coed, segregated by floor or "pods" for freshmen and "blocks" for upperclassmen, each of which has a shared bathroom, microwave oven, and other amenities. Described by one student as "becoming increasingly plush," the dorms have recently been updated to incorporate more modern facilities and internet connectivity.

Students call the chaplaincy "traditional, but welcoming." The Benedictine heritage remains very much a living tradition at St. Vincent, which the vast majority of students consider beneficial; students are able to interact with monks inside and outside of class, and some of the monks have managerial roles on campus.

There is plenty to do at St. Vincent, and students are encouraged to get involved on campus, especially in the area of what is generally termed "volunteering." The college believes especially that physical activity is important for a balanced and holistic education. This normally translates into athletics, but at St. Vincent it takes a more practical turn as well: since the 1960s, the college has had its own fire brigade, staffed by a mix of students, monks, seminarians, and staff. Recently an emergency medical unit was added.

There is a wide range of athletics to choose from at St. Vincent: men's and women's lacrosse, basketball, track, soccer, golf, and tennis, to mention but a few. The afternoon baseball games on campus are especially popular with students, as are the midnight madness pep rallies, though football is currently generating a lot of excitement with the impending reestablishment of the college's team, the "Bearcats," in 2007, after a forty-five-year absence. In the long list of college clubs several cater to the physically active student: cheerleading, fencing, health and fitness, snowboarding, and ultimate Frisbee.

SUGGESTED CORE
1. English 235: The Epic (*closest match*)
2. Philosophy 101: Ancient and Medieval Philosophy
3. Religious Studies 201/ 214: Old Testament I / Four Gospels
4. Religious Studies 225: History of Christian Thought
5. Political Science 130: Western Political Thought (*closest match*)
6. English 314/315: Shakespeare
7. History 106: U.S. History to 1865
8. No suitable course.

For students not entirely inclined to athletics, St. Vincent has a number of clubs of a more cerebral nature, including the Democratic and Republican clubs, as well as those for drama, education, English, and sociology. Also available is the Pittsburgh Cultural Series, which enables groups of students to take in Pittsburgh's cultural events, either free of charge or at a large discount. These include evenings at the symphony, opera, ballet, theater, and so on, with students sometimes able to take backstage tours or meet the performers. Afterwards, they typically refresh themselves at a local bistro or café. The music department puts on many classical concerts and attracts renowned musicians, while the English department hosts many respected poets and authors for readings of their work. The college also has its own art collection and gallery.

With 160 years of history and close proximity to a graveyard, it was probably inevitable that sooner or later the college would be considered haunted. St. Vincent is currently listed as among the top five haunted colleges of America. Students seem to enjoy this reputation—and insist that their enthusiasm is shared by the college's monks. The founding of the school is celebrated annually at the end of November with a large banquet for faculty, alumni, and students, at which the college's Christmas tree lights are turned on and fireworks lit off, allowing students to describe Founders Day as a cross between the Fourth of July, Thanksgiving, and Christmas.

Located in the small town of Latrobe and enveloped in a rather rural setting, students can sometimes feel isolated at St. Vincent. This explains why some make the forty-mile drive to Pittsburgh on the weekends.

Crime is rare; the school reported just one aggravated assault and four burglaries in 2004. However, disciplinary actions for liquor-law violations grew between 2002 and 2004 from seventy-nine to 180. This may reflect a tighter enforcement of college rules. No alcohol is allowed in the freshmen dorms—nor are empty bottles or even alcohol posters allowed in any dorms—and one student described security as "excellent." The school asserts that illegal drug use is punished "severely."

St. Vincent has succeeded at keeping tuition costs to a comparatively moderate $21,679. Room and board add $6,874. Virtually all students—98 percent—receive some need-based financial aid.

SAMFORD UNIVERSITY

BIRMINGHAM, ALABAMA • WWW.SAMFORD.EDU

Established by Alabama Baptists in 1841, Samford University has gone through a lot, ultimately not only surviving but truly thriving. The school has witnessed two destructive fires, the devastation of the Civil War, Reconstruction, and several relocations on its way to becoming Alabama's largest private university. Dedicated to liberal learning in a Christian environment, today Samford is an affordable school that offers students strong academic programs in a nurturing and structured community.

The university, founded as Howard College, originally took its name from the eighteenth-century English prison reformer John Howard. The school reorganized as a university in 1965 and was renamed for the chairman of its board of trustees, founder of Liberty National Life Insurance, Frank Park Samford. The institution relocated from its original site in Marion to the East Lake area of Birmingham in 1887; it moved again in 1957 to its present serene suburban campus in Homewood, six miles from downtown Birmingham.

Samford is affiliated with the Alabama Baptist Convention and governed by a board of Baptist trustees. The school is said to enjoy both academic independence and good relations with the Alabama Baptists—and its board of trustees wants to keep things that way. In June 2006, it welcomed its new president, Andrew Westmoreland. "He's a wonderful combination of an educator who has a grasp for academics and fundraising, people skills and, at the same time, a sincere, deep Christian commitment," search committee cochairman Hobart Grooms told the *Alabama Baptist*. "He's also a relationship kind of guy. He has a real concern for the students and their spiritual welfare." That pretty much sums up Samford's attitude toward education.

Academic Life: The Truth Shall Set You Free

Every Samford undergraduate must complete the University Core Curriculum and General Education Requirements, sets of courses that, added together, occupy a fair chunk of a student's credits. By insisting on these courses, Samford ensures that every graduate receives a sturdy, broad liberal arts education in addition to expertise in his or her chosen major. The school's rationale for this insistence speaks well for it. The required courses are meant to "strengthen the foundations for understanding human experience, in the hope that students will lead lives characterized by broad vision and independent thinking. Consistent with Christ's teachings that 'the truth shall set you free,' a broad liberal arts foundation echoes the Latin *libertas*—the freedom—from one's own limited experiences in favor of an intellectual framework based on awareness of other perspectives and the thinking of past generations," says the catalog. Students must complete the following:

- "Biblical Perspectives," a course examining scripture for its historical and theological content and its value in shaping everyday life;
- "Cultural Perspectives I," part of a two-semester introduction to the humanities that views the Western intellectual tradition within a global context. The first semester examines works of Plato, Sophocles, Augustine, Virgil, Machiavelli, and Shakespeare, plus selections from the Bible;
- "Cultural Perspectives II," which moves from the Renaissance into the Protestant Reformation and up to the present day—and which also includes some study of the Middle East and Islam. Readings include more selections from the Bible, texts by Luther, Galileo, Voltaire, Paine, Austen, Wordsworth, Darwin, and Marx, and one non-Western novel;
- "Communication Arts" I and II, a course sequence that combines writing and speaking skills with real-world experience. Students engage in several hours of community service, write and speak about their experiences, and read and analyze relevant texts. Service projects range from work in after-school tutoring programs and homeless shelters to environmental clean-up efforts;
- two natural science classes;
- one social science course, chosen from a short list that includes "Economics I," "World Regional Geography," "Mass Communication and Society," "Modern Britain," "Introduction to Political Science," "General Psychology," and "Introduction to Sociology";
- one mathematics class;
- tests or coursework to demonstrate literacy in a second language. Choices include French, German, Spanish, Arabic, Chinese, Hindi, Italian, Japanese, Portuguese, Russian, Greek, Latin, Thai, and Swahili;
- two fine arts courses. The three choices are "Art Appreciation," "Music Appreciation," and "Theatre Appreciation";
- one humanities course chosen from a short list. Representative courses include "The West in Global Perspective," "Latin American Studies," and "Introduction to Philosophy"; and
- "Concepts of Fitness and Health." This includes aerobic fitness and health education, plus two fitness-based activity courses.

The Honors Program at Samford supplements and complements the regular curriculum. Selected students take honors sections of the University Core Curriculum, as well as general education classes their first two years. An interdisciplinary seminar, team-taught by two professors, is taken in the junior year. In the senior year, every student writes a thesis and defends the project before the University Honors Council. About 10 percent of the freshman class is admitted into the program. A GPA of 3.5 or higher at graduation leads to a separate honors diploma.

In addition to offering nearly seventy bachelor's degree programs in six colleges serving undergraduates, Samford offers a multitude of master's and first professional degrees in business, environmental science, divinity, law, music, nursing, and pharmacy, as well as joint master's programs of study. The school also maintains doctoral programs in divinity, education, law, and pharmacy. In recent years, Samford has been nationally recognized for its education department—at many other schools, the weakest link. In 2000, the university was cited by the secretary of education as one of four model teaching programs in the United States. An alumna, Betsy Rogers, was named National Teacher of the Year in 2003.

Students are encouraged to do at least a portion of their language study at academic programs hosted by schools in Asia, South America, and Europe, where they can live both the language and the culture on a daily basis. An estimated 8,000 students and 125 faculty members have studied at the Daniel House in London since 1984, when the school purchased the Georgian townhouse. Students select courses taught by Samford professors and teachers at British schools, internships that take students into the midst of British life and work, a fine-arts directed independent study, and independent studies arranged through campus departments. For students interested in an earlier phase of our culture, the Department of Classics conducts students on tours of ancient ruins and historic sites in Italy and Greece during the January term.

Most disciplines at Samford remain traditionally oriented. Philosophy majors are required to complete two history of philosophy classes, courses in introductory logic, moral ethics, metaphysics, and a senior seminar. Students speak well of the courses—even though the department boasts only two full-time faculty members. History majors at Samford are required to take reliable survey classes, including "The West in Global Perspective," "Early America to 1877," "Modern America since 1865" and the historiography course "The Historian's Class." The department calls for six upper-level courses, nearly all in European or American history. Students also complete either a senior seminar or an independent research project.

VITAL STATISTICS
Religious affiliation: Baptist
Total enrollment: 4,507
Total undergraduates: 2,941
SAT/ACT medians: SAT V: 570, M: 570; ACT: 25
Applicants: 2,025
Applicants accepted: 65%
Accepted applicants who enrolled: 54%
Tuition: $14,642
Room and board: $5,616
Freshman retention rate: 85%
Graduation rate: 51% (4 yrs.), 68% (6 yrs.)
Courses with fewer than 20 students: 58%
Student-faculty ratio: 14:1
Courses taught by graduate students: none
Most popular majors: business/marketing, education, communications/journalism
Students living on campus: 65%
Guaranteed Housing for four years? no
Students in fraternities: 27% sororities: 43%

The English department offers a well-structured major containing a high proportion of foundational courses. A three-course sequence on American and British literature and both a critical theory and Shakespeare class are required. Majors also choose a writing course that examines a particular literary genre (poetry, the short story, the novel, drama, and film) and two survey courses of different literary periods. Students demonstrate their ability to research and analyze literature in depth by writing a senior thesis. Finally, a comparative literature capstone course in the senior year includes a comprehensive oral examination on English and American literature.

Courses in the religion department tend to be foundational, too, including "Philosophy of Religion," "History of Christianity," "Studies in the Law-Torah," "Pastoral Theology," "World Religions: Traditions in the Modern World," and "Christian Ethics." At Samford, the preoccupation with ethnic or sexual grievances that dominates many religion departments seem blessedly absent. Some students have complained that theologically conservative undergrads feel belittled by some of the religion faculty—particularly when their ideas are "undeveloped" and based solely on their church upbringing. But this is not a Bible school; it is fitting that students learn in college religion classes how to defend their beliefs. The school adheres, officially, to the Baptist Statement of Faith and Message (1963); however, serious attention is given to all major theological traditions and students are welcome from all Christian denominations.

The largest undergraduate majors are business and marketing, journalism and mass communications, and education. Among Samford's strongest departments are biology, English, philosophy, classics, and political science.

Recommended undergraduate teachers include James Brown in history; Douglas Clapp in classics; William Collins in political science; Mike Howell and Ronald Jenkins in biology; Christopher Metress, Julie Steward, and Nancy Whitt in English; Thomas Woolley in business; Dennis Jones in journalism and mass communications; Keith Putt and Dennis Sansome in philosophy; and Stephen Chew in psychology.

Each student is assigned an advisor working through the academic departments of his declared major. Before that, students are assigned to the dean of freshmen for advice in choosing courses and a department. The student-faculty ratio at Samford is 14 to 1 and there are no teaching assistants. Faculty normally teach three courses each term—a moderate load. Students say most professors have an open-door office policy and are very accessible.

"I find the faculty to be high caliber, very cooperative, and collegial," says a non-Baptist faculty member who previously had been at a large state university. He says, "At Samford I have found a community, both faculty and students, who take the Christian vocation seriously. The school is in the Baptist tradition, but it made a break from the increasingly fundamentalist Southern Baptist Convention a couple of years back." Another professor notes that the faculty is stable and committed, and that teaching is emphasized in tenure decisions.

Most meetings of faculty and administration at Samford include prayer. "Prayer is acceptable anywhere at any time. In short, one's faith is taken seriously, and the college is intentional in other ways about its Christianity, though I think in the professional schools and business school this might not be taken quite as seriously as in arts and sciences," say a professor.

Although they are tempered with a certain southern decorum, Samford has witnessed its share of controversies—most recently over the theory of Intelligent Design (ID). A planned lecture scheduled for February 2006 by ID proponent John Lennox, a research fellow in mathematics at Oxford University, upset faculty who didn't want the school to be seen as endorsing theoretical alternatives to evolution. One supporter of Lennox's appearance complained of "a coterie of natural scientists who oppose anything that even remotely smells anti-evolutionist. . . . The usual protests filled the e-mails for several weeks, and an e-mail controversy raged between the majority of conservative (note: for free speech and giving all points of view a hearing) faculty and the scientific promoters of censorship." In the end, the school did host Lennox. Samford's then-president explained, "This is a university and you are supposed to talk about ideas."

Both Birmingham and Samford are historically associated with past southern racial crises, and Samford hasn't forgotten. In addition to the prevalence of faculty research on and class discussions and lectures about civil rights on campus, the class of 2009 orientation included faculty-led small-group discussions centered on the theme "Journey to Birmingham: Race, Community and Christianity in the Magic City."

"I find the faculty to be high caliber, very cooperative, and collegial. At Samford I have found a community, both faculty and students, who take the Christian vocation seriously."

Samford belongs to the Birmingham Area Consortium for Higher Education (BACE), an intercollegiate organization that allows students to take classes at the University of Alabama at Birmingham, Miles College, University of Montevallo, and Birmingham-Southern College.

Student Life: Sweet Home Alabama

Located in the foothills of the Appalachian Mountains, Birmingham is Alabama's largest city, with a population of nearly a million people. The state's industrial, business, financial, and cultural center, it retains many of the better traditions of the small-town South. One can enjoy asparagus salad with roasted pecan dressing at an elegant restaurant for lunch, and later have supper at a café serving country-fried steak and butter beans. People are friendly and life really does move more slowly than up North.

Samford's charming campus impresses visitors. Its 200-acre suburban physical plant in Homewood, a "Mayberryesque" city of 25,000, was designed by Charles Davis Jr. With its Georgian-colonial architecture, hills, and shade trees, Samford is a beautiful place. On the school's quad, a plaque commemorates a slave named Harry who worked at the school in 1854, the year of a midnight fire—and who saved student and faculty lives by helping them evacuate. His name can also be found on the popular coffeehouse on campus. The Sciencenter houses the biology, chemistry, and physics departments, thirty-five labs, Alabama's largest planetarium and a medicinal plant conservatory. Slated for completion in 2006 is a 32,000-square foot recital hall that will house Samford's orchestral and band programs. A multipurpose 5,000-seat arena and fitness center will be built in 2007.

Attendance at chapel/convocation is compulsory and students are expected to earn at least eight convocation credits each semester. "The purpose of convocation is to nurture students in faith, learning and values from a distinctly Christian perspective," says the school's website. Convocations consist of worship services, lectures, cadres (small-group discussions led by faculty), and cultural and artistic programs such as plays and concerts. Sometimes the lecture forum coincides with topics—e.g., the Reformation—covered in Cultural Perspectives classes. Academic, Samford Business Network, and student speakers address a variety of topics including business, science, social justice, and poverty issues. Recent lecture titles were "God and Science: Asking the Right Questions" and "The Interface of Spirituality and the Arts." Cadre active-learning groups have focused on exploring students' talents, interests, and career choices, built a Habitat for Humanity house, and examined the book *But Is It Science?* which considers the Intelligent Design debate.

Ninety-four percent of freshmen and more than half of the upperclassmen live on campus. Housing is located in Beeson Woods, Central Campus, and West Campus. Beeson Woods is a student residential village that features twelve buildings with apartment-style units for 500 students. Central campus houses mainly freshmen. In addition to single-sex buildings, students live in fraternity and sorority houses. The school's seven sororities and fraternities play a visible role in campus life. "The Greeks are strong among women," reports a professor. Samford's visitation policy does not allow members of the opposite sex to visit each other in a student's room or other nonpublic areas of residence halls or apartments except at designated times.

Samford students are expected to live by the school's Code of Values, which expresses Christian moral standards in specific rules and regulations about student behavior regarding alcohol and drugs, conduct between the sexes, and personal accountability. The alcohol and drug policy in the student handbook states that "the use of illicit drugs or alcohol by faculty, staff or students on campus, or in connection with or affecting any school-related activity, is strictly prohibited. Violations of this policy will result in the imposition of disciplinary sanctions up to and including termination of faculty and staff, and expulsion of students." However, a professor says that the campus does not have a "bed check tone," and the environment "makes for a very nice place to study and grow up."

Generations of families attend Samford in succession. "The students have incredible loyalty to the institution," says a professor. Most Stamford students have strong religious affiliations—about 30 percent are Baptist, and a little over 8 percent are either Methodist or Lutheran. Catholic students at this heavily Protestant school will find ample support at the headquarters of the national Catholic broadcasting network, Eternal World Television Network, headquartered in Birmingham.

Samford students tend to be affluent, and more than 70 percent are drawn from southern states. Until the college brings the percentage of undergraduate male students up from 37 percent, it will be easier for men to be admitted than women. A professor describes students at Samford as "a little bit conformist 'conservative.'" Another professor says they are "very eager to learn but their idea is to sit down and write down what the teacher says."

Samford undergrads should have no trouble finding clubs that interest them, whether academic, service, social, or religious in nature. Political-oriented clubs are scarce—although there is one for Republicans. There are several singing groups, including the renowned Samford A Cappella Choir, a jazz ensemble, Samford University Theatre, and a school band that includes marching and symphonic bands. The *Samford Crimson* is a weekly student-run newspaper. The school is host to Air Force ROTC.

SUGGESTED CORE
1. Cultural Perspectives 101
2. Philosophy 301: History of Philosophy: Ancient and Medieval
3. English 309.01 Special Topics: The Bible as Literature
4. Religion 302: History of Christianity
5. Political Science 345: Modern Political Theory
6. English 340: Shakespeare
7. History 217: Early America to 1877
8. Cultural Perspectives 102 (*closest match*)

Students find plenty of outlets on campus to foster their spiritual development; there are regular worship services, prayer groups, Bible classes, and mission opportunities. Hundreds of students are involved in local missions and community outreach. Members of the Baptist Student Ministry support their Bulldogs football team and reach out to fellow students by cosponsoring tailgate parties with local churches and working concessions at the games to support summer missions.

Samford attracts beauty queens. Literally. The Miss Samford Scholarship Pageant, organized by students, is a Miss Alabama preliminary held for women enrolled at Samford. The campus also has participated in Miss Alabama competitions. Deirdre Downs, a 2002 graduate of Samford, was crowned Miss Alabama in 2004 and Miss America in 2005.

The biggest events on campus are Homecoming, Step Sing, and Spring Fling. Country music singer Brad Paisley headlined the homecoming concert in fall 2004 and comedian Bill Cosby performed in 2005. The homecoming weekend includes a football game, banquet, and Alumni of the Year recognition and a dance. Samford's love of tradition is carried out when Samford's marching band opens its games with "Sweet Home Alabama" and ends football-day activities by singing the alma mater and doxology and playing the hymn "It Is Well with My Soul." Step Sing, the major Student Government Association event of the year, finds most student organizations participating in a music and choreography competition. Students welcome the warm weather in April with games, music, and food on the quad during Spring Fling.

The Samford Bulldogs participate in the NCAA Division I and are members of the Ohio Valley Conference. Intercollegiate men's and women's sports include basketball, cross-country, golf, indoor track, tennis, and track and field. In addition, women participate in softball, soccer, and volleyball and men compete in baseball and football. The school was recently ranked in the top ten nationally by a new NCAA system designed to track how student-athletes are progressing toward degree completion.

The Samford campus is a safe place. In 2005, the school reported only a single crime—a burglary. Samford is also generously endowed (more than $230 million) and affordable, with the cost of tuition at $14,642, and room and board another $5,616. About 36 percent of students receive need-based financial aid. The average student loan debt of a Samford graduate is around $17,500.

SEATTLE PACIFIC UNIVERSITY

SEATTLE, WASHINGTON • WWW.SPU.EDU

Opened in 1891 as Seattle Seminary, Seattle Pacific University began as a college preparatory school where "students would be educated and trained for missionary service by teachers whose lives represented the highest in Christian values." The school added college-level classes in 1910, and in 1915 changed its name to Seattle Pacific College. In the 1920s, a normal school was added to the college, and as enrollment began increasing, an accredited liberal arts program was started in 1936. The school continued to grow, and more programs were added, until the college became Seattle Pacific University in 1977. (Today, the school offers fifty-five undergraduate majors, twelve master's degree programs and three doctoral programs.) The common curriculum, a set of general education requirements that takes up half of an undergraduate's credit hours, was instituted in 1998—and it is this curriculum, along with the school's faithfulness to its religious mission (SPU is still operated under the guidance of the Free Methodist Church), which should attract the attention of a serious Christian student.

Despite the many changes in size and scope it has experienced over the years, Seattle Pacific University remains committed to the Wesleyan tradition. The university describes its Christian character as "historically orthodox," "clearly evangelical," "distinctively Wesleyan," and "genuinely ecumenical." And the school continues to uphold its founding mission of "engaging the culture and changing the world by graduating people of competence and character, becoming people of wisdom, and modeling grace-filled community."

Academic Life: Engaging the Culture, Changing the World

Unlike many schools—even some religious colleges—Seattle Pacific emphasizes an integrated curriculum, one firmly grounded in the liberal arts and Christian doctrine. Even allowing for its understandable emphasis on theology over philosophy, SPU has one of the strongest curricula in the country. All students, regardless of major, must complete the following requirements:

- "University Seminar," a first-semester introduction to the liberal arts through the study of a special topic. Seminar instructors serve as faculty advisor to students in their seminar through the freshman year;
- "The Arts and the Christian Community." This class treats the religious and existential questions raised by art across the ages;
- "The West and the World," which "explores the history of interaction between the West and the World from the dawn of the modern global age (about 1500) to the present";
- "Belief, Morality and Modern Mind." Here students consider "questions about Christian faith and practice that arise from modern developments in philosophy and science";
- "Christian Formation." Focusing on Christian life and its "distinctive beliefs, practices, attitudes and virtues," this class looks at "texts, written and non-written, ancient and modern";
- "Christian Scriptures," a course introducing students to "the literature and theology of both Old and New Testaments";
- "Mentoring Freshmen," a practicum that allows upperclassmen to serve as mentors to incoming freshmen in their first University Seminar;
- "Christian Theology," in which students study the "basic doctrines and practices of historic Christianity";
- either coursework or tests to demonstrate mathetmatical competency;
- either coursework or tests to demonstrate writing competency;
- either coursework or tests to demonstrate competency in a foreign language at the intermediate level. Languages offered at SPU include French, German, Latin, Russian, and Spanish;
- one (or more; see below) course in art, music, or theater;
- one (or more) course in humanities. Examples are "Ancient Civilization," "Public Speaking," and "Survey of Western Philosophy." Students also must take one additional course in either art or humanities;
- one introductory social science course in psychology or sociology, and one in history, geography, economics, or political science;
- one class in biological science, and one in the physical sciences; and
- one course in mathematics.

Evaluating the core courses on Western civilization, one professor notes, "They're more respectful [of the Western heritage] than on most campuses, but not what they need to be. The influence of multiculturalism is felt here, just not as strongly as at most places. The curriculum itself is very good. Students read good stuff, but tend to get a left-of-center perspective on it." There is, however, "a strong respect for Christianity and the Bible." Another professor reports that teachers at Seattle Pacific are "very respectful of Western classics." He also points to the school's excellent University Scholars option as "basically a Great Books program. There is an attempt to integrate this with at least two core classes that emphasize global traditions; but the emphasis is on the need for reconciliation, and doesn't denigrate Western tradition in any way."

The academic year at Seattle Pacific is divided into quarters, so that the autumn, winter, and spring quarters make up the regular school year. Classes are usually held either for fifty minutes five days a week, or for ninety minutes three times a week; hence, most classes are worth five credits, rather than three.

SPU offers a wide variety of majors, including both liberal arts and preprofessional programs. The philosophy, English, and sociology departments are particularly recommended by faculty, both for displaying traditional rigor and for offering strong teachers. "Theology," warns one faculty member, "has some excellent professors, but also some that are into the more fashionable stuff." In the vocational and science programs, nursing, education, biology, and business are recommended as strong departments with good reputations. Particularly recommended faculty include Gregory Wolfe (editor of the Christian arts journal *Image*) and Suzanne Wolfe in English, Alberto Ferreiro in history, and Reed Davis in political science.

Professors agree that "teaching is most important" on campus, rather than research. "Teaching is everything," says one faculty member. "You can't get tenure without it. Student evaluations are very important." The school makes an effort to keep classes relatively small, especially in the freshman Common Curriculum. In addition to this, professors are readily available to students, both during their office hours and informally. "Students here can ask professors out to lunch or coffee; we often meet informally in small groups. There is a lot of mentoring, a lot of one-on-one time," remarks a professor.

The university offers a large study-abroad program. Students may take English classes in Great Britain or in South Africa, complete a nursing practicum in Honduras, study Spanish at the University of Salamanca, study marine biology in the Caribbean Sea or Pacific Ocean, or study language, history, and culture in Germany. There is also a European Studies program, which is offered two quarters a year and held at various sites across the continent, depending on the faculty teaching the courses. One particularly recommended study-abroad opportunity is the Normandy Studies Program, which includes classes in French and early modern French political thought (including, for example, Montesquieu, a seminal influence on the American founding). The university also provides opportunities for students to participate in a number of internships across the United States.

Although Seattle Pacific remains committed to its Methodist origins, the school welcomes students of all religious backgrounds. The majority of students, however, are

---

VITAL STATISTICS

Religious affiliation:
  Free Methodist
Total enrollment: 3,873
Total undergraduates: 3,022
SAT/ACT midranges: SAT V: 510–610, M: 510–620; ACT: 21–27
Applicants: 1,714
Applicants accepted: 93%
Accepted applicants who enrolled: 40%
Tuition: $21,447
Room and board: $7,400
Freshman retention rate: 85%
Graduation rate: 37% (4 yrs.), 61% (6 yrs.)
Courses with fewer than 20 students: 72%
Student-faculty ratio: 14:1
Courses taught by graduate students: none
Most popular majors:
  psychology, business administration, nursing
Students living on campus: 58%
Guaranteed housing for four years? no
Students in fraternities or sororities: none

ALL-AMERICAN COLLEGES

249

evangelical Christians. Faculty members are required to be Christians, but not to swear to any set creed or church; there are at least fifty denominations represented on campus among faculty and students. Instead of focusing on denominational particulars and mandating attendance at chapel, Seattle Pacific has a distinctive "Christian Faith Exploration Requirement," which can be met in a variety of ways. This requirement consists of "ten hours of campus-based faith exploration events and five hours of community service," and may be fulfilled through chapel services, faith learning forums, various prayer and Bible study groups, and through a variety of service projects in the Seattle area.

While there is a diversity of thought at SPU, the students especially tend to be somewhat conservative, and faculty report that there are no departments which would be unwelcoming to such students. "That's an impossibility here," comments one professor. "The majority of our students are conservative evangelical Christians, and you can't teach well if you don't like your students." Another professor adds, "Students tend to be conservative, but liberals have a voice. There are pockets of political correctness, but on balance, political diversity and freedom of expression at SPU are strong points."

By emphasizing its common curriculum, and by encouraging students to integrate their academic activities with experience in the community around them, the university strives to fulfill its mission to "graduate people of competence and character."

By emphasizing its common curriculum, and by encouraging students to integrate their academic activities with experience in the community around them, the university strives to fulfill its mission to "graduate people of competence and character." Seattle Pacific offers its students a stimulating atmosphere where they can stretch their minds without abandoning their convictions. "It's a good place for Christians to study who do not wish to set their faith aside from their academic work," says one professor.

Student Life: Service in Seattle

Located in a residential neighborhood about ten minutes from downtown Seattle and half a mile from the Fremont business district, Seattle Pacific gives students plenty of access to urban attractions in one of America's most pleasant, cosmopolitan cities. In addition, the school's proximity to Puget Sound, Mt. Rainier National Park, and the Olympic National Park offers students plenty of opportunity to enjoy the natural beauty of the northwest. Students can explore waterfalls, tide pools, and ice caves within a day's trip from campus. In addition, the school operates two island campuses: Camp Casey on Whidbey Island is used for retreats and workshops, while at the environmental preserve on Blakely Island, students can study life near (and even under) the sea.

Seattle Pacific offers students and faculty a state-of-the-art campus. In 1994, the four-story Seattle Pacific Library was opened, with over 190,000 volumes, a collection which grows by about 6,000 volumes a year. The library also includes more than 1,300 print journals and access to 8,000 online journals. One professor remarks upon the "outstanding library staff," and the fact that there are "millions of books available conveniently through the SUMMIT system." Through interlibrary loan and their library privileges at Northwest University and Pacific Lutheran University, students have access to over 31 million books. The campus also has numerous computer labs, including a networking lab, a music keyboard lab, and an art center with computers for instructional uses in fine arts and visual communication.

Because Seattle Pacific is "committed to the education of the whole person," students are required to live in campus housing at least until their junior year. The school sees this as beneficial because it immerses students more fully in the educational experience and community life of the school. Within this requirement, however, there are a number of choices for student residence, including residence halls and on-campus houses and apartments. Boarding costs vary according to the type of accommodation selected. Residence halls are coed, but segregated by floor, with intervisitation permitted from noon to 11 p.m. Campus houses and apartments are open for intervisitation twenty-four hours a day, although members of the opposite sex are not permitted to sleep there. Peer advisors on each floor and in each apartment complex enforce regulations and oversee residence life services and programs. Each residence hall elects hall council officers, who promote hall activities and address hall concerns, and more than forty student ministry coordinators lead prayer and Bible study groups on each floor.

Chapel services at Seattle Pacific are held in the First Free Methodist Church sanctuary. They are described as "creative, multi-traditional, student-led worship service[s] with speakers from the SPU campus and around the world." Attendance is not mandatory. Students are encouraged to attend the services of their own denominations.

The school's behavioral expectations for students consist mainly of basic prohibitions of illegal activity, dishonesty, possession of weapons, and the like. In addition, sexual misbehavior and all use of alcohol and tobacco are forbidden. The ban on alcohol was recently questioned by a large percentage of the students, but the administration upheld the rule. As part of the application for undergraduate admission, students sign an agreement to abide by the university's standards if they are admitted.

Seattle Pacific offers its students a wide range of extracurricular activities in which they can become involved. "Athletics are huge at SPU," comments one faculty member. There are several intramural leagues and also many one-day tournaments, as well as

> ## SUGGESTED CORE
>
> The required Common Curriculum is quite good but incomplete. Supplement with the following courses: Classics 3104: Survey of Ancient Greek Literature; Philosophy 1004: Survey of Western Philosophy; Political Science 4642: Theories of the Political System: Modern; English 4445: Shakespeare; and History 2502: The U.S. to 1876.

ALL-AMERICAN COLLEGES

twelve intercollegiate sports teams. "Basketball and soccer are especially exciting," says a student. Besides sports, there are many clubs, academic (such as the French Club and Accounting Society), political (College Republicans, Political Union Club), and special-interest groups.

The school offers a long list of service clubs and opportunities to become involved in the local community. At Seattle Pacific, there is a strong emphasis on being active in the world as Christians—which explains the five hours each semester students must spend performing community service. Many students belong to clubs that focus on serving the needy and get involved visiting prisons and nursing homes, staffing homeless shelters, and providing recreation for the disabled. The university encourages service learning, which involves students working with faculty on a community-based project, such as tutoring in a public school or volunteering at a library for the blind. These activities reinforce a student's learning in the classroom and count toward academic credit. Through SPRINT, Seattle Pacific Reach Out International, students can participate in service projects across the United States and in other countries during academic breaks.

Despite its proximity to a large city, Seattle Pacific has a safe campus. Burglary is the most commonly reported crime, with seventeen cases being reported in 2004, the last year for which statistics are available. During that year, one case of aggravated assault and seven motor vehicle thefts were also reported.

Seattle may be a relatively expensive city, but in comparative terms SPU is moderately priced. Tuition runs $21,447, and the average room and board charge is $7,400.

SHIMER COLLEGE

CHICAGO, ILLINOIS • WWW.SHIMER.EDU

What do Shimer College and Italian auto-mobiles have in common? Plenty, according to William Rice, former Alfa Romeo mechanic and current president of Shimer College. Rice, in his 2004 inaugural address, compared the college to the elite sports cars in terms of its small scale and extraordinary output, an inefficiency that requires "high-octane fuel and intense upkeep." With a student body of only 110, a student-faculty ratio of 8 to 1, and one of the country's few

discussion-based Great Books curricula, Shimer's interdisciplinary core and intimate community are certainly as rare and distinctive as one of those tiny Italian cars. And just like a sophisticated automobile, Shimer has had its share of technical difficulties. As of fall 2006, the undergraduate school will leave its barebones campus in Waukegan, Illinois, to share a campus with the Illinois Institute of Technology on the south side of Chicago (some of the school's graduate offerings will remain in Waukegan). This move will allow the school to offer amenities such as food service and athletic facilities, which it has not provided up to now. But the college promises to keep alive the close-knit community and intense academic program that made its reputation as "the Great Books college of the Midwest."

Academic Life: Great Books at a Small School

Shimer's curriculum is known as "The Hutchins Plan" in honor of Robert Maynard Hutchins, who pioneered the integrated curriculum of original sources and discussion classes in the 1930s at the University of Chicago, where he served as president. The approach, designed to teach "how to think, not what to think," is Shimer's hallmark. One student says, "It's impossible to go through Shimer's curriculum without learning how to interact with a text of social analysis or poetry or music or prose. And philosophic inquiry is the end result of everything." This end is accomplished through a common core, a curriculum that is shared by all students and faculty and only "changes gradually, by evolution rather than revolution. . . ." All students must take the following:

- "History and Philosophy of Western Civilization" (two semesters). This anchor of Shimer's Great Books program covers seminal works of our culture from the *Epic of Gilgamesh* and the *Iliad* up through the *Divine Comedy* in the first semester. The second class covers writers from Chaucer to Nietzsche;
- "Art and Music," in which students explore Plato, Balzac, Kafka, Aaron Copland, and various texts on aesthetics;
- "Poetry, Drama, and Fiction." Texts include works by Homer, Sophocles, Shakespeare, Conrad, Dostoevsky, and Beckett;
- "Philosophy and Theology." Students in this course read Plato, the Bible, Augustine, Anselm, Teresa of Avila, Descartes, Pascal, and Locke;
- "Critical Evaluation in the Humanities (Enlightenment to Present)." Authors studied include Matthew Arnold, Schiller, Nietzsche, Woolf, Kant, Kierkegaard, Buber, Wittgenstein, and Auerbach;
- "Society, Culture, and Personality," a class that introduces students to the works of major social analysts such as Margaret Mead, Freud, Piaget, DuBois, Durkheim, Marx, Engels, and Weber;
- "The Western Political Tradition." This class covers Plato, Aristotle, Aquinas, Machiavelli, Hobbes, Locke, Rousseau, Jefferson and other American founders, Adam Smith, Montesquieu, and Mary Wollstonecraft;
- "Modern Theories of Politics and Culture." Thinkers covered include Tocqueville, Mill, Hegel, Marx and Engels, Freud, Sartre, Arendt, Huxley, and Beauvoir;
- "Theories of Social Inquiry," a course that moves through the twentieth century to the present, covering authors such as Weber, Durkheim, Freire, Mannheim, and Foucault;
- "Laws and Models of Chemistry." This chemistry course "begins with the ancient Greek philosophers and continues into the early twentieth century";
- "Evolution, Genetics, and Animal Behavior." This class covers thinkers on biology from Aristotle, Mendel, and Darwin to Stephen Jay Gould;
- "Light, Motion, and Scientific Explanation," a physics course that examines "gravitation, light, electromagnetic forces, and relativity";
- "Physics and Philosophy." This class explores modern quantum physics and genetics in a philosophical context;
- "Logic and Rhetoric," a course on literary analysis that uses texts by Plato, Aristotle, Copernicus, and Martin Luther King Jr.;
- "The Nature and Creation of Mathematics." Here students gain "an understanding and appreciation of mathematics" and "the axiomatic method by examining various mathematical and geometrical systems throughout written history"; and
- a senior thesis.

The curriculum is so integrated that Shimer has no departmental divisions, just a list of faculty members. Following the classical model of education, Shimer uses primary sources for readings rather than textbooks. Classes (which never include more than twelve students) are taught using the Socratic method of discussion, with students and teacher seated around a table.

The curriculum is divided into three areas: humanities, social sciences, and natural sciences, although the courses often cross boundaries. Students may choose to major in one of these three areas or earn their degree in Liberal Studies. One student says, "Shimer excels at the humanities and the social sciences because of the critical and analytical approaches that both fields require." Shimer's approach to the natural sciences is historical, following questions such as "What is light?" through history. "Consequently," says one professor, "we are not as dependent on state-of-the-art equipment as more conventional science departments might be."

Two-thirds of the Shimer bachelor of arts program consists of required courses (divided into the Basic and Advanced Core) that introduce students to the Western intellectual tradition. The other third of the curriculum consists of electives. After completing the Basic Core, students must pass a comprehensive exam before moving on. The Area Comprehensive Examination tests the student in his major area. In the student's final year he takes a two-semester course on Western civilization and writes a senior thesis.

There are two kinds of electives at Shimer. Skills courses are offered in the arts, writing, mathematics, and languages; workshops are offered in theater, art, creative writing, and math. With the approval of the dean, students may take private music or dance lessons or participate in internships in the arts. Classical Greek and Latin are offered as well as modern languages such as French and German. Shimer's small size, of course, can sometimes be a weakness. "Since Shimer has so few faculty members it can only offer a limited number of electives in which the teaching faculty member is truly expert," says a former student. "The result is that an elective will be requested by students and offered by the college, but the faculty member may be only tangentially knowledgeable of the subject." Examples of recent elective course offerings include "Shake-speare and Performance," "Women in Literature," "Calculus," and "The Historical Jesus."

Indeed, Shimer's use of the Socratic method, which teaches by asking rather than telling, presents unique opportunities and challenges for professors. For example, Homer's *Odyssey* is viewed as a work of literature in one course, and primarily as a historical document in another. This integration creates among faculty and students

VITAL STATISTICS

Religious affiliation: none
Total enrollment: 111
Total undergraduates: 108
SAT/ACT medians: SAT V: 680, M: 580; ACT: 27
Applicants: 42
Applicants accepted: 71%
Accepted applicants who enrolled: 45%
Tuition: $18,650
Room and board: $3,000 (room only)
Freshman retention rate: 75%
Graduation rate: 28% (4 yrs.), 47% (6 yrs.)
Courses with fewer than 20 students: 100%
Student-faculty ratio: 8:1
Courses taught by graduate students: none
Most popular majors: n/a
Students living on campus: 65%
Guaranteed housing for four years? yes
Students in fraternities or sororities: none

"a viewpoint which recognizes the interrelationships among the various aspects of human thought and aspirations," according to the school.

The faculty focus squarely on instruction rather than research. "Teaching is what we do at Shimer," says one professor. Another reports, "I've taught at seven institutions and none of them has come even close to Shimer's emphasis on teaching." One student says, "Shimer faculty are universally approachable. . . . I've never seen a syllabus without the faculty member's home or cell phone [number]." Close student-faculty relationships are inevitable with Shimer's small classes, discussion-based curriculum, and democratic governance. Students and teachers eat meals together, discussions often continue outside of the classroom, and teachers and students consider each other peers.

Students' praise for the faculty (which numbers only about twenty-four) is enthusiastic. Steven Werlin's deep thinking and passion made one student "not only envy the people who work with him regularly, but also want to grow up to be him." Another says that longtime professor Eileen Buchanan "effectively passes [her] excitement on to the people in class." Ann Dolinko is a "relentless critic, but in a way that forces a student to improve, not in a way that stifles engagement." Conversations with Jim Donovan about science and religion "intertwine in wonderful and unexpected ways," says another. David Lukens "is possibly the smartest person ever . . . interested in exploring everything." One student "loved every moment of classes" with John Meech. Don Moon, president emeritus, is described as "irreverent and brilliant . . . a cross between a nuclear physicist and a reverend." Of David Shiner's class on Plato, one student says, "To tell the complete truth, I don't think a week has gone by since that class that I haven't made some reference to Plato's *Republic*."

> *"It's impossible to go through the curriculum without learning how to interact with a text of social analysis or poetry or music or prose. And philosophic inquiry is the end result of everything." This end is accomplished through a common core curriculum.*

Faculty too are proud of the education they provide. One faculty member says, "I believe that our students get one of the best groundings in the classic liberal arts tradition in the country." President Rice calls Shimer "one of the most serious institutions of higher learning in the world."

Politics are not overly intrusive in the classroom, though one professor describes the campus as "generally politically left." Nevertheless, both students and faculty believe that all students are encouraged to express their viewpoints and that all reasonable opinions are respected on campus. One student says, "If a student is committed to working intelligently and nondogmatically in an atmosphere of open conversation and respect for all, she or he will find Shimer an ideal intellectual atmosphere. If however, a conservative, liberal, or irreligious student is dogmatic about her or his religiosity or antireligiosity or liberalism or conservatism, she or he will be attacked mercilessly." A professor says, "I do recall a couple of incidents in which a religious student felt visibly uncomfortable, but it was the subject (Darwin's writings) rather than the class discussion that was at issue." Another student says, "Shimer is an extremely liberal college and the student body has at times been hostile to conservative views. Although I imagine that was felt in an undertone during classes, for the most part I believe it remained separate from class."

The dominant subject of conversation on campus in 2006 was the school's impending move to Chicago. Although some students fear the change threatens their tightly knit community, the school claims that its relocation will not alter its character. "While things will surely change, we are reasonably confident that we can retain much of the 'community' feel of the school at our Chicago location," says one professor. The college also hopes relocation will encourage growth, one major goal of Rice's presidency. "The Illinois Institute of Technology's invitation to Shimer proved attractive because the two institutions have much to offer each other academically and intellectually," Rice said. "Shimer will strengthen the liberal arts on the university's campus, reinvigorate the Great Books tradition with deep roots in Chicago, and Shimer students will benefit from IIT's strengths in science and technology," he added. The decision to expand to Chicago will have no effect on Shimer's unique curriculum; regardless of location, Shimer's primary focus will remain the life of the mind. And with impressive results: Shimer produces the third-highest percentage of Ph.D. recipients in the United States, behind only Cal Tech and Harvey Mudd College.

Student Life: One Big Family

With a student body of only 110, meaningful, personal attention is readily available to all students who seek it out, with ample opportunities to interact with peers and professors. "Because Shimer is such a small school the addition or subtraction of merely four or five people can completely change the school culture," says one former student. Dialogue is such a big part of life at Shimer that the Ethics Statement officially requires Shimerians to "demonstrate respect and sensitivity for the ideas, feelings, and needs of others." Shimerian sensitivity also extends to egalitarianism on campus. Sororities and fraternities and other organizations which "promote exclusivity based on sex, age, national origin, economic, or academic status, or any other basis, are not permitted." Shimer is self-governed by faculty, students, and staff. The Assembly, composed of all community members (students, faculty, and staff) directs most of the college's operations, including the recent decision to relocate. Students serve on every major committee and serve as voting members of the board of trustees. Faculty members are expected to participate in college administration.

With so much to talk about, Shimerians apparently don't have much time for extracurricular activities. The college website lists only one student organization, the "Shimer College Quality of Life Committee." Other community activities listed on the

ALL-AMERICAN COLLEGES

website include "potluck dinners, chess, and topical discussions." Lectures and theater are a big part of campus life as well. Intercollegiate and intramural athletics are nonexistent. Instead, students may participate in community games of softball, basketball, volleyball, or perhaps a game of soccer with children from the after-school program. One professor says, "The institutional culture is such that we get few party animals or strongly career-oriented students." In a recent poll, the educational goal most selected by students was "Developing a philosophy of life." Another professor says, "Students themselves are avid readers and intellectually curious people; if they were not, they would not have enrolled at Shimer."

Many students participate in Shimer's Oxford Program. There they study with a Shimer faculty member who directs the program and with Oxford tutors for their elective work. Since 1950, Shimer has offered an Early Entrant Program for high school students, many of whom found high school stifling and unsatisfying. "Motivation, willingness to learn and intellectual curiosity" are the most important qualifications for early admittance, according to the school. One early entrant says, "Shimer offered a radically different education, one based in genuine inquiry and conversation." High school students can also participate in summer Great Books workshops.

Homeschoolers, already accustomed to an unconventional approach to education, often shine at Shimer. The college actively recruits them—offering middle school and high school science labs to local home school and high school students. The Every-Third Weekend Program is designed for adult students who wish to acquire a classical education while maintaining a career. The Foundations of Science Graduate Program serves K-12 teachers who need additional credit toward certification.

Yearly tuition at Shimer is on the low side at $18,650. It is $3,000 extra for a double occupancy room (board plans are not yet offered). Over 90 percent of Shimer students receive some kind of financial aid. Shimer offers a variety of need- and merit-based scholarships, including scholarships for homeschoolers, early-entrants, and other nontraditional students. Still, the average student loan debt among recent graduates is a stiff $35,000.

SOUTHERN VIRGINIA UNIVERSITY

BUENA VISTA, VIRGINIA • WWW.SOUTHERNVIRGINIA.EDU

Southern Virginia University is the only independent liberal arts college in the country that serves members of the Church of Jesus Christ of Latter-day Saints (LDS). It does not, unlike Brigham Young University, have official ties to the LDS church, but it does provide, in a small-school setting, a traditional and rigorous education in an atmosphere and culture consistent with the moral standards espoused by the Mormons.

The university is relatively young. In 1996 a group of Mormon educators and businessmen had the idea of founding an LDS-based college in the East. To that end, they acquired Southern Virginia College, a coed junior college on the brink of closing its doors. The school reopened in the fall of 1996 as a four-year liberal arts institution in the LDS tradition. It took the name Southern Virginia University in 2001 and gained full accreditation in 2003. Ninety-two percent of the students at SVU are Mormons. Total enrollment at the school during its first decade has risen from seventy-four to 656 students and is expected to reach 1,000 students by 2010.

The university's catalog says that in order to achieve its mission, the school "will provide a superior faculty committed to their faith and to rigorous instruction in the arts, letters, and sciences. Students will be encouraged to reflect on their studies in light of the gospel of Jesus Christ." For students of an LDS background, SVU provides a sound East Coast alternative to (the excellent) Brigham Young.

Academic Life:
Laying Solid Foundations

Rodney K. Smith, SVU's president since 2004, calls SVU's approach to education "an honors program for every student." School provost Paul S. Edwards told the school's newsletter, *Tidings*, that "through a liberal education, the discerning student can gain an appreciation for the beliefs, culture, and institutions that allow for human flourishing. The discerning student of Western civilization can appreciate how it is that the West was able to achieve and maintain the framework for the rule of law and economic prosperity." In keeping with this vision, the school imposes admirable general education requirements, which come close to the old ideal of a core curriculum. They are as follows:

- "English Composition." Students must also produce an "advanced writing paper" in one of their classes;
- "Technology Tools," which introduces students to online research methods (individuals may test out);
- either the first semester of "Literature of Western Civilization" (which covers the ancient to Renaissance periods) or the second (Reformation to the present). Texts here are chosen from among Western literary classics;
- one of two history classes, "Western Civilization" I or II;
- "History of Philosophy," either I or II;
- one course in art history, music, or theater history;
- An additional two-course survey sequence in history, literature, philosophy, or the history of art, music, or theater;
- "American Civilization," a class that "considers what it means to be an American citizen." Tocqueville's *Democracy in America* constitutes the central text;
- one course in either chemistry or physics, and one in biology—at least one of which must have a lab;
- "Introduction to Logic" or one course in mathematics;
- coursework or tests to show intermediate facility in a foreign language. Choices include French, German, Latin, Greek, Chinese, and Spanish;
- four service courses; and
- three physical activity courses (for a total of three credits) and a "Health and Wellness" course.

This curriculum guarantees that students receive a wide-ranging exposure to the liberal arts, philosophy, American history and civics, and the historical development of at least one discipline. "We try to encourage as much intellectual curiosity as we can get from our students. Most general education classes emphasize participation in class discussions and require student presentations," says a professor.

The strongest majors at SVU include English, philosophy, and history. The English major at SVU is challenging and comprehensive, ensuring that students are confronted with the most influential authors and texts in the Western literary tradition. Majors are required to take six specific courses that include two "Literature of Western Civilization" courses (ancient to medieval and Renaissance to modern), "Studies in Shakespeare," "Approaches to Literature," and two genre-studies classes in fiction and poetry. Students go on to complete six electives and a senior paper or creative work. Orson Scott Card, the prolific and bestselling author of science fiction and fantasy novels, is a new member of the English department, where he teaches writing and literature.

Requirements for philosophy majors include "History of Philosophy: Justice and Virtue," "History of Philosophy: Knowledge and Reality," "Introduction to Logic," and a course in epistemology or metaphysics. The department also has students complete an additional fifteen hours of electives and a significant writing project in the senior year. It is reported that the faculty are "brilliant, passionate, and involved" and that students in the small noncompetitive program learn from one another. However, a philosophy major notes that "some of the classes conflicted with one another and so it was difficult to take every class you wanted to without a good deal of planning."

A graduate says, "I was privileged to attend a number of history classes at SVU and I found each to be genuinely respectful of Western heritage and American institutions." The professors in the department "know you, know your work, and push you," says a student majoring in history. They "encourage us to engage in primary research and teach us that we can make a real contribution to the field of history." Although the school is small and less well known than "a big name school," one student says he has been given the opportunity to present papers at academic conferences. "You just have to work at it a little harder here," he says. Major requirements include two survey courses in "Western Civilization," after which students go on to complete seven electives chosen from such courses as "Colonial and Revolutionary America," "American Civil War and Reconstruction," and "American Politics and Foreign Policy since World War II." Finally, seniors complete a writing project and take a general examination upon completion of their coursework.

The natural sciences are also strong at the school. The school catalog reports that SVU graduates have enjoyed great success in being admitted to medical schools. Students in the health preprofessional program are thoroughly prepared to take the MCAT, DAT, and other graduate school tests, says a student. The program includes a seminar that addresses topics related to preparing for medical, dental, and veterinary school, as well as a class in which students have a "one-on-one clinical experience shadowing local doctors, dentists, or veterinarians," says the course catalog. "Four or five evenings a week the students gather and the professors of biology, chemistry, and physics take turns prepping students for the test and they take practice tests," says a student. "All of the science faculty are amazingly dedicated, but the one who stands out most of all is Dr. Barbara van Kuiken, who is also the premed advisor. She probably spends more time on campus working with the students than any other professor in any field. If anyone does not excel under her, it was not her fault."

VITAL STATISTICS

Religious affiliation: Mormon-founded, nondenominational
Total enrollment: 656
Total undergraduates: 656
SAT/ACT midranges: SAT V: 480–600, M: 460–580; ACT: 21–26
Applicants: 816
Applicants accepted: 98%
Accepted applicants who enrolled: 49%
Tuition: $15,350
Room and board: $4,300
Freshman retention rate: 31%*
Graduation rate: 8% (4 yrs.), 13% (6 yrs.)*
Courses with fewer than 20 students: 78%
Student-faculty ratio: 14:1
Courses taught by graduate students: none
Most popular majors: business, liberal arts, English
Students living on campus: 62%
Guaranteed housing for four years? no
Students in fraternities or sororities: none

Many Mormon students take two years off after their freshman year to serve as missionaries, which skews some of these statistics.

The school has been adding to its foreign language faculty during the past three years, hiring new professors to teach Spanish, French, and German. But some students say that a few of the foreign language classes have ranked among their least favorite. SVU offers study-abroad experiences in Italy, France, England, Germany, and Spain. In the past, student groups have also studied Chinese language and culture in China at Liaoning Normal University, and classical art, literature, and philosophy in Greece. Many SVU students spend eighteen to twenty-four months living in a foreign country after their first year of school to serve in missions for the Church of Jesus Christ of Latter-day Saints.

Students and professors name the following faculty members as some of the best at the university: John M. Armstrong and Jan-Erik Jones in philosophy; C. Randall Cluff and Scott A. Dransfield in English; W. Todd Brotherson and E. Susan Kellogg in business; Steven K. Baldridge in government and education; and Lora L. Knight and Francis MacDonnell in history.

According to the provost, "Through a liberal education, the discerning student can gain an appreciation for the beliefs, culture, and institutions that allow for human flourishing . . . , the development of the rule of law, and economic prosperity."

With a student-faculty ratio of 14 to 1 and an average class size of fifteen, student-faculty relationships are close at SVU. The faculty do not have teaching assistants. A professor says, "In some disciplines, publications play a larger role in tenure decisions than in others. We tend to have the attitude that where more university research support is given, more research is expected, but teaching has typically been a bigger factor." Students say that the faculty are highly accessible and put in many hours with students outside of class time. "If you just see them in passing they are willing to stop and talk, read over a draft of your paper, or talk about post-graduation plans or just how life is going. They are mentors to us," says a student. Another says, "Every student that is willing has a personalized learning program because the professors truly care about them." A recent graduate says, "I will be attending law school in the fall, and without any family in the legal profession it was my professors and President Smith who encouraged me to take the LSAT, helped me with my applications, and gave me advice on different schools."

A professor says that students at SVU have a "fair bit of intellectual curiosity" and that when they've completed their degrees, "they've received more from their experience from our faculty—in terms of knowledge, skills, and challenges—than they would have at a larger institution. We have a 'value-added product.'"

The only things not freely debated on campus are the LDS church and its leaders, says a student. "Many professors are Democrats, but political correctness is not an issue. If anything, this university has taught me critical thought. Debate is encouraged and thrives. Most students have a conservative slant and you will probably never hear anyone argue for abortion, but I have never seen a professor put someone's opinion down if it was well presented and well supported." Another student says that the professors "teach us that we need to be able to explain and defend what we believe in and be aware of other opinions, but they never tell us what to think or how to believe. I have never felt stifled, but I have never been uncomfortable or shocked either." An alum says, "Many of the professors were LDS but not all were and each was respectful of every religion. I never heard a negative word towards any belief. If there was debate over an issue it was welcome as long as it was mutually respectful." A professor notes, "This is not a Rush Limbaugh vs. Michael Moore atmosphere. There are debates, and there is a fair bit of intellectual activity in and out of the classroom, but it's eerily respectful."

SVU does not require any religion courses for graduation. Students can earn, on a pass/fail basis, up to eight religion credits toward graduation by taking classes at the LDS Institute of Religion on campus.

"Learn That Life Is Service" is SVU's motto. A leader-servant, according to the *Tidings*, is someone "who leads by example, governs with love, and gives back to the people by performing acts of service." Each student is required to take four "Service-Learning" classes and to complete a minimum of sixty-eight service hours. Service obligations can be fulfilled on campus via athletics and at the library, local hospitals, Chamber of Commerce, schools, senior centers, juvenile correctional facilities, and health care centers. The equestrian club is the group on campus with the most volunteer hours. Members dedicate their biweekly activities to caring for horses in the local area. They also spend time working with Hoofbeats, an organization that uses horseback riding as social therapy for the mentally and physically handicapped. Six miles away in Lexington is the Virginia Horse Center, one of the largest equestrian centers in the United States. Groups from the school travel every year for the university-wide service project at the Mormon Temple in Washington, D.C.

Student Life: Shenandoah Sunsets

Southern Virginia University is located in Buena Vista, a town of about 6,000 residents situated in the heart of the beautiful Shenandoah Valley of the Blue Ridge Mountains. The town is approximately 165 miles southwest of Washington, D.C. There are numerous major historical sites in the area, including Monticello, Appomattox, Williamsburg, and Yorktown, and the nearby mountains offer opportunities for skiing, biking, horseback riding, fishing, camping, and other outdoor activities.

The university's 155-acre campus consists of ten major buildings and sixteen homes, which are used for housing and office space. The focal center on the scenic campus is the Main Hall, formerly the Buena Vista Hotel. Built in 1891, it is a state landmark, painted red with a wraparound porch in the elaborate Queen Anne Victorian style. The huge building houses administration offices, conference rooms, lounges, a cafeteria, a ballroom, residence halls for women (on the upper three floors), a chapel, Student Health Services, and laundry facilities.

1. English 210: Literature of
   Western Civilization:
   Ancient and Medieval
   (*closest match*)
2. Philosophy 210/215:
   History of Philosophy:
   Knowledge and Reality /
   History of Philosophy:
   Justice and Virtue
3. Religion 201-202/ 211-
   212: Old Testament I-II /
   New Testament I-II
4. No suitable course.
5. No suitable course.
6. English 345:
   Studies in Shakespeare
7. History 323:
   Colonial and
   Revolutionary America
8. History 215:
   Western Civilization II
   (*closest match*)

Due to the small size of the university's Von Canon Library, a portion of the school's book collection is stored at an auxiliary library. The libraries at Washington and Lee University and Virginia Military Institute in Lexington share reciprocal borrowing agreements with SVU. Recent additions to the campus include a new laboratory for chemistry classes and the Stoddard Activities Center, which houses SVU's assemblies, dances, movie nights, dinners, and graduations.

The university requires single freshmen and sophomore students under the age of twenty-one to live on campus unless they live locally with their parents. Sixty-two percent of the students live on campus in resident halls, residential and modular homes, or in townhouses. Housing is single-sex, and limited housing for married students is available. The university's honor code is based on the teaching and values of the Church of Jesus Christ of Latter-day Saints. Enrolled students, staff, and faculty, regardless of their faith or personal philosophy, pledge to live by the standards of the SVU Honor Code on and off campus and to share the responsibility of assisting others to fulfill their commitments to do the same. Principles include honesty in all areas of life and prohibitions against sexual intimacy outside of marriage, alcohol, tobacco, coffee, tea, cursing, gambling, pornography, and illicit drugs. Dress and grooming standards are supposed to promote modesty and cleanliness. Visiting hours for members of the opposite sex in dorms are set by the school and enforced. "There are lobbies and public areas where the men and women can spend time together, but the dorms are more for quiet time, study, as well as spending time with your roommates and other students on your floor," says a student.

The marriage-and missionary-friendly Mormon culture is very much alive at SVU. In the class of 2005, 31 percent of students served missions for the LDS Church, and 47 percent were married (four couples graduated together).

"Students who thrive at SVU are serious about their education and serious about knowledge. They believe that knowledge is its own virtue. They are balanced individuals and excel at many things. They are not focused solely on sports or their social lives," says a student. "Because it is so small, SVU has a great sense of community. Students are really involved in all sorts of activities, and are there to support one another," a recent graduate reports. "SVU is not a competitive environment. Study groups are encouraged and free tutoring is available to anyone at the Student Support Center. I have come away from SVU with many lifelong friendships."

The *Paladin* is the Student Association's official newspaper. Additional student groups include the Knight Classic Film Society, Oratorical and Debate Society, academic clubs and honor societies, Multi-Cultural Student Association, a literary maga-zine, a Democratic club, and the Service Counsel. Performing arts groups on campus include a capella vocal bands, a comedy troupe, pep band, choirs, (including a flute choir), and an orchestra. Recent theater department productions have included *The Importance of Being Earnest*, *The Tempest*, and *Fiddler on the Roof*. Beginning in 2005, the music and theater programs began collaborating to produce their first full-scale opera, Gian Carlo Menotti's *Old Maid and the Thief*.

Annual homecoming events on campus include soccer and basketball games, a tennis tournament pitting faculty and staff against students, and a traditional pep rally, football game, bonfire, and dance. SVU hosts many forums, devotionals, fire-sides, and various conferences featuring LDS church members and civic and business leaders from a variety of political, social, and religious backgrounds.

Approximately 40 percent of students participate in intercollegiate sports. The Southern Virginia University Knights are an independent member of the National As-sociation of Intercollegiate Athletics. Many SVU athletic teams also compete against NCAA Division III, II, and I schools. In its ten-year history, SVU has won twenty-three national championships for small colleges. Sports programs offered for men are: base-ball, basketball, football, track and field, golf, cross-country, soccer, and wrestling. Women can take part in basketball, soccer, softball, track and field, golf, cheerleading, cross-country, and volleyball. The sports arena is equipped with a gym, training facili-ties, weight room, and classrooms. The student union houses a swimming pool and a dance studio.

Crime is not usually an issue at SVU or in Buena Vista, say students. "People often leave their cars running while they go into the store, and people rarely lock their homes during the day," says a recent graduate. "There was one incident [in 2005] in-volving some young men living in the dorms who were stealing from other students and from the bookstore. They were caught, however, brought before the honor council, and asked to leave the school. They were also turned into the police." The school has at least one security officer on patrol at all times and provides an escort service for loca-tions on campus. In 2004, the school reported two sex offenses and twenty burglaries.

Tuition at Southern Virginia University in 2005–6 was quite low for a private college: $15,350, with room and board at $4,300. Sixty-seven percent of students at the school receive need-based financial aid. One loan program mirrors the "Perpetual Edu-cation Fund" of the Church of Jesus Christ of Latter-day Saints. Students who demon-strate financial need are loaned money from SVU, to be repaid upon their graduation, free of interest, over a period of ten years. The repaid money replenishes the loan fund and is in turn given out to new students. The average student loan debt of recent gradu-ates is $14,479.

UNIVERSITY OF THE SOUTH

SEWANEE, TENNESSEE • WWW.SEWANEE.EDU

The southern dioceses of the Episcopal Church established Sewanee just before the Civil War and grandly named it the University of the South. The school saw decades of hard times both during the war (when invading troops blew up the cornerstone of the chapel) and afterwards, when it closed for a time. It reconvened in 1868 with nine students and four professors. Oxford and Cambridge universities sent books to help stock the struggling school's library, and with time and dedication, Sewanee became a seat of gentility, learning, and maturation for generations of southern men. It became coed in 1969 and abolished mandatory Saturday classes in the 1980s. Through it all, the school has maintained a reputation for academic excellence, producing twenty-five Rhodes Scholars—two in the last three years—the most per capita of any school in the nation.

The college is located on one of the most beautiful campuses in the country. Known for its "remoteness without cultural dislocation," the Domain (as the campus is called) is adorned with beautiful buildings and thousands of acres of forest and fields and includes the town of Sewanee itself. Tradition holds that the mountain is so beautiful that angels once lived here. As students pass through the university gates they touch the roof of their car to take a guardian angel with them while they're away from Sewanee. When they return, they touch the roof to release it. In 1941, poet William Alexander Percy wrote of Sewanee, his alma mater: "It is so beautiful that people who have been there always, one way or another, come back. For such as can detect apple green in an evening sky, it is Arcadia—not the one that never used to be, but the one that many people always live in; only this one can be shared."

Academic Life: The Thames and the Tiber

Sewanee has historically imposed a fairly traditional set of distribution requirements on its students. Recently, under new dean Rita Kipp and the influence of outside (i.e., Yankee) consultants, some attempts were made to overhaul the curriculum to make it more "relevant." However, according to one professor, those efforts "ground to a screeching halt" in the face of staunch faculty opposition—at least for now. (Dean Kipp is doing her part to implement what changes she can, teaching an exciting, oh-so-transgressive new course in the women's studies department called "Cross-Dressing Cross-Culturally: Gender in Reverse.") In the midst of this simmering culture war, a professor says, "Sewanee still offers one of the most broad and rigorous basic liberal arts educations available among the top one hundred liberal arts colleges in the country. This is, however, beginning to crumble under pressures brought to bear by departmental interests attuned more to fads of the professional organizations than to the holism of liberal education." Nevertheless, insists another professor, "Our liberal arts curriculum is still strongly oriented toward the cultural legacy of Europe and toward canonical texts in most disciplines. This is a campus where the most popular major is English and where the two most popular classes in that major are [in] Shakespeare and Chaucer." Another professor says, "In the context of the region, we are considered liberal. But in the context of our peer (especially East Coast) schools, there is a small measure of political correctness here. It is a matter of comparison." In setting degree requirements, the college aims to "inspire personal initiative in social consciousness, aesthetic perception, intellectual curiosity and integrity, and methods of scientific inquiry while encouraging moral growth." All B.A. students must complete the following:

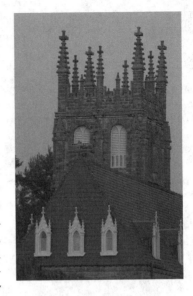

- "Literature and Composition." This course on writing "focuses on several plays by Shakespeare, introduced by an examination of lyric poems—either by Shakespeare or by one of his contemporaries. The course is designed to develop the student's imaginative understanding of literature along with the ability to write and speak with greater clarity";
- two more writing-intensive courses;
- a foreign language at the third-year level or above. The school offers majors in French, Spanish, German, Greek, Latin, and Russian as well as instruction in Italian, Chinese, and Japanese;
- one course in mathematics;
- two courses in the sciences. One of these must be a laboratory course; options include "Biology and People" and "Introduction to Forestry";
- "Topics in Western Civilization," which covers the development and impact of Western civilization upon the human community;
- one course in anthropology, economics, or political science. "Women, Family, and Work in the Muslim World" and "The Anthropology of Gender" would both qualify;
- one course in either religion or philosophy. Choices include "Ancient Philosophy from Homer to Augustine" and "Feminist and Womanist Religious Ethics";
- one course in the arts (art, art history, music, or theater). Courses range from "Greek and Roman Art" to "The Films of Alfred Hitchcock"; and
- two semesters of physical education.

This generally admirable curriculum resembles a traditional core and ensures that students have a more or less common foundation on which teachers of their more

Religious affiliation:
  Episcopalian
Total enrollment: 1,528
Total undergraduates: 1,432
SAT/ACT midranges: SAT V:
  588–670, M: 570–660;
  ACT: 25–29
Applicants: 2,027
Applicants accepted: 67%
*Accepted applicants who
  enrolled:* 31%
Tuition: $28,528
Room and board: $8,160
Freshman retention rate: 88%
Graduation rate: 79% (4 yrs.),
  82% (6 yrs.)
*Courses with fewer than 20
  students:* 72%
Student-faculty ratio: 10:1
*Courses taught by graduate
  students:* none
Most popular majors: English,
  history, economics
Students living on campus:
  94%
*Guaranteed housing for four
  years?* yes
Students in fraternities: 70%
  sororities: 68%

advanced courses can build. Students who want a more complete introduction to the cultural history of the Western world should take the Interdisciplinary Humanities Program, a sequence of four chronologically arranged courses. Beginning with "Tradition and Criticism in Western Culture—the Ancient World," and continuing with courses in the medieval, early modern, and modern eras ("Modern World—Romantic to Postmodern"), the plan allows students to fulfill four distribution requirements while reading Great Books—Plato's dialogues, the *Odyssey*, the *Aeneid*, St. Augustine's *Confessions*, the *Canterbury Tales*, *Paradise Lost*, and many others—and by exploring the art, history, politics, and music of each period as well. One professor calls it one of the most rigorous course sequences in the college.

According to the 2005 results of the National Survey of Student Engagement, the University of the South is in the top 10 percent of colleges nationwide in terms of "academic challenge, student-faculty interaction, enriching educational experiences, and supportive campus environment." A student says, "Our teachers are eminently accessible. One of Sewanee's strongest reputations is for engagement and personal relationships between professors and students. I consider some professors here among my closest friends. Office hours are only the beginning; many professors invite students to their houses for dinner and other social activities. The social atmosphere at Sewanee facilitates real relationships." One professor says the close connection is a result of the small community: "We see students outside the classroom all the time. Interaction with students is not only common, it's expected." Another professor says that Sewanee has "enough serious students who are grateful for the leisure to study to make teaching here rewarding." The student-faculty ratio is 10 to 1, and the average class size for freshmen is nineteen students, with just thirteen students in the typical upper-level course. The university's Writing Center, staffed with students skilled in the craft, is open every day.

The English department—the most popular major on campus—has been home over the years to many literary figures of national note, including Monroe Spears, Andrew Lytle, Allen Tate, and Caroline Gordon. Building on its golden reputation, the department has recently added the School of Letters, which offers an M.A. in English and American literature and an M.F.A. in creative writing, which can be completed in four or five summers "on the Mountain." The library stores an extensive collection of original Faulkner papers and students may take a course that studies them. Home of the nation's oldest and most prestigious literary quarterly, the *Sewanee Review*, the department is traditional in focus; for example, majors are still required to take two courses in Shakespeare and two others in pre-1750 English literature. Medievalist professor Robert Benson is called by one student "a shining example of faith and reason." Dale Richardson, a Shakespeare scholar, is known as the "most intelligent and well-read professor in the college and is familiar with the prevailing modes of philosophical and literary critical thought," says another. Students also recommend Thomas Carlson, William Engle, Pamela Macfie, Kelly Malone, Jennifer Michael, and Wyatt Prunty.

The classical languages department is also strong. As one student puts it, "These departments [English and classical languages] pick up the slack as the advocates of the Western canon, Christian orthodoxy, and traditional academic philosophy in which other departments are sorely lacking." Students say Christopher McDonough is "a very fine teacher, extremely well regarded among students and faculty." Another member of the department, Jon Bruss, an ordained Missouri Synod Lutheran pastor, is one of the most popular young faculty members on campus. According to one student, he has promoted much-needed changes in the department and has been instrumental in recruiting many new majors. Students also recommend Donald Huber and Doug Seiters.

In contrast, the religion department "refuses to teach courses in theology, or any course in Christianity which is not deconstructionist in nature," complains a student. Students and professors report that conservative and religious views are not tolerated within the department. "Views contrary to the prevailing academic liberalism are considered backward, patriarchal, and unintellectual," says a student. A professor concurs, reporting that the department has been ruined by a "wholesale adoption of postmodern criticism; so pluralist as to exclude the Christian tradition in recognizable form."

"Our liberal arts curriculum is still strongly oriented toward the cultural legacy of Europe. . . . This is a campus where the most popular major is English and where the two most popular classes in that major are Shakespeare and Chaucer."

In the history department, which is excellent, majors are required to declare a focus on the history of the United States, Europe, Great Britain, or Africa/Asia/Latin America, and then to take at least five courses in this concentration and four outside of it. Classes in American and British history are required for all history majors. Students recommend William Brown Patterson, Charles Perry, Woody Register, and Susan Ridyard in this department.

The environmental studies program is also said to be excellent. The university's immense land holdings offer an unparalleled outdoor laboratory. Both conservationist and environmentalist voices are represented among faculty. The department is interdisciplinary and offers four types of major. Faculty members are also on staff in other university departments like anthropology, biology, forestry, and geology. According to one professor, the school "teaches evolution as science and Intelligent Design as theology."

In other departments, students recommend Chris Conn and James Peters in philosophy; Gayle McKeen in political science; and Mishoe Brennecke and Greg Clark in art and art history.

New students should consider Sewanee's First-Year Program, which is designed "to provide an intensive academic experience that seeks to integrate rigorous classroom work with out-of-class experiences." Classes are team-taught and kept small. According to the college, 95 percent of students completing the course would recommend it to incoming freshman. The catalog lists fifteen or so seminar-style courses on topics like "God, Death, and the Meaning of Life," "The Struggle between Good and Evil," and "Philosophy through Film: Socrates, Jesus, and Cowboys." According to one professor, however, the program has recently suffered substantial funding cuts, reducing its out-of-classroom initiatives.

The university also offers opportunities for study abroad through its own programs or through partnerships with other colleges and universities. Students enrolled in the European studies program choose one of two study options: "Ancient Greece and Rome: The Foundations of Western Civilization" or "Western Europe in the Middle Ages and the Renaissance," and spend four weeks at Sewanee before heading overseas to York, Durham, and Oxford.

Student Life: Et in Arcadia Ego

Sewanee is located in south-central Tennessee between Nashville and Chattanooga, the nearest metropolitan areas. The 10,000-acre campus sits atop the Cumberland Plateau, a tableland of sandstone that rises more than a thousand feet above the Tennessee River Valley. The "University Domain" is the second largest campus in the nation and includes the town of Sewanee (pop. 2,300), as well as a remote and rugged paradise of ridges, ravines, caves, and waterfalls.

Indeed, the university's grounds and architecture are a bit of heaven on earth. Wide, expansive lawns are ringed with huge trees and numerous flowers and surrounded by structures made of native sandstone. Campus buildings include a new dining hall that looks as if it had been constructed a century ago, when the collegiate Gothic style enjoyed wide popularity. If you are considering Sewanee, visit the campus; you'll never want to come home.

With over 130 student organizations, students may participate in club sports, honorary societies, language clubs, service organizations, and various student publications. Through organizations such as the Emergency Medical Service, Habitat for Humanity, and the Volunteer Fire Department, many students are also active participants in the Sewanee town community. Despite the administration's preoccupation with obtaining liberal respectability, students are generally "moderately right leaning," says one. "There tends to be a strong majority of students who favor conservative social positions. . . . However, there is a large minority of center-left students as well."

For outdoor enthusiasts, the Domain includes sixty-five miles of trails and 8,000 acres of undeveloped land for biking, hiking, climbing, backpacking, and spelunking. The Sewanee Outing Program (SOP) promotes outdoor activities both "on and off the Mountain." The SOP offers weekend excursions, weekday trips, and extended trips to National Parks as wells as clinics with some of the country's top climbers, cavers, and kayakers. It also operates a low-cost bike shop that rents outdoor equipment and has a self-help bicycle repair facility. The SOP recently added a sixty-foot-long, indoor bouldering wall for students, faculty, and staff to hone their climbing skills before heading out into the wilderness. The Carter Martin Whitewater Club Boathouse serves as the gathering point for the college's canoe team and weekend paddlers.

Summers are a busy time on campus. Touted for its "remoteness without cultural dislocation," some of the nation's most notable writers and scholars gather in the summer for the Sewanee Writer's Conference. Tennessee Williams left funds to the university to support this conference. Since 1957, Sewanee has also hosted the Sewanee Summer Music Festival, a five-week program for advanced music students. The college also offers a variety of sports camps, language camps, and summer schools. In fact, a professor says, "many of [the students] do anything they can think of to remain on campus during the summer."

SUGGESTED CORE
1. Classical Studies 351: Greek Literature in Translation
2. Philosophy 203: Ancient Philosophy
3. Religion 141: Introduction to the Bible
4. Religion 321: Christian Theological Paths
5. Political Science 302: Recent Political Theory (*closest match*)
6. English 357/358: Shakespeare I and II
7. History 227: Intellectual and Cultural History of the United States I
8. History 398: European Cultural and Intellectual History, 1750–1890 (*closest match*)

All Saints Chapel is the hub of religious activity on campus. In addition to Sunday services, the chapel offers a variety of programs such as Bible studies, a centering prayer group, a *Chronicles of Narnia* study group, and the University Choir, which sings for weekly and special services. The choir is renowned for its quality. Through the All Saints Chapel Outreach Program, students travel to mission sites around the world.

The University of the South is officially Episcopalian, and nearly a third of the student body belongs to that church. One professor says the school's church identity "forms the foundation for all the ceremonies of the college." Sewanee even refers to its academic year with terms from the church calendar: the year is divided into the Advent and Easter semesters, not fall and spring. But other denominations are supported as well. Baptist Christian Ministries and the Sewanee Catholic Community are both active. Sewanee also houses the School of Theology, a residential seminary that offers a master of divinity, master of arts in theology, and other graduate studies programs, giving the school its university status.

ALL-AMERICAN COLLEGES

The college motto is taken from Psalm 133, which translates, "Behold how very good and pleasant it is when kindred live together in unity!" Virtually every student does in fact live on campus. Sewanee has a variety of housing options, from single-sex dorms with suites to apartments and special-interest and language houses. There are eleven fraternities and nine sororities at Sewanee, involving 70 percent of the student body, which accounts for a thriving party scene. Some of the residence halls are converts from the campus's days as a hospital, inn, and military academy. Emery Hall, once a morgue, is now a small women's dormitory. Not surprisingly, ghost stories abound.

For more than one hundred years, Sewanee has operated under the Honor System, to which students commit themselves in writing upon acceptance into the university. The system works. According to one professor, exams are not proctored, and cars and dorm rooms are habitually left unlocked. The code prohibits lying, cheating, stealing, plagiarizing, and removing books from the library without checking them out. All tests, quizzes, and papers carry the written pledge: "I hereby certify that I have neither given nor received unauthorized aid on this paper." More simply, the word "pledged," followed by a student's signature, carries the same promise. Most professors won't accept papers or exams that are not "pledged." The Honor System is maintained and administered by a student-run Honor Council; penalties for violations are harsh. For example, plagiarizing almost always carries the penalty of automatic expulsion.

One of Sewanee's most treasured traditions is the "Order of Gownsmen," a carry-over from the school's Oxford-and-Cambridge roots. Faculty wear gowns in the classroom, although, according to one professor, a few teachers grumble and choose not to participate. Students of academic distinction wear gowns in class as well, though this tradition, too, has faded somewhat over time. In general, students do dress up more for class here than is typical elsewhere. Outside the classroom, "preppy" is the predominant look, which one professor describes as "studied and expensive." It's not uncommon to see students in polo shirts with shorts, flip-flops, bowtie, and a gown. "Sewanee's students are, for the most part, rich kids from traditional, conservative, southern families," says a faculty member. "That's just the nature of the place." Another faculty member says, "Students are extremely polite. It's a joy to teach here."

Despite the Sewanee administration's best efforts, the student body remains fairly homogenous. The admissions department holds a special weekend each year for prospective minority students. If they enroll, they are offered a special freshman orientation retreat. But Sewanee's student body remains less than 10 percent black, and though this is sometimes decried in the student newspaper, the *Sewanee Purple*, the makeup of the university's student body has changed only slightly over the past couple of decades. "We're known as a conservative school with a mostly white student body," says a faculty member. "As much as Sewanee tries to change that, it's hard for people to get over a longtime stereotype."

Perhaps due to the respected Honor Code, crime is remarkably low (in fact, not a single assault has taken place in years). The only crimes in 2004 were fifteen burglaries and one stolen car. One security brief attributed the general increase in burglaries on campus to an increase in gadget-sized technology.

Sewanee was one of twenty-eight private institutions to be named a Fiske Guide's Best Buy School for 2006. But that doesn't make it cheap. Tuition is high at $28,528, with room and board at $8,160. About 60 percent of students receive some sort of financial aid; admissions are need-blind; and the school uses its sizable endowment of $240 million to provide 100 percent of each student's demonstrated need.

SOUTHWESTERN UNIVERSITY

GEORGETOWN, TEXAS • WWW.SOUTHWESTERN.EDU

Southwestern University is an intriguing mix of old and new, of liberal and conservative. In some ways it tracks the trends of other secular, modern universities. But it is also one of the few remaining American colleges offering a major in the classics. It is a church-affiliated institution that nevertheless is known for its easygoing approach to morality (if not to alcohol). And it is a place that can be extremely frustrating to the conservative-minded in religion and politics, yet will nevertheless yield both academic and personal rewards if one knows where to look. In many ways, its current divisions and contradictions, strengths and weaknesses, mirror those of its parent denomination, the United Methodist Church.

Although the university opened at Georgetown in 1873, its roots are even more deeply embedded in Texas's past. Previous attempts to found a Methodist college in Texas had all foundered for one reason or another. What was then called Texas University began in 1873; in 1875 it took the more abstract moniker of Southwestern University, but still claimed descent from Texas's five previously chartered Methodist colleges. This is why SU today considers itself to be "Texas's First University."

The school explains its ethos as follows: "Dogmatic rigidity is alien to our institutional spirit; we hold that ethical commitments and spiritual identities must welcome and support the swift advance of knowledge. Believing that none has a permanent monopoly on truth, Southwestern is fundamentally committed to academic freedom, to the informed debate in which new knowledge, new ethical insights, and richer spiritualities are grounded. Southwestern also shares the traditional Methodist concern for social justice: we seek to promote a sense of social responsibility, and are committed to offering the benefits of higher education to those who confront adverse financial and social circumstances." The school seems best suited to old-fashioned liberals and others who come into college without strong religious commitments, but who are curious about the liberal arts and humanities and eager to study with like-minded students and dedicated professors.

Academic Life: Maintaining the Classics

At the heart of a Southwestern education are the school's general education requirements, which are fairly loose—mirroring those at most major secular universities. Each student must take the following:

- "First-year Seminar." Students choose among special topics courses that are supposed to provide "stimulating and challenging academic experiences to help prepare incoming students to be successful in a rigorous liberal arts college environment";

- "Writing and Critical Thinking," a freshman composition course;
- one class in mathematics;
- one course in "American and Western Cultural Heritage." This may include any one of a scattershot of such classes ranging from "Greek Civilization" to "A Journey Through the Civil Rights Movement," and innumerable other survey courses on the civilization, literature, music, or drama of every major European nation;
- one course in "Other Cultures and Civilizations." Options (literally) come from all over the map, from "Introduction to Anthropology" to "Women in World History";

- one course in "The Religious Perspective." Options range from a general survey course, "Dimensions of Religion," to "The Christian Tradition" and include classes on Eastern faiths;
- one course in "Values Analysis." This is to be chosen from the following: "Schools, Society and Diversity," "Introduction to Ethics," "Contemporary Moral Problems," "Theories of Race," "Biomedical Ethics," "Values and the Liberal Arts," "American Political Thought," "Parenting: Theories and Realities," and "Theories of Race";
- two courses in "The Natural World." One course must be in physical science, the other in life or experimental behavioral science;
- two courses in "Aesthetic Experience." One of these must be a classroom/lecture-based class, such as "Italian Renaissance Art" or "History of Dance"; the other must feature performance/production, such as "Modern Dance," "Creative Writing," or "Public Speaking";
- two courses in "Social Analysis" from two different departments. At least one of these must be from the social sciences department. These include: "Introduction to Women's Studies," "Chicago: Studies in Urban Sociology," "Principles of Macroeconomics," "Survey of Exceptionalities," "Principles of Psychology," and "Social Patterns and Processes";
- at least one course that requires computer skills and has "assignments which require the use of word processing, web-based resources for research, spreadsheets, e-mail, or other kinds of discipline-related software";
- one class that includes a "Continued Writing Experience." This is essentially any course requiring written papers to demonstrate a student's composition skills;

Religious affiliation:
   United Methodist
Total enrollment: 1,276
Total undergraduates: 1,276
ACT midrange: 24-29
Applicants: 1,888
Applicants accepted: 66%
*Accepted applicants who
   enrolled*: not provided
Tuition: $23,650
Room and board: $6,700–
   $8,628
Freshman retention rate: 88%
Graduation rate: 74%
*Courses with fewer than 20
   students*: not provided
Student-faculty ratio: 10:1
*Courses taught by graduate
   students*: none
Most popular majors: social
   sciences, history,
   psychology
Students living on campus:
   83%
*Guaranteed housing for four
   years?* no
*Students in fraternities or
   sororities*: 30%

• an "Integrative or Capstone Experience." The catalog defines this as a "special course or project in which students are expected to bring together and apply what they have learned, a comprehensive written examination, or other experience appropriate to the area of specialization";

• two semester hours of fitness and recreational activity courses; and

• coursework or tests to "demonstrate proficiency at the fourth-semester level in . . . a foreign language." Options include French, German, Spanish, Chinese, Greek, and Latin.

Since these requirements are so loose, it's possible to drift through Southwestern without acquiring a genuinely worthwhile liberal arts education—and equally possible to acquire a solid foundation, if one chooses courses judiciously (see our suggested Southwestern core).

Students seeking a more intensive educational challenge should look into the school's Paideia Program, effectively an honors college that offers smaller courses and more interaction with teachers. The program works by "integrating in-class and out-of class academic and nonacademic activities. The Paideia Program fosters and promotes connections between academics, intercultural experiences, leadership, service-learning, and collaborative research and creative works through a series of one-credit-hour seminar courses and through frequent one-on-one meetings with Paideia professors." Students interested in the program must complete an application that requires several essays.

Upon entering SU, each student is assigned a faculty academic advisor. After the first semester, a student may request a change in academic advisor. It is intended that the advisor will help guide an individual through the innumerable class offerings. There are thirty-five different majors offered at SU, most in various aspects of the liberal arts, including communication, education, English, history, modern languages and literatures, political science, psychology, religion and philosophy, and sociology and anthropology. In addition, Southwestern is one of the relatively few schools where one can still pursue a traditional classics major. The requirements and coursework in this admirable program are said to be as rigorous as any offered in this country or in Europe. Classics students may pursue semester or academic year study at College Year in Athens, at the Intercollegiate Center for Classical Studies in Rome, or in archaeological excavation at Hacimusalar, Turkey—which the school accurately describes as "a unique opportunity for students at the undergraduate level." More than half of all Southwestern students spend some time abroad as part of their education. Other options offered by the school include a semester in London, exchange programs with Osnabrueck University in Germany and the University of Kansai Gaidai in Hirakata, Japan, and over one hundred locations around the world approved by the International Student Exchange Program.

Less promising than classics is Southwestern's vigorous feminist studies program, which offers courses in the standard range of ideologically charged topics, including "queer theory."

The students we consulted say it is important to choose courses and professors judiciously. One art teacher, Thomas Howe, comes highly recommended for lectures on topics such as archaeological site preservation, in which he is a world-renowned expert. Southwestern has, according to one student, "Some of the best professors I've heard of, and since it's a small school they are very willing to help you in any way." Another reports that there are no teaching assistants. According to a current undergrad: "The two departments in which I spend most of my time are theater and English. The faculty in these two departments are astounding." There's a reason why professors seem to be to pupils' liking: students are involved in hiring them. According to the influential book *Colleges That Change Lives*, Southwestern is one of relatively few colleges where undergrads have a voice in which prospective faculty are employed by the school. Other highly praised teachers at SU include Aaron Prevots in French, Tim O'Neill in political science, and Kenny Sheppard in music.

"SU is certainly not right for everyone, but it is a great place for motivated students for whom academics come first. . . . To more liberal-minded students, SU can feel way too conservative; however, conservative students often think it's extremely left-wing."

Students note that some faculty, for instance in the English department, use feminist theory as a filter through which to view course material. It's best to ask around before registering for a class if you wish to avoid this sort of thing. One student tells us "The ideology of some of the instructors does make an appearance [in the classroom], if usually not too offensively." "Attacks on Christianity occurred occasionally, most were humorous in nature and the profs admitted their lack of knowledge," says another.

Overall, "Southwestern provides an extremely valuable learning experience to all students who are willing to cultivate relationships with the faculty and other students. This is definitely not the place to be if you truly want to be a number and to disappear with the masses. All of my professors have been extremely bright and concerned with the quality of my education, as well as how I am doing personally," one student raves.

One department that might be worth a skeptical look is psychology, according to another undergrad. As one student majoring in that field complained in a published online discussion, "Research is the key focus of this school, despite its lack of resources.

The professors are condescending if you are not one of their favorites. Moreover, grades are all anyone (students and faculty) cares about and it gets in the way of actual learning."

Whether or not this is true of that student's department, it seems not to reflect the school as a whole. Perhaps more representative was the student who wrote

> SU is certainly not right for everyone, but it is a great place for motivated students for whom academics come first with campus involvement a close second. There are tons of things to get involved with, and none of them are exclusive to a "certain type" of person. To more liberal-minded students, SU can feel way too conservative; however, conservative students often think it's extremely left-wing. I guess that just shows that everyone will find something to complain about, but I think that's true anywhere you go.

Notable Southwestern alumni include Red McCombs, former owner of the San Antonio Spurs, Denver Nuggets, and Minnesota Vikings; Pete Sessions, congressman from Texas; Major League pitcher Mike Timlin; John Tower, senator from Texas; and actor Jerry Wayne Hardin. Southwestern is currently rated by college ranking organizations as the top national liberal arts college in Texas and the Southwest.

Student Life: The Complexity and Ambiguity of Changing Interpersonal Relationships

Georgetown, Texas (pop. 28,339), where SU is situated, is the seat of Williamson County. Located on the edge of the Texas Hill Country, what it lacks in cultural opportunities (outside the university itself) it makes up for with outdoor recreation. Horseback riding, canoeing, hiking, cycling, camping, and rock-climbing are all with easy reach at many of Texas's best parks, rivers, and lakes, Gulf of Mexico beaches, Hill Country trails, and climbing spots. Best of all, when traffic isn't bad the school is only half an hour away from artsy, laid-back cosmopolitan Austin.

Georgetown was founded in 1848 by Tejanos, Swedes, Czechs, Germans, Anglos, and blacks—all of whom left a cultural impact. The downtown has a large number of Victorian architectural gems, centered on the courthouse square, which play host to art shows, festivals, and live music. The Art Deco Palace Theatre features entertainment ranging from classic movies and live music to community plays, and such structures as the neoclassical Williamson County Courthouse and the Williamson County Historical Museum are well worth seeing.

The student body itself is, according to one student, "extremely diverse . . . 60 percent women, with a high gay/lesbian population." It is also close knit: "Everyone knows everything here at school, rumors fly all over the place." One self-described Christian writes online of the inherent tensions: "I don't regret my choice to attend Southwestern, even though the political correctness is ridiculous in its implementation sometimes . . . and the workload is enormous. I am a true fish out of water I guess—a political moderate in a group of extremes, a conservative fiscally amongst liberals, a virgin amongst the atmosphere of casual sex and 'hooking up.'"

Another student wrote of the school (on a college critique website, StudentComment.com): "The student body is a mixture of very liberal . . . and highly conservative, so wars of words via the e-mail listserv will clog your boxes. But I love the atmosphere and the curricula, which were the deciding factors for me."

Historically, American Methodists have harbored grave suspicions regarding alcohol: they originated the custom of serving grape juice at Holy Communion. In keeping with this, SU "supports abstinence from alcoholic beverage use," but does not enforce it for students of legal age. All sorts of anti-alcohol and anti-drug instruction and assistance are available to students, both in and out of the residence halls.

Living on campus is key to an SU education, according to the school, which strongly encourages it for upperclassmen and requires it of underclassmen. Some 83 percent of students live on campus. The "varied living options, from traditional residence halls to apartments, both single gender and coed," contribute to what the university optimistically calls "exploring interpersonal relationships and becoming comfortable with the complexity and ambiguity of changing interpersonal relationships." Ahem.

SUGGESTED CORE
1. Classics 07-203: Greek and Roman Mythology (*closest match*)
2. Philosophy 18-313: History of Western Philosophy: Ancient
3. Religion 19-123/19-133: Introduction to the Hebrew Bible / Introduction to the New Testament
4. No suitable course.
5. Political Science 32-613: Political Philosophy (*closest match*)
6. English 10-703: Shakespeare
7. History 16-233: U.S. Civilization
8. Philosophy 18-333: History of Western Philosophy: Nineteenth Century (*closest match*)

Activities on campus include NCAA baseball, basketball, cross-country, golf, soccer, swimming/diving, tennis, and volleyball for both sexes. The school long ago abolished sports scholarships. Two eating and entertainment centers on campus are the Commons and the Cove. Annual events include Homecoming, Mall Ball, Sing, Brown Symposium, Parents' and Grandparents' Weekend, SU Day of Service, and Late Night Breakfast. Moreover, the Office of Student Activities and the University Programming Council put on a number of weekly events such as the Cove Concert Series every Wednesday, the Friday Night Live performances, and Cinematic Saturday movies.

Some students party hard at the wide array of Greek events offered on weekends, while others stick to their books. Although their numbers have dropped to around 30 percent since the 1960s, when a majority of students pledged, Greek organizations are still prominent on campus. "The Greeks try to control all facets of social life on campus, what little there is, which always felt cliquish to me. However, there are nearly one hundred organizations on campus, so if you want to fit in without beer and parties, you don't have to go Greek to do it," one student writes.

More than ninety extracurricular clubs on campus "represent interests that range from student legislation to social activism, literary publications to Greek life," says the

ALL-AMERICAN COLLEGES

school. "If you cannot find an organization that suits your interest, then create your own. Organizations are classified in eight categories: Departmental, Governing Bodies, Greek/Social, Religious, Sport Clubs/Athletics, Scholastic/Honorary, Special Interest, and Student Media." Politically, student divisions are represented by thriving College Republican and Young Democrat chapters, as well as the Sexual Orientation Awareness League, whose stated goal is to be "an open forum for the discussion of gay, lesbian, bisexual, and transgender issues." The student paper is the *Megaphone*.

Despite SU's Methodist background and ethos, religious organizations also reflect student diversity, as shown by the Jewish Student Association, Canterbury of SU, Catholic Student Association, Cross Training, Fellowship of Christian Athletes, Kappa Upsilon Chi, Lutheran Students at SU, Muslim Student Association, Sigma Phi Lambda, and (not too surprisingly) the United Methodist Student Movement. These play an important role at SU, because, "while the University Chaplain offers programs, services and pastoral care, most of the opportunities in religious life are student organized and student led." The Lois Perkins Chapel is a beautiful Gothic structure completed in 1950 that offers weekly interdenominational services—on Thursdays. Other special events throughout the year include "Candlelight," a service of lessons and carols in honor of Advent, and Ash Wednesday services. Catholics on campus might prefer to venture into Austin, perhaps to the beautiful downtown cathedral. Episcopalians' local parish, Grace Church, occupies a relatively new building.

The campus is said to be quite safe. In the period from 2002–4 it witnessed five rapes and thirteen burglaries.

As private schools go, Southwestern is not so bad (in relative terms, of course), with tuition of $23,650 and room and board ranging from $6,700 to $8,628. The school reports that "46 percent of students get need-based financial aid averaging a little more than $17,790 a year, with another 33 percent receiving merit scholarships averaging $8,294 a year." Much of this largesse is made possible by earnings from the university's permanent endowment, which exceeds $280 million.

THOMAS AQUINAS COLLEGE

SANTA PAULA, CALIFORNIA • WWW.THOMASAQUINAS.EDU

Deep in the southern California countryside there is a tiny college that aims at grand things: preserving the ways and ideals of old Christendom. According to the college, "Fundamental in the Catholic intellectual tradition is the conviction that learning means discovering and growing in the truth about reality. It is the truth that sets men free and nothing else. Since truth concerns both natural and supernatural matters, the college's program has both natural and divine wisdom as its ultimate objectives." In pursuit of this wisdom, the school employs no textbooks, instead putting all students through a "prescribed, four-year interdisciplinary course of studies . . . based on the original works of the best, most influential authors, poets, scientists, mathematicians, philosophers, and theologians of Western civilization. In every classroom, the primary teachers are the authors of the 'Great Books' from Aristotle, Homer and Euclid to St. Thomas Aquinas, T. S. Eliot and Albert Einstein." Instead of lectures, students go through "tutorials, seminars, and laboratories guided by tutors who assist students in the work of reading, analyzing, and evaluating the great works which are central in the collected wisdom of Civilization." There are no more than twenty students in each class, and everyone receives "daily practice in the arts of language, grammar, and rhetoric; in reading and critical analysis of texts; in mathematical demonstration; in laboratory investigation. . . . There are no majors, no minors, no electives, no specializations. The arts and sciences which comprise the curriculum are organized into a comprehensive whole."

The philosophical basis of this unusual setup is, quite simply, Catholicism, which the college feels is indispensable to understanding reality, declaring that "education is responsible first and foremost for helping its students perfect their intellects under the light of the truths revealed by God through the Catholic Church." Thomas Aquinas College takes its commitment to the church seriously. It is one of the few "Catholic" universities and colleges in the United States where teachers of theology follow Vatican policy and swear fidelity to church teaching.

The school was opened in 1971 by a group of Catholic academics disillusioned by the fragmentation and secularization of church-sponsored

schools in the late 1960s. The school has grown tremendously since then in its physical plant, the size of its student body and faculty, and in academic renown. Commencement speakers have included Mother Teresa and Cardinal Francis Arinze. In 1999, *U.S. News & World Report* ranked the college the third "Best Buy" among all national liberal arts colleges nationwide.

The college's founders said that they "wanted not to return to some earlier form of education in America, but to something that resonated with the kind of academic excellence that flourished in ancient Greece or in the great medieval universities in Europe. Simply put, they wanted to return not to the 1950s, but to the 1350s. At the same time, they were thinking ahead," recalls the school. If that vision appeals to you, and if you are strongly committed to exploring a specifically Catholic (read, Thomistic) tradition of learning, TAC may be the place for you.

Academic Life: Our Future Is the Past

At Thomas Aquinas College, all students follow the same course of studies. On completion of this course, they each receive the same degree: a B.A. in Liberal Arts. Students take the following courses:

- "Freshman Seminar." Readings include Homer, Plato, Aeschylus, Sophocles, Herodotus, Aristotle, Plutarch's *Lives,* Euripides, Thucydides, and Aristophanes;
- "Freshman Language." Students work on introductory Latin and English composition;
- "Freshman Mathematics." The central text is Euclid's *Elements*;
- "Freshman Laboratory," in which students cover the scientific texts of Aristotle, Galen, Goethe, Harvey, Linnaeus, Pascal, Archimedes, Mendel, and several contemporary authors;
- "Freshman Philosophy." Authors include Plato, Porphyry, Aristotle, and St. Thomas Aquinas;
- "Freshman Theology," which focuses on the Bible;
- "Sophomore Seminar." Authors covered include Virgil, Lucretius, Cicero, Livy, Plutarch, Tacitus, Epictetus, St. Augustine, Boethius, Dante, Chaucer, Spenser, and St. Thomas Aquinas;
- "Sophomore Language," a course that covers intermediate Latin, using Horace, St. Thomas Aquinas, and the text of the Roman liturgy;
- "Sophomore Mathematics." Students read Plato, Ptolemy, Copernicus, Kepler, and Archimedes, among others;
- "Sophomore Laboratory." Authors include Aristotle, St. Thomas Aquinas, Lavoisier, Dalton, Pascal, Mendeleev, and an atomic theory manual;
- "Sophomore Philosophy," which covers the Pre-Socratics and Aristotle;
- "Sophomore Theology," in which readings include St. Augustine, St. Athanasius, St. Anselm, and St. John Damascene;
- "Junior Seminar." Readings include Cervantes, St. Thomas Aquinas,

Machiavelli, Bacon, Shakespeare (histories, tragedies, sonnets), Montaigne, Descartes, Pascal, Hobbes, Locke, Berkeley, Hume, Swift, Milton, Gibbon, Corneille, Racine, Rousseau, Spinoza, Adam Smith, Kant, and Leibniz, plus the Articles of Confederation, the Declaration of Independence, the U.S. Constitution, and *The Federalist Papers*;

- "Junior Music," in which students explore selected writings of Plato and Boethius and the sonatas of Mozart;
- "Junior Mathematics," where the "teachers" are Descartes, Archimedes, Hippocrates, Pascal, Leibniz, Bernoulli, Newton, and Berkeley;
- "Junior Laboratory." Students read and examine experiments by Descartes, Galileo, and Newton;
- "Junior Philosophy," which focuses on Aristotle's *Nicomachean Ethics* and *Politics*;
- "Junior Theology," a class centering on St. Thomas Aquinas's *Summa Theologiae*, *On Sacred Doctrine*, *On God*, and *On Law*;
- "Senior Seminar." Authors include Tolstoy, Goethe, Hegel, Flaubert, Feuerbach, J. S. Mill, Marx, Melville, Willa Cather, Engels, Darwin, Nietzsche, Mark Twain, Jane Austen, Freud, Jung, Newman, Kierkegaard, Ibsen, Dostoevsky, Eliot, St. Pius X, Leo XIII, Pius XI, Pius XII, Plato, Vico, Tocqueville, Husserl, Flannery O'Connor, and St. Thomas Aquinas, plus selected documents of Vatican II and the Lincoln-Douglas debates;
- "Senior Mathematics," in which students read Pascal and Lobachevski, among others, in their study of calculus;
- "Senior Laboratory." Authors include Newton, Huygens, Maxwell, and Einstein;
- "Senior Philosophy," which returns students to Aristotle and St. Thomas Aquinas; and
- "Senior Theology," which concludes with a study of Aquinas's *Summa Theologiae*.

Tutors (as faculty are called at TAC) stick to original sources, rather than textbooks, which as "secondary sources" are thought to be two steps removed from reality: "thoughts about thoughts." At too many schools, TAC faculty complain, the impact of great works and great ideas is blunted by teachers who "historicize" them out of all relevance to the present. At Thomas Aquinas, students encounter and evaluate these

---

VITAL STATISTICS

Religious affiliation: Roman Catholic
Total enrollment: 359
Total undergraduates: 359
SAT/ACT midranges: SAT V: 630–740, M: 570–650; ACT: 24–29
Applicants: 196
Applicants accepted: 81%
Accepted applicants who enrolled: 64%
Tuition: $19,300
Room and board: $6,000
Freshman retention rate: 88%
Graduation rate: 68% (4 yrs.), 73% (6 yrs.)
Courses with fewer than 20 students: 98%
Student-faculty ratio: 12:1
Courses taught by graduate students: none
Most popular majors: n/a
Students living on campus: 99%
Guaranteed housing for 4 years? yes
Students in fraternities or sororities? none

works based on their actual merits—and in the process sharpen their own faculties of reasoning.

All works are taught via the Socratic method. "Each one of us brings certain fundamental ideas to education which must be made explicit before learning can advance," says the school. "Discussion is the optimum means to bring them forth. The student must, as it were, give them birth; the teacher, as a good midwife, only assists the labor." Thus, the tutor at TAC may guide the discussion, doing his best to keep it on track and to ensure that all students are involved. But it is not his role to interpret the work under discussion. Rather, it is to make sure that each student is engaged to the utmost. For this reason classes must be kept to fewer than twenty, lest the discussion become unwieldy or some students manage to escape participation.

Teachers at TAC suggest that secular schools approach works by the likes of Augustine and Aquinas as if they were merely museum-goers looking at an exhibit of fragments of a dead past. Instead, tutors and students at TAC view them as portals to some aspect of Truth. TAC holds that we can know Truth and strives to help students discover it for themselves. Since the school unabashedly regards the Catholic synthesis of faith and reason as the best approximation of that Truth, church teaching and authority inform most classes.

"In every classroom, the primary teachers are the authors of the 'Great Books,' from Aristotle, Homer, and Euclid to St. Thomas Aquinas, T. S. Eliot, and Albert Einstein."

Teaching is decidedly "low tech." Not only are lectures not used, but computers, calculators, and audio-visual techniques are all banned as "shortcuts" that allow one to escape actually thinking. No one would be caught dead carrying Cliff's Notes around campus.

The school intends that each student should acquire "intellectual virtue," a burning desire to educate himself for the rest of his life. Here, TAC aspires to the same heights of the pursuit of wisdom that characterized medieval universities. That they have succeeded to a great extent is revealed by the occasional emergence of intellectual conflicts among students (and sometimes faculty) as bitter as any that divided the University of Paris in the days of Abelard and William of Champeaux. The circulation among the student body in the 1990s of a privately prepared "Book of Leo" still resonates as an example of such controversy. Some saw the book, a compilation of writings by Pope Leo XIII and other authorities on Catholic social teaching, as an attack on the American political system. The debate over its contents led, on at least one occasion, to a fistfight. In the end, the administration ordered the document suppressed because of its "divisiveness." Other topics that occasionally cause similar episodes are monarchy versus democracy and the old Platonist/Aristotelian rift that agitated so many campuses in the Middle Ages. If reading this makes you nostalgic, for heaven's sake, go to TAC: you couldn't possibly choose more wisely.

Arcane as these disputes may seem, they do suggest the college's success in getting students to take scholarship seriously and to make the quest for wisdom a key part of their lives. Says one observer of the TAC scene, "These episodes may be embarrassing, but they are proof that the students are serious in their views. And if they get worked up now, they will surely stand strong for principle in the real world."

SUGGESTED CORE

The school's required core curriculum suffices.

Tutors and their close personal involvement with students make education at TAC an adventure, rather than a slog through old books. Students particularly recommend professors Mark Clark, Richard D. Ferrier, John W. Neumayr, John Nieto, and Laurence L. Shields. Although, because of the intensity of their work, faculty members at TAC may not publish as much as those at other colleges, one comes across their articles in prestigious publications from time to time.

If students have a complaint, it is of a certain rigidity among core faculty, who act as if Aristotle and Aquinas held a monopoly of truth between them—as interpreted by the version of Thomism regnant at the school. But this self-confidence does not descend into dogmatism. One student says, "Most of the students in my class were basically Platonists. They often disagreed with the teacher, but so long as they could prove their points, he was okay with it; I saw none of the students penalized for their views—as long as they could defend them."

Student Life: A Hamlet on a Hill

TAC lies between two small towns—the still rural but rapidly sprawling Santa Paula, and the somewhat more sophisticated (and oddly New Age) Ojai. Between them, the two towns offer a full range of cultural and culinary experiences. But there can be no doubt that the college itself is the real center of the students' lives. TAC is a tight-knit community, with all the advantages and disadvantages that this implies. There is warmth and closeness, "but everybody knows everybody else's business—or thinks they do," a student says.

The 360 faculty and staff all live on or near campus. The love of conversation encouraged by the curriculum carries over into other facets of life. TAC students talk—a lot. The visitor will be impressed by many of the casual conversations he overhears, informed as they are by considerations of philosophical virtue and Christian fidelity. Students are refreshingly polite and well groomed.

The college's own description of a typical day runs as follows: "Classes typically begin at 8:30 in the morning and, with a break from 11:00 until after lunch, continue from 1:00 until about 3:30 in the afternoon. Freshmen have 18 hours of classes each week, so this amounts, for a freshman, to about three hours of classes each day. Freshman seminar runs from 7:00 until 9:00 on Tuesday nights. On average, a freshman puts in an hour of preparation for each hour in class. School is, roughly, a forty-hour per week effort." This synopsis is spot on, according to our sources. Breakfast is served in the Commons from 7:30 until 8:15, lunch from 11:45 a.m. until 12:45 p.m., and dinner from 5:30 p.m. to 6:15 p.m. in the evening.

In the midst of all this activity, TAC students find time for music and drama practice, visits to Ojai and Santa Paula, and the ever-present joys of discussion. On the weekend, dances, poetry readings, choir and musical ensemble practice, and trips to nearby beaches, Los Padres National Forest, the mountains, Santa Barbara, Los Angeles, and, of course, Ojai's Bart's Books are all part of the ritual of life.

All unmarried students are required to live in the school's dormitories. The college maintains that "[l]earning is not confined to the classroom but can take place whenever there is a meeting of the minds . . . in the dining hall or coffee shop, along the campus walkways, in classrooms and study rooms, in the dormitory common rooms, even on the basketball court. These meetings are more likely to occur in a residential community than when students see each other infrequently because their education is but one facet competing with busy off-campus lives." There is no lodging available for married students.

Men live in SS. Peter and Paul Hall, Blessed Junipero Serra Hall, and St. Bernard's Hall, while women take up residence in St. Monica, St. Therese of Lisieux, or St. Katharine's halls. Dormitory rooms are suitable for two students. "Freshmen are assigned roommates; in ensuing years, students generally select their own roommates," says the school. Male and female dormitories are always off limits to the opposite sex.

"The possession or use of alcohol or illegal drugs in the dormitories—as elsewhere on campus—is strictly forbidden and may entail expulsion from the program," the school warns. It has recently enforced these penalties.

Student prefects selected by the dean and the assistant dean for student affairs maintain discipline within the dorms. Each dorm comes equipped with a large common room, which serves as the focus for the "family life" of the dormitory. Many lifelong friendships are forged at TAC, to say nothing of many marriages—and not a few religious vocations.

Of course, Catholicism is a huge part of life at TAC. While non-Catholic faculty (outside of theology classes) and students are welcome, it must be remembered that they are in a comparable position to Catholics at schools like Wheaton or Biola (both covered elsewhere in this book). None of our sources had heard that any non-Catholics at the school were disrespected or experienced discomfort—but they did note that everyone at TAC must conform to some degree to the school's ethos. There are no non-Catholic services on campus, but nearby Ventura is host to a number of conservative and evangelical congregations, including Grace Church of the Lutheran Missouri Synod.

Four years of Catholic theology and Thomistic-centered philosophy are only the beginning of the Catholic influence at TAC. The liturgy offered is the Novus Ordo in Latin, with scrupulous adherence to the rubrics—three times daily and on Sunday. Once a month, a Tridentine Mass is offered. The school retains three chaplains: Fr. Michael Perea, O.Praem., Fr. Wilfred Borden, OMI, and Fr. Cornelius M. Buckley, SJ, a former dean of San Francisco University and a renowned scholar in his own right with a Ph.D.

from the Sorbonne. This trio plays an influential role in campus life, not merely by saying Mass, but also in spending many hours counselling students.

There are many extracurricular activities—dramatic, musical, and athletic—available at the college, mostly organized by students. According to the school, "Two seniors are chosen each year by the assistant dean to plan activities and events both on and off campus. [These include:] formal and informal dances, barbecues, intramural sports, backpacking and snow skiing trips, sightseeing excursions, the annual St. Patrick's Day party, [and] Trivial and Quadrivial Pursuit, a favorite 'stump the student' game played by the student body and faculty on St. Thomas Day." The dances are particularly important: "Those who arrive at the College unfamiliar with the two-step, the swing, and the waltz can plan to learn and distinguish themselves in these essential arts," the college notes.

There is a plethora of clubs, primarily cultural or religious. The closest thing to political action is "TACers for Life," whose members make weekly trips to abortion clinics to pray and offer counseling. The choir, schola, dramatic troupe, and two campus magazines offer plenty of opportunities for those who wish to stretch their creative wings.

Not surprisingly, with such a small, self-contained campus and so few students, serious crime is nonexistent.

TAC has largely succeeded at keeping costs down; tuition is under $20,000, while room and board runs at $6,000 or so. Since the college receives no federal campus-based funds or contracts, some federal aid normally available to college students elsewhere is not available at TAC. The college does, however, have its own aid program that is funded through contributions made by benefactors of the college. This program includes both Service Scholarships (work-study) and grants. Some 69 percent of student receive need-based financial aid. The average student loan debt of a recent graduate is a middling $14,000.

THOMAS MORE COLLEGE OF LIBERAL ARTS

MERRIMACK, NEW HAMPSHIRE • WWW.THOMASMORECOLLEGE.EDU

At many colleges, students spend their time collecting blue ribbons and jumping hurdles—all in preparation for forty-five years in a cubicle. The ethos at Thomas More could not be more different. The school was created out of the love of a handful of dedicated educators for a way of learning that seemed, in the 1970s, to be vanishing. It wasn't a romantic nostalgia for antiquity that pushed them on; it was the notion that the tradition of educating the whole person, of enriching him with the life of the mind and the soul, was particularly needed to meet the challenges of our time. That hope, almost thirty years later, still animates this college, located just thirty miles north of Boston in the heart of the higher education capital of this country—beautiful, rural New England. Thomas More College is steeped in the church's heritage of uplifting and humanizing culture; the result is orthodoxy that flows from a joyful spirit. If you're looking for an intense, authentically Catholic liberal arts education in a close-knit community, there is probably no better choice than TMC.

Academic Life: More Is . . . More

Thomas More's mission centers on the courses in its fantastic core curriculum. In addition to courses in their majors, all students must take the following:

- "Humanities I—The Ancient World: Ancient Literature, Politics, and Philosophy." Readings include Homer, *The Epic of Gilgamesh,* the Old Testament, Herodotus, Hesiod, Heraclitus, Parmenides, Plato, and Aristotle;
- "Humanities II—The Ancient World: Ancient Literature, Philosophy, and Politics." Texts covered include Aeschylus, Sophocles, Euripides, Aristophanes, and Thucydides;
- "Humanities III—Rome and the Early Middle Ages: Early Medieval Theology

and Literature." Readings include Virgil, Livy, Plutarch, Cicero, the New Testament, Augustine's *Confessions, The City of God*, and *Beowulf;*

- "Humanities IV—The High Middle Ages: Medieval Philosophy, Medieval Literature." Texts include Anselm, Francis of Assisi, Bonaventure, Duns Scotus, Thomas Aquinas, Dante, Chaucer, and Alfarabi;
- "Humanities V—The Renaissance and Reformation: Renaissance Philosophy, Renaissance Literature." Works include Machiavelli, Thomas More, Erasmus, Shakespeare, Milton, Calvin, Luther, Marlow, Bacon, Ignatius of Loyola, the Council of Trent, Teresa of Avila, and John of the Cross;
- "Humanities VI—Early Modern Studies: Modern Philosophy, Literature, Politics." Works covered are by Cervantes, Descartes, Hobbes, Locke, Rousseau, Pascal, Flaubert, Melville, Dostoevsky, Conrad, Kant, and Burke;
- "Humanities VII—American Studies: American Politics, American Literature." Students read the Constitution, *The Federalist Papers,* Tocqueville, Hawthorne, Thoreau, Emerson, Twain, Fitzgerald, and Faulkner;
- "Humanities VIII—The Late- and Postmodern Era: Contemporary Philosophy, Twentieth-Century Literature." Readings include Marx, Freud, Nietzsche, Heidegger, Guardini, Joyce, Hemingway, and Dostoevsky;
- "Writing Workshop" I, II, III, and IV. Students engage and write about readings in the humanities courses, as well as works of Robert Frost, Richard Wilbur, Yeats, Keats, Donne, T. S. Eliot, Hopkins, and Joseph Pieper;
- "Theology I—Christology and Ecclesiology";
- "Theology II—Sacraments";
- "The Art and Architecture of Rome," taught in Rome;
- "Introductory Latin" I and II and "Intermediate Latin" *or* "Introductory Greek" I and II and "Intermediate Greek";
- "General Biology," "General Chemistry," and "Mathematics" I and II; and
- a junior project, based in one's major, as well as a senior thesis.

The humanities portion of the core curriculum is structured in a four-year rotation so that everyone in the whole school can take the same class together. Founding president Peter Sampo arranged this intentionally, in order to confront each class of students with a "fresh batch" of ideas every year. Furthermore, he meant for upperclassmen to learn alongside newcomers, sharpening their ideas and helping them develop communication skills that would serve them well after graduation. Teachers say that older students undertake a kind of "servant-leadership" in grooming new students and bringing them up to speed. In the tradition of liberal arts education delineated by John Henry Newman, learning at Thomas More is intended to shape young people in the discipline of understanding and independent thinking, within the context of a broadly accepted faith tradition.

The reading and writing load at the school is heavy; freshmen and sophomores are required to write a paper a week on a topic related to the humanities coursework. Such an emphasis on writing has its practical benefits. A chief complaint of employers is the decline of college grads' writing skills. Their recruiters may want to visit TMC.

ALL-AMERICAN COLLEGES

289

Religious affiliation:
  Roman Catholic
Total enrollment: 105
Total undergraduates: 105
SAT midranges: V: 620–690,
  M: 520–600
Applicants: 52
Applicants accepted: 95%
*Accepted applicants who
  enrolled*: 61%
Tuition: $11,100
Room and board: $8,000
Freshman retention rate: 85%
Graduation rate: 88% (4 yrs.)
*Courses with fewer than 20
  students*: 70%
Student-faculty ratio: 11:1
*Courses taught by graduate
  students*: none
Most popular majors: litera-
  ture, philosophy,
  political science
Students living on campus:
  93%
*Guaranteed housing for four
  years?* yes
*Students in fraternities or
  sororities*: none

Many schools have study-abroad programs, and several offer semesters in Rome, but at no other school is the time spent in the Eternal City so pivotal to the educational experience. At TMC, the second sophomore semester in Rome is mandatory; indeed, Peter Sampo considers this interlude the crucial moment in each student's journey. "I've seen students who couldn't pass any of my exams make a complete turn-around," he says. More likely, it's the effect of experiential learning—of seeing, hearing, smelling, tasting, and touching the artifacts of a culture that incarnate the otherwise abstract ideas students encounter in the Great Books. Students speak with great enthusiasm of their Rome semester, particularly of the class in church history through art and architecture, conducted in the churches, excavations, and outdoor cafés of Rome by their irrepressible teacher, Paul Connell. Other lessons learned in Rome can be of lifelong value—for instance, the cooking classes provided by the owner of the Italian restaurant that the school employs to feed its students all semester. Newly hatched student foodies return to enliven fare in the school cafeteria. According to Sampo, "We have other ethnic-food nights, but Italian food night is by far the best."

The most recent class to return from Rome brought back some particularly special memories. These students were in Rome during the passing of Pope John Paul II and the election of Benedict XVI. They speak of being "grateful" to have had the chance to witness history at first hand. One said that he felt they had "been given a gift of being in the right place at the right time, from being in Rome on the night the pope died to being right under the window as the new pope came out to greet Catholics for the first time." The fact that TMC slots its Roman term during the sophomore year is unique, and wise. Students have logged just enough time at the college to appreciate the opportunity, and they have plenty of time afterwards to benefit from it.

When they return from Rome, juniors settle on a major discipline. Or as one professor says, "It is hard to say whether a student chooses a discipline or the discipline chooses the student." The areas of study from which they may choose are literature, philosophy, political science, and biology.

The biology major is a recent addition to the Thomas More curriculum. The school operates on a small scale and does not offer the kind of research-related work (or lab facilities) that a larger college could. But one student felt that the personal training and mentoring she received more than made up for this limitation. Aspiring doctors who attend Thomas More certainly will come away with the kind of humanist education and ethical understanding one wishes were more widespread in that profession.

The Junior Project entails an intense study of one influential author or historical figure covered within the student's major. Working closely with a faculty advisor, a student explores the primary texts of the subject, building up to an extensive oral presentation given before faculty armed with questions, who then grade the student. This project produces student "experts" who go on to contribute to the discussions held in the humanities class. One professor comments, "We can read the *Republic* and ask a student: what would Nietzsche think of that idea?"

The capstone of a Thomas More education is the Senior Thesis, a formal presentation on a given topic within the student's chosen area of study. Each student prepares a substantial research paper, delivers it before the entire school, then passes a comprehensive exam in his or her subject area. The level of academic work attained by most students can be gauged by the fact that a healthy number of Thomas More students go on to excel in graduate work in one of the humanities.

The one question mark that had hovered over Thomas More in the last year or so had concerned its search for a new president. Founding president Peter Sampo had announced he was retiring, and at such a unique (and young) institution, identifying the right successor was by no means easy. But in June 2006, the college announced that Jeffrey O. Nelson, longtime senior vice president at the Intercollegiate Studies Institute (the publisher of this college guide) had been selected to follow in Sampo's footsteps. An intellectual historian with a strong institution-building track record, Nelson's challenge will be to maintain—and build on—the delicate but exceptionally fruitful balance Thomas More College has found between Catholic orthodoxy and humanistic liberality. According to Nelson, "The Catholic understanding of the fundamental unity that envelops the variety and mystery of human existence has been the keystone of Western civilization's achievements. Shoring up that foundation through an integrated liberal arts education is therefore essential for the proper formation of the person. This transformational understanding of education is at the center of the Thomas More College vision." Many believe that Nelson's arrival marks an exciting second chapter to the school's history as it seeks to increase its student body and related activities several times over. He will no doubt draw upon the rich deposit of writing left by his famous father-in-law, the conservative writer Russell Kirk, to chart the future of the college.

> *In the tradition of liberal arts education delineated by John Henry Newman, learning at Thomas More is intended to shape young people in the discipline of understanding and independent thinking, within the context of a broadly accepted faith tradition.*

Student Life: Spontaneous Orthodoxy

Drive up to the Thomas More property and at first you may wonder if you have the correct address. There are only five buildings on campus. In addition to separate dorms for men and women, the campus comprises a colonial-era house used by the administration, a renovated barn, which houses the dining facilities, and the Warren Memorial Library, which looks and feels like it would have been perfectly congenial to Thomas Jefferson. Students say that there is plenty of space for reading and studying. The large rooms host classes, student-led theater, campus films, and visiting lecturers.

It is hard to imagine a college that is more like an extended family. Everyone eats the cook's fine fare together (after saying grace), and groups of students alternate on clean-up duty. The curriculum is well integrated into the daily lives of the students, so the discussion at the table will most likely have to do with the current readings. In season, the chef posts his football picks—which adds some lively digressions to the conversation. But you aren't likely to hear much about the contemporary Beltway political debates. Students here dwell on a more theoretical and intellectual plane, and polemic seems out of place. Both students and faculty would challenge any opinion, leftist or right-wing, which was not well thought out. Students mention that they are given the rhetorical skills to hash out ideas, but that some perennial issues still go back and forth. At this school, no one would argue in favor of legal abortion, for instance, but there are lively debates on subjects where Catholics are free to disagree—for instance, on the death penalty.

There's a surprising range of ordinary human diversity at TMC—athletes, grinds, wannabe poets, and shameless flirts. This makes for fun at such social events as Bad Poetry Night, American Idol for Intellectuals, and the Halloween "dress as a famous intellectual or artist" party. An annual favorite event is the Mock Dating Game. In this version, three bachelors are put to the test with questions like, "Which of Virgil's characters are you most like?" At Thomas More, few men are liable to answer "Dido." The school's most prevalent vice (if vice it be) is smoking.

Friday nights the school hosts a lecture series, and sometimes a speaker will stay on campus and join the students for breakfast. This lecture series is an important part of the school's attempt to keep the students plugged into the world and to keep things from getting too (figuratively) incestuous. The school often brings in lecturers who are experts in the fields being studied in the humanities course that semester. When students were studying the ancient Greeks, Dr. Nalin Ranasinghe and Dr. Glenn Arbery were invited to speak on Plato and the *Iliad*, respectively. Things aren't always so sober; other recent speakers have included a Catholic chef discussing her light-hearted cookbook celebrating the feast days of the saints.

A school operated on this scale could probably plan all its social events over a meal, but Thomas More does have a social council that organizes activities. Otherwise, as one student noted, "Things just happen. Someone remembers that we had an Advent wreath last year, and they go look for it and put it out." Student clubs regularly sprout up, based on the interests of the current class. Informal gatherings are more the norm, since free time arrives sporadically. But don't let the academic seriousness throw you off: TMC students are a fun-loving group. Music, movies, and hiking are favorite activities. Off-campus drinking is common, and many students, especially upperclassmen, head to the nearby town of Nashua to drink margaritas alongside undergrads from St. Anselm's (also covered in these pages). Both Boston and Concord, Massachusetts, are less than an hour away for students who want to visit fantastic sites related to our nation's political and literary history.

The school doesn't have any organized sports, but there is a "Y" across the street with a $20 monthly membership fee. Thomas More men do partake in the annual "mud bowl" just before the annual Christmas Dance event. The college chef serves as referee and the teams become "The Sinners" and "The Saints" for the duration.

Mass and confession are available on campus as well as at two local Catholic parishes. Lovers of traditional rites can make the trek to the exquisitely chanted services at Manchester's Melkite Catholic parish, Our Lady of the Cedars. The college has plans to build a beautiful new church dedicated (appropriately, given its location) to the North American Martyrs. Incoming president Jeff Nelson will be charged with realizing this goal as one part of larger campus development initiatives.

In a recent essay in the *Atlantic Monthly,* a successful management consultant wrote, "If you want to succeed in business, study philosophy." Thomas More alumni prove his point. Graduates hold senior executive positions at companies like Microsoft; are increasingly finding success at leading financial institutions, fund companies, and law firms; direct or teach at secondary schools; attend prestigious graduate schools; work at national and state-based think tanks; and go into religious life. Another practical but underappreciated advantage of the TMC experience is that many students find their future spouses as a result of the time they spend at this idyllic New Hampshire campus.

The campus is very safe; in a recent three-year period (2002–4) the only crime reported was a single burglary.

Tuition at Thomas More is a relatively inexpensive $11,100, plus $8,000 for room and board. Students are quick to point out that the school is very generous with financial assistance. Most are on a ten-hour-a-week work-study program that keeps them busy working around campus on repairs, landscaping, and cleaning. The school is committed to meeting 70 percent of the cost to attend and the average student leaves the program about $20,000 in debt. The savvy high school student can participate in the annual Faith and Reason Scholarship essay competition; if they nail the first prize, they will receive a 50 percent scholarship.

UNION COLLEGE

SCHENECTADY, NEW YORK • WWW.UNION.EDU

In 1795, Union College became the first college chartered by the New York State Board of Regents. During the nineteenth century it became quite famous—at one point the equal of any member of the Ivy League in its reputation and in the distinction of its graduates. Founded as a secular liberal arts school in Schenectady, New York, with the ideal of fostering a leadership class for the new American nation, Union counts among its alumni President Chester A. Arthur, noted electrical engineer Charles Steinmetz, and the secretaries of state for both the Union and the Confederacy during the Civil War. (Portraits of the two, Robert Toombs and William H. Seward, hang side by side in the college president's house.) Overall, Union has educated "fifteen United States senators, ninety-one members of the House of Representatives, thirteen governors, fifty important diplomats, more than 200 judges, forty missionaries, sixteen generals, and ninety college presidents, including the first presidents of the University of Illinois, the University of Iowa, the University of Michigan, Vassar College, Smith College, and Elmira College," the school reports. The college keeps alive many of its nineteenth-century traditions, which it considers vital not only in building camaraderie among students but in carrying on the best of the college's past into its future. It also works hard to offer students of "hard" science subjects such as engineering a genuinely humane education. This often-overlooked school with a venerable past and a strong curriculum deserves consideration by passionate students of the liberal arts.

Academic Life: Civilized Studies

Union College requires that a substantial portion of a student's education revolve around its well-thought-out general education requirements. All students must complete the following:

- "First-Year Preceptorial," which is "an introduction to general education, with the goals of improving student writing; developing critical reading skills; stimulating class discussion; becoming knowledgeable about cultural differences; and being exposed to varieties of good writing";
- A two-course sequence in history; students choose either "History of Greece" and

"History of Rome"; "History of the United States to the Civil War" and "History of the United States Since the Civil War"; or "History of Europe" I and II, which go from the fall of Rome to the present;

- two more courses that match the chosen history sequence—"either two courses in literature . . . at least one of which is a survey course . . . or one course in literature and one course in civilization";
- one introductory course in anthropology, economics, political science, psychology or sociology;
- one course in mathematics;
- two courses in basic or applied science, one of which must include laboratories;
- either any sequence of three courses in a classical or modern foreign language or "any related group of three courses in Africana Studies, East Asian Studies, or Latin American Studies." Languages offered include Greek, Latin, French, Spanish, German, Chinese, Japanese and Russian. Students can partly fulfill this requirement through study abroad; and
- at least five courses from at least two different divisions that have been certified as "Writing Across the Curriculum courses" and a "Senior Writing Experience," such as a senior thesis or a senior seminar paper.

Those who wish to supplement the relative rigor of these requirements should look into Union's Scholars Program, which top freshmen are invited to join. It offers extra seminars, research opportunities, trips abroad and mentoring programs, along with a colloquium to accompany the honors students' senior theses.

Students report that campus politics don't get in the way of learning at Union, although political issues naturally come up in class discussion. "I was a conservative student in a class where the most outspoken students and I suspect the professor didn't share my opinions. But the professor didn't ever shut me down. My opinions were valuable and I was appreciated for expressing them," says one satisfied student.

The history department offers more courses than almost any college of comparable size and selectivity. Majors take at least twelve courses in the discipline, including a junior seminar and a two-term senior project. Between the general education requirements and those of the major, anyone specializing in this subject will have to study a good deal of American history—which certainly can't be said of many other colleges.

VITAL STATISTICS
Religious affiliation: none
Total enrollment: 2,180
Total undergraduates: 2,180
SAT/ACT midranges: SAT V: 570–660, M: 590–690; ACT: 25–29
Applicants: 4,230
Applicants accepted: 47%
Accepted applicants who enrolled: 29%
Tuition: $44,043 (includes room and board)
Freshman retention rate: 91%
Graduation rate: 80% (4 yrs.), 84% (6 yrs.)
Courses with fewer than 20 students: 69%
Student-faculty ratio: 11:1
Courses taught by graduate students: none
Most popular majors: economics, political science, psychology,
Students living on campus: 87%
Guaranteed housing for four years? no
Students in fraternities: 24% sororities: 30%

Sometimes a political bias seems suggested by a course description. For instance, a class titled "Since Yesterday: United States History, 1974–2000" features scare quotes around anything smacking of conservatism: "This course looks at the emergence of new social movements (e.g., the women's and environmentalist movements), the rise of the 'new right,' the Reagan 'revolution' in domestic policy. . . ." Still, one history major says that the school is small enough that students who feel they "can't sit still in a class with a bias can avoid some professors by reputation. However every professor in my experience has been fair and respectful to students no matter what views they express."

The philosophy department similarly offers a large selection of courses covering logic, ethics, metaphysics, and the history of philosophy. An off-the-wall-sounding course like "Cyberfeminism," which "will investigate the impact that digital technology has had on human perception, labor, and self-identity, including socialist feminist arguments about the restructuring of work and the possibility of women's liberation due to technology" is offered infrequently, and nobody is forced to take it.

"I was a conservative student in a class where the most outspoken students and I suspect the professor didn't share my opinions. But the professor didn't ever shut me down. My opinions were valuable and I was appreciated for expressing them," says one satisfied student.

The English department offers a wealth of excellent courses for students looking to study the great corpus of English literature. Majors are required to take a series of classes on major English authors, from Chaucer through Keats, Tennyson, and Joyce. They are also, as in traditional English programs, required to take a course in Shakespeare. The department offers numerous courses in American literature and particular studies in nature and environmental writing, the self, and the American Southwest. In some of the higher-level courses, literature is looked at from feminist or black perspectives. But these courses comprise but a few electives. Courses at the 300 level deal with specific periods of literature and the development of major literary forms, such as the novel.

Union does house a women's studies department, a traditional bastion of leftist ideological cant, but it can be easily avoided. Very few courses are exclusive to the department, though in most humanities departments several courses are taught from a feminist perspective.

Top faculty at Union, recognized for both their teaching and their research, include Suthathip Yaisawarng in economics, Hans-Friedrich Mueller and Mark Toher in classics, Teresa Meade and Mark Walker in history, Robert B. Baker and Raymond Martin in philosophy, Ilene Kaplan in sociology, Ann Anderson in mechanical engineering, Hilary Tann in music, Robert Olberg in biology, and William Zwicker in mathematics.

Union offers extensive study-abroad programs for a school of its size. Students can choose to spend terms in Australia, France, Germany, Italy, Vietnam—even Fiji and

Tasmania. In Ireland, Union students take courses taught by the National University of Ireland in Galway in Contemporary Irish culture and Irish history, including electives such as "Medieval Irish Annals," "The Short Plays of Samuel Beckett," and "The Irish Famine." The modern language department offers a French term in Rennes, a German term in Vienna or Freiburg, a Spanish term in Seville or Cuernavaca, and terms in China, Japan, Switzerland, and Russia.

Union makes a special effort to provide future engineers with top-notch undergraduate educations in their fields as well as a serious liberal education. On top of the general education courses, the school encourages such students to obtain a liberal arts minor.

Undergraduate research is considered one of Union's "Five Pillars," and the school pushes students to get their hands dirty in their fields. Currently, engineering students are doing research on new technologies intended to enhance internal combustion engines. "These students have conducted research in diverse areas such as Hydrogen Internal Combustion Engines, Camless valve trains, and the associated alternative engine cycles made possible by this technology, the oxidative stability of Biodiesel fuels, and the design of a thermo-acoustic musical instrument!" boasts the school. Union also offers specialties in computer and electrical engineering.

Union recently announced the appointment of a new president, Stephen Charles Ainlay, recently professor of sociology and anthropology at the College of the Holy Cross in Worcester, Massachusetts.

SUGGESTED CORE
1. Classics 161: Survey of Ancient Epic
2. Philosophy 150: Ancient Philosophy
3. Religious Studies 200: The World of the Bible (*closest match*)
4. Philosophy 131: God and Evil in the Middle Ages: Medieval Philosophy (*closest match*)
5. Politics 330: Enlightenment and Its Discontents
6. English 125: Introduction to Shakespeare
7. History 101: History of the United States to the Civil War
8. Politics 233: Intellectuals and Politics (*closest match*)

Student Life: Father of the Frats

Schenectady is a thriving small city located near Albany, New York, and students can find plenty to do within a short drive of campus. Six Flags New England, the amusement park, is a common day trip for many. Other forms of entertainment may be found at the Albany Symphony Orchestra or the Schenectady Symphony Orchestra. Skiers can take day trips to the Killington and Okemo mountains in Vermont. Hikers have Albany Pine Bush and Gore Mountain. Those who prefer the city will find plenty of cafés and shopping in Schenectady itself or in nearby Albany.

Union's student body of about 2,200 is evenly divided between men and women. All first-year students live in Davidson, Richmond, Webster, or West halls, all of which are coed dorms. There are some single-sex floors in each dorm, and West divides the sexes between two halves of the building. First-year students are matched up by computer based on the living habits they describe in a series of forms. Turning in a form late could mean a bad match regarding sleep and study habits. "My freshman room-mate and I were vinegar and water. So I spent a lot of time hanging out at Green, which was as good a refuge as any," recalls one student.

Upperclassmen have the option of living in one of the school's "Minerva Houses" (see below), in theme or Greek housing, or in on-campus apartments. The houses are self-governing, and students may soon find themselves taking on leadership roles in their houses. Theme houses are touted as helping to build the Union community and are organized around some particular interest. Wells House is dedicated to community service, while Symposium House hosts professor-student conferences and discussions. Two language houses offer students a chance to immerse themselves in the academic study of a foreign language.

Union College is actually the "father" of several fraternities, including the first three founded in the U.S.: Kappa Alpha, Sigma Phi and Delta Phi, each of which had its first chapter at Union. Because of the relatively small size of the school, the Greek organizations do not exert the malicious influence seen at schools of 20,000 or more. "Yes, we host parties and yes, people drink. But there isn't any anonymity at Union. Pretty much everyone knows everyone and takes care of each other. The frats are an extension of that in some ways," says a fraternity brother.

The Minerva Houses—Blueth, Blue, Golub, Green, Orange, Wold and Sorum—are closer to the center of student life than are the Greek residences. Each student belongs to a Minerva House, which has its own "government, budget and spirit," and often an associated professor. Each house has a seminar room, work room, kitchen, and grill. During some hours the work room is reserved for Peer Assistant for Learning (PAL). Minerva Houses sponsor events like small concerts or ones centered around food. Green House recently sponsored breakfast for every Wednesday in April, offering coffee, bagels, muffins, and the *New York Times*, as well as a barbeque and bluegrass on Saturday afternoons. Sorum House offers a 9 p.m. group viewing of *The Family Guy* every Saturday, and maintains a den dedicated to the Class of 1941, including many mementos and articles associated with that class.

Religious chaplaincies exist at Union, but conservative believers may wish to be wary of what they offer. The Catholic program advertises its emphasis on "social jus-tice issues," while the Protestant program describes its minister's job as providing a "non-judgmental listening presence." However, more traditional students at Union have plenty of options in Schenectady. St. John the Evangelist Catholic Church is across the street from Payne Gate and Catholic students have no shortage of options for Mass or devotions. Some 15 percent of Union's student population is Jewish, and Schnectedy offers Reform, Conservative, and Orthodox synagogues. One senior says, "Religion isn't a source of great controversy at Union—the campus is pretty secular. I have friends who went to more religious schools and sometimes I wish it was more of a presence on campus, but those who wish to be part of a community can just walk across the street or take a short ride into town."

Union provides some of the comforts of home to students who miss it. Parents can order a birthday party from the Union Dining Service. For about thirty dollars, the package includes a personalized round layer cake, candles, soda, and a balloon. Students enjoy having an almost "childlike" party. "A couple of my friends asked for cakes or cupcakes and balloons on their birthdays because of its ironic appeal to college-age students. I think it's just comforting," says one student. The meal plans are similar to other schools, offering a set number of meals a week in the "Caf" and an allowance for the cash-and-carry Rathskeller. One freshman mentions that she got the fifteen-meal plan to try and avoid "the freshman fifteen. You can eat too much on the larger meal plan, so a couple of friends and I try to get some healthier food to make in the dorms," she explains.

Crime is not a major concern at Union, though students do urge caution about leaving one's room unlocked. "Schenectady and Union are safe as long as you have common sense," says one. In 2004, the school reported five forcible sex offenses, one robbery, one aggravated assault, thirty-one burglaries, two stolen cars, and two arsons on campus.

Union College carries an elite-school price tag, with "comprehensive fees" (tuition, room, board, and other charges) set at an imposing $44,043 per year. However, financial aid is generous, with 48 percent of students receiving need-based assistance. As a result, the average student loan debt of a recent graduate who borrowed money (not all do) is a moderate $15,132.

VIRGINIA MILITARY INSTITUTE

LEXINGTON, VIRGINIA · WWW.VMI.EDU

Few Americans today are likely to mention the liberal arts and military colleges in the same breath. But the fact is that apart from the three federal service academies (all of which specialize in engineering), the nation's four military colleges and five military junior colleges are all liberal arts schools. In fact, when *U.S. News & World Report* published its 2005 *America's Best Colleges*, its choice as the "top public liberal arts college" in the country was none other than Virginia Military Institute. It seems that cadets can indeed both chew on great ideas and march in time.

Anyone who has attended one of these academies will not find the *U.S. News* ranking surprising; VMI, like its sister institutions, still holds firm to the notion that it is forming the "whole man" through an education that builds all-round leaders, developed physically and mentally, who are capable of guiding their country and community in peacetime and defending it in times of war. If you aspire to become such a person, this school should be one of your top choices.

Founded in 1839, VMI closed briefly during the War between the States—which was rigorously contested by a great number of its graduates and faculty. The latter included physics professor Thomas Jonathan "Stonewall" Jackson. Once the school had been rebuilt from the rubble, it reopened in late 1865. During the Vietnam War, over 300 alumni made the ultimate sacrifice in service to their country, and two alumni were killed during Operation Desert Storm, in which over 500 alumni served. Many are now serving in Iraq and Afghanistan. Jacob G. Hornberger of the Future of Freedom Foundation asserts that "VMI, by producing graduates who do not blindly follow authority and blindly obey orders, produces superior officers to those of the professional military academies." Notable alumni include Benjamin Franklin Ficklin, a founder of the Pony Express, and George Marshall, Army Chief of Staff during World War II and a Nobel Peace Prize winner, among many other luminaries—the most recent being Kenyan immigrant Michael Lokale (Class of 2003), a Rhodes scholar and famous distance runner.

Academic Life: The Arts of War and Peace

As a school with a definite mission, VMI "carefully limits the scope of the academic program in order to ensure curricular and extracurricular offerings of the highest quality." There are fourteen majors and twenty minors, as well as a number of special offerings, including the Institute Honors Program and the Undergraduate Research Initiative, the Office of International Programs, and the Institute Writing Program.

The core or "Rat" curriculum, which all freshmen must take, is impressively substantial. All cadets study in their first year:

- two courses in English composition, which must be passed with a C or better;
- at least two mathematics courses (science and engineering majors take three);
- two courses in chemistry;
- with a few exceptions, at least two semesters of world history;
- two courses out of these three: "Aerospace Studies," "Military Science," and "Naval Science";
- two semesters of physical education (this on top of all the drilling and marching that is required);
- two semesters of a foreign language (for liberal arts majors). Choices include Arabic, French, German, Japanese, and Spanish; and
- two writing-intensive courses, at least one of which must be within one's major department.

There is no classics major at VMI and neither Latin nor Greek is offered. The liberal arts majors are English, fine arts, history, international studies, and modern languages and cultures. Each of these is taught in an interdisciplinary fashion. For example, "English majors . . . take a variety of courses in literature, philosophy, history, foreign languages, classics, the fine arts, and the sciences. With twenty-seven hours of free electives, they are also able to pursue minors in other departments, as well as concentrations in writing or fine arts."

The school sees education in the liberal arts as a means of making graduates more effective as soldiers and leaders. With a results-oriented outlook that seems fitting in a military academy, the English department notes that its alumni "have been successful in graduate schools of law, business, medicine, theology, psychology, and art, as well as English. The department has placed its graduates in some of the best graduate schools in the country, and about 55 percent of our English majors earn advanced degrees, primarily MBAs and law degrees. English graduates are equally successful on the job market. In a recent survey, approximately 70 percent of English alumni reported earned income over $60,000 a year. One-third of English majors reported earned income over $100,000 a year."

This sort of pragmatism may rankle those devoted to scholarship and knowledge as ends in themselves. However, it has positive side-effects; one alumnus says of the school, "There are no 'fluff' electives or gender studies, and the instructors are extremely respectful of the canon." Moreover, the coursework is rigorous, demanding the development of keen writing and research skills. Noted faculty include Drummond

VITAL STATISTICS

Religious affiliation: none

Total enrollment: 1,300

Total undergraduates: 1,300

ACT median: 23

Applicants: 1,479

Applicants accepted: 55%

Accepted applicants who enrolled: not provided

Tuition: $4,382 (in state), $18,582 (out of state)

Room and board: $5,666

Freshman retention rate: 87%

Graduation rate: 66% (4 yrs.)

Courses with fewer than 20 students: 74%

Student-faculty ratio: 11:1

Courses taught by graduate students: none

Most popular majors: business/managerial economics, history, engineering

Students living on campus: 100%

Guaranteed housing for four years? yes

Students in fraternities or sororities: none

Ayres, Col. Bill Badgett, and Col. John Leland in English; Col. Malcolm Muir and Col. Bruce Vandervort in history; Maj. Benjamin Kleinerman and Clifford A. Kiracofe Jr. in international studies; and Mary Ann Dellinger and Brig. Gen. Alan Farrell in modern languages. By and large, the teachers are "an extremely devoted group, with a higher dedication to their students than I saw in the Ivy League," one graduate says.

Of course, the biggest difference between VMI and other top-notch liberal arts schools is that its students wear uniforms and answer the call of the bugle—which governs their daily lives. A VMI cadet has to be ready to dash away from a calculus exam to a field training exercise—or vice versa. The school maintains that at VMI, "you will enter an environment steeped in tradition—where academic quality is paramount, where performance of body and mind intersect, and where development of character is essential." Despite the uniforms and discipline, however, VMI is not aimed at turning out a standardized batch of interchangeable parts. Indeed, students tell us that the hallmark of the VMI experience is the individual attention they receive, made possible by a low (11-to-1) student-faculty ratio, and the relationships forged in barracks life.

The institute's military tradition is a proud one. Since the Mexican War, every one of this country's conflicts has prominently featured VMI grads. Not surprisingly, the institute served its native state during the Civil War. Indeed, 98 percent of all VMI graduates—regardless of age—served in that struggle. When Union forces came close to Lexington, the cadets themselves were deployed against them. The result was the 1864 battle of New Market, the only time in the nation's history when an entire student body has fought as a unit in pitched battle. In tribute to the ten cadets who died and the forty-seven who were wounded, to this day VMI cadets are allowed to parade with fixed bayonets. Six of the fallen cadets are buried on the VMI grounds, and the Corps of Cadets pays annual tribute to them in formal ceremonies on May 15. Today, all cadets participate in one of the Reserve Officers' Training Corps (ROTC) programs offered by the Army, Air Force, and Navy/Marine Corps. Although actual service in the armed forces is not required of VMI grads, it is strongly encouraged.

Student Life: The Thin Gray Line

Lexington, Virginia, is a small town in the Blue Ridge Mountains. But given the presence of both VMI and Washington and Lee University, the town offers that paradoxical combination of sophistication and "down-home" flavor so common to rural academic centers in the South. Admission to VMI means entering a world all its own, with manners and ritual foreign (and sometimes repellent) to outsiders. Of course, many VMI grads someday will find themselves doing things that most outsiders will not, like leading soldiers into battle. This calls for a different sort of preparation than what is offered at most colleges—something that reporters, outside activists, and meddlesome judges seem not to understand.

Key to VMI's way of life is the "Rat" system, analogous to that of "Knobs" at the Citadel or "Plebes" at West Point. Encompassing the first year a cadet spends at the institute, the Rat system is administered by "Old Cadets," as upperclassmen are called. According to the school, the system's purpose is to teach New Cadets, in the shortest period possible:

- "excellence in all things";
- "military bearing, discipline, and conduct";
- "self-control, humility, and self-restraint";
- "respect for authority and the forms of military courtesy";
- "habits of neatness, cleanliness, orderliness, punctuality, and the importance of attention to detail"; and
- "the history and traditions of VMI and cadet life."

Unstated goals include the promotion of class unity and the "brother rat" spirit. Friendships forged in a stern and demanding environment often last a lifetime, surviving challenges both on the battlefield

Ninety-eight percent of all VMI graduates—regardless of age—served in the Civil War. When Union forces came close to Lexington, the cadets themselves were deployed against them. The result was the 1864 battle of New Market, the only time in the nation's history when an entire student body has fought as a unit in pitched battle.

and in civilian life. Being a Rat strips one of whatever self-importance (born of wealth, prowess, or social rank), he might have carried in with him, putting all New Cadets on an equal playing field. One succeeds or fails strictly according to one's abilities and willingness to cooperate.

Much of the Rat system involves seemingly meaningless or bizarre activities: "Throughout most of the first year, the new cadet walks at rigid attention a prescribed route inside the barracks known as the 'rat line,' and double-times up and down barracks stairs. The cadet must be meticulous in keeping shoes shined, uniform spotless, hair cut, and in daily personal grooming. Additionally, the new cadet must memorize school songs, yells, and other information," the school warns. This "is intended to instill pride, discipline, brotherhood, and a sense of honor in the students. A Rat faces many physical and mental challenges and must memorize rules, school songs, and facts about the school and its history. The Ratline is among the toughest and most grueling initiation programs in the country. It is best described as a longer version of the Marine Corps boot camp combined with rigorous academics."

Each Rat is appointed a first-classman (senior) who serves as his mentor throughout the year. But his main source of support will be his fellow Rats. The reason for all of the "sweat parties," early morning and late night runs, and countless push-ups is to help Rats learn to think under pressure and use a team approach to overcoming challenges. After a "Break Out" event in the second semester, Rats become fourth-classmen, and their lives become a bit easier—though nothing is made really easy for cadets at VMI.

Another key element at VMI, as at all military colleges, is the Honor System. This is centered on the Honor Code, which states that "a cadet will not lie, cheat, or steal, nor tolerate those who do." Operated and enforced by cadets themselves, the Honor System is intended to maintain the practice (and punish infractions) of the Code. Should a cadet be reported for breaking the Code, he will be brought up before the Honor Court. If there is sufficient evidence to warrant a trial, it is conducted with randomly chosen cadets as the jury. If the accused is found guilty, there is only one penalty: expulsion—which, however, must be approved and executed by the Superintendent. For students expelled, there is a "Drumming Out" ceremony. Cadets are "awakened in barracks late in the night by the sound of a long snare drum roll followed by a single bass drum beat, repeated over and over again. They then listen in the darkness to an announcement from the president of the Honor Court that a cadet has 'placed personal gain above personal honor, and has left the Institute in shame.' The name of the cadet is never to be mentioned inside the four walls of VMI again," the school reports.

A third key element of life at VMI is the Regimental System. While the ROTC classes are organized into Army, Navy, Marine, and Air Force units, the basic structure of the VMI Corps of Cadets is that of an infantry regiment consisting of two battalions of four rifle companies each and the Regimental Band. The regimental system is overseen by the Commandant of Cadets and his staff, but cadets drill as infantry troops under their own company leadership. Demonstrated qualities of leadership and skill in military and academic studies are the basis of cadets' appointments to noncommissioned and commissioned cadet rank. The First Captain, the highest-ranking cadet, is commander of the regiment. Much of the administration of the Corps of Cadets is given over to cadet officers and their staffs. The whole framework of a cadet's life is based on the structure of the regiment. As might be expected, housing for all cadets is in barracks, and most meals are served in the mess hall.

Physical training is an essential element of a VMI education. If one does not want to join one of the fifteen intercollegiate "Keydets" athletic teams at the NCAA Division I level (about a third of the 1,300 cadets take part), VMI offers more than twenty sports clubs and a number of intramural programs. Everyone must participate in athletics at some level.

According to one cadet: "The VMI Corps of Cadets is mostly self-contained. Cadets go to the Palms Bar and Grille and to Washington and Lee University parties.

There are many clubs within the corps from the Semper Fi Society to the dance club. Dating within the corps is allowed except between freshmen and seniors. Most relationships do not last at VMI, due to the stresses of VMI life. The relationships that do work usually result in marriage."

There are more than fifty cadet clubs, club sports, and organizations at VMI. Among these are military organizations, musical and performance groups, religious organizations, and service groups. The Office of Cadet Life oversees three cadet publications: *The Bomb* (VMI's yearbook), the *Cadet* (the weekly newspaper) and *Sounding Brass* (VMI's literary magazine). The Glee Club is famous and venerable (it dates to 1885), performing up and down the eastern seaboard. Unlike many military schools, VMI permits political clubs. Although the general tenor of student thought at VMI is rather conservative, there are College Democrats as well as College Republicans present on post.

Religion plays an important role at VMI. The Baptist Student Union, the Canterbury Club, the Newman Club, the Officers of Christian Fellowship, and a local Hillel group, which offers services for Jewish students, are all present. The chaplain to the Corps of Cadets is an important figure on campus, and according to the school, "Cadets are encouraged to mature in their faith through prayer (the Jackson Prayer Brigade meets weekly for breakfast), Bible study (small Bible study groups meet on each stoop weekly), fellowship (numerous religious groups assemble on and off campus each week), worship (local churches offer weekly services and a nondenominational Protestant service is held in Jackson Memorial Hall), community service (students are encouraged to participate in activities benefiting those in need), and missions." Jackson Memorial Hall, which is dedicated to the memory of Stonewall Jackson, is an imposing military-Gothic structure. It was built in 1915 with funds paid by the federal government in restitution for damages inflicted on the institute during the Civil War.

It is precisely in the religious sphere that VMI lost a major battle recently—against federal judges. The school came under legal assault for its nefarious practice of offering nondenominational, non-Christian prayers at dinnertime—for instance, on Mondays: "Almighty God, we give thanks for VMI, for its reputation, spirit and ideals. Let Your favor continue toward our school and Your grace be abundantly supplied to the Corps." Two cadets, deeply offended (or perhaps suborned by activists), asked the school to change the prayers. When VMI refused, the lawyers got involved, and in 2002 a three-judge panel of the Circuit Court of Appeals ruled, "Put simply, VMI's supper prayer exacts an unconstitutional toll on the consciences of religious objectors." The following year, the Supreme Court refused to overturn this decision, and so the ominous sound of dinner prayers fell silent.

A far more damaging conflict began in 1989, when feminist pressure on VMI to admit women reached its climax. Given the school's Rat System and Regimental Sys-

SUGGESTED CORE

1. English 374: Classics in Translation
2. Philosophy 201: History of Greek and Medieval Philosophy
3.–4. No suitable courses.
5. Politics 331: Political Theory (*closest match*)
6. English 310: Shakespeare
7. History 205: History of the United States
8. No suitable course.

tem, and the close quarters in which all cadets must live, VMI's leaders (as well as the overwhelming majority of alumni and current cadets) did not feel that the institute was a good place for women. Once again, judges immune to the consequences of their own actions decided that they knew best, and in 1996 the U.S. Supreme Court ruled 7-1 that VMI would have to admit women.

The institute leadership has done its best to integrate the patriotic young women who arrive to join the Corps. But parents and their daughters who are interested in such quaint notions as "modesty" and "virtue" may well wonder if the pressure-cooker environment of VMI is the best environment where they may be pursued. As innumerable harassment incidents in the coed military and in other military colleges have shown, putting young men and women in close proximity leads to all sorts of mischief—and worse.

Security at the institute is not left up to the Honor Court alone: the VMI police are a permanent, professional, state-recognized force who look after both cadets and property. The only crimes of note in 2004 consisted of one rape and thirty-eight burglaries. As might be guessed, VMI is one of the safest campuses in the country.

It is also one of the least expensive—if you're from Virginia. In the 2005–6 year, residents paid $4,382 in tuition; $5,666 in room and board; a $2,606 "auxiliary fee" (for medical services and the like); a $1,678 "Quartermaster Charge" (for uniforms and the like); and a $200 security deposit, coming to a grand total of $14,532. While nonresidents paid no more for the other fees, their tuition was $18,582, raising their total cost to $28,732. The institute's financial aid office is quite zealous in helping prospective cadets "who otherwise would be unable to attend." A number of federal and institutional grants and loans are available for all cadets, and Virginia offers more still for residents. The institute reports that 62 percent of students receive financial aid.

WABASH COLLEGE

CRAWFORDSVILLE, INDIANA · WWW.WABASH.EDU

For nearly 175 years, this small college in central Indiana has been educating young men to "think critically, act responsibly, live humanely, and lead effectively." Dedicated to the serious pursuit of learning and grounded in the liberal arts, the college maintains a distinctive identity that produces what the college calls "a lifetime of loyalty." "Dear Old Wabash, thy loyal sons shall ever love thee," says the old college fight song, written in 1899. Its assertions ring true: Results from a recent student survey indicate that 87 percent of graduating seniors would "definitely choose Wabash if starting over." And school loyalty extends beyond graduation. Another national survey places the college in the top twenty-five among all colleges in alumni giving.

The use of "sons" in the college song is no sexist oversight. Wabash proudly remains one of the few remaining all-male colleges in the land. (It's easy to forget that most schools were single-sex before the 1960s.) In July 2006 the college will inaugurate its fifteenth president, Patrick White, formerly of St. Mary's College, an all-female school in Notre Dame, Indiana. His predecessor, Andrew Ford, headed up the successful "Campaign for Leadership" that brought in over $136 million in gifts, doubling the college's investments. With a $330 million endowment, the college ranks first in endowment-per-student among schools in the Great Lakes Colleges Association (GLCA) and among the top thirty colleges nationally. This permits the school to provide top-notch facilities and generous financial aid, along with small classes conducted by dedicated teachers.

Academic Life: Tradition, Excellence, Challenge

The preamble to the Wabash curriculum states, "We, the Faculty of Wabash College, believe in a liberal arts education. We believe that it leads people to freedom, helps them choose worthy goals and shows them the way to an enduring life of the mind." With the aim of educating its students "broadly in the traditional curriculum of the liberal arts," the college has rigorous general education requirements. All students must complete the following:

- one freshman tutorial. This course is designed to help students "read texts with sensitivity, to think with clarity, and to express one's thoughts with conviction and persuasion." Topics vary widely at the discretion of the professors. Recent course titles included "Science Fiction and Philosophy," "Medievalism and Middle Earth," "Men and Masculinity," and "Global Warming: Fact or Fiction";
- one two-semester common course titled "Cultures and Traditions." Essentially a Great Books sequence, this yearlong class changes annually, according to faculty preference, but it invariably covers high points in the civilization of the West and other traditions. In fall 2005, students read ancient Chinese, African, and Greek literature; the next semester, they studied modern poetry, Mary Shelley, Adam Smith, Marx, the Bible, Ralph Ellison, and W. E. B. DuBois;
- one course in rhetoric, English composition, creative writing or classics;
- three courses in art, music, theater, or literature;
- three courses in economics, political science, or psychology;
- three course, including two labs, chosen from biology, chemistry, mathematics, or physics;
- one course from a selected list in computer science, mathematics, philosophy, economics, political science, or psychology;
- two courses in history, philosophy, or religion;
- tests or coursework to demonstrate proficiency both in English and one foreign language (choices include French, German, Greek, Latin, Russian and Spanish); and
- a written and oral comprehensive exam in their major field.

A student senate representative says, "Wabash is challenging and time-consuming. Most students become completely enveloped in their studies, fraternity, athletic team, social organization, and leadership positions. Students quickly learn that motivation and self-determination are the keys to success. Professors will assist development in every way they can but they will not pamper students. Extension and late assignments without penalty are rare. Grading is strict but reasonable. I have never felt that my grade did not reflect the quality of my effort and knowledge. There are times when severity seems disheartening, but being strict prepares the Wabash man for the world outside of Crawfordsville.... Wabash ensures that each student is well-rounded, confident, educated and prepared to confront and overcome any obstacle faced after he leaves the hallowed halls of her campus."

A graduate says, "Wabash forces students to take a hefty portion of courses from outside their majors or areas of interest. Having majored in English, I was pushed to my intellectual limits in science and math courses and challenged to synthesize disparate disciplines in my 'Cultures and Traditions' (C&T) course."

Wabash sophomores have been taking C&T for over twenty-nine years. During a recent semester, students read Homer's *Odyssey* and studied the ancient cultures of Israel, classical Greece, and classical China. "The purpose of 'Cultures and Traditions,' says a former student, "is to develop students' understanding of not just the Western and American cultural heritage, but the legacies of most of the world's great cultures and civilizations. This course is respectful of the Western tradition and, in some respects, exposes students to other cultures as a way of setting apart the grandeur of the Western/American tradition."

Wabash offers twenty-one majors, a 3-3 program in law with Columbia University, and a 3-2 dual-degree engineering program with Columbia and Washington universities. The student body of 900 enjoys a 10-to-1 student-teacher ratio. Approximately 75 percent of Wabash students go on to graduate or professional school within five years of graduating from Wabash. They are prepared for the demands of graduate school by the written comprehensive exam they must complete in any major, which also entails facing a panel of three professors for their senior oral exam, the "culminating component of a Wabash man's liberal arts education," says a student.

Conservative students will find the political climate at Wabash both accepting and challenging. "While Wabash attracts a conservative student population, the faculty, which like most academic institutions leans more to the left than to the right, is not overtly political inside the classroom," says a student. "Professors have reputations or political bias, but their views usually only become known in their publishing, public speaking, and one-to-one informal conversations with students," he continues. Another student says, "I am extremely conservative and I am challenged by conservative and liberal professors daily. These discussions are stimulating and lead to higher productivity and more critical thinking for students. . . . The political, academic, and social freedom makes Wabash unique and exceptional."

Wabash attracts top-notch professors who are revered among students. A recent graduate says, "They come to Wabash, many of them at least, because it's a place that espouses cutting-edge academic research as much as it does excellence in teaching and student mentoring. . . . By my senior year, I had dined or had drinks with most of my professors and felt like I knew them as people. Wabash professors, especially Warren Rosenberg and William Placher, mean the world to me. . . . I graduated with the feeling that I knew my professors not merely as scholars or intellectuals, but as people."

The religion department is one of Wabash's strongest disciplines. The department focuses primarily on Christianity, but offers courses on Islam, Judaism, and other religions as well. Faculty members have distinguished careers and many are nationally recognized for their scholarship. Students report that expectations are high and that

---

VITAL STATISTICS

Religious affiliation: none
Total enrollment: 871
Total undergraduates: 871
SAT/ACT midranges: SAT V: 530–650, M: 550–660; ACT: 23–28
Applicants: 1,358
Applicants accepted: 51%
Accepted applicants who enrolled: 36%
Tuition: $22,964
Room and board: $6,728
Freshman retention rate: 89%
Graduation rate: 66% (4 yrs.), 70% (6 yrs.)
Courses with fewer than 20 students: 74%
Student-faculty ratio: 10:1
Courses taught by graduate students: none
Most popular majors: English, economics, history
Students living on campus: 91%
Guaranteed housing for four years? yes
Students in fraternities: 65%

the classes are both difficult and lively. One student marvels, "My older brother, who arrived at Wabash with no expressed interest in theology, left Wabash with a B.A. in religion, largely due to the larger-than-life professors." Especially recommended departmental faculty include David Blix, William Placher, Robert Royalty, Steve Webb, and Raymond Williams. The department benefits from the Center for Teaching and Learning in Religion, which is housed on campus. The center "seeks to strengthen and enhance education in North American theological schools, colleges, and universities." Professors from all over the country come to Wabash during the summer to discuss ways they might improve their teaching of religion.

English, history, and classics are also exceptional, though some members of the English department are deemed quite liberal. One student says that the English faculty "knows how to engage students and elicit vibrant class discussions," and that the department is seen as "one of the more dynamic academic programs" on campus. Recommended professors in English include Joy Castro and Warren Rosenberg. Students also speak favorably of the history department, which "boasts tremendous scholars, some leaders in their field," says a student. David Kubiac in classics is a campus-wide favorite.

"Wabash forces students to take a hefty portion of courses from outside their majors or areas of interest. Having majored in English, I was pushed to my intellectual limits in science and math courses and challenged to synthesize disparate disciplines."

The sciences are vigorous at Wabash. According to the college website, over the past ten years medical schools have accepted Wabash students at a rate of 81 percent, about twice the national average; acceptance rates into dental and other health professional schools were even higher. David Krohne, John Munford, and David Polley are particularly recommended in biology. A biology major says, "Dr. Polley is a special teacher. I felt as though I disappointed him and let myself down if I did not work diligently everyday in his class. He is very popular among students because he is extremely well-rounded intellectually."

Nearly 25 percent of Wabash students study abroad with programs in more than 140 countries. Unlike most schools, Wabash will apply the student's financial aid to the cost of the trip, making overseas study more feasible. One student spent a semester in Australia. He says, "For me, the experience was amazing. I was enveloped by a culture in a country thousands of miles away from home. As a student of the liberal arts, this experience was instrumental in my growth as an individual. I heard intense criticism of America daily and found myself defending, rather than applauding, our nation for the first time in my life." The college also has an immersion learning program where professors take their classes to locations around the country and abroad that are relevant to classroom topics. These trips are available at no additional cost to the student and usually take place during spring break or other short recesses. Wabash encourages internships and collaborative student-professor research projects throughout the academic year and during summer breaks.

Wabash houses the Center of Inquiry in the Liberal Arts, whose mission is "to explore, test, and promote liberal arts education, and to ensure that its nature and value are widely understood in an increasingly competitive higher education market." Among other projects, the center is currently involved in a collaborative nationwide research effort studying the effectiveness and outcome of a liberal arts education.

Student Life: Testosteronopolis, Indiana

Crawfordsville, Indiana, is a community of 15,000 located forty-five miles northwest of Indianapolis and 150 miles southeast of Chicago. *Ben-Hur: A Tale of the Christ,* by General Lew Wallace, was researched and written under a beech tree near Wallace's home in Crawfordsville. The general also served as a state senator, governor, ambassador, and jurist in the trial of John Wilkes Booth. (Wabash claims Wallace as one of its most famous alumni. There is, however, some debate as to whether he actually qualifies as a Wabash alumnus. Wallace was only thirteen when he attended the college's affiliated preparatory school.) Known as the "Athens of Indiana" for the number of writers it has produced, Crawfordsville is ranked forty-third in Norman Crampton's *100 Best Small Towns in America.* The historic downtown has more than 200 small businesses, cafés, art galleries, and other attractions.

Wabash's sixty-acre wooded campus is beautiful. Brick buildings of Georgian architecture are surrounded by immaculate grounds. Students begin and end their careers at Wabash with the ringing of a bell in Pioneer Chapel, a tradition that started with Caleb Mills, the first professor at Wabash. The college president rings in freshman during orientation and rings out seniors at commencement using the same bell Mills used over 170 years ago. The Malcolm X Institute for Black Studies, which "promotes educational, cultural, and social programs," moved to a new $2 million building in 2003. The $30 million Hays Hall, dedicated in 2004, is the 80,000-square-foot home of the biology and chemistry departments. The recent $5 million renovation of Goodrich Hall expanded classrooms, improved research facilities, and added equipment for the mathematics and physics departments. The $20 million Allen Athletics and Recreation Center, which was built in 2001, includes a fieldhouse with multipurpose courts and indoor track, fitness center, and pool, among other facilities. The Lilly Library holdings include more than 434,000 books and 5,530 serial subscriptions and an extensive media collection.

SUGGESTED CORE
1. Classics 102: Greek Drama (*closest match*)
2. Philosophy 140: Philosophy of the Classical Period
3. Religion 141/162: Hebrew Bible / History and Literature of the New Testament
4. Religion 171: History of Christianity to the Reformation
5. Political Science 335: History of Political Thought: Hobbes to the Twentieth Century
6. English 216: Introduction to Shakespeare
7. History 141: America to 1877
8. History 131: Nineteenth-Century Europe (*closest match*)

Undoubtedly, its all-male student body (one of only three in the county) is Wabash's most distinctive trait. But the campus is not entirely devoid of women. There are a number of female faculty members, and young women from Butler, Indiana, Purdue, and DePauw universities frequently come to socialize. A student says, "There are more honest and intense discussions at Wabash than there would be at a coeducational university. Men seem to be more comfortable in the classroom without females' presence. Men are less intimidated and more confident in their ideas at Wabash and this stimulates fervent discourse in and out of the classroom."

The college has a strong Greek identity. Two-thirds of the student body lives in one of the ten fraternities on campus. Those students who choose not to go Greek live in one of five on-campus residence halls with the option of single, double, or triple rooms. Juniors and seniors may live off campus. One student says, "Living in a fraternity has changed my life. Going beyond the friendships, brotherhood, and parties, living in a fraternity has taught me responsibility, accountability, loyalty, and cooperation."

There are plenty of organizations and clubs for the Wabash man. A recent graduate says, "Since Wabash is a small school, opportunities to get involved with extracurricular organizations abound." Students can choose from sports clubs like the Cricket Club, which is devoted to the promotion of "the gentleman's sport." There are a number of service organizations, foreign language clubs, musical groups, religious groups, and preprofessional societies. Several organizations are dedicated to "the understanding of diverse cultures and lifestyles," such as the Muslim Students Association and 'shOUT, the official student organization for "gay, bisexual, questioning and supportive students dedicated to campus awareness of the issue." The college also has a variety of campus publications and a radio station, WNDY. With over ninety participants, this station is the largest student-run organization on campus.

The Brew Society is one of the newest clubs on campus. It was approved by and received funding from the student senate. "Most schools would prohibit such an organization and funding from the college would be considered absurd," says a biology major. "At Wabash, this club was not only formed, but applauded by many faculty. Brewing beer is a very meticulous time-consuming process utilizing biochemical knowledge to manipulate the yeast's enzyme activity. The Brew Society became a forum for discussion about cellular biology and protein properties." This Wabash man has a fine future in public relations, we expect.

The Wabash "Little Giants" compete in the North Coast Athletic Conference (NCAA Division III) in ten varsity sports, with nearly half the student body participating at the varsity level. One student boasts, "Chadwick Court is known as the loudest and most intense environment in the NCAC because the student body's passion is palpable and saturating."

The Wabash versus DePauw University contest for the Monon Bell is one of college football's greatest rivalries and dates back to 1890. Wabash won the 2005 game and regained the coveted trophy, a 300-pound locomotive bell from the Monon Railroad. The game draws a large crowd of alumni, local community members, and nearly the entire student body. To date, the two teams have played each other 112 times. Wabash leads the series 52-51-9.

In another longstanding Wabash tradition, over 200 screaming freshman belt out the lengthy school song, "Old Wabash," in competing to win the annual "Chapel Sing" for their fraternity. "It's unlike anything you'll see elsewhere," says a former Wabash student.

A single regulation governs all aspects of campus life. "The Gentleman's Rule" states that a Wabash man will "conduct himself at all times, both on and off the campus, as a gentleman and a responsible citizen." No other regulations exist, so students must take personal responsibility for their actions. The interpretation of the rule resides with the dean of students, who is said to be "very fair but stern when addressing breaches of the Gentleman's Rule," according to a student. The rule extends to issues of academic honesty as well as social life, including the use of drugs and alcohol on campus. It must be working. There has not been a single drug or alcohol violation reported in the last three years. There were, however four burglaries and one aggravated assault on campus in 2004.

The estimated comprehensive cost of attending Wabash for 2005–6 was $32,116, which includes $22,964 for tuition and $6,728 for room and board, plus personal expenses, the cost of books, and other fees. Students who live in fraternities pay anywhere from $5,600 to $6,800 for room and board. Wabash's substantial endowment underwrites a generous program of merit-based scholarships. Almost three-quarters of Wabash students receive need-based aid; Wabash meets 100 percent of demonstrated financial need. Each spring, during the Honors Scholarship Weekend, high school seniors compete for over $3.5 million dollars in scholarship awards. The average recent Wabash graduate owes $17,328 in student loans.

WHEATON COLLEGE

With its strong commitment to both the liberal arts and Christian orthodoxy, Wheaton College has earned its reputation as the most respected conservative Protestant institution of higher learning in the United States. Students who enter Wheaton emerge inspired and transformed. One student says, "There is no other school in the country that combines extraordinarily rigorous academics with an authentic and committed Christian faith. I was challenged and stretched intellectually and spiritually by being here. The Bible says that as iron sharpens iron, so one man sharpens another. There is a lot of sharpening happening at Wheaton." A recent graduate with plans to work in economic development and conflict resolution says, "Wheaton had a profound impact on the way I approach my engagement with the church and society. Like no other liberal arts institution could, Wheaton gave me the Christian framework within which I could best understand the world God has created. Like no other Christian institution could, Wheaton gave me the first-rate scholars and mentors who pushed me to think critically and creatively about Christian citizenship." For students of an evangelical bent, there are few schools which offer a comparable synthesis of faith and reason at such a high level of academic excellence.

Academic Life: "Here I stand; I can do no other."

The purpose of general education at Wheaton College is "to introduce men and women to an understanding and appreciation of God, His creation and grace, and to our place of privilege and responsibility in the world He has made," says the school. Wheaton's curriculum "encourages students to ground all aspects of life in the Word of God, leading to a firm commitment to Christ and His kingdom." This is accomplished in part through Wheaton's general education requirements, which, though they do not constitute a true core, do impart an understanding of the fundamentals of Western culture and history. As one student says, "Wheaton students come to understand that in order to be most effective for the future, we must understand our civilizational past, in both its triumphs and its tragedies." All students must complete the following:
- "Theology of Culture";
- one or two courses in the Old Testament, and one or two courses in the New Testament (students may test out of an introductory class in each case);
- two classes in Christian thought, chosen from a short list of solid offerings;
- one philosophy class, such as "Issues and Worldviews in Philosophy,"

"Contemporary Moral Problems," or another approved course;

- one of three history courses—either "World History," "World History: Ancient to Modern," or "World History to 1600";
- two classes in social sciences, with choices like "Introduction to Anthropology," "Comparative Politics," "Third World Issues," and others;
- coursework or tests to show competency in a foreign language (French, German, Spanish, Greek, Latin, or Hebrew);
- coursework or tests to show competency in quantitative skills;
- test scores or coursework to prove competency in oral communication;
- test scores or coursework to demonstrate competency in writing skills;
- one introductory lab course in a "hard" science, plus another upper-level class, including at least one class in biology or geology and one in astronomy, chemistry, or physics;
- one course in literature, possibly "Classics of Western Literature" or "Survey of Spanish Literature";
- one class in the fine arts, such as "Introduction to Music" or "Arts Survey";
- a three-hour course in wellness, plus one hour of physical education; and
- a senior capstone course in the student's major.

The college offers forty majors to its 2,400 undergraduates. There are many fine departments, the most popular being English, business/economics, music, communications, and psychology. Wheaton also has many outstanding professors. A student says, "If I were forced to limit my praise to a single aspect of Wheaton College, it would undoubtedly be the professors. Professors teach virtually all classes, office hours are useful, and mentoring opportunities abound." Students say that almost without exception, professors are accessible, open, and helpful.

The "biblically grounded" biblical studies and theology department is legendary, with many internationally renowned scholars and top professors. Students say some of the best teachers in the department are Vincent Bacote, Lynne Cohick, Gene Green, and Andrew Hill.

In the English department, Roger Lundin, known for routinely reciting extended literary passages from memory, is highly recommended. One student calls him "the most intelligent and passionate professor from whom I have ever taken a class." Alan Jacobs, also in English, teaches "Modern Literary Theory," a "must-take" course for anyone interested in learning the art of hermeneutics. Wayne Martindale is a "kind and patient teacher who manages to bring literature to life," says a student. Kent Gramm and Lee Ryken are also recommended.

Peter Hill in economics offers wide-ranging, multidisciplinary analysis on economic matters and is "one of the most well-rounded academics I have ever met," says a student. "He is a great teacher who consistently turns down the opportunity to go to big research universities because he loves to teach," says another. David Iannuzo and Kevin Carlson in the applied health sciences department are both said to be excellent. Students report that the department has become a serious and rigorous academic program in recent years, drawing a number of premed students because of the intensive lab work and research opportunities it provides.

The Department of Politics and International Relations is very strong. "The faculty are recognized scholars in their fields of study and committed to teaching students. Professors encourage thoughtful dialogue and rigorous debate about the important issues relating to faith and politics," one student reports. Mark Amstutz and Sandra Fullerton Joireman come particularly recommended. (Wheaton has the second highest pass rate in the nation for first-time takers of the foreign service exam, and it has had students accepted into twenty-four of the top twenty-five law schools in the country.) Other favorite professors at Wheaton include Edith Blumhofer in history and Bruce Benson in philosophy.

Wheaton's Conservatory of Music produces graduates who have pursued advanced degrees in music at Eastman, Peabody, Indiana University, New England Conservatory, Julliard, and Yale. The department boasts more than 200 majors, plus another 200 liberal arts students who participate in departmental programs such as the Symphony Orchestra, Concert Choir, private music lessons, and music ministry opportunities. I

According to Franklin and Marshall University's latest survey of over 900 private colleges and universities, Wheaton ranked ninth in the nation in the number of graduates who went on to earn doctorates. The college has produced thirty college presidents or provosts, 1,500 corporate leaders, 250 government and foreign service professionals, 1,000 medical professionals, and over 3,000 graduates working in ministry and evangelism. Among its most famous alumni are Speaker of the House of Representatives Dennis Hastert, evangelist Billy Graham, symphony conductor John Nelson, and September 11th hero Todd Beamer. A recent ranking placed Wheaton among the top fifty science departments at liberal arts schools.

Wheaton offers study-abroad programs in Asia, England, France, Germany, Latin America, Spain, and the Holy Land. Wheaton-in-England, an eight-week summer program in English literature, is a student favorite.

The school is emphatically not for everyone. According to the college's mission statement, Wheaton "exists to help build the church and improve society worldwide by promoting the development of whole and effective Christians through excellence in programs of Christian higher education." Guided by this mission, the college has developed a "Statement of Faith" intended to outline its vision of evangelical Protestant Christianity, to which students and faculty must adhere. It is this Christian character that defines and unites the campus. Faculty members are expected to integrate their faith and teaching. New faculty members are required to participate in a yearlong "Faith and Learning" program designed to help them unify their Christian faith and academic enterprises.

If the school knows what it believes, it also knows what it rejects. In 2005, Joshua Hochschild, a young but highly regarded philosophy professor, converted to Catholicism—and was told he would have to leave or be fired. Hochschild believed that he could still sign the school's Statement of Faith in good conscience; the school thought otherwise. In response to the ensuing controversy, college president Duane Litfin told the *Chicago Sun-Times* that Wheaton follows a "systemic model where the entire institution, root to branch to leaf, is about that sponsoring religious tradition. If you are going to be that kind of institution, you have to have people there who embody that tradition. . . . Our hiring policy says you embody what you stand for. This institution cannot exist without that." Wherever one comes down on the university's action—and keep in mind that Hochschild was not in the theology department, but was hired to teach medieval philosophy—it is still rather refreshing to see a religious school take its faith commitments so seriously.

Within the boundaries of Protestant orthodoxy, "Wheaton does foster free and vigorous debate," says a student. Still, the college grapples to set the proper limits for that debate. "If anything, Wheaton is currently erring on the side of caution," comments a student. "The effect on dissent has been somewhat stifling." Another student says, "Rather than an 'anything goes' kind of debate, the opinions that Wheaton students and faculty express, while diverse, move towards the common goal of building the church and society. Wheaton is a Christian liberal arts institution that simultaneously embraces its evangelical heritage and aspires to contribute to the liberal arts tradition from a self-critical stance."

For the most part, the campus fosters open intellectual inquiry. One student says:

> Professors here do not have a particular line that they are trying to impart to you. I found that if you can defend your position, you will be respected—but they make you work to defend your position, whatever it is. Conservative students will feel right at home, if not because of their professors, because of their peers. That is not to say that everyone here is a conservative, in fact, I think that many of the students graduate less conservative than when they arrived—not because they are influenced . . . but because youthful passions mature and are moderated over the course of four years.

VITAL STATISTICS
Religious affiliation: Nondenominational Protestant
Total enrollment: 2,932
Total undergraduates: 2,417
SAT/ACT midranges: SAT V: 630–730, M: 620–710; ACT: 27–31
Applicants: 2,163
Applicants accepted: 51%
Accepted applicants who enrolled: not provided
Tuition: $21,100
Room and board: $6,660
Freshman retention rate: 95%
Graduation rate: 76% (4 yrs.), 86% (6 yrs.)
Courses with fewer than 20 students: 51%
Student-faculty ratio: 12:1
Courses taught by graduate students: none
Most popular majors: English, business/economics, music
Students living on campus: 90%
Guaranteed housing for four years? yes
Students in fraternities or sororities: none

Another student says, "At Wheaton, you will find interesting and intelligent Christians of all stripes"—just no Catholic professors.

Wheaton seeks to enroll professed Christians with strong academic backgrounds. The college can afford to be selective in its admissions; it has only about a 50 percent acceptance rate. Nearly half of the incoming class are from the top 10 percent of their high schools, and about 10 percent of each class are National Merit finalists. Each student applying to Wheaton must provide an academic recommendation from a teacher, a pastor's recommendation, and a 500-word essay on his or her "personal experience of coming to faith in Christ." A student says, "The student body here is very ambitious, but have goals that are substantively different from a lot of other places in terms of the things they want to accomplish." Students at Wheaton, he says, are less interested in "prestige" than in making an "impact" in the world.

> *"Professors here do not have a particular line that they are trying to impart to you. I found that if you can defend your position, you will be respected—but they make you work to defend your position, whatever it is." Another student says, "At Wheaton, you will find interesting and intelligent Christians of all stripes."*

Student Life:
The Lord and the Dance

Wheaton, Illinois (pop. 55,000), is located twenty-five miles west of Chicago. The city of Wheaton and the college grew up together. The village was incorporated in 1859 by the Wheaton brothers, who donated land to the college (which was founded in 1860). Blanchard Hall, named after the first president, is the center of campus and is listed in the National Register of Historic Places. The eighty-acre campus is a blend of Colonial, Victorian, Federal, and Georgian architecture, with many of the newer buildings designed to retain its historic flavor. The newest facility, the Todd M. Beamer Student Center, is named after one of the heroes of United Airlines flight 93; like his widow, Lisa, he was a Wheaton graduate. The $22 million center opened in 2004 and boasts an auditorium, bakery, convenience store, offices, and the Anderson Commons dining facility. Wheaton is rated as one of the best campus food providers in the country. All food is prepared fresh from scratch. Daily, chefs prepare 200 pounds of vegetables, 450 pizzas, and 6,000 homemade cookies. The $15 million Sports and Recreation Center was completed in 2000. It includes a 2,650-seat arena, weight room, three gyms, a running track, and more.

The Wade Center research library holds the most complete collection of C. S. Lewis's material outside of England, including a black oak wardrobe carved by Lewis's grandfather. Whether or not this is the wardrobe through which the children entered Narnia is a point disputed by Westmont College in California, which owns another of

Lewis's old wardrobes. Wade also houses a collection of the works and personal libraries of other Oxford "Inklings," including J. R. R. Tolkien, Owen Barfied, Charles Williams, and Dorothy Sayers, and kindred spirits G. K. Chesterton and George MacDonald. Wheaton holds the complete papers of Madeleine L'Engle, Malcolm Muggeridge, Fredrick Buechner, and other prominent Christian writers.

The Student Activities office exists "to prepare students in becoming whole and effective servants of Christ." To that end, much of the college's cocurricular programming is geared specifically toward developing students' spiritual lives. The Office of Christian Outreach, whose mission is to "transform our cities and the nations by mobilizing worshippers and witnesses," provides opportunities for weekly service projects and a multitude of mission work programs at home and abroad. The chaplain's office administers the Discipleship Small Group Ministry, which consists of student-led groups of four to six who meet for prayer and mutual support. Students are required to attend the three weekly interdenominational chapel services.

The lengthy list of clubs and organizations is refreshingly devoid of some of the more politically correct organizations found on many campuses. Rather, the emphasis is on music, sports, and academic clubs. However, you will find both College Republicans and College Democrats, as well as Amnesty International, Student Global AIDS Campaign, and the provocatively named Students for Biblical

SUGGESTED CORE
1. English 101, Classics of Western Literature
2. Philosophy 311: History of Philosophy: Ancient Greece through the Renaissance
3. Biblical and Theological Studies 211 or 212/ 213 *or* 214: Old Testament Literature and Interpretation / New Testament Literature and Interpretation
4. Biblical and Theological Studies 315 or 316: Christian Thought
5. Political Science 347: Renaissance and Modern Political Thought
6. English 344: Shakespeare
7. History 351: American Civilization to 1865
8. History 463: Enlightenment Modernity and Its Discontents

Equality. The college also maintains an Office of Multicultural Development (OMD), which tries to ensure that Wheaton's minority students feel comfortable and affirmed. There are a number of "diversity" organizations on campus, such as Koinonia, an Asian American fellowship; Unidad Cristiana, a Latino fellowship; and the Wheaton College Gospel Choir, a multiethnic choir.

Wheaton is a member of NCAA Division III in athletics and competes in twenty-two men's and women's sports, winning thirty-four conference titles in the last five years. The college also offers a number of club and intramural sports.

Campus life is governed by Wheaton's Community Covenant, which outlines the Christian goals and ideals of the college. Students and faculty alike must adhere to the Covenant's standards of behavior, which President Litfin calls "a positive statement of our biblical aspirations for life together at Wheaton College." The covenant was revised in 2003, permitting social dancing on campus for the first time in the college's 143-year history. It still requires that members of the Wheaton community affirm biblical standards, live the Christian life, exercise responsible freedom, and embrace college standards. These standards, in short, prohibit undergraduates from drinking, smoking, or gambling while enrolled in the college. Prior to the revision, faculty members and other adults were also required to refrain from alcohol, but under the new covenant, they "will use careful and loving discretion in any use of alcohol." (That sound you hear is C. S. Lewis and G. K. Chesterton clinking their mugs in approval.)

A student says, "I think the fact that students are not allowed to drink or smoke is a terrific benefit. You learn to have good, clean fun—and students do have a lot of fun here. That is not to say that no drinking and smoking happens, but when they do they are in out of the way locations and limited to a select few people."

Because Wheaton believes that Christian growth is aided by community life, all undergraduates must live on campus in college-owned residence halls, apartments, or houses. All residence halls and floors are single-sex. Visitation is permitted on Wednesdays from 7 p.m. to 10 p.m. and on Fridays from 7 p.m. to 11 p.m. Doors must stay open. "I found this (restricted visitation) to be a great thing for building community and friendships on the floors. There are healthy, platonic relationships among men here—unlike many, many other schools," says one student. Apartment buildings are coed and members of the opposite sex may visit until 2 a.m.

Partly because the college is located in an upper-middle-class suburban neighborhood, the campus is generally safe. In 2004, the school reported one aggravated assault, one burglary, one stolen car, and one arson.

Wheaton's costs are not so bad, compared with other selective private colleges. Tuition for 2005–6 was $21,100; room and board added $6,660. Approximately 49 percent of enrolled students receive need-based financial aid. The average recent graduate emerged with a student loan debt of $17,936.

WHITMAN COLLEGE

Walla Walla, Washington • www.whitman.edu

Although it is named for a pair of spectacularly unsuccessful Presbyterian missionaries, this college (founded in 1883) is secular. Amidst the cool, green (and Green-Party) setting of its coastal zone, Whitman College manages to accommodate local environmentalist and multicultural concerns while retaining many of the virtues of a traditional liberal arts college. Courses in Western civilization are still required, and Whitman's humanities programs are vigorous, making this college a prime choice for old-fashioned liberals. That is, for people who might not share Cardinal Newman's theology, but still respect his ideal of humane education—and who want to pursue it in one of the country's most beautiful, unspoiled regions.

Academic Life: A Whittled-Down Core

Whitman College was the first school in the nation to make undergrads complete comprehensive examinations in their majors. In 1919, it opened the first chapter of Phi Beta Kappa in the region. Today, the school has the best graduation rate and the largest endowment per student of any college or university in the Pacific Northwest. Its relative wealth permits the school to maintain a low student-teacher ratio (10 to 1), small classes, and a moderate teaching load—so students can count on extensive interaction with teachers. Whitman also imposes respectable general education requirements. All students must complete the following:

- an abbreviated, but worthy, two-course core sequence, "Antiquity and Modernity." In it, students encounter a sampling of the great works of Western literature and history from the ancient and modern periods;
- two classes in social sciences. Choices range from "Argument in the Law and Politics" to "Introduction to Gender Studies";
- two courses in the humanities. Options range from "Renaissance Art" to "Sexuality and Textuality";
- two classes in the fine arts. Choices here include "Music History: Medieval through 1700" and "The Wardrobe Artist in the Theatre";

ALL-AMERICAN COLLEGES

- two classes in natural science, including one lab section;
- two courses that count as "Alternative Voices." In addition to a variety of politics-infused multiculturalist classes, students can fulfill this through upper-level language courses, history courses, or classes at foreign universities;
- one course in quantitative analysis. Any mathematics or computer science course, as well as classes in symbolic logic or advanced music theory, will qualify;
- a mandatory, and typically rigorous, comprehensive examination on the contents of their major; and
- a public presentation at Whitman's Undergraduate Conference. Modeled on academic conferences, this event features studio art exhibits, original plays, recitals, papers, and research. Whitman cancels classes so that all students can attend.

The two-semester core class, "Antiquity and Modernity," features students meeting in seminars of no more than twenty. Sections are presided over by professors from different disciplines; thus, a biology professor may teach Shakespeare, and an English teacher might teach Darwin. Some of the texts studied in this yearlong course include the *Odyssey*, poems of Sappho, Aeschylus's *Agamemnon* and *Eumenides*, Sophocles' *Antigone*, Euripides' *Medea*, Plato's *Symposium*, several Old and New Testament books, Virgil's *Aeneid*, Augustine's *Confessions*, and works by Galileo, Descartes, Shakespeare, Locke, Rousseau, Kant, Darwin, and Nietzsche.

"Antiquity and Modernity" is mostly popular among the students. Says one, "The core courses create a built-in platform for dialogue in upper-level classes and outside the classroom. Students have a common ground." Some teachers suggest that "Antiquity and Modernity" does not spend enough time on the classic texts that are assigned. One professor says, "The core does offer readings in substantial works in the Western tradition, but in some cases this is in snippets (the Bible), and a frequent complaint is that an insufficient amount of time is spent on individual texts." The quality of the core classes "varies a little depending on the professor," reports one student. "Most of the faculty who teach the course really like it, and like the texts they teach, and want the students to like them too. A minority, but an all too vocal minority, hate the course, hate the texts, and teach the students to hate them too. Such have been pushing for either the inclusion of more 'voices' (such as the trivial and annoying Emma Goldman) in core or for radically changing it altogether. Fortunately, there seems to be a consensus on campus for keeping core, and keeping it based in the Western tradition. The big flaw . . . is that it has no medieval texts, but surveys Homer to Augustine—and then Descartes to Toni Morrison. So no Chaucer, no Dante, no Aquinas." There remains a common syllabus for all sections of these core courses, which restricts instructors from altering their content too greatly. According to one professor, "There is a reluctance to radically change the curriculum. Any changes mostly amount to one year reading the *Iliad* and the next year reading the *Odyssey*."

Says one instructor, "Students can get a solid grounding in the liberal arts at Whitman, but merely meeting the requirements for graduation will not guarantee this.

Students should discuss how to accomplish this with their premajor advisors as soon as they get to campus." Another says, "It is possible to get a strong liberal arts education at Whitman, if a student chooses wisely from the potpourri of diverse offerings, and if a student gets solid direction from his/her advisor."

There are no graduate students at Whitman, and hence no grad student instructors. However, "there are a significant number of adjuncts teaching regular courses at Whitman, especially in the First-Year Core," notes a teacher. The quality of the teaching and the rigor of the discussions is said to vary from section to section, even in core classes. Students don't choose their sections, and transferring to other sections, a professor warns, "is difficult to do, and students are discouraged by the school." Some faculty members bemoan Whitman's lack of a foreign-language requirement, pointing out that enrollment in classes teaching major European tongues has been declining at the school.

When a student enrolls at Whitman, he is assigned a faculty advisor, whom he is expected to visit several times throughout the first year. In addition, student academic advisors (SAs) live in first-year residence hall sections, organizing weekly study sessions. Professors lead discussions in the freshman residences.

Whitman offers forty-two majors and thirty-four minors. Some of the most popular departments are history, biology, physical sciences, and psychology. When a student chooses a major, he also picks a faculty advisor. "Some advisors take an active approach with pizza parties and such. Others let the students come to them," remarks one student.

The necessity of preparing students for comprehensive exams in their senior year helps make up for sometimes anemic course requirements. English majors must take one introductory course ("Approaches to the Study of Literature"), four period courses in English and American literature, one course focusing on a major English writer (Chaucer, Shakespeare, or Milton), and one senior-level seminar. One teacher complains, "Because of the many options open to students, it is possible for them to avoid hundreds of years of English literature, traditional major authors, and important periods." Nevertheless, every English major is responsible for knowing a long list of classic works that appear on his senior exam.

The politics department maintains that it has "earned a reputation of resisting the trend toward narrow specialization." Unfortunately, the department's courses don't always live up to its claim. They include "The Christian Right in the United States," "Welfare in America," "Capital Punishment," "Politics of Race, Ethnicity, and Reli-

VITAL STATISTICS

Religious affiliation: none
Total enrollment: 1,454
Total undergraduates: 1,454
ACT midrange: 27–32
Applicants: 2,318
Applicants accepted: 50%
Accepted applicants who enrolled: 32%
Tuition: $30,806
Room and board: $7,840
Percentage of students receiving aid: 43%
Freshman retention rate: 93%
Graduation rate: 77%
Courses with fewer than 20 students: 70%
Student-faculty ratio: 10:1
Courses taught by graduate students: none
Most popular majors: history, biology, psychology
Students living on campus: 60%
Guaranteed housing for four years? No
Students in fraternities: 34% sororities: 32%

gion," and several concerning environmentalism. An overwhelming number of the politics courses—even those with innocuous titles like "Nations and Nationalism"—emphasize race, ethnicity, and gender. Still, quite a few classes use primary sources. For instance, in the unpromising "Sexuality and Textuality," students at least read Plato, Sappho, and Shakespeare. One student charges that this department is "known for throwing its leftist views in your face. . . . The political leaning of both the faculty and the student body is so liberal that conservatives like myself are frequently verbally attacked and affronted with regularity. There are no right-leaning politics professors, and it is almost suicide to be a conservative politics major. The atmosphere of many courses is like this, and it certainly influences the content of social science courses like history and politics." Another says, "It would be hard to be a conservative here."

One professor insists that although faculty members are overwhelmingly liberal, "We don't wear our politics on our sleeves." One conservative teacher agrees, "Overall, Whitman is, despite the political leanings of its faculty, still a fairly old-fashioned, small liberal arts college—and as such, a very good place to learn."

"Overall, Whitman is, despite the political leanings of its faculty, still a fairly old-fashioned, small liberal arts college—and as such, a very good place to learn."

Another professor says, "From my observations, the strongest departments in the humanities are the English and the classics programs. The English department has a very varied faculty, specializing in both literature and creative writing and covering a wide variety of periods. . . . [It also has] a number of very intelligent and very rigorous teachers (in particular Theresa DiPasquale and Jeanne Masteller). The classics department has only two full-time faculty, Dana Burgess and Elizabeth Vandiver, but both are erudite, fun, and very demanding of their students; and both have a deep appreciation for the liberal arts as classically understood. The mathematics faculty are very strong and uniformly genial. Their students do well in getting into graduate school." Other comparatively strong departments include biology, chemistry, history, music, religion, and some of the foreign languages. There is no major in gender studies (only a minor), and the program has no full-time faculty members devoted to it.

Whitman employs many excellent faculty. Students say the best teachers include Delbert Hutchison in biology; James Russo and Leroy G. "Skip" Wade in chemistry; Dana L. Burgess in classics; Jan Crouter in economics; Walker Percy scholar John F. Desmond in English; Robert J. Carson in geology and environmental studies; David F. Schmitz in history; Bob Fontenot, Pat Keef, and Laura Schueller in mathematics; David Glenn and Susan Pickett in music; David Carey and Patrick Frierson in philosophy; Rogers Miles and Walter Wyman Jr. in religion; Robert Sickels in rhetoric and film studies; and Keith Farrington in sociology.

Faculty are said to be focused on students. "Teaching is completely and utterly central. Research is expected, but subsidiary. The professors are highly accessible, form close relationships with their students, and very much like teaching. It's a 3/3 load, which seems to work out pretty well, as class sizes are generally under thirty, and often in upper-division classes under fifteen," reports one professor.

Some classes meet at professors' homes (most faculty members live within walking distance). Students praise the accessibility of professors, most of whom give students their home phone numbers. Teachers and students play intramurals together, eat together, and socialize on Whitman's small campus. The admissions office recounts how one mathematics professor, for instance, explained a difficult concept to a couple of students in the frozen juice section of a local grocery store. A religion major comments, "I would have to say the best part of Whitman College is the faculty-student relations. I've always received help from my professors, and they sometimes go out of their way for me. Even the president of the college likes to mingle with the students. On finals week, it is common to see him roaming the library handing out cookies."

As for the students themselves, one professor says, "There is a certain cultural flavor. . . . Students are more laid-back about things, more well-rounded, and more cooperative in group projects. To generalize, they're not selfish about learning." Whitman students are "bright and happy people with a lot of interests," reports another instructor. And a third says, "The students here are tremendously curious. They are some of the most willing students I've ever taught, in terms of dealing with material thrown at them and trying to make sense of it. They also take the initiative outside class to further their learning, with lots of involvement in theater, creative writing, art, et cetera."

Whitman maintains a sterling study-abroad program, cosponsoring international programs in Sri Lanka, Scotland, New Zealand, China, Argentina, Spain, and dozens of other locations; 40 percent of juniors participate. Environmental interdisciplinary majors can take a "Semester in the West," an adventure term of field work with working ecologists. Numerous opportunities to conduct original research are available to science (including premed) majors. Prelaw students can, with six years of study, combine a Whitman B.A. degree with a J.D. from Columbia University.

Student Life: Snowboarding and Granola

Although relatively remote, Walla Walla is one of the oldest cities in the region and boasts a number of cultural attractions and historic buildings. Its up-and-coming downtown offers sidewalk cafés, restaurants, and art galleries. Even so, some students complain that the town is "extremely boring," which may explain why most undergrads bring cars. Within a short drive are opportunities for rock climbing and boating at Lake Chelan, and sites for skiing and snowboarding in the Cascade Mountains.

Whitman's campus is lovely. The administration plants dozens of trees every year and maintains a creek and duck pond. Students (who call themselves "Whitties") create their own entertainment—including one of the country's top debate programs, an active theater and music performance series, a highly competitive skiing program, and

1. General Studies 145: Antiquity (*closest match*)
2. Philosophy 201: Ancient Philosophy
3. Religion 201/202: The Hebrew Bible / The New Testament and Early Christianity
4. History 202: European Intellectual History 386–1300 (*closest match*)
5. Politics 222: Modern European Political Theory
6. English 351/352: Shakespeare
7. History 105: Development of the United States (1607–1877)
8. General Studies 146: Modernity (*closest match*)

a popular student-run radio station. The student paper is the *Pioneer*. There are usually parties on weekends, guest lectures (recent invitees have included Seamus Heaney, Robert Pinsky, Louise Gluck, Adrienne Rich, Derek Wolcott, Billy Collins, and Maya Angelou), and coffeehouse music performances. One student says, "I know too many people who consider getting drunk a good way to spend their free time. But once the weekend ends, it is back to work." Half the student body spends time on community work, for instance through Whitman Mentors and the Cross-Cultural Outreach program.

All students under twenty-one must live on campus for at least four semesters. After that, they're free to move to fraternities and sororities on campus—and about a third do just that. Indeed, the Greek organizations are said to more or less govern on-campus social life. On-campus residence halls are coed, except for one that houses first-year women. However, except for special-interest houses, all residence hall bathrooms are single-sex. Douglas Hall, a twenty-four-hour quiet hall, is an option for upperclassmen. A housing official says that each year a handful of students opt for coed dorm rooms (they must have parental approval). For all of this, one student claims, "The on-campus housing just plain sucks. When it gets overcrowded, they just stick you in the common room of the dorm."

Whitman's eleven interest houses include La Casa Hispana, La Maison Française, Tekisuijuku (Japanese House), Das Deutsche Haus, Asian Studies House, Outhouse (an environmental studies house), Fine Arts House, Community Service House, MECCA House (i.e., Multi-Ethnic Center for Cultural Affairs), Global Awareness House, and the Writing House.

Religious students who come to Whitman should "actively seek out a faith community on or off campus and become as active as possible," one professor advises, noting "only a minority of students are religiously active." Faith-based groups include Catholics on Campus, InterVarsity Christian Fellowship, and Shalom, a Jewish club. Interesting communities in Walla Walla include St. Silouan Greek Orthodox Church—which is composed mostly of former Episcopalians who worship in English using a modified Book of Common Prayer.

The mores and politics of the region predominate. "There is no respect for open debate, and a true scrutiny of political issues is rare," complains one conservative student, who laments a "lack of religious and political diversity." One professor reports that "both students and administrators have called for greater openness to Republicans, Christians, as well as the more usual minorities." This professor sees "more support for students all along the political spectrum than in the past" at Whitman.

Another professor says, "Generally Whitman is overwhelmingly left-leaning, but at the same time there is a strong respect for freedom of speech and opinion. Recently, when the Whitman Christian Fellowship put up unattributed quotes from the Bible on campus and in campus mailboxes, some students—and sad to say, some faculty—protested about 'proselytization.' But the majority of students and the vast majority of the faculty backed the right of the students to express their opinion. And the signs were approved by the administration. Having said that, there is a recent push for campus diversity, unfortunately defined predictably as race and sexual orientation, which I think is having a dampening effect on freedom of expression. The new president has shown himself maladroit with regard to some issues, particularly in encouraging 'subdued' holiday decorations in offices lest anyone get offended by Christmas. Fortunately, most of the faculty found his e-mail idiotic, but it may be a harbinger of things to come."

A different professor adds, "I'd say it'd take some courage to be an outspoken conservative on this campus (the College Republicans a few years ago sponsored a 'come out of the closet' day for Republicans), but you'd probably get a lot more flak from fellow students . . . than from teachers." In a student body of nearly 1,500, the College Republicans have almost seventy members, meet biweekly, and are trying to become more active and vocal. One student says, "There are a good number of conservative students who are afraid to express their views because they are in a minority. I only really talk when asked my views; I don't go looking for fights."

The Whitman Missionaries compete on twenty intercollegiate varsity sports for men and women in soccer, volleyball, cross-country, golf, basketball, swimming, alpine and Nordic skiing, tennis, track and field, and baseball. Club sports for men and women include lacrosse and rugby, with coed leagues in fencing, volleyball, water polo, and ultimate Frisbee. Intramural clubs offer still more options. A renovated athletic center accommodates most of these activities.

The campus and the surrounding area are quite safe; on-campus crime statistics for the past four years list one burglary and sixteen forcible sex offenses. However, eight of those sex crimes took place in 2004.

Whitman is every bit as expensive as its eastern elite-school counterparts, with 2006–7 tuition at $30,806 and room and board at $7,840. Financial aid is said to be generous, however. About 50 percent of students receive need-based financial aid, and (among recent grads who borrowed) the average student loan debt is $16,900.

YESHIVA UNIVERSITY

NEW YORK, NEW YORK • WWW.YU.EDU

Yeshiva University, located at several sites throughout the borough of Manhattan, put down roots in 1886 in the Lower East Side as a *cheder* elementary school, teaching the basics of Judaism and Hebrew. The Rabbi Isaac Elchanan Theological Seminary and Yeshiva College (the school's original full name) was founded in 1928 in Washington Heights. In 1954, after a gift from the late industrialist Max Stern, Yeshiva opened the Stern College for women in midtown Manhattan. In 1970, against the protests of some students and professors, Yeshiva revised its charter to become a secular school and transformed its high schools into affiliates. However, the educational philosophy of Yeshiva remains "Torah Umadda," about which Rabbi Norman Lamm wrote: "Torah, faith, religious learning on one side and Madda, science, worldly knowledge on the other, together offer us a more overarching and truer vision than either one set alone. Each set gives one view of the Creator as well as of His creation, and the other a different perspective that may not agree at all with the first. . . . Each alone is true, but only partially true; both together present the possibility of a larger truth." This viewpoint has sometimes been called "Centrist Orthodoxy," and it has guided Yeshiva through decades of academic excellence.

According to the university's literature, its "guiding vision is the confidence that the best of the heritage of contemporary civilization—the liberal arts and sciences—is compatible with the ancient traditions of Jewish law and life." On the undergraduate level, this belief is embodied in the dual curriculum, under which students pursue a full program of Jewish studies while taking college programs in the liberal arts, the sciences, and business—receiving specialized preparation for advanced work in any discipline or profession. Another worthy goal of the institution "is to serve the general and Jewish communities of the city, the nation, and the world by preparing well-trained professionals in many fields and providing pioneering resources for community service." The scientific research conducted at Yeshiva's graduate schools regularly produces medical breakthroughs that keep this distinctive school in the news. The university fills a distinctive and important place in American education, which should commend it to the attention of students who wish to integrate the Jewish tradition with a top-flight humanities education.

Academics: Athens and Jerusalem

The general education requirements at Yeshiva offer exactly what the school's mission promises—a broad exposure to the liberal arts, as well as to the Torah and Jewish tradition. All students at Yeshiva (men's) College must take the following:

- one class in English composition;
- one approved course in mathematics, computer sciences, or statistics;
- two courses in physical education;
- two literature courses, chosen from a short list including "World Literature: Ancient and Classical" and "American Literature through the Civil War";
- two courses in history, philosophy, or a foreign language other than Hebrew (options include Greek, Latin, French, and Spanish);
- an introductory class in art, music, or a foreign language other than Hebrew;
- two courses chosen from economics, political science, psychology, or sociology;
- two semesters of a laboratory science;
- "Introduction to the Bible," plus three additional two-credit Bible courses;
- "Intermediate Hebrew"; and
- two Jewish history classes, such as "Classical Jewish History," "Medieval Jewish History," or "Jewish Intellectual History" (a multipart sequence broken up chronologically).

Particular to Yeshiva are its requirements in Jewish studies. Students are required to take courses in Hebrew and encouraged to do so early, as the Hebrew language becomes necessary for more advanced courses in the Jewish studies department. Options for completing the biblical requirements include in-depth studies of certain books (including Exodus, Leviticus, and Numbers) and thematic courses in biblical exegesis.

At the Stern College for Women, the requirements are also demanding. All students must study the following:

- one semester of English composition;
- two semesters of physical education;
- a speech class;
- one additional course chosen from computer science, mathematics, or statistics;
- four classes in humanities "chosen from courses in foreign language (other than Hebrew and Yiddish), art, English, music, and philosophy. . . . [N]o more than three credits may be taken in art, no more than three credits in music, and no more than six credits in any other discipline";

Religious affiliation:
   Modern Orthodox
   Judaism.
Total enrollment: 6,371
Total undergraduates: 2,931
SAT/ACT midranges: SAT V:
   550–670, M: 560–680;
   ACT: 23–29
Applicants: 1,875
Applicants accepted: 78%
*Accepted applicants who
   enrolled*: 69%
Tuition: $26,100
Room and board: $7,880
Freshman retention rate: 84%
Graduation rate: 80% (4 yrs.),
   82% (6 yrs.)
*Courses with fewer than 20
   students*: 72%
Student-faculty ratio: 11:1
*Courses taught by graduate
   students*: none
Most popular majors:
   business administration,
   psychology, biology
Students living on campus:
   82%
*Guaranteed housing for four
   years?* yes
*Students in fraternities or
   sororities*: none

- three courses chosen from economics, history, political science, psychology, and sociology, with "no more than three credits . . . in psychology . . . no more than three in sociology, and no more than six in any other discipline";
- one year of a single laboratory science: biology, chemistry, or physics;
- three electives in a foreign language (not Hebrew or Yiddish) or in disciplines outside the student's major;
- six semesters of "Core Segment," which is "a unit of three Jewish Studies classes consisting of eight to nine hours of lecture per week"; and
- fourteen additional Jewish Studies credits, chosen from classes in the Bible, Judaic studies, Jewish history, Jewish philosophy, and Hebrew.

Beyond the excellent foundations which it lays, the departments in various disciplines at Yeshiva are solid, traditional, and serious. For instance, the history department offers a robust menu of courses. Students majoring in history must take two classes surveying the development and sources of Western civilization and two in American history—from a list of outstanding choices. Beyond the basics of America's founding and development, students can take courses specializing in the history of the American South, the New Deal, even the history of New York City. Advanced history courses look at history thematically. One course, "War in Western Civilization," explores the "relationship of war, in its broader ethical, intellectual, religious, technological, and purely military aspects, to Western civilization," as well as the "concept of the Just War, war crimes, terrorism, guerrilla warfare, [and] nuclear war." When asked if professors have political axes to grind in the classroom, one student says, "Not really." One sophomore says that occasionally "you hear a professor grumble about this or that but there is always an open discussion in the classroom. The courses in history and in other departments are geared toward conveying information and ideas—not in turning you into someone who votes for one party or another."

The English department offers a traditional menu of courses in the great works of our vernacular literature. Intermediate-level courses are offered in Chaucer and the Victorian era. Majors are encouraged to take two semesters of Shakespeare. More advanced courses include consideration of American literature in relation to the city or to rural America. Only two courses out of several dozen focus exclusively on Jewish American literature, and no courses import modern gender or identity politics into the discipline. The English department helpfully offers courses in technical writing: students can take courses in writing advertising copy, for instance.

Unsurprisingly, Yeshiva offers one of the best Jewish studies departments in the country. Thirty courses on Jewish laws and customs are offered—including courses about Jewish law and custom on the Sabbath. There are courses covering the development and differences between Sephardic and Ashkenazi laws and customs. Jewish studies majors have ample options to study the Torah, Mishnah, and the work of Maimonides. In accord with ancient custom, students looking to take a course on the Kabbalah must fulfill a prerequisite in Jewish philosophy.

The Jewish philosophy department offers a wide selection of classes in every major period of Jewish thought. One student who took the introductory coursework in Jewish philosophy in order to fulfill general requirements was enthralled by what he found. "I was basically a secular Jew, and in some ways maybe I still am. But when I took the intro courses in Jewish philosophy a lot of it made sense to me. It was fascinating. It helped me understand the 'whys' of other required coursework at Yeshiva." Majors in Jewish philosophy can cap off their education with an undergraduate thesis closely advised by the staff.

"I was basically a secular Jew, and in some ways maybe I still am. But when I took the intro courses in Jewish philosophy a lot of it made sense to me. It was fascinating. It helped me understand the 'whys' of other required coursework at Yeshiva."

Award-winning and highly recommended faculty members at Yeshiva and its associated graduate schools (some of whom teach undergraduate classes as well) include David C. Kahn in accounting; Peter Lencsis in finance; Michael Brownlee, M.D., in the medical school; Vern Schramm in biochemistry; David Glaser in music; David Schnal in management; Jeffrey S. Gurock, Libby Klaperman, and Alvin Schiff in Jewish studies; Rabbi Melech Schachter in rabbinics; Rabbi Moses D. Tendler in medical ethics; Rabbi Joseph Weiss and Rabbi Gershon Yankelewitz in Talmudic studies; and Deborah Y. Cohn in marketing.

For students who wish to go abroad, Yeshiva offers a Summer in Israel program that includes classes in film, archeology, the Torah, and political science. Students in the archaeology course stay on a kibbutz near Tell es-Safi. According to the program directors, "Students will participate in supervised seminar discussions in Jerusalem, addressing current topics such as developments in Israeli politics and society (including the secular-religious divide), developments on the Palestinian side (including the implications of the recent elections), the regional situation, and wider political issues, such as the role of nongovernmental organizations in the Arab-Israeli conflict." One student reports, "You go into the program thinking you know something about the politics there, but you really don't until you've walked the streets in Jerusalem. It was the most eye-opening experience of my college life."

ALL-AMERICAN COLLEGES

Apart from Yeshiva College and the Stern College for Women, Yeshiva includes the undergraduate Sy Syms School of Business, which "offers professional preparation with a broad base in liberal arts studies." The curriculum emphasizes Jewish tradition as a framework for business ethics, in addition to the usual business courses. Graduates earn a bachelor of science degree. Students in the Syms School "simultaneously attend one of four schools of Jewish studies."

The university offers a wide array of graduate programs through affiliated institutions: the Albert Einstein College of Medicine, Benjamin N. Cardozo School of Law, Wurzweiler School of Social Work, Ferkauf Graduate School of Psychology, Azrieli Graduate School of Jewish Education and Administration, Bernard Revel Graduate School of Jewish Studies, and Rabbi Isaac Elchanan Theological Seminary. Each of these schools has produced its share of luminaries in the fields of business, medicine, natural science, social science, and law.

Student Life: Orthodox Hipsters

Life in New York City is familiar to many students at Yeshiva, but a substantial number of students hail from other states or from Israel—and are delighted to explore the city one student calls "the center of the world." "I've been to the new Museum of Modern Art, I've been to the Guggenheim. And, it's a cliché, but my friends and I can party like hipsters in Williamsburg [Brooklyn] if we want to," he says.

Hipster partying aside, the campus itself maintains rather traditional rules and mores. At the Wilf campus for undergraduate men, most of the 1,100 students on campus live in traditional dorm housing—two students per room with common microwaves and kitchens. For some upperclassmen there is apartment-style housing available. There is no curfew for students, but the dorms remain single-sex. Female guests can be in men's rooms only to help them move in on check-in day, and are permitted during the daytime only in common areas such as the lounges and dining halls. Similarly, the woman's campus restricts the presence of male visitors to lounge areas, and even there only during certain portions of the day. Overnight guests are welcome at each campus but must be same sex and college-aged.

Yeshiva has more than its share of student-run clubs. Popular groups at the Stern College for Women include the Dance Club, the Debate Club, and Brainstorm, a book club that aims to gather book lovers together every few weeks for "tea and crumpets" and a good read. The men's college has a number of clubs dedicated to politics, foreign languages, and other interests. Recently the men's college held a "battle of the bands."

There are student-run newspapers at both the men's and women's colleges. One is called the *Commentator*, affectionately known by its staff as "the Commie." Another student paper, *Hamashkif*, is published in Hebrew. In a recent editorial one graduating senior pondered the identity of Yeshiva: "We are so much defined as a people by our religious identities that polarity, instead of broadness, rules the day. Maybe it's just me, but I found that at Yeshiva it was exceedingly difficult to relate to kids I grew up with who decided that Modern Orthodoxy just wasn't good enough, and opted for a more 'authentic,' more rigid, Judaism," he wrote. Such a concern about division among students was echoed to us once or twice by undergrads, who found that the study of Judaism often led to disputations among students. However, some find it exhilarating. "I know people can be pretty harsh and judgmental about their religious habits and yours, but I found the discussion stimulating. I learned a lot about my Jewish friends while I was here and sometimes a little disagreement is the price of self-discovery," he says.

Religious life is of course integral to Yeshiva, despite its officially maintained secularity. Students live a "kosher" lifestyle in keeping with Modern Orthodox Judaism. The colleges run programs in order to encourage student participation in Shabbat. "The Shabbat Enhancement Program, sponsored by the Office of Student Affairs, is designed to make Shabbat on campus relevant to all segments of the . . . college community. With subsidized meals, a warm, vibrant atmosphere, and an array of themed Shabbatonim sponsored by a wide variety of clubs, Shabbat on campus allows you to share a unique experience with fellow students and friends from other colleges whom you invite as your guests,"

SUGGESTED CORE
1. English 4201: Masterpieces of World Literature
2. Philosophy 2170: Ancient and Medieval Philosophy
3. Bible 1015: Introduction to the Bible (*Hebrew Scriptures only*)
4. Philosophy 2170: Ancient and Medieval Philosophy (*closest match*)
5. Politics 1810: Modern Political Philosophy
6. English 2331/2332: Shakespeare I/II
7. History 2005: Survey of United States History I
8. History 1602: European Intellectual History

says the school. Also, S'gan Mashgichim programs are a resource for students in need of additional counseling to help get through the sometimes difficult college years. A small staff of "the greatest rabbis" will inquire of students: "'How are your *chavrusas*?' Or 'How is *shiur* going?' They keep office hours throughout the week," reports one student.

Crime is not a major problem at Yeshiva. Security guards are posted at each dorm both at the Wilf campus in Washington Heights and at the Berean campus in midtown Manhattan. Students look out for each other. The Washington Heights area, which has a long-standing Jewish community that predates Yeshiva, has been gentrifying in recent years—a Starbucks can now be found on 181st Street—and crime has been in steep decline. One student did complain about being hassled by homeless people in the neighborhood, but in the past five years, says one professor, the neighborhood has gotten a lot friendlier and is experiencing a revival. In 2004, the Yeshiva College campus reported no crimes other than nine burglaries. The Stern College campus reported seven burglaries.

Tuition for undergraduates at Yeshiva is a tad over $26,000, plus about $7,000 per year for room and board. This makes Yeshiva competitively priced with other top-tier undergraduate schools in New York.

ADDITIONAL SERVICES FROM ISI

All-American Colleges has been produced by the staff of the Intercollegiate Studies Institute (ISI), a nonprofit, nonpartisan educational organization. Since its founding in 1953, ISI has supported efforts to strengthen liberal arts curricula at colleges and universities nationwide.

ISI's Student Self-Reliance Project, of which ISI's college guides are the foundation, is a comprehensive program designed to ensure that students have access to the intellectual tools they need to make the most of their education. The project consists of a broad selection of programs and publications that will help students navigate through their schools' academic, social, and political environments.

Students can turn first to *A Student's Guide to Liberal Learning*, by Georgetown University professor James V. Schall, for wise counsel on how to read well, mature intellectually, and gain insight into the nature of education. Mark C. Henrie's *Student's Guide to the Core Curriculum*, included in this book, will help them build a concrete foundation for their studies. It also demonstrates that, by choosing electives carefully, students can obtain the education they deserve even at schools that abolished their core curricula decades ago.

As students progress through their college years, they will find that our unique student guides will keep them ahead of the class. These brief essays by nationally known scholars on a number of topics and disciplines—including classics, psychology, U.S. history, economics, literature, philosophy, political philosophy, natural science, religious studies, American political thought, and the study of both history and law—serve as superb introductions to the most important fields in the liberal arts. Forthcoming guides will treat the disciplines of sociology and music. Readers are invited to visit www.isibooks.org for more information.

Conferences, lectures, fellowships, books, and journals round out the services provided by ISI to tens of thousands of students and professors each year. ISI organizes conferences on important intellectual problems as well as career development seminars throughout the nation. Lecturers sponsored by ISI speak on more than two hundred college campuses annually on a vast array of topics. Graduate students in the sciences, social sciences, education, and humanities may apply for our prestigious fellowships. And ISI publishes and distributes a range of scholarly and opinion journals every year, as well as nearly twenty serious books of nonfiction through its national trade imprint, ISI Books.

Whatever your stage of education—homeschool, high school, college, graduate school, or lifelong learner—ISI offers programs and publications designed to help you make the most of your talents. And whether you are a student or teacher, professor or parent, you can benefit from our resources and expertise.

To learn more about the Intercollegiate Studies Institute, a nonprofit 501(c)3 organization, or to make a donation to ISI, visit our website at www.isi.org or e-mail us at collegeguide@isi.org. You may also call us at (800) 526-7022 or mail us at: ISI, P.O. Box 4431, Wilmington, Delaware, 19807-0431. ISI Books titles may be ordered by calling (800) 621-2736 or by visiting www.isibooks.org.

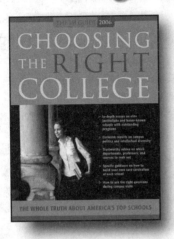

More College Guides from ISI

If you liked *All-American Colleges*, you will love ISI's Guides to the Major Disciplines. They are indispensable introductions to a lifetime of learning. Elegantly written by leading scholars, each title offers a reliable and informative tour of a major discipline: its history, distinguishing characteristics, and most accomplished and influential practitioners. All who treasure the world of ideas will be motivated by these original and stimulating presentations.

"These slim volumes come close to constituting mini–great books in themselves." —**Wall Street Journal**

**A Student's Guide to
THE STUDY OF LAW**
GERALD V. BRADLEY
$8 paper • 80 pp. • 1-882926-97-8

**A Student's Guide to
CLASSICS**
BRUCE S. THORNTON
$8 paper • 90 pp. • 1-932236-15-5

**A Student's Guide to
PSYCHOLOGY**
DANIEL N. ROBINSON
$6.95 paper • 70 pp. • 1-882926-95-1

**A Student's Guide to
RELIGIOUS STUDIES**
D.G. HART
$8 paper • 90 pp. • 1-882926-58-9

**A Student's Guide to
AMERICAN POLITICAL THOUGHT**
GEORGE W. CAREY
$8 paper • 100 pp. • 1-932236-42-2

**A Student's Guide to
LIBERAL LEARNING**
JAMES V. SCHALL, S.J.
$8 paper • 54 pp. • 1-882926-53-6

**A Student's Guide to
POLITICAL PHILOSOPHY**
HARVEY C. MANSFIELD
$8 paper • 75 pp. • 1-882926-43-9

**A Student's Guide to
LITERATURE**
R.V. YOUNG
$6.95 paper • 74 pp. • 1-882926-40-4

**A Student's Guide to
PHILOSOPHY**
RALPH M. MCINERNY
$7 paper • 75 pp. • 1-882926-39-0

**A Student's Guide to
ECONOMICS**
PAUL HEYNE
$8 paper • 64 pp. • 1-882926-44-7

**A Student's Guide to
THE CORE CURRICULUM**
MARK C. HENRIE
$7.95 paper • 112 pp. • 1-882926-42-0

**A Student's Guide to
U.S. HISTORY**
WILFRED M. MCCLAY
$7.95 paper • 96 pp. • 1-882926-45-5

**A Student's Guide to
THE STUDY OF HISTORY**
JOHN LUKACS
$6.95 paper • 50 pp. • 1-882926-41-2

**A Student's Guide to
NATURAL SCIENCE**
STEPHEN M. BARR
$8 paper • 88 pp. • 1-882926-92-9

ISI BOOKS   **A UNIVERSITY IN PRINT** *Wilmington, Delaware 19807-0431*

AVAILABLE AT FINE BOOKSTORES. *To order, call (800) 621-2736; fax (800) 621-8476. Domestic shipping & handling: $4 for 1st book, $1 for each additional book. Order online at: www.isibooks.org*